National Intelligencer and *Washington Advertiser* Newspaper Abstracts 1806-1810

Joan M. Dixon

HERITAGE BOOKS
2006

HERITAGE BOOKS
AN IMPRINT OF HERITAGE BOOKS, INC.

Books, CDs, and more—Worldwide

For our listing of thousands of titles see our website
at
www.HeritageBooks.com

Published 2006 by
HERITAGE BOOKS, INC.
Publishing Division
65 East Main Street
Westminster, Maryland 21157-5026

International Standard Book Number: 978-0-7884-0596-9

NATIONAL INTELLIGENCER NEWSPAPER
WASHINGTON, D C
1806-1810

TABLE OF CONTENTS

PREFACE
Daily National Intelligencer Newspaper Abstracts
1806-1810
Joan M Dixon

The National Intelligencer & Washington Advertiser is hereafter the Daily National Intelligencer. It was the first newspaper printed in Washington, D C; Samuel H Smith, the originator. The same was transferred to Jos Gales, jr on Aug 31, 1810; on Nov 1, 1812, the paper was under the firm of Jos Gales, sr, & Wm W Seaton. The Library of Congress has microfilm of the paper from the first issue of Oct 31, 1800 thru Jan 8, 1870, the final paper. The Evening Star Newspaper of Jan 10, 1870 reports: The Intelligencer is discontinued: the proprietor, Mr Alex Delmar, says that having lost several thousand dollars, & being in poor health, he has resolved to discontinue its publication.

Included in the abstracts are advertisements; appointments by the President; Hse o/Rep petitions; passed Acts; legal notices; marriages; deaths; mscl notices; social events; tax lists; military promotions; court cases; deaths by accident; prisoners; & maritime information-crews. Items or events which might be a clue as to the location, age or relationship of an individual are copied.

No attempt has been made to correct the spelling. Due to the length of some articles, it was necessary to present only the highlights of same. Chancery and Equity records are copied as written.

All surnames and *land/tract names* are included in the index.

ABBREVIATIONS:

AA CO	**ANNE ARUNDEL COUNTY**
CO	**COMPANY/COUNTY**
CMDER	**COMMANDER**
CMDOR	**COMMODOR**
D C	**DISTRICT OF COLUMBIA**
ELIZ	**ELIZABETH**
ELIZA	**ELIZA**
MONTG CO	**MONTGOMERY COUNTY**
PG CO	**PRINCE GEORGES CO**
WASH	**WASHINGTON**

BOOKS IN THE NATIONAL INTELLIGENCER NEWSPAPER SERIES: 1800-1805/1806-1810/1811-1813/1814-1817/1818-1820/1821-1823/1824-1826/1827-1829/1830-1831/1832-1833/1834-1835/1836-1837/1838-1839/1840/1841/1842/1843/1844/1845/1846/
SPECIAL: CIVIL WAR 2 VOLS, 1861-1865

The National Intelligencer and Washington Advertiser
Washington, D C

1806

WED JAN 1, 1806

Election of reps from Ga: Cowles Mead had 4438 votes & Thos Spalding-4269 votes-Mead elected. Hse o/Reps voted 66 yeas & 52 nays, on Thos Spalding being entitled to the seat.

Jas Thecker, insolvent debtor, confined in Wash Co prison, for debt. -Wm Brent, clk.

Bankruptcy issued on Apr 10, 1802 against Wash Bowie; claims against the est of said Bowie by Feb 1. -Walter Smith, surviving assignee of Wash Bowie. Gtwn.

Oliver Evans has taken the iron foundery, So Wark bet Front & 2d & Queen & Christian Sts, Phil, for executing his own casings for his steam engines, etc.

FRI JAN 3, 1806

Ranaway-Bill Wood, mulatto man, age ab't 20 yrs, from Geo Bayly, living in Fred'k Co, Va, nr Front Royal.

Philip B Key declines undertaking any new business in Wash; his ofc remv'd to the hse lately occupied by Chas Wayman where Francis S Key will conduct as an atty at law.

Louisiana Terr-In the General Crt, Oct 1805. Pierre Menard, vs J L L Sarpy, on petition. Persons interested in late firm of Tardiveau & Co & their claims; also why the money now in the hand of Pierre Antoine Laforge, being proceeds of sale of prop of Tardiveau & Co & of Louis Vander Benden, dec'd, shd not be pd over to said P Menard. -Wm Prince, Ck G C.

B Henry Latrobe, srvy'r of U S public bldgs, Wash.

MON JAN 6, 1806

For sale: four farms, nr Gum Spring, Loudoun Co, Va, 800 acs; part of 15 tracts in Western Va & in Ky, viz, 8 tracts in Monangshela Co, 8,513 acs, 4 tracts in Wood Co, 45,223 acs; 2 tracts in Kanhawa Co, 4,500 acs. Am desirous of selling this prop, living very remote & apart -John Spencer, living nr mouth of Kanhawa Rvr, Wood Co. Or apply to Messrs Israel Lacy, Chas Lewis, Jos Lewis jr & Benj James, in Loudon Co. Any claims against me deliver to Mr Benj James. -J Spencer.

Order of Crt of Calvert Co, sale at late resid of Nathan Smith, dec'd, 414 acs, nr Nottingham & 6 miles from *Pig Point*. -Jos Blake, Chas Williamson, Richd Ireland jr, com'rs.

Order of Orphans Crt of PG Co. Sale at hse of Caleb Taylor in PG Co, all prsnl est of heirs of late John Clark. -Abraham Clark, Geo W Willitt, grdns, PG Co, Md.

WED JAN 8, 1806

Mrd: Dr Benj Prathers, of PG Co, Md, to Miss Eliza Tomkins, of Gtwn, Jan 2, by Rev Mr Balch.

FRI JAN 10, 1806

Jas Ogilvie will resume the instruction of youth in Milton, Albemarle, Va.

Appt'd by the Pres: John Cox, Capt of Cavalry in 1st Legion of Militia of D C vice Wm Brent, rsgn'd.

Hse o/Reps: Memorial of Stanley Griswold, Sec of Terr of Mich, praying for augmentation of salary.

Cmtee of merchants of New York, Dec 26, 1805:
John Broome, chrmn
cmte:

		Oliver Wolcot
John Franklin	Wm Edgar	Isaac Lawrence
Thos Carpenter	Henry I Wyckoff	John Taylor
Thos Farmer	Geo M Woolsey	David M Clarkson
Robt Lenox	Goold Hoyt	Elisha Coit
J B Murray	L Lefferts	Saml A Lawrence
Saml Russell	Jos Blackwell	John Murray
M Clarkson	John B Coles	Archibald Gracie
Wm W Woolsey	Benj Minturn	Wm Bayard
Gulian Ludlow	Eben Stevens	Reusselaer Havens
Wm Lovett	Geo Griswold	Henry Post jr
Jas Arden	John R Livingston	John Clendining
Wm Henderson	John P Munford	Benj Bailey
Isaac Clason	Wynant Van Zant jr	Edmund Seaman
P Schermerhorne	Jas Scott	Wm Coleman
Chas McEvers jr	John Kane	

Ctzns opposing erecting a bridge below the town will meet at Graham's Tavern, Gtwn. John Gozzler, Henry Foxall, Wm H Dorsey, John Threlkeld, Anthony Reintzel, Adam King, Thos Mudd, Marshum Waring, Wash Bowie. Gtwn.

Richd & Laude Elliott have a grocery store in Gtwn.

MON JAN 13, 1806

Mr Mankins, mgr on est of late Jesse Ewell, of Va, has used pit coal as a manure with success. -Thos Ewell

Stolen or strayed, bay mare. -John Staynes, at sign of the schnr *Enterprize,* Navy Yard, Wash.

Enoch Spalding appt'd collector of fines for 1st Legion of Dist of Col. -Wm D Beall, clk.

WED JAN 15, 1806

Certify that Thos Brian, brought before me a trespassing stray, a sorrel mare. -Saml Hamilton, Wash Co, D C.

Order of Orphans Crt of PG Co, Md. Sale at Mr Elisha Jones' nr Broad Creek, part of the prsnl prop of Jos Gill, dec'd. -Mary Gill, admx.

FRI JAN 17, 1806

Orphans Crt of Wash Co, D C. Jan 17, 1836. Prsnl est of Geo Beal, late of Wash Co, dec'd. -Walter T Greenfield, adm, PG Co, Md.

Strayed or stolen, mare & colt. -John Sinclair, *Greenleaff's Point*, Wash City. [or to Ed Burrewes or David Waterstone]

Ranaway: John, appr boy, taylor by trade, from Thos Carpenter-one cent reward.

MON JAN 20, 1806

Partnership of Jos Cassin & Jos Costigan is dissolved by mutual consent. Cassin will settle accounts.

Bay mare was stolen from my stable. -John Ball, Sen, Alexandria Co, D C.

Died: A C Hanson, Chancellor of State of Md. [No date-recent]

WED JAN 22, 1806

Deserted aboard the U S frig, *U S*: Jas Mihan & Wm Coles. -John Cassin, Wash Navy Yard. Reward-$10 ea.

Ranaway: Ben, age 29, negro; from John Moore, Mt Tirzah, N C.

Richd & Lynde Elliott-groc store, Water St, Gtwn.

FRI JAN 24, 1806

Died: Col Jeremiah Jordan, Jan 12, age 73 yrs, Reg of Wills for St Mary's Co, Md.

Gabriel Duvall, appt'd Chancellor, v Alex'r C Hanson, dec'd. [Maryland]

First Light Infantry-Phil, Dec 21, 1805. Francis Shallus, Capt; John Stratten, Lt; John Hufty, Ensign. -Henry Dearborn, esq, Sec at War, Wash.

For sale in Wash-lot 1-60 acs; lot 2-42 acs; lot 3-102 acs; lot 4-19 acs; lot bet John Tayloe & Dr Worthington, 80 to 100 acs. Apply to Jas White or Rev John Breckenidge nr the prop.

Notice: I forewarn all persons from taking a note of hand from me to Zachariah Hazle of PG Co, for $50; fraudulently obtained. -Barton Carico.

MON JAN 27, 1806

On the declension of Gabriel Duval, Wm Kilty is appt'd Chancellor of Md.

Desirous of mvg to Ky-sale of my est at Falls of Rappahannock, 1,031 acs nr Fredericksburg, Va. -Francis Thornton

WED JAN 29, 1806

Chas Tompkins, insolvent debtor, confined in Wash Co prison for debt. -Wm Brent, clk.

Reward: $20 for Andrew, mulatto, hired from Mr Jos Thomas who keeps the Middle Ferry to Alex. -G B Causin or Dr N P Causin, Port Tobacco, Chas Co, Md.

For sale: Iron Works & Mill, Wash Co, Md, bet 7 & 8,000 acs. -Alex'r Henderson, Jas M Lingan, John Henderson, Wm Stuart, excs of Richd Henderson. [John Ritchie on premises]

For sale or rent: wharf; formerly occupied by R & G Barry as a lumber yard. -Garret Barry, Twenty Bldgs, Wash.

FRI JAN 31, 1806

For sale, the farm I now occupy, nr 300 acs, Isaac Polock, *Fruit Hill*, 5 miles from Gtwn & Wash. Apply to Mr John Thompson, Gtwn, or Dr Wm Thornton, Wash, or Wm Searly also residing on the farm.

Jas Forrest is appt'd by Leg of Md, Reg of Wills for St Mary's Co in place of Edmund Key, esq, appt'd a Judge for the Dists of St Mary's, Chas & PG cos.

For sale: tract of land I purch'd from Mrs Mary Jenkins, St Mary's Co, Md, ab't 700 acs. -Wilfred Manning, *Great Mill*.

MON FEB 3, 1806

Quiet & peaceful hse for entertaining travellers & drovers. -Peter Glasscock, Paris, Va.

Charleston, Jan 15. Mr Anthony Butler from High Hills of Santee has informed that the hse of Gen Sumter at Statesburgh, with all out ofcs, was consumed by fire Jan 7.

Committed to my custody, John Williams, negro, absconded from his mstr nr Alex, Va; says he was purch'd of a John Dorsey, of St Mary's Co, Md. -N Rochester, Shrff, Wash Co, Md.

Wm R King, insolvent debtor, confined to Wash Co prison for debt. -Wm Brent-clk

WED FEB 5, 1806

For sale, per deed from John Withers to secure payment of a debt due to Jonathan & Mahlon Schoefield: 129 acs Fairfax Co, Va, on Old Leesburg Rd above Capt Slacombs & joins the lands of Benj Dulany & Carlisle Whiting. -Andrew Schoefield, Thos Cook, trustees.

Partnership bet Dan'l Rapine, Mich'l Conrad & John Conrad, bksellers, is dissolved by mutual consent. Business will continue under Dan'l Rapine, Capitol Hill, Wash.

Stray red cow came to my plantation. -Hos Stillings, Wash Co.

My wife, Mgt, & I have agreed to part by mutual consent, I am determined to pay no debts of her. -Wm Brooks.

I beg attention to reports in Montg Co, are false; 1st report, that I had made over all my property to my son Matthew in Ky & was recorded in Montg Co for fear of Thos Orme; 2nd I had published Thos Orme in public papers; 3rd my son Laurence had altered a figure in a certificate for weight of hay. -Wm Lodge.

Wm Kilty will dispose of a few articles of hsehld furn.

FRI FEB 7, 1806

Merchants & traders in Balt City: Robt Gilmor, Chrmn

J A Buchanan	John Hollins	Jas Calhoun
Alex'r McKim	David Stewart	Saml Sterrett
Wm Patterson	John Donnely	Hugh Thompson
Luke Tiernan	John Swan	Wm Lorman
Wm Wilson	Lemuel Taylor	Mark Pringle
Thos Hollingsworth	Thos Tenant	Wm Taylor
John Sherlock	Benj Williams	John Stricker
Geo Stiles	Henry Payson	Jos Sterett
Stewart Brown		

Attempted assassinate-Thos Paine, in his hse at new Rochelle, N Y last Dec 25; was shot by a musket thru a window & it missed him.

Bickley vs Blodget. Jan 25, 1806. Ratify report of Dan'l Carroll Brent; part of prop in decree was sold by him, am't-$20,713.75. -Wm Brent, clk.

Crct Crt of Wash Co, D C. John Blagge, John P Van Ness, adms of Wm Laight & Chas Laight, dec'd, against Geo Walker, dfndnt. Bill to revive proceedings in original case; Geo Walker is not a resid of D C at this time. -Wm Brent, clk.

Lost a pkt bk bet my hse in Gtwn & Wash. -Saml Turner jr.

MON FEB 10, 1806
Ranaway-Lewis, negro, age 30. -John Willis, Orange Co, Va.

WED FEB 12, 1806
R S Bickley, vs Thos Peter, Thos Monroe, Robt Brent, Benj Stoddert, Elias Boudinot Caldwell, Wm Thornton, John Stickney, Adam Lindsey, Edw Frithy, Jas Dougherty, Francis Lowndes, Saml Blodget, Thos McEwen, Wm Davidson & Wm Smith. Report made by Dan'l Carroll Brent, trustee, be ratified; sold prop for $20,713.75. -Wm Brent, clk.

FRI FEB 14, 1806
Ranaway -Ned, negro. Purchased of Mr Enoch Millard in Gtwn ab't 9 yrs ago. -David Lynn, Cumberland, Alleghany Co, Md.

Committed to my custody, Davy, negro, says he is the prop of Wm Cook of Chas Co, Md. -Sutton Weems, Sheriff, Calvert Co, Md.

For sale: 2 story brick hse, 7th St, formerly occupied by Mr Jas Friend, baker, now prop of Saml Rusk.

Miniature painting. J D Mallat at Mrs Thompson's Six Bldgs. [Local ad]

MON FEB 17, 1806
Strayed or stolen from Carlton Petticords store nr Goshen, a black horse. -Wm Adams, Montg Co, Md.

Lease for number of yrs, 200 tracts of land on side of Mad Rvr, 8 miles from Ohio, apply to Jacob Broadwell, resident nr Cincinnati. -John Smith, of Ohio.

Deserted on board the U S frig, *President*, Edw Thompson, black seaman. -John Cassin, super, Navy Yd, Wash.

WED FEB 19, 1806
For sale: 971 acs in Albemarle, Va, on both sides of the Hardware River, & a hse. -Chas Wingfield, on the premises.

FRI FEB 21, 1806
Died: Eliz Louisa Smith, age 14 yrs, Feb 9, d/o Sec of the Navy; her parents were also afflicted with the loss of a boy of 3 yrs of age who died a few days since. -Balt. Feb 10 [R Smith is Sec of the Navy]

To be sold at Ann Arundel Co jail, Richd, negro. -Jasper Edw Tilly, Sheriff.

For sale: land cld *Non Such*-280 acs, Wash, D C. -John Masters.

Jos Cassin has commenced the groc business nr the Navy Yd.

Died: Capt Jas Fenwick, Feb 3, of St Mary's Co, Md.

MON FEB 24, 1806

Collectors for Ohio:

Thos Scott	Chillicothe (Va Army lands)	A Goforth	Cincinnati
Jas Herron	Zanesville	Wm Skinner	Marietta
Jas Hilman	Warren	Chas Maxwell	Steubenvle

-Thos Gibson, Auditor

Orphans Crt of PG Co, Md. Feb 11, 1806. Prsnl est of Geo Hatton, late of PG Co, dec'd. -Basil Hatton, adm.

Order of Orphans Crt of PG Co, Md. Sale of prsnl est of Wm Wilson, dec'd, at Mill town. -Alex'r Gibbons, PG Co, Md.

Wilmington, N C in ashes: fire found in the bake hse occupied by John B Gamache; devoured the new brick hse of John Lord & Dr N Hill; Mr John Martin's bldg escaped the fire as did a small bldg of Maj Walker's nr the wharf owned by Messrs Richd Bradley & Alex'r Hostler & a warehse belonging to est of Peter Mallet.

Runaway: Wallace, negro. Reward-$20. -Townsend Dade, King Geo Co,Va.

FRI FEB 28, 1806

Orphans Crt of PG Co, Md. Feb 24, 1806. Prsnl est of Walter Mackall, late of PG Co, dec'd. -Jas S Morsell, adm.

Order of Orphans Crt of PG Co, Md. Sale of prsnl prop of Fielder Rawlings, dec'd, at Magruder's Ferry; schnr *Nancy & Nelly*. -Richd B Gardiner, adm.

MON MAR 3, 1806

Dr Ebenezer Brooks, only s/o a ctzn of Phil, died in Wash Co, Va, in 1799.

For sale-all rght & title of Thos Clark, of Gtwn: lot 13 with brick hse; lots 173, 174, 175; 50 acs nr Gtwn. -Jas S Morsell, trustee.

For sale-brick hse on lot 10 sq 728, East Capitol St, Wash. -Saml Tyler.

Virtue of a deed of trust from Rev Geo Ralph to Saml Tyler, dec'd, & Mary Pottinger, will sell at Mr Chapelier's Tavern, Charlotte Hall Acad, St Mary's Co, Md, land cld *Hulston,* 150 acs & 6 negroes. -Mary Pottinger, survivor of Saml Tyler. PG Co, Md.

For sale-at Bowling Green in Caroline Co, Va, the stud of the late Col John Hoomes. -John G Woodfolk & John Hoomes

John Dobbin has opened a porter cellar at the Navy Yd, Wash.

WED MAR 5, 1806
Dan'l Pettibone, ntv of Conn, offers the patent rights to welding of cast steel to iron or other steel; on Smith bellows; pots & kettles. -Dan'l Pettibone, Wash City. His affairs may also be handled by Mr John Abbot, at War Dept.

Ranaway-Chas Cokelin, negro, purch'd from Capt Robt Beall, of PG Co, Md, by Saml Beall, of Montg Co, Md. -S Beall.

Richmond, Va. Richmond Republican Blues, a vol corps of light infantry: Geo Wm Smith-Capt; Wm Davidson-Lt; G W Dixon-Ensign.

For sale: 500 to 600 bushels of coal. -Jos Huddleson.

FRI MAR 7, 1806
Old copper & brass wanted. -Matthew Hart, Pa Ave nr Centre Mkt.

Heirs of Stephen Reynolds, who died on his way from the Western country in Aug 1803, supposed to be ntv of N H; apply to John Rine, adm, living in Cumberland, Alleghany Co, Md.

Ranaway: Rachel, negro, ab't 20 yrs of age, from subscriber when living in Balt, Md, Jun 1, 1804. -Francis Clark.

MON MAR 10, 1806
For sale: 2nd hand coachee. Apply to Wm A Washington, esq, of *Rockhill.*

Partnership of Thos Hunton, of Fauquier, & Geo Britton, of Shenandoah, was dissolved on Aug 2, 1805.

WED MAR 12, 1806
To avoid the necessity of a refusal, I request no one will ask for credit; my bk debts are nrly $900. -Geo Pitt, Gtwn, D C.

FRI MAR 14, 1806
For sale: 5 to 600 bushels of Jas Rvr coal, nr the hse of Jos Huddleston, Pa Ave. -John Stephen, auct.

MON MAR 17, 1806
New work of Thos Ewell, M D of Gtwn, entitled *Plain Discourses on the Chemical Laws of Matter*.

In Chancery, Mar 7, 1806. Levin Luckett & Richd L Hall against *Jas Simpson & *Juliet his wife, *Wm Gibson Luckett, *David Lawson Luckett & others, heirs of David Luckett, dec'd. Bill-decree for sale of rl est of David Luckett, dec'd, for payment of his debts. [*reside out of Md.] -Saml H Howard, R C C.

Order of Orphans Crt of PG Co, Md. Sale of part of the prsnl est belonging to orphans of Benj Wight; hsehld furn etc; at the hse of Mr Gerrard Borman on rd from the Capt to Bladensburg. -John Wight, grdn to orphans of B Wight-D C.

Matched horses for sale at my repository, 7 North 7th St, Phil, Pa. -Wm Davidson.

For sale: Ploughs; Mr G W Riggs will attend to orders. -John Thomas 3d & Co.

For sale: Dwlg plantation of the late Wm Digges, 230 acs 4 miles from Gtwn, subject to the life est of a lady upwards of 70 yrs of age. At the same time, a plantation on *Rock Creek*, 215 acs, nr Wash. -Jos B Clagett, Philip B Key, trustees.

Pblc sale by Order of Chancery Crt of Md. 519 acs, Montg Co, Md, part of the est of Gen Geo Washington, dec'd; of same estate-500 acs lying in said Co & State. -Bushrod Washington.

WED MAR 19, 1806

To rent or let in Apr: frame hse on F St, Wash, now occupied by Mr Jas Hewitt. Apply to Mr Geo Way in adjoining hse or to John Barnes, Gtwn.

Ltrs of adm on prsnl est of John Boyce, dec'd. -Sarah Boyce.

FRI MAR 21, 1806

Ranaway: Ann, negro, age ab't 20 yrs; formerly belonged to John Brent, esq, nr Port Tobacco, Chas Co, Md. -Geo Gloyd, one of the constables of Gtwn.

Died: Genr'l Jas Jackson, Rev hero, Mar 18, Senator from Ga; remains interred at Rock Creek Chr.

Election for Directors of Columbian Library on Wed. -David Wiley-Sec.

MON MAR 24, 1806

Died: Wm Pitt, at his hse at Putney, Jan 23. -London, Jan 25.

WED MAR 26, 1806

For sale: new hack carriage at Vendue Store nr Navy Yd. -Nichs L Queen.

Orphans Crt of Calvert Co, Md. Mar 19, 1806. Prsnl est of Saml Whittington, late of Calvert Co, dec'd. -Wm Whittington, adm & assignee of Francis Whittington, surviving partner of S Whittington & Co.

FRI MAR 28, 1806

John Lowry jr, advertises svcs as srvy'r-West'n country or any other part.

MON MAR 31, 1806
Ebenezer Purdy has rsgn'd as Senator in the Leg at N Y on plea of indisposition.

Appt'd by Cncl o/Md: Jos Hopper Nicholson, Chf Judge o/6th Judicial Dist.

John Langdon, re-elected Gov of N H, without opposition.

WED APR 2, 1806
Line of Stages will be established bet Phil & Wash. It will leave McLaughlin's Hotel in Gtwn. -Thos Harris, *Rock Hall*, David Wetherspoon, Middletown.

FRI APR 4, 1806
Act of Relief for Peter Landais was approved by the Sen & Hse o/Reps: late a Capt of armed vessel of U S, $4000 for his claim to prize money, accruing from captures made & carried into Bergen, in 1779; to be deducted from money which may be obtained from the Danish Gov't for said claim.

Act to incorporate the trustees of Presby Congregation of Gtwn: that Stephen B Balsh, Wm Whann, Jas Melvin, John Maffit, John Peter, Joshua Dawson, Jas Calder, Geo Thompson, Richd Elliot, David Wiley & Andrew Ross, & their successors, have continuance forever as trustees titled above.

St Mary's Co Crt, Mar Term, 1806. Nath'l Washington, insolvent debtor, to appear at the crt hse in Leonard town Jul 19. -Jos Harris, clk of St Mary's Co Crt.

Persons with claims against est of Uriah Forrest accruing since his bankruptcy, present same to Philip B Key. -Rebecca Forrest, Excx.

The Black Sultan will stand at the farm of John Tayloe, Petworth. -Chester Bailey, mgr for J Tayloe

Ranaway: Dennis, negro. -Simon Sommers, Alexandria Co.

Partnership bet Elisha Riggs & Romulus Riggs is dissolved by mutual consent. Business will be cont'd by Romulus Riggs-Gtwn.

For sale: an ample printing ofc. Wm Duane, Pa Ave, Wash.

MON APR 7, 1806
Persons are warned from taking assignment on bond issued John Phillibrown, dec'd, in Apr 1804. -John Beckley, Wash City.

All persons indebted to est of Wm Rutherford, an insolvent debtor, will please make payments. -Thos Herty, trustee.

Crct Crt of Wash Co, D C. Jas Barry, cmplnt, vs Dorothy O'Brien, Jas O'Brien, Mary Anne O'Brien & John O'Brien, dfndnts in Chancery. Pblc auction of land in Wash. -Lewis Ford, trustee.

For sale: the prop where I now live, hse & lot in Gtwn. -Henry Schnivly.

WED APR 9, 1806
Died: Miss Mary Scott, d/o late Gustavus Scott, age 22 yrs, Apr 4, in Wash.

Sale of prop & late resid of Anthony Holmead, dec'd, 146 acs, lots adjoining Wash & *Rock Hill*, the seat of Col W A Washington. Number of lots in Wash City. -John & Anthony Holmead, excs of Anthony Holmead, dec'd.

Wm H Dorsey, atty at law, opened an ofc in Gtwn.

Ladies with ltrs in Wash P O-Apr 1, 1806:

Phillis Burr	Eleanor M Brown	Mrs S Bacon
Dores Chrous	Mary A Caton	Mrs Rebecca Bickly
Miss Dur	Miss Cath Derrer	Miss Sally Davis
Eliz Flanagan	Mrs Charlotte Fitzhugh	Eliz Evanans
Cath Gardiner	Miss Susannah Hutchins c/o Richd Cutts, esq	
Eliz Hughes	Mary Horner	Johanna Gallaspy
Susan Johnson	Miss Sarah Lowmox	Cath Jauvier
Mrs Hannah Maxwell	Eliz R Morris	Mrs Jane Murray
Miss Frances W Nance	Rebecca Nalley	Miss Ann Pryse
Miss Milly Perry	Mrs Price	Miss Ridenhouse
Madame La Bland De La Rochelaucault		Eliza Shorter
Miss Eliza Swaine	Mrs Merier Smith	Miss E Thomas
Molly Wright.		

FRI APR 11, 1806
Pblc auction-deed of trust from heirs of John Brown, late of PG Co, Md, dec'd. Land nr Robt Sewell, 7 miles from Piscataway, 360 acs. -Chas D Hodges.

Creditors of Peter Van Wagener, late merchant in N Y C, an insolvent debtor; payments to be made. -Jos T Baldwin, assignee, Newark N J.

Runaways, Hamer & her chldrn, Mial & Bell; says she is the prop of Elisha Berry of PG Co, Md. -Sutton Weems, Shrf-Calv Co, Md.

MON APR 14, 1806
Died: Hon Jas Winchester, esq, Apr 5, at his resid in the country, late Judge of the Dist Crt of Md. [Balt, Md.]

For sale: prop where I now live; 2 lots in sq 88 on Water St. -John Stephen.

WED APR 16, 1806
Died: on Apr 10, Hon Horatio Gates, Lt Genr'l in svc of U S during Rev War, age 78 yrs; was a Whig in England & a genuine American. -New York.

For sale: the land I live on, 5 to 600 acs. -Geo Lee, Chas Co, Md.

Wm King jr has remv'd his cabinet shop to his dwlg hse on Jefferson St, below Valentine Reintzell's bldg. -Gtwn.

For sale: At Bath, Berkeley Springs, Va, hse & lot, prop of Thos Palmer, dec'd. Apply to John Davidson, Wash City, or Wm Alex'r, esq, Bath.

Fire at lumber yard occupied by Mr Griffith Coombe, Apr 11. -Wash Item.

FRI APR 18, 1806

Negroes to be sold: Jack, says he was sold ab't 2 yrs since to a Mr Kennell, from est of Gen Bradley, in Sussex Co, Va; also, Billy Evans, age ab't 26 yrs, says he was born free in Nothumberland Co, Va; he is thought to belong to Mr Shadrach Carter, Amherst Co, Va. -Dan'l C Brent-Mrshl of D C.

Ranaway: Jim Ellimer, negro, age ab't 20 yrs, from Wm B Beanes, Upper Marlboro, Md.

MON APR 21, 1806

For sale-brick hse in Bladensburg, where I reside. -Alex'r McDonald.

Died: Hon Edw Shippen, age 78 yrs, Apr 15, late Chf Justice o/Sup Crt of Pa. -Phil.

WED APR 23, 1806

Certify that I, Jacob Watts, of Montg Co, N C, at request of John K Carson, did find gold at *Rock-Hole*, lands formerly prop of Thos Carson, dec'd, in N C. -Jacob Watts. J Brooks, J P. Testimony: Elias Horn-Cucumber Creek; Jacob Cagle-Branch of Isl Crk; Andreas Strow-Island Crk; Wm Johnstons, Demcy Honeywilt; Paul Daniel-Branch of Isl Crk; Christpher Osborn-Branch of Rock Hole Crk; Wm Long-Rock Hole Crk; Thos Croton; Moses Osborn; Jacob Watts; Thos Black-one of the head branches of Rock Hole Creek.

For sale-per decree of Sup Crt of Chancery, Richmond, Va: 1097 acs in Loudon Co, prop of Thos Atwood Diggs, esq, cld *Valley Tract*; also *The Green Hill Tract* ab't 1940 acs nr the Blue Ridge. -Thos Swann, Wilson C Selden-com'rs.
[Article below was underneath above advertisement]
Proper to warn any person inclined to purchase same that the degree was obtained in a most secret manner & he will not give any aid in procuring title. -Thos A Digges, Warburton, Md.

FRI APR 25, 1806

Died: Dr Starling Archer, age 24 yrs, Apr 21; by a wound rec'd in a duel of Apr 17; late of the Navy; interment in Gtwn with Military Honors.

Pblc auction-brick hse & lot nr Centre Mkt. -John Bloor

MON APR 28, 1806

Taxes due Wash Corp on rl est of:

Capt Addington	John B Anderson	Adam Aults heirs
Mahlin Atkinson	Saml Blodget	John Barnett
Ignatius Boone	Matthew Brown	Jesse Burch
Benj Bacon	John A Burford	Dan'l Bussard
Geo Betz	Jos Bently	Saml Aker
Mrs Bull	Benj Bryan	John Brackenridge
Joel Brown	Quintin Bain	Richd & Augustine Boyer
Richd B Brashears	Bishop Clagett	Crow & Wright
Wm Cross	John Craigg & others	Dan'l Caffray
John Christy	Crookshanks & Thompson	
Timothy Caldwell	Wm Duncanson	Jas Dant
Tristram Dalton	Deolois & Nicholson	Alex'r Davidson
Jasper De Carnap's heirs	Hugh Densly	Richd Delphi
John Dempsie	Eliz Ditterly	Jos Dove
Lewis Deblois	Evan Evans	Elizius Edelin
Richd Frazier	Edw Fatton	Bennet Fenwick's heirs
Jas Foulkner	Joshua Gregg	Richd Gridley
Jas Graham	Edw Griffin	Peter Hull
Wm Herron	Danl Hurley	Peter Hamm
Geo Jacobs	Wm Johnson	Alex'r Graham
Andrew Jameson	Thos Jones	Absalom Joy
Jas Knight	John Kennedy	Thos M Kirk
Jas Kennedy	Wm Lovell	Henry Luddington
Chas F Lovering	Jas Lyon	Wm Lowry
Jas M Lingan	Geo Lyles	Notley Maddox
John McCarthy	Henry Moscrop	John Mc Elwee
Andrew McDonald	Lewis Morin Sr	John Moore
Chas McDonald	Jas O'Brien	Bern'd McDermott Roe
Susannah Osborne	Francis Pratt & others	Isaac Pollock
Wm Prentis	Robt Ware Peacock	Philips, Grout & Washington
Isaac Reid	Rhodes & Higden	Mich'l Shanks
John Swank	John Story	Alex'r Shaw
Stoddert & Templeman	John Sutton	Jos Saul
Roger Smith	Shreeve & Unthank	Geo & Sarah Sweeny
John Stewart	Shaw & Birth	Calhoun Smith & Co
Nicholas Spoher	Jas Topkins	Patrick Tool
Philip Tool	Geo Thompson	Thompson & Veitch
Colin Williamson's heirs	Ambrose White	Thos Wilson
John Wilson	Nathan Walker & Jas Thompson	
Robt Wilson	Jas Waugh	Geo Walker
Joshua Warl	Geo Washington's heirs	Thos Webb
John B Winsett	Mary Yeats	Jas H Blake

-Wash Boyd, Treas Wash City.

The pblc is notified that the prop of Thos Atwood Digges, Leesburg, being clearly vested in & belonging to Wm Dudley Digges of Md, an infant under age. -Robt

Brent, atty in fact for est of Wm Dudley Digges. -Wash City.

For sale: prop belonging to est of Geo French, dec'd; hse & prop I now occupy-3 story brick hse nrly opposite the Bank of Columbia; & lots in Wash & Gtwn; 100 acs on rd leading to Fred'k Town; 301 acs-part of Friendship. Mr Warren will show it. Also, ab't 3 to 400 acs above Little Falls, Mr Barnes resides there; 2 tracts in Allegany Co, 750 acs, & *Castle Hill*-50 acs. -Auana French, devisee of Geo French, dec'd. [Auana-Ariana is correct per Apr 30]

WED APR 30, 1806

New York-Apr 25. The sloop *Richd*, from Brandywine, was fired at by the *Leander*, a ball struck John Pierce, bro to the Capt, in the neck. He was instantly killed. [See May 2]

Partnership bet Chas A Burnett & John B Rigden, Gtwn, is dissolved by mutual consent. Burnett will continue the business at their old stand-jewelry & fancy articles. -Gtwn.

Partnership bet Saml Lowdermilk & John Banks, nr the Navy Yd, has been dissolved by mutual consent. Lowdermilk will continue the groc & hardware business-L St so & 8th east.

Pblc sale: bill of sale from Miss Finigan; furn etc. -Benj Waters.

Died: Maj Gen Jas Jackson, commanded the 1st Div of Militia; Senator of Ga in Cong of U S. [Ltr-Hdqrtrs, Ga. Louisville, Apr 8, 1806.] His colleague Abraham Baldwin was with him when he died. -Geo R Clayton, Cmder in Chf.

FRI MAY 2, 1806

Funeral of John Pearce [See Apr 30] Procession to move from City Hall to St Paul's Chr the place of interment; Americ vessels at half mast; committee-Jas Fairlie, Jacob Mott, John D Miller, City Hall, N Y. *Leander* was a British ship of war & within a qrtr mile of Sandy Hook.

Ranaway-negro Tom Monk, age 26. -Edw Gantt jr, Calvert Co, Md.

For sale: millinery, nr the Navy Yd. -Francis Wayne.

MON MAY 5, 1806

For sale: apparel, bks, spy glass etc, of Mr Mark Stockwell, dec'd. -John Smith & Robt Underwood, excs.

WED MAY 7, 1806

Act for relief of Gilbert C Russell, late a Capt of Co of mounted infantry of Tenn, sum of $617.95, for provision & forage, etc, supplied by him, on tour of duty from Tenn to the Natchez. -Nath'l Macon, Spkr of Hse o/Reps.

To rent: hse on Pa Ave nr the Centre Mkt, formerly occupied by Hugh Somerville, dec'd. -Jos Huddleston, David Somerville.

FRI MAY 9, 1806

Elected directors of No Carolina Gold Mine Co: John F Mercer, Thos Tudor Tucker, Philip Barton Key, Dan'l Carrol of Dud'n, John P Van Ness, Littleton D Teakle & Wm Thornton, M D.

MON MAY 12, 1806

Annual sheep shearing took place at Arl, Apr 30; Ludwell Lee, esq, of *Belmont*, Loudoun Co, Va-annual premium for finest ramb lamb of 1 yr old.

Order of Orphans Crt of PG Co, Md. Sale of all the prop of Justinian Greenwell, dec'd: negroes, hsehld furn, stock, etc. -Ann Greenwell, admx.

WED MAY 14, 1806

Died: Robt Morris, esq, May 8, svcs to his country during Rev War are well known throughout the U S.

FRI MAY 16, 1806

Died: Maj Bowles, in the cells of Moro Castle, Havannah, early in Apr; bro to Carrington Bowles, of print shop memory, on Ludgate Hill, London.

Order of Orphans Crt of PG Co, Md. Sale at hse of Ignatius Boone, in Nottingham; negro boy age ab't 10 yrs; to satisfy debt due from est of late Mrs Ann Bradly Cox, of PG Co, dec'd. -Aquila Beall, adm, PG Co, Md.

MON MAY 19, 1806

In Chancery-John Hoy & Benj Stoddert vs Benne Penn, Robey Penn & others. Object of bill is to annul 3 deeds executed by Chas Penn, Sen, one on Mar 22, 1792 to Benne Penn, Robey Penn & Zacheus Penn; deed of same date to Betsy Penn, Wm G Penn, Sarah Penn & Caleb Penn; 3d dt'd May 7, 1792 to Chas Penn jr & Wm Penn; on ground that the said deeds were fraudulent & executed by said Chas Penn Sr, for purpose of defrauding his creditors. Benne & Robey Penn do not reside in Md. Saml Harvey Howard, R C C.

Orphans Crt of Wash Co, D C. Ltrs of adm on prsnl est of Susanna Osborne, late of said Co, dec'd. -Dan'l Rapine, adm.

Mrd: Ninian Pinkney, esq, Sec of Exec of the State of Md, to Mrs Amelia Hobbs, May 1, by Rev Mr Higgenbotham.

WED MAY 21, 1806

Sale by auction-at store lately occupied by Peter Heally, dec'd, on N J av, sundry groceries. [Wash Item.]

Henry Schnively, insolvent debtor, confined to Wash Co prison, for debt. -Wm Brent, clk.

FRI MAY 23, 1806

Orphans Crt of Wash Co, D C. May 19, 1806. Prsnl est of John Pitman Lovel, late of Wash Co, dec'd. -Alex Cochran jr, adm.

Geo St Clare brought before me a stray horse. -Saml Smallwood, Justice of Peace, Wash Co, D C.

For sale: 2 tracts of land in Monangalia Co, Va; one nr Kingswood, 315 acs; the other 4 miles distance, 200 acs, with a log hse. -Jas E Beall, lvng on premises.

MON MAY 26, 1806

Died: Mrs Eliz Carter, May 19, in PG Co, Md, nr Marlboro, after painful confinement of 9 mos, consort of Mr John Carter, formerly of Wash City.

WED MAY 28, 1806

Ranaway: Jack, negro, age 50 yrs, from Richd Brandt, living in Pomonkeynick, Chas Co, Md.

From the Republican-Petersburg, May 22. List of victims to British atrocity; May 11 as the ship *Eliza*, Capt Perry, from Londonderry came into the Capes of Va, she was brought to by the British frig *Cleopatra*-Capt White, who dragged 16 of her passengers from on board the said ship & retains them in violation of the laws: Saml Sample, Hugh McCaken, Anthony Griffin, Andrew Johnston & Alex'r McConnel o/Donegal; Wm Findly o/Astra-Co of Tyrone; Wm Stuart o/do; Thos Ballentine o/do; Wm Teiny, Hugh Quig & Wm Gilchrist o/Derry; Jas Miller o/Stewart's Town; Saml Patrick o/Tyrone. Signed.-A Friend To Liberty. [They were dragged amidst the lamentations of their wives & chldrn.]

FRI MAY 30, 1806

Jacob Bishop, a black man, will preach at the Baptist meeting hse this evening. [Wash Item]

Election for City Cncl will be held-1st Ward at tvrn of Ann Bradley; 2d Ward at tvrn of Lewis Morin; 3d Ward at Mr Stelle's Hotel; 4th Ward at Hugh Drummond's Tvrn.

MON JUN 2, 1806

Ranaway-George, negro, ab't 24 yrs of age, from Richd Murray, living nr Tenley town, Wash, D C.

Pblc sale: all right, title, & claim of Robt Brown in lot 4 sq 320 with brick dwlg hse, at suit of Saml Davison, Crct Crt of Wash Co, D C; & right, title & claim of John Moore [miller] in sq 535, late the prop of said Moore, at suit of Saml Davidson. [2 Splgs of Davison-Davidson] -Danl C Brent, Marshal.

WED JUN 4, 1806

Wash City-elected for City Cncl:

First Chamber:	John Dempsie	Saml N Smallwood	Jeremiah Booth
	Wm Prout	Robt Alex'r	Saml H Smith
	Thos H Gillis	Fred'k May	Jas Hoban
Not elected:	John Nowland	Saml Fowler	Thos Carberry
2d Chamber:	John Sinclair	Matthew Wright	Alex'r McCormick
	Peter Lenox	Henry Herford	Phineas Bradley
	Jos Bromley	Nicholas King	Henry Ingle
Not elected:	Robt Cherry	Cornelius Cunningham	John Beckley
	John Davis	Buller Cocke	Saml Lowdermilk

FRI JUN 6, 1806

Lt Alfred Sebastian, of U S 2d Reg infantry, found not guilty at Crt Martial held at New Orleans, Jan 4, 1806.

Wanted an apprentice, where fine arts combined with mechanical practice will be taught. -Mr Lewis Clephan, F St.

MON JUN 9, 1806

Reward-$10 for strayed colt. -Jas Scaggs, lvng on Eastern Branch, PG Co, Md.

Pblc sale-decree of High Crt of Chancery. Dwlg plantation of the late Richd Williams, dec'd, in PG Co, Md, 300 acs. -Wm Williams, trustee.

WED JUN 11, 1806

Directors of the Tyber Creek Navigation will meet at the hse of Thos Thorpe, chrman, Sat.

Taxes due by Mar 1, 1807. -J Pleasants jr, kpr of the rolls. Richmond. Va.

Jos Flaut, insolvent debtor, confined to Wash Co prison, for debt. -Wm Brent, clk.

Strayed or stolen-bay gelding. -Randol Morris, PG Co, Md.

FRI JUN 13, 1806

John Suter, insolvent debtor, confined to Wash Co prison for debt. -Wm Brent-clk.

Dissolution of partnership: Andrew Ross & Stephen Pleasanton, by mutual consent; store crnr of Wash & Bridge Sts, Gtwn. Business cont'd under Andrew Ross & Robt Getty. [groceries]

MON JUN 16, 1806

Died: Geo Wythe, age 80 yrs, Jun 8, Patriot, Chancellor of Richmond, Va. [See Jun 30, 1806]

Ice for sale: J Boothe & G Barry, So Capt St & Ga Ave, nr Barry's wharf.

Official ltr to Hon Robt Smith, esq, Sec of the Navy, Phil, 7 Sep, 1805 by Thos Truxtun. Cmdor Truxtun wrote that on Mar 3, 1802 he was unwell & in Norfolk; was remv'd to his farm in N J & confined to his bed; this is in regard to his order to assume command of the frig *Chesapeake* & Cmdor of the Mediterranean squadron. By order of the Pres, the resignation of Cmdor Truxtun thus tendered was accepted. Richd Dale writes to Chas Biddle, Phil, Sep 7, 1805, that he did not understand that Cmdor Truxtun was resigning his commission. Decision in ltr dt'd Feb 10, 1806 to Truxtun by R Smith:-you cannot now be re-instated.

My son, Richd Anderson, left me without just cause, forwarn persons on crediting him on my account. -Saml Anderson.

For sale: *Swan Point*, Chas Co, Md, 214 acs, prop of Dr Chas Lancaster. -John Lancaster Sr & Benj Lancaster, *Cob Neck*. Also, 142 acs adjoining *Swan Point*. -Benj Lancaster.

WED JUN 18, 1806
Ranaway-Wm Dent, age 14 yrs, apprentice. -Edw Fennell, Wash.

Brethren of Columbia Lodge-No 35, to meet Tue. -Jas Grady, Sec.

FRI JUN 20, 1806
My wife, Mary, has eloped from my bed & board. I will not pay any debts contracted by her. -Azariah Gatton.

Ice for sale, bushell or peck, my hse on F St. -Honore Julien.

MON JUN 23, 1806
Thos Patterson has supplied his store on F St with medicines & drugs. Wash City.

Ship-*Western Trader*, was built at Pittsburg & owned by Jas Berthoud. The ship-*Thos Penrose,* was built at Maysville, Ken, & owned by Messrs Hollingsworth & Gallagher.

Jos Bentley, insolvent debtor, cnfnd in Wash Co prison, for debt. -Wm Brent, clk.

For sale: *Harvey's Meadows* patented Dec 31, 1805, 341 acs; also *Mount Parnassus*, 298 acs; both in Allegany Co, Md. Mr Thos Beall, of Cumberland & Dan'l Clark & Robt Cowden Stone, esq, are acquainted with the land. Saml J Coolidge, Upper Marlborough, PG Co, Md. [Saml has never seen the land]

WED JUN 25, 1806
Reward-$5 for ladies wearing apparel; person suspected is a Mrs Williams. -Geo Rice, nr the Navy Yd

FRI JUN 27, 1806
Crt of Common Pleas, Carlisle, Cumberland Co; Jas Corbet & Mgt his wife, late Mgt Clark widow & relict of John Clark, late of Allen Township in Cumberland Co, dec'd, in right of said Mgt; support of last will of said John Clark, dec'd. Wm Lyon, Prothonetary, Carlisle.

MON JUN 30, 1806
Ranaway: Rafe, negro, ab't 20 yrs of age, from Benedict Boarman, living nr Bryantown, Chas Co, Md. Reward-$20.

Richmond, Va-Jun 25. Geo W Sweeney was cld before the Examining Crt on charge of poisoning his gr uncle, Geo Wythe, & a srvt boy. Trial to be held Sep next. [See Jun 16, 1806]

WED JUL 2, 1806
John Konkapot jr, of the Stockbridge Tribe of Indians, thanks the gentlemen of Wash & Gtwn for relieving him from pecuniary embarrassment. -Jun 30, '06.

Thos Fry, insolvent debtor, cnfnd in Wash Co prison, for debt. -Wm Brent, clk.

MON JUL 7, 1806
My wife Mable Farrell has eloped from my bed & board; I have determined to live with her no longer; I will not pay any debts that she may contract. [Retraction of same, Jul 9 -Patrick Farrell] -Patrick Farrell.

Reward-$60 for Bill Stewart, mulatto; was prop of Honore Martin who sold him to Rich Contee, who sold him to me. -Walter Bowie living in PG Co, Md. Also Harry & Joe Grimes alias Graham.

In Chancery: Thos Law vs Richd Gridley; ratify sale of mortgaged prop for $425. -Wm Brent, clk.

WED JUL 9, 1806
For sale: decree of High Crt of Chancery-sale o/plantation where the late Nicholas Blacklock formerly lived in Chas Co, Md, 514 acs. -John Spalding, trustee.

In Chancery, Jun Term 1806. Jas Barry vs Dorothy O'Brien & others. Ratify sale by Lewis Ford, trustee, saving to the said Dorothy O'Brien her legal right of dower, premises sold for $500. -Wm Brent, clk.

Ranaway negro, Bill, ab't 19 yrs of age; from *Pettworth* farm of John Tayloe, esq, nr Wash. Thos T Page, agent for John Tayloe, esq, at *Neabsco Furnace*, nr Dumfries, Va.

FRI JUL 11, 1806
W Blanchard, chemist & druggist, has opened his new store on First & High St, one of Mr Thos Corcoran's new hses. -Gtwn.

In Chancery, Jun 25, 1806. Wm Stewart vs Isaac Polock & David Polock. Ratify sale by Jos Forrest, trustee, for sum of $2,260. -Wm Brent, clk.

MON JUL 14, 1806

Ranaway: Wat, negro, ab't 33 yrs of age; formerly prop of Sarah Clagget nr Upper Marlboro, PG Co, Md. -Jos Fowler

David Easton, insolvent debtor, confined in Wash Co prison for debt. -Wm Brent, clk.

WED JUL 16, 1806

Elected trustees of the Wash Acad by the City Cncl: Thos Jefferson, Wm Cranch, Nicholas King, Abraham Bradley, Wm Brent, Fred'k May, Saml Hanson [Wash]

To rent: the wharf & warehse of the late Mr Griffith Coombe, in this City. -Robt Brent.

Mrs Reagan has opened an acad on F St bet Capt Jas Hoban & Josiah W King.

FRI JUL 18, 1806

Republican Delegates met at Mr David Levy's hse in Fred'k Town, Md, to unanimously endorse Patrick Magruder. -John B Colvin, Sec.

Orphans Crt of Wash Co, D C. Application of Christiana Berrs for ltrs of adm on prsnl est of Wm Sykes, late of U S Navy, seaman, dec'd. -John Hewett, Reg.

Died: Mrs Mary Eliz Robinson, age 76, Jul 14, at the hse of Dr Thornton in Wash, in whose family she had resided for many yrs; ntv of Pa.

MON JUL 21, 1806

Wash City-Trial of Mr Duane, editor of the Aurora, against Peter Meirkin, for assault & battery, jury found verdict in favor of the plaintiff, $600 damages.

Ranaway: Romulus, negro, age ab't 14 yrs. -John Eversfield, living in PG Co, nr Nottingham, Md.

Ladies with ltrs in Wash P O, Jul 1, 1806:

		Hannah Bond
Mrs Buddy	Miss Mary Bloor	Mrs Annie Davis
Eliz Hughes	Mrs Mgt Heasket	Miss Jackson
Miss Sarah Lomax	Mrs Jane Lolier	Miss Nancy Prout
Miss Ann Price	Mrs Lucy Smith	Mrs Sarah Slater
Miss Polly Touler	Mrs Molly Thompson	Miss Sally Thompson
Mary Waters.		

Benj Hawsey brght before me a stray horse. -Saml Hamilton, Wash Co, D C.

Crct Crt of U S. N Y Dist. U S vs Col Wm S Smith.
Jurors cld & sworn:

John Sullivan	John Rathbone jr	Lewis C Hamersley
Cortlandt Babcock	John P Haff	Gold Hoyt
John A Fort	Jas Masterton	Schuyler Livingston
Henry Panton	Geo Forman	Augustus Wyncoop.

Witnesses examined in behalf of the prosecution:

Dr Romaine	David Gelston	John McLean
General Stevens	Richd Belden	Jonathan Ogden
John Jacob Astor	Benj Haigh	Bernard Hart
Abram Vannest	Jonathan Fay	Wm Fosbrook
Saml G Ogden	Wm Allen	

FRI JUL 25, 1806

U S vs Col Wm S Smith-N Y Crt. [See Jul 23, 1806]
Witnesses on part of the prosecution:

Danl Ludlow	Wm Wallace	Jos Price
Thos Stevenson	Jno Moore	Wm Shields
Saml Corp	Cornelius Brinekerhoff	John McBride
Wm Weyman	John Corre	Martin Boorham
Jas Cleliand	John Murray	N Ward
Jas Burbank	Anthony Bird	Geo F Hopkins
John Gantz	Francis Gantz	John Swartwout
Jonas Mapes	Thos Stokes	Peter Rose
Richd Platt	Augustus Fleming	John Fink
Newinton Grenard		

[Jul 28-Verdict, not guilty-high misdemeanor]

Died: Maria Antoinette of Naples, Princess of Asturias, age 21 yrs, May 20.

MON JUL 28, 1806

Masonic meeting on Jul 29 to lay corner stone of Prot Episc Chr. -Jas Burges, Sec.

Died: Miss Elinor Ann Lee, age 67 yrs, Jul 17, at the Glebe of Wm & Mary, Chas Co, Md; latest surviving d/o Hon Richd Lee, last Pres of Md.

WED JUL 30, 1806

Convention bet U S & Creek Nation of Indians, Nov 14, 1805;
Signed & Sealed in presence of: Jas Madison, Rt Smith, Benj Hawkins, Timothy Bernard-interpreter, John Smith, & Andrew McClary; his Mark X: Oche Harijo, Wm McIntosh, Tuskenehau Chapco, Tuskenehau, Enehau Thlucco, Chekopeheke Emaettau. Seal of U S affixed Jun 2, 1806: Th Jefferson, Pres.

Died: Mr Simon Smith, midshipman, Jul 6, suddenly on board the U S bomb ketch *Vengeance*; ntv of R I; one of the Americ prisoners in Tripoli.

Died: Lt Seth Cartes, last Apr, at Syracuse, Cmder of Gun Boat #10, ntv of R I, & Mr Brent, midshipman, on board the U S cutter, *Hornet*.

Died: Lt Jos Maxwell, of U S N, at Syracuse, Feb last.

Orphans Crt of Wash Co, D C. Application of Mich'l McCormick for of adm on prsnl est of Wm Gough, late of U S N, seaman, dec'd. -John Hewitt, R C C

Strayed from the Commons, Wash City, grey horse. -Wm Simmons nr the President's square, Wash City.

FRI AUG 1, 1806

Dept of State requests proof of citizenship for: Richd Smith, Peter Jennings, Christopher Beckman, Geo Jemison, Chas Hancock, Wm Barrett & Edw Duncan, detained in British svc, in order that application may be made for their release.

MON AUG 4, 1806

Died: Mr John White, age 58 yrs, Jul 28, at his plantation a few miles from Wash; mbr of old family in this vicinty; sacrament was administered to him by Rev Mr McCormick. Funeral, Jul 29 with sermon preached by Rev Mr Reed at dec'd's hse.

WED AUG 6, 1806

Quarry of marble stone has been discovered on the plantation of Mr John Henkel, nr Harper's Ferry. -Alexandria, Jun 21.

FRI AUG 8, 1806

For sale: 356 acs, Harrison Co, nr Clarksburgh; 238 acs, Campbell Co, Va. -John Plummer, Wash City. Desirous of purchasing lands in state of Ohio.

MON AUG 11, 1806

Ranaway-Stephen Tarleton, negro, ab't 35 yrs of age. Reward-$30. -Thos P Willson, Montg C H, Md

Wash Academy West, Richd White, principal.

WED AUG 13, 1806

Benj Austin, loan ofcr, acknowledged he had circulated an infamous falsehood ab't my prof conduct, & having refused to give the satisfaction due to a gentleman in similar cases, I hereby publish said Austin as a coward, liar, & scoundrel. -Thos O Selfridge, Boston, Aug 4, 1806.

Died: Mr Chas Austin, age 19 yrs, eldest s/o Hon Benj Austin, esq, from a pistol discharged in State St; expired instantly. Coroner's inquest returned verdict of wilfull murder by the hand of Thos O Selfridge, with malice aforethought. -Boston-Aug 6, 1806.

Wanted: info ab't Mr Renderts, left Holland ab't 1787 or the West Indies; then left for the U S; supposed to be a resid of this country. Will by writing Mrs Anna Moore, Wash City, rec info of his dght, who with her mthr, [long since dead], remained in Dockurn, West Friesland, when her fr sailed from Amsterdam.

Calvert Co Crt, Md. May Term, 1806. Application of Wm Spencer & wife, 2 of the reps of John McDowell, dec'd: if his est wld admit of division. Some of the reps: Ann Blackburn, Jas Ellis & Dolly his wife, & Alice Blackburn live out of Md. -Wm S Morsell, clk.

Died: Gen John Williams, age 53 yrs, Jul 23, in Salem, Wash Co, formerly a mbr of Cong of U S.

FRI AUG 15, 1806

Horrid murder-Augusta, Maine-Jul 9. Capt Jas Purrington, of said place, murdered his wife & chldrn & slashed his throat; dghts were aged 19 yrs, 10 yrs, & 18 mos; sons were 8 yrs & 6 yrs; eldest son age 17 yrs escaped & ran to Mr Dean Wyman, a nr neighbor; another dght barely survives her wounds. Capt Purrington was 46 yrs of age & lately remv'd from Bowdingham to Augusta.

Boston Chronicle: T G Selfridge, lawyer of this town, ab't 34 yrs of age, was committed by Justice Gorham, for his murder of Mr Chas Austin, oldest s/o Hon Ben Austin, esq.

Dept of State wants proof of ctznship of the following now detained in the British svc:

John Williams	John Badd	Roles Morris
John Hays	John Dickson	Wm Mills
Henry Pierce	John Collin	Henry Kirlpatrick
Jas Vent	John Jameison	John A Mott
Jacob Bonequaid	John Days	Nath'l Perry

In Chancery-Chas Co, Md. Ratify sale by John Spalding, trustee, of rl est of Nicholas Blacklock, dec'd; 514 acs in Chas Co sold for $8,159.75. -Saml H Howard, R C C

Those indebted to me must make immediate payment. I am closing my books. -Romulus Riggs, Gtwn.

Ranaway: Kizziah, negro woman, age ab't 24 yrs. -Robt Alexander, Wash.

MON AUG 18, 1806

Ranaway: Jack, negro. -Abram B Hooe, living at Hooe's Ferry, King Geo Co, Va. or notify Henry Suttle, Gtwn.

Wanted: a journeyman chair-mkr. -Saml Russ, Navy Yd, Wash.

Wish to exchange ab't 800 acs in Fairfax Co, formerly Loudon Co, for land in western country. -B Dade, Alexandria.

Murder of the crew of the ship *Atahualpa*, of Boston; from Mr Joel Richardson who was armorer on board. Murdered was Capt Oliver Porter, 2 mates, Mr Lyman

Plumer, & 6 seamen. Ship left Boston in Aug 1803 bound for nw coast of Americ; arrv'd there in Jan 1804. [Lyman Plumer is nphw of Theodore Lyman, esq, of Boston the ship's owner]. Indian Chief Kiete, who had traded on board a few visits before, returned & with 200 indians attacked all on board; Capt Porter was daggered & taken captive to the shore where he lingered for 15 days. Killed on board-Mr John Hill, chief mate, Danl Gooding, 2nd mate, John G Ratstraw, Capt's clk, Peter Spooner, Luther Lapham, Mr Lyman Plumer, seamen, Isaac Sammes, cooper, John Williams, cook. Wounded: Ebenezer Baker, seaman, Henry Thompson, seaman, Ebenezer Williams, seaman, Luke Bates, seaman, Jos Robinson, carpenter, Thos Edwards, steward & Wm Walker. When the decks were cleared of the indians we set sail & buried the dead in Queen Charlotte's Sound.

WED AUG 20, 1806

Henry Ingersoll, prisoner taken on board Miranda's schnr, is s/o Mr Jonathan Ingersoll of Stockbridge, in this county. He went to N Y last Nov & rashly embarked with the Spanish adventurer, he was under 21 yrs off age.
-Pittsfield Sun.

For sale: 500 acs belonging to the est of late Richd Henderson, in PG Co, Md. Mr Jos Wilson lives on the land. -Jas Longan, John Henderson, excs.

John C Smith has rsgn'd his seat in the Hse o/Reps of U S.

FRI AUG 22, 1806

Partnership of Rufus Elliott & John Gregory is dissolved by mutual consent.

Nath'l Macon, of N C, re-elected a rep in Congress.

MON AUG 25, 1806

I forwarn all persons trusting my wife, Matilda; I will not pay any of her debts.
-Peter Joseph, X his mark.

Saml Vail & Co propose publishing a wkly newspaper, Missouri Correspondent & Illinois Gazette, in La Terr at St Louis.

WED AUG 27, 1806

Editor wanted for the Salem Register due to the death of its editor, Mr Carlton.

Miss White, of England, intends opening a school for young ladies. Cards to Mrs White's hse next to Columbia Bank.

For sale: hse & lot now occupied by Mr Geo Southerland, North G St nr the War ofc, now rented for $175 per annum. Apply to F H Gilliss, Wash City.

Died: John Dennis, esq, of Somersett Co, [M.] age 35 yrs, was rep in Cong of U S for several yrs.

Anacostia Library Co. -Benj Moore, librarian.

Died: Meriwether Jones, com'r of loans, Aug 9, nr Sweet Springs; left a widow & his son, his only child. [Aug 29 paper-*Warm Springs*, Bath Co, Va, age 41 yrs]

FRI AUG 29, 1806

Ltr to Cmdor Jno Rodgers, by ofcrs of Americ squad, in Mediterranean, previous to their departure for the U S, noting their high respect for him. Signed: Theodore Hunt, Jas Laurrence, Ben Smith, Saml Elbert, Arthur Sinclair, Wm Crane, Ralph Izard, Humphrey Magrath, John Henly, A C Harrison & Nath'l Haraden. -Ship *Constitution,* Gibraltar, May 27, 1806.

Mr Stedman, of N Y, fell into the hands of the Spaniards & was killed-he had resided in Port-Au-Prince for ab't 7 or 8 yrs; others recognized as dead were Messrs Ledlie & Donahue & Capt Gardner. Aug 8 the Miranda was to be publicly burnt at Laguira. Capt Suter informs that the Spaniards rejoiced at the proceedings. -Phil True Am. N Y, Aug 26. Jas Ledlie, Capt Geo Kirkland & Mr Lippincott, persons mentioned to be hung at Carraccas, were not on board *Miranda's* captured schnrs; this affords hope that the acc't of the execution is premature.

Phil-Aug 23: Crew of the 2 schrs belonging to *Miranda* who were put to death & their heads exhibited: Jas Ledlie of Phil; Mr Lippincott-connections in Phil; Capt Donahue of Phil, left a wife & family; Mr Geo Kirkland, formerly a Capt in the Provisional Army of U S; Paul George & Capt Gardner-no info; Mr Smith-butcher of N Y & a Polish gentleman.

MON SEP 1, 1806

Correct list of persons executed as pirates, at or nr Laguira: Jas Garnder, Gus Adolphus Bergudd-a Polander, Chas Jonson, Miles Hall, John Farris, Francis Farquahasen, Thos Donahue-of Phil, Thos Villop, Danl Kemper, Paul F George-Portuguese.

Jason Jones-insolvent debtor, confined to Wash Co prison for debt. -Wm Brent, clk.

The new mkt hse nr the Navy Yd in Wash will be opened Sep 1. -L White, clk of Eastern Branch Mkt.

For sale-order of Orphans Crt of PG Co, Md; plantation of late Jas Beall, dec'd, & prsnl prop. -Jas Beall jr & Obid Beall-excs.

Orphans Crt of Wash Co, D C. Aug 30, 1806. Applic of Mich'l McCormick for ltrs of adm on prsnl est of Hugh McCormick, late of U S N, dec'd. -Jno Hewitt, ROC.

A skow has taken adrift nr *Carrolls Point.* Owner apply to Saml Anderson or Saml McPherson.

WED SEP 3, 1806
Memoirs of Jos Priestley were written by himself up to the yr 1795; the continuation until his decease is by his son, Jos.

Died: Baron De Melas, Genr'l o/Cavalry, at an advanced age; at Elbe-Teinitz, Bohemia; commanded the Austrian Army at Battle o/Marengo.

Shipwreck of the *Rose in Bloom:* left Charleston Aug 16; violent storm arose off S C; passengers who got into the sea, Miss McPherson, helped up the companion by Mr John Rutledge; Gen McPherson numbered among the dead, also Mrs Booth & her only son. Rescued by the British brig, *Swift*, of St Johns, [Capt Richd Phelan:]-Capt Stephen Barker, Capt Oliver Champlin, Hon John Rutledge, Miss Eliza MacPherson, Messrs M Brennan, Jos W Page, B Booth, D Botifeur, John Davis, H Turner, N Perry, D Crooker. Seamen: Benj Brayton, W Van Eightten, John W Gibbs, Randal Cornell, Lloyd B Brut, John Hathway, Wm Dawson, Lewis Riley, Jas Quin, Thos Conly, Wm Cowan, Baptiste Hajardie, John Murray & Henry Davis, last 3 of colour. List of those who were lost: Gen MacPherson & svt; Mrs Booth & son; Messrs Clark, Jas Miller jr, Thos Tait, Henry Bowering; Dr Ballard & svt; svts' of Mr Botifeur & D Crooker. Passengers & seamen: Wm Whiteledge, John Forcha, D McCarty, Wm Robinson, Chas Bryce, Fortune Johnson, John Trusty, Adam Knot & Harry Kid, last 3 men of colour. [Mr Tait was of the hse of Tait & Wilson in Charleston]

Crt of Enquiry. Capt Danl Carmick, of U S M C, for disrespect to his cmndng ofcr. Crt will be formed by following ofcrs: Lts Henry Caldwell, John R Fenwick, John Williams. Judge Advocate, Elias B Caldwell, esq. Franklin Wharton, Lt Col Commandant Marine Corps. Capt Carmick found not guilty.

FRI SEP 5, 1806
Reps in ensuing Congress from N C: Nath'l Macon, Jas Holland, Evan Alex'r, Richd Stanford, Willis Alston, Wm Blackledge & Thos Kenan.

Springfield bridge in Mass, skill & industry of Jonathan Walcott, of Windham, Conn; piers & stone work under superintendance of Mr Israel Reed, of Harvard, Worcester Co.

Farm to rent in Montg Co, Md, at Falls of Seneca, 18 miles from Gtwn. -Jos Forrest, Wash.

MON SEP 8, 1806
Elected reps in Cong from N C: Thos Blount, Lemuel Sawyer, & John Culpepper.

Leonard town, Jockey Club Races. E J Millard, sec.

Re-elected mbrs of Cong for 6 dists of Ky: Matthew Lyon, John Boyle, John Rowan, R M Johnson, Benj Howard & Jos Desha.

Electors of Md. Montg Co: Robt P Magruder & Upton Beall. PG Co: Walter Bowie & Edw Calvert. Annapolis: Benj Ogle.

WED SEP 10, 1806

Runaway: Philip, negro, committed to Fred'k Co, Md jail, says he belonged to Mr Wm Boyd, of Fred'k Co, Va & after his death was sold to John Henderson of one of the Carolinas. Also committed: Geo Morgan, runaway, says he belongs to Isaac Brewill, of Mecklenburgh Co, Ohio. -Geo Creager, Shrf, Fred'k Co.

FRI SEP 12, 1806

Died: Chas Francis Sheridan, esq, Jun 24, at Tunbridge Wells, historian of the Rev of Sweden, & bro of senator & poet, Richd Brinsley Sheridan.

Ranaway: Joe, mulatto fellow, age ab't 30 yrs. -Singleton Burgee, living in Fred'k Co, Md, nr New Market.

Died: Chas Pettit, Sep 10, patriot of the Rev; born in N J; after declaration of peace Mr Pettit chose Phil for his resid; age 70 yrs; chldn survive him.

MON SEP 15, 1806

Mrd: Mr Jas Bury to Miss Mgt Coons, both of Wash, Sep 9, by Rev Mr McCormick.

WED SEP 17, 1806

Those indebted to the firm of Brohawn & Byus will make payment to Saml Speak or to R W Goldsborough.

Died: Wm Patterson, Sep 9, at Albany, Judge of Crct Crt of U S.

MON SEP 22, 1806

Countryman, Benj West, eminent painter, will return to Pa in a few days. -Am Daily Advertiser.

Died: Hon Wm Patterson, at mansion of Stephen Van Rensselaer, in Albany, N Y, Sep 16; Patterson ctzn of N J & Judge.

Dr David Ramsay, of Charleston, S C, has written a *Life of Washington*; he also wrote The History of The Americ Rev .

Murder has been comitted on Chas Nevitt, jr, of PG Co, by a negro man, slave of Basil Soper, cld Wall, who has absconded. Govn'r Robt Bowie offers reward of $100. -Ninian Pinkney, clk.

WED SEP 24, 1806

Richd Ross brought before me 2 stray horses. -Gabriel P Vanhorn.

Nehemiah Knight & Isaac Wilbour, elected Reps to Cong from R I.

Died: Col Fred'k H Baron De Weissenfels, age 78 yrs, at New Orleans, May 14; born nr Elbing, a Hanse town in Prussia in 1728, of a noble family; town in Germany named by his family; came to Americ in 1756; joined the Americ Army & in 1779 was made Lt Col Commandant of the 4th N Y Regt.

Hugh Maguire, late a prof in St John's College, Annapolis, intends to open a school for gentlemen in Upper Marlboro, Md.

FRI SEP 26, 1806

For sale: prsnl est of Chas McLaughlin, dec'd; furn, negroes, horses, stock; order of Orphans Crt of Wash Co. -P McLaughlin, adm.

Goshen farms for rent-300 acs, Montg Co, Md; & dwlg hse. -R M Boyer, Gtwn-D C.

State of Conn vs Selleck Osborn & Timothy Ashley.

Jurors:

Jabez Gillet	Ashbel Spencer	Medad Munson
Benj Hale	Norman Griswold	Josiah Upson
Wm Taylor	Titus Darrow	Stephen Diler
Levi Watson	Luke Loomis	Platt Starr

Support of prosecution:

Chas Deming s/o Julius	Jos Adams	Julius Deming

For the Defense:

Ebenezer Picket	Ashahel Wilson	John Welch
Moses Seymour jr	Capt Simmons	Seth Griswold
Deacon Ozias Lewis	Russel Hunt	Norman Buell
Gen Skinner	Aaron Page	Ebenezer Picket
Job Simmons	Hicks Smith	

[Libel case] Osborn & Ashley, both convicted as common libeller-fine $100, cost of prosecution, & bonds of $500 ea.

Lost or stolen-black mare. -Chas Minifie, Wash City.

MON SEP 29, 1806

Orphans Crt of Wash Co, D C. Sep 29, 1806. Prsnl est of Jos Taylor, late of Wash City, dec'd. -John Davidson; Wash Boyd, excs

Patent threshing mach, inventor-Jas Deneale, Dumfries, Va. To wit for same: Stephen Milburn, Beverley's Ford, Fauquier Co, Va; Wm Champe Carter, Culpepper, Va; John Strode, Culpepper Co, Va.

WED OCT 1, 1806

For sale: prop adjoining Bank of Columbia, Gtwn, now occupied by Mr Wm Graham as a tavern. -Osborn Sprigg, PG Co, Md.

FRI OCT 3, 1806

Wash Jockey Club: John Tayloe, Pres; John Mason, Thos Peter, Henry O'Reilly, Nathan Lusborough, Stewards; Dennison Darling, Sec & Treas; Chester Bailey, clk of the course.

MON OCT 6, 1806

Reward: $500 for 2 ltrs from Messrs Walker & Kennedy at Phil to Messrs Jas & John Dunlop at Petersburg, Va; ea with $2000 bank notes. -Gideon Granger, Postmaster Genrl.

In Chancery, Sep 24, 1806. Ratify sale made by Jas S Morsel, trust of est of Thos Clarke, dec'd; sum of $3,847 & another part for $210. -Saml H Howard, R C C.

WED OCT 8, 1806

Ladies with ltrs in Wash P O-Oct 1, 1806:

		Mrs Cath Belt
Miss Bayly	Betty Chandler	Cath Cornon
Miss Mgt R Chesnut	Polly Crane	Miss Mary G H Dulany
Miss Ann Gallay	Mrs Henry Hutchens	Miss Ann Heart
Mrs Jane Lottor	Cath Nigly	Molley Sharp
Mrs Ann Smith		

FRI OCT 10, 1806

John H Barney, insolvent debtor, confined to Wash Co prison, for debt. -Wm Brent, clk.

MON OCT 13, 1806

Balt & Fredericktown Turnpike Rd Co: Pres-Jonathan Ellicott, Treas-Wm Cooke. Mgrs: Thos Sprigg, John McPherson, Geo Baer jr, John E Howard, John Ellicott of John, John Donnell, Solomon Etting, Lewis B Smith. -Petersburg, Oct 2.

Orphans Crt of Montg Co, Md. Sale of prsnl est of John Holmes & Mary Holmes, late of said Co, dec'd. M Browning adm D B N of John Holmes & adm of Mary Holmes, dec'd. To be rented-the late farm of Mary Holmes, 500 acs. -M Browning, Clarksburg, Md.

Delegates from PG Co, Md: Francis M Hall, Benj Hodges, Henry A Colles & Thos Woodward. Archibald Van Horne is elected to Rep the Dist of PG & A A cos, in Congress of U S.

WED OCT 15, 1806

Reps in Assembly *Fred'k Co,* Md: Thos Hawkins, Joab Waters, Henry Kuhn, Benj Biggs. *Wash Co*: John Bowies, Tench Tinggold, Martin Kershnor, David Schebly, ____ Webb & John T Mason

FRI OCT 17, 1806

Sale at auction, hsehld furn at hse of his Britannic Majesty's Envoy Extra & Mnstr Pleni to U S-Wash. -N L Queen, Auct.

Tan yard for sale in Wash City; & 20 lots. -Robt Underwood, Treas Dept.

Died: on Oct 16, Mrs Mary Davidson, w/o Jas Davidson, cashier of ofc of Discount & Deposit of Wash. Funeral is Oct 17.

MON OCT 20, 1806
Mrd: Lt Jos Tarbell, of U S N, to Miss Eliza Cassin, d/o Capt John Cassin, Oct 16. [No date-recent: Wash City news item.]

WED OCT 22, 1806
Wm Campbell, bill of interpleader, in case of Henry Pratt, Thos W Francis, John Miller jr, John Ashley & John Baker, cmplnts vs Wm Mayne Duncanson & Saml Ward, dfndnts. Bill filed by Campbell in case now depending in Chancery in Crct Crt of Wash Co, D C. Bill states that Robt Morris, John Nicholson & Jas Greenleaf, & others were seized of sqs in Wash City; conveyed same to Duncanson against bills of exchange & notes held by Saml Ward; same have been fully discharged; Campbell states that Duncanson is indebted to him for a large sum of money; Ashley, Baker & Ward do not reside in Wash, D C. -Wm Brent, clk.

Died: Mr Fragonard Sr, age 74, Aug 22; French school loses an esteemed painter; he has left a son who will follow in his fr's footsteps. -Paris Argus.

FRI OCT 24, 1806
Ranaway: Milly, mulatto, ab't 30 yrs old. -Andrew T McCormick, Wash.

Genrl Assembly convened at New Haven-John C Smith, spkr; Lyman Law & Uriel Holmes jr, clks. -Hartford, Oct 13.

Durham Parish, Chas Co, Md, wishes to employ a clergyman of Prot Episc Chr. -Wm Browner, reg.

MON OCT 27, 1806
Medicines prepared by Richd Lee & son, Balt, must apply to Mr Danl Rapine, Capt Hill, Wash, or Dr John Ott, Gtwn.

WED OCT 29, 1806
John Ragan, insolvent debtor, confined in Wash Co prison, for debt. -Wm Brent, clk.

Hartford: Theodore Dwight, esq, chosen to rep in 9th Cong of U S, vice John C Smith, esq, rsgn'd. Jona O Mosley, Lewis B Sturges, Timothy Pickin jr, Benj Tallmadge, Epaphrodisus Champion, Saml W Dana, & John Davenport, esqs, chosen to rep in the 10th Cong of U S. -Conn.

Rms for rent: apply to Anne Shaw, living on Capitol Hill, in yellow frame hse, nr Mr McCormick's store. -Ann Shaw.

Orphans Crt of PG Co, Md. Sale of est of Benj Leitel, late of PG Co, Md, dec'd. -Thos Leitel, adm

FRI OCT 31, 1806

Stolen or strayed from City Commons, a bay horse. -Henry Gird, living in the rear of the bank. Reward-$5.

MON NOV 3, 1806

N J election-reps in next Congress: Henry Southard, Wm Helms, John Lambert, Thos Newbold, Ezra Darby & Jas Sloan. [Rpblcns]

Pblc congratulates Lewis & Clark on the happy termination of their expedition; some details are in a ltr by Capt Clark to his bro, Gen Clark, nr Louisville. -St Louis, Sep 23.

WED NOV 5, 1806

The following have been impressed into British svc for lack of proof of ctznship of U S:

Thos Morris
Francis Nicholas
Henry Connor
Jas Fowler
John Lein
John F Cook
John Chase
John Donalds
Billy Chissers
John Miller
John Herbert
Nath'l Roach
Wm Allen
Jas Bennett
Robt Silver
Jas Oppa
Augustus Tomkins
David Hayes
Wm C Bree
Robt Briton
Jas Lind
Francis Cormick
Wm Witherald
John Jones
John Lock
Wm Ambrose
Thos Pierce
David Johnson

-Dept of State, Nov 3, 1806.

Mrd: Mr John Ott to Miss Ann Ritchie, both of Gtwn, at Fred'k Town, by Rev Mr Wagner.

FRI NOV 7, 1806

Pres of U S appt'd Jas Mather Sr & Pierre Foucher, mbrs of Leg Cncl of this terr, vice P Sauve & J N Destrehan, rsgn'd. -N Orleans, Sep 25.

Died: Chas Jas Fox, Sep 13, in the arms of his nphw Lord Holland; age 58 yrs. -London [Nov 10 paper-age 57 yrs; died at Chiswick; born Jan 13, 1749; & died Sep 13, 1806.]

Jas S Stevenson, druggist, has purch'd Dr John Bullus' medical establishment nr the Navy Yd, Wash.

MON NOV 10, 1806

David Duncan, late collector of the Port of Machinae, to remit by March the am't of their bond given to the U S. -Robt Abbott, Jno Dodemead; Detroit.

WED NOV 12, 1806

Died: Gen Knox, Oct 25; swallowed a sharp chicken bone which perforated his bowels & produced mortification. [Warren, Maine, Oct 26.]

Lottery-St Paul's Parish, Balt, Md. Mgrs: John Merryman, Mark Pringle, Jas Carroll, Wm Lorman, Geo Grundy, Isaac Philips, Geo Hoffman, Godert Haskins.

Mary Gibbons will petition to Congress at next session to divorce her from her hsbnd, Wm Gibbons. Wash City.

FRI NOV 14, 1806

American Hotel opened; east of the Capitol; was occupied for several yrs by Mr P D Stelle. -Frost & Quinn.

Order of High Crt of Chancery. Sale of dwlg plantation of late Richd Williams, dec'd, in PG Co, Md-300 acs. -Richd Isaac, trust.

Robt Wright is elected Govn'r of the State of Md, with no opposition.

MON NOV 17, 1806

Reps to Cong from S C: Robt Marion, Wm Butler, David R Williams, John Taylor, Richd Winn, Levy Casey, Thos Moore & Lemuel Jas Alston.

Order of Orphans Crt of PG Co, Md. Sale of dwlg place of John Hughs, late of PG Co, dec'd, nr Magruders Ferry, stock & furniture. -Wm Weems, adm.

WED NOV 19, 1806

Teacher wanted-apply to Rev Mr Thos Harrison of Pr Wm Co, Va, or to Mr David Boyle, merchant of Dumfries, Va.

Died: Mr Benj Bannecker, age 73 yrs, black man, at his resid in Balt Co, Md, immediate descendant of an African fr.

Maj Ferdinand L Claiborne, with 250 Dragoons & mounted infantry, crossed the Mississippi at Natchez on Sunday on their march to assist Genr'l Wilkinson in repulsing the Spanish Troops. Ofcrs commanding the cos: Capts Benj Farrar, Geo Poindexter, Alex Bisland, Basil Abrams, Wm T Voss, Ralph Regan. Dragoons from Jefferson Co, under Capt Thos Hinds, will join them in a few days. Natchez, Oct 7. All except Capt Farrar's Co has returned -Oct 14.

FRI NOV 21, 1806

Orphans Crt of PG Co, Md-sale at dwlg plantation o/the late John Baden of Thos, part o/his prsnl est: stock, utensils, etc. -Clement Baden & Jos N Baden, excs.

St Mary's Co, Md, Crt -Aug Term, 1806. Petition of Saml Greenwell to ascertain the division of the rl est of Martin French; division wld be prejudicial to the parties. Reps of said French: Jas French, Raphael French, John French & Eleanor French reside in Ky. -Jos Harris.

I, John L Ramage, Cnsl of U S for island of Cuba & resid of Havanna, certify that Thos B Bennett, mstr, Thos Lynch, mate, & Giles Williams, seaman, belonging to the schnr-*Aagenoria*, of Balt, were boarded by Lt Foley, Cmder of British schnr-*Haddock*; said Foley took Edw Williams, Henry Hara, Giles Williams & Jos Fraley; later he released all but Edw Williams & Henry Hara; Foley then made sail with the 2 impressed men. -Thos B Bennett, Thos Lynch, Giles [X] Williams. Sep 1, 1806, John L Ramage.

MON NOV 24, 1806

Troop of Cincinnati Light Dragoons, Capt Jas Ferguson, proferred their svcs to the Pres to march against the Spaniards if it is found necessary. -Cincinnati, Nov 4.

Wm A Burwell of Franklin Co, Democrat, elected to Congress, vice-Christopher Clark, rsgn'd. -Lynchburg, Va, Nov 13.

Died: Haydn, great musician, ab't Sep 1. -A Paris paper.

WED NOV 26, 1806

Pblc auction, at hse of Mathias Hart, dec'd, on *Greenleaf's Point*; hshld furn & gunsmith's tools. -N L Queen, auct.

Sale by auction-all the hshld furn, stock, etc, at hse of Dr Benson in Pa Ave -John Stephen, auct.

FRI NOV 28, 1806

Died: Chas Hodges, merchant, age 28 yrs, Nov 20, at Upper Marlboro, Md.

Mr Wm O'Neale advertises his boarding hse-Jefferson st, Gtwn. Apply to O'Neale or Capt Jno Mitchell, Gtwn. West Mkt, Wash City.

Francis P Hamilton, has commenced the prac of law; ofc on Capitol Hill in hse formerly occupied by Mr Claxton.

Boarding & lodging -John Doyne, Pa Ave, Wash City.

MON DEC 1, 1806

John C Shindle has opened a tin & sheet iron business nr Pa Ave, Wash, opposite the Centre Mkt.

Leg of Md elected Philip Reed, Sen in Cong of U S, vice, Robt Wright, appt'd Gov of Md. Mr Reed is a decided Rpblcn. Elias Glenn, appt'd a mbr of Senate of Md, in room of John Thompson Mason, not duly qualified to take a seat.

Thos Spalding, late Rep of Ga, has rsgn'd his seat.

TUE DEC 2, 1806

Thos Thorpe on F St, Wash, has fitted his hse for travelers.

Tunis Cravan has opened a new Dry Goods Store nr the Navy Yd.

Chas A Burnett-Gtwn, has rec'd watches & jewelry from London.

Ranaway: Joe, negro ab't 24 yrs of age; purch'd him 10 or 12 yrs ago of Dr John Emory, since dec'd, on the Eastern Shore. -Wm Briscoe, living nr ChaptiCo, St Mary's Co, Md. [St Clement's Bay, St Mary's Co, Md]

FRI DEC 5, 1806

Money found in red Morocco pktbk -Timothy Caldwell, nr West Mkt, Wash City.

MON DEC 8, 1806

Orphans Crt of PG Co, Md. Nov 25, 1806. Prsnl est of Jas Haddock Smith, late of said Co, dec'd. -Thos Crandell, Walter Smith, excs.

Wash Co, D C. Gerrard S Boarman brought before me a stray horse. -Saml N Smallwood.

Orphans Crt of PG Co, Md. Sale in Piscataway, prsnl prop of John Alex'r, dec'd, at his tavern. -B Bowling, adm.

Wash Co, D C-in Chancery, Jan 1806. Gedion Snow, cmplnt, vs Abigail Perkins, widow & adm & Hannah Perkins, sister & heir of Jos Perkins, dec'd, & Nathan Bond, dfndnts. Jos Perkins, formerly of Boston, dec'd, indebted to the U S for duties-$757.50; cmplnt was obliged to pay same; Jos Perkins died intestate leaving no lineal heirs & leaving a wid & sister both who reside in Boston; prays for sale of lots 5 & 6, sq 408, in Wash City. -Wm Brent, clk.

Those with demands against Levi Holden, insolvent debtor, meet at the hse of John Baird, innkpr, in town of Heckensack. -Jonathan Baldwin, assignee.

Orphans Crt of Wash Co, D C. Dec 8, 1806. Prsnl est of John Stenger, late of Wash City, dec'd. -Solomon Stenger, adm

Orphans Crt of PG Co, Md. Isabella Wood & Osborn Belt jr, adms of Elijah Wood, late of PG Co, Md, dec'd, to make distribution to heirs & leg reps of said Wood. Lashly Wood, Eleanor Swaine & Robt Wood reside out of Md. -Trueman Tyler, Reg of Wills

Reward-$50 for apprehending Richd Gotier, who broke from jail; was a sailor in U S svc. -Danl C Brent, mrshl of D C.

Hse o/Reps: petition from Josiah Whitney, atty for heirs of Phineas Miller, late of Ga; referred to committee of claims.

Ranaway: Moll, age 25, negro woman. -Geo French, Gtwn.

Wm H Cabell re-elected Govn'r of Va without opposition.

Committed to Cecil Co, Md, jail-John, negro, ab't 23 yrs of age; says he belongs to Jas Bailey of Henrico Co, Va. -Jos Baxter, Sheriff, Elkton, Cecil Co, Md.

Benj Hodges of Thos, Up Marlboro, Md, wishes to purchase negro girl ab't 16 to 21 yrs.

Crct Crt of Wash Co, D C. Augustus Fricke, cmplnt, vs Thos Carpenter, dfndnt. Pblc auction part of lot 15 sq 141, Wash, with 2 story framed dwlg hse.
-Lewis Ford, trust.

Teas, wines, brandy, etc for sale. -Walter & Clement Smith, Gtwn.

FRI DEC 12, 1806

Thos Scott, Chilcotke, Ross Cy, Ohio, will act as agent for non-resid proprietors of land in Ohio.

Land for sale: resid of late Col John Gordon, 860 acs, North-Cumberland Co, Va, cld-*Exeter Lodge*. 200 acs in Fauquier Co, adj Mrs James & Mr Eustace, nr Elk Run Chr. In Caroline Co, 2,700 acs, part/o *Beverly Chace*. 100 acs in Spotsylvania Co, adj Col Jos Brock, Messrs J Brock & S Schoolers. Culpeper Co-960 acs, joins Landon Carter's farm. 815 acs adj Wm C Carter & Col M Green.
-Colin & Jas Ross, Fredericksburg, Va.

MON DEC 15, 1806

Creed Taylor, esq, appt'd by Leg of Va as successor to the late Judge Wythe, in High Crt of Chancery. Lewis Harvie, esq, of Richmond, elected mbr of Privy Cncl or Cncl of State, vice Lyne Shackelford, esq, dec'd. [Va]

WED DEC 17, 1806

Mary A Pic, of Gtwn, carries on business at her old store; articles of separation bet her hsbnd & herself & authority to conduct business for her own profit are recorded. -Gtwn.

Orphans Crt public sale: prsnl prop of Dan'l Eldridge, dec'd, consisting of wearing apparel, Navy Yd. -David Dobbin, Wash.

For sale: seasonable goods. -Chas Herstons, Gtwn.

FRI DEC 19, 1806

Died: Presly Thornton, late of Va, at Bath, in Genesee, N Y, Nov 17.

Mr Louis Francois Leloup, appt'd by Emperor of French & King of Italy, as Provisional Commissary of Commercial Relations, Balt, Md. -Thos Jefferson, Pres; Jas Madison, Sec of State.

Stolen from my plantation, a sorrel horse. -Dan'l Clarke,

Philip Reid, esq, of Kent Co, Md, elected Senator for 5 yrs.

MON DEC 22, 1806

Ltr from Pittsburg, Pa, to mbr of Congress, Dec 8, 1806. Some men of this town have set out to join Col Burr in his expedition against Mexico. Morgan Nevill, s/o Gen Presly Nevill; Thos Butler, s/o late Col Butler; Mr Forward, printer & editor of Tree of Liberty.

Final distribution at dwlg o/late Dan'l Kent, dec'd, Calv Co, Md. -Jos Kent, adm.

WED DEC 24, 1806

Andrew Moore, esq, elected Brig-Genr'l, vice, Genr'l John Bowyer, dec'd; in the 13th Brigade, Va.

Will of the late Hon Chas Jas Fox, of St Anne's Hill, Parish of Chertsey, county of Surry. Monies: Unto my nphw, Henry Fox, s/o Gen Fox; moiety unto Robt Stephen-youth living with Lord Viscount Bollingbroke, in America; annuity to my wife Eliz Bridget, exec, which after her decease-unto Harriet Willoughby. Wit: Edw Kenn, Chas Pembroke, Robert Giles. -C J Fox, Jul 21, 1802. [Extracts only]

Andrew Price, Capt; Jas Crawford, 1st Lt; John McIvain, 2d Lt; The Claibrone Volunteers are organized to serve at a moments warning. -Orleans Gazette.

Jesse Franklin is elected Senator of U S for North Carolina.

MON DEC 29, 1806

Frankfort, Ky, Dec 5. Charges against Aaron Burr & John Adair. No testimony to incriminate either person. Jury: Abraham Hite [foreman], Wm Steele, Geo Madison, John Patrick, Thos Lewis, Richd Apperson, P B Ormsby, Geo Greer, Richd Davenport, E M Covington, Abraham Owen, Thos Johnston, Robt Johnson, Nicholas Lason, John Kenton, N Miller, J Winlock, Richd Fox, Richd Price, Nathl Hart, John Bacon, & Thos Respass. -Thos Tunstall, C K D C.

La Genr'l Crt, Oct Term, 1806. U S vs Rufus Easton. Conduct of Mr Easton, dfndnt, in relation to contract made with David Fine was fair, honorable & honest; Mr E is not guilty. St Louis, Nov 1, 1806. Jurors: Nathan Bush, Anthony C Pormer, Green Dewitt, Chas Lucas, Henry Matz, Jas Berry, Saml Solomon, Darius Shaw, John Boly, Wm Johnson, Nichs Boilvin, Anthony S Badyly -Russel E Hicok, St Louis, Nov 13.

Orphans Crt of PG Co, Md. Sale at dwlg place of Saml D Beck jr, late of PG Co, Md; all prsnl est, stock & furn. -Andrew Hamilton, adm.

Ranaway: Peter, negro, ab't 35 yrs of age, from Jacob Barr living ab't 3 miles from Hagerstown, Wash Co, Md. $20-rwd.

Thos Munroe is postmaster, Wash City, D C.

WED DEC 31, 1806
Capt Meriwether Lewis arrived in Wash City after an absence of nrly 3 & 1/2 yrs, exploring the western country.

Zephaniah Farrell, of Wash, D C, pblc collector of pvt acc'ts, offers his svcs.

1807

FRI JAN 2, 1807

Geo Masters rsgn'd ofc of Chief justice of Ky, Thos Todd appt'd his successor. Felix Grundy appt'd in room of Benj Sebastian. Jas L Cathcart, esq, appt'd Cnsl of U S for Madeira, vice Mr Lemar, dec'd. Dennis Smelt, new mbr from Ga, elected in rm of Thos Spalding, rsgn'd.

Ranaway: Cato, negro man, from Eliz Willson, living in Pg Co, Md, nr Piscataway town. Reward-$10.

MON JAN 5, 1807

Ltr from Capt Hugh G Campbell to Patrick Simms, esq, dt'd U S ship *Constitution,* Lisbon Harbor, Oct 15, 1806. Rg death of Dr Patrick Simms, your son, on Oct 1; he was interred in Church Corpo Sauto, with all rites & ceremonies due.

Died: Mr Geo Dearborn, s/o Genr'l Dearborn, on his passage to this country.

Portrait painting: C Boyle paints likenesses in oil, in bldg formerly occupied by Mr G Stewart, Pa Ave, Wash.

WED JAN 7, 1807

Saddle & harness making, Pa Ave, Wash. -John Peltz

Died: John A Seitz, at Orleans, Jul 1804.

Legislature of Ky-charges against Benj Sebastian, Judge of Crt of Appeals charging him with receiving a pension from the Spanish Gov't. Testimony presented by Thos Bullitt, Chas Wilkins, Jas T Martin, Christ Greenup, Richd Steele, Wingfield Bullock, Danl Weisiger-adm with Harry Innes of the late Saml M Brown dec'd, & Harry Innes. Dec 2, 1806. [Ltr included from Thos Power, Louisville, Jul 19, 1797.]

FRI JAN 9, 1807

Info wanted: by young woman by name of Elliott, came with me from Clones, County Monaghan, Ire, expecting to find her Uncle ab't 40 miles of St Augusta or Savanna, Ga; his name is Wm Williamson, been in this country ab't 18 or 20 yrs, age ab't 40 yrs. -Wm McKilden, Wash City.

Leg of Ky, Dec 2, proceedings against Judge Sebastian. Testimony presented by: Thos Todd, Jos Crockett, Achilles Sneed, Geo Madison, Jos Hamilton Daveiss, John Brown. [See Jan 7, 1806]

Runaway: Joe, negro, confined to Fred'k Co, Md, jail; says he belongs to Col Jas King, of Sullivan Co, Tenn. -Geo Creager, Sheriff.

Died: Hon John Breckenridge, late Atty Genr'l of U S, at his seat nr Lexington, Ky, on Dec 14, 1806, age 47 yrs.

MON JAN 12, 1807

Present editor of the Commonwealth determined to relinquish his editorial duties-offers the same to any competent person of pure Republican principles. -E Pentland, Pittsburgh.

WED JAN 14, 1807

Died: Col John Bayard, age 69 yrs, at New Brunswick, Jan 7. -Philadelphia, Jan 12.

Died: Hugh Lennox, Dec 1, at Kingston, Jamaica; Cnsl of the U S in that island.

Resolution in favor of a present to Geo W Mann for his gallant conduct at Derne, unanimously passed the Genr'l Assembly of Md. -American.

Genr'l Assembly of Md will bestow 3 swords & belts to Chas Gordon, John Trippe & John Davis, for brave & gallant conduct in attacks on enemy gun boats off Tripoli.

For sale: part of lot 46, on Bridge St, adjoining Mr John Lairds's counting rm. Apply to Gen John Mason.

FRI JAN 16, 1807

New Jersey Dist-U S Crt. Indictment of Luther Baldwin for sedition. Baldwin, late of Newark Twnshp, Essex Co, N J, waterman; malice towards the Pres on Jul 27, 1798 in aforesaid Dist. Lucius Horatio Stockton, Atty of U S for N J Dist. [Congress-Hse of Reps, indictment read by Mr Eppes, Jan 9, 1807, during debate on bill for the punishment of crimes against the U S]

Edw Tiffin, esq, present Gov of Ohio, appt'd Senator of U S for 6 yrs from Mar 3, vice, Mr Worthington, whose term expired.

For sale: lease on sq 452 in Wash, improved by David Hepburn, gardner, now dec'd. -Alice Hepburn-adm, Tyber Spring Garden.

MON JAN 19, 1807

Orphans Crt ordered Isaac Pomroy, adm of John Deleitz, dec'd, that he sell prsnl prop of dec'd. -John Hewitt, reg.

WED JAN 21, 1807

Act of relief for Geo Little, damages, interest, & charges in the case of the brig, *Flying Fish*, captured by him while Cmder of the frig *Boston*, in svc of the U S, in 1799. -Nathl Macon, spkr of Hse o/Reps; Geo Clinton, VP of U S; Thos Jefferson, Pres;-Approved.

Andrew Gregg elected Senator of U S from Pa, vice Geo Logan. N B Beileau & John Steele were also in the election.

FRI JAN 23, 1807

Sale by auction-rl est of Dr Robt Pottenger, dec'd, lying in PG Co, Md, ab't 5 miles from Queen Anne, 800 to 1,000 acs. -Thos Buchanan, trustee.

Auction sale at hse of Thos Barwise, formerly Geo Walker's, in Wash-stock, blacksmith's tools & shop. -N L Queen-auct.

Wash, Dec 12, 1806. Lt Jas Thompson, paymaster of this Corp, to be replaced by Lt Robt Greenleaf. -Franklin Wharton, Lt Col Commandant M Corps. [No breach of trust, Signed-Wharton]

English horse, *Brilliant*, prop of John Tayloe, esq, of Mt Airy, will stand at Mr J Miltons, Fred'k Co, Va, nr Berryville, next season.

MON JAN 26, 1807

Erick Bollman & Saml Swartwout are confined in Wash Co, D C, at Marine Barracks under Military Guard.

Applied to be placed on the pension list; disabled by wounds rec'd in Rev War:

N H	Robt B Wilkins	Noah Robinson		
MA	Jonas Farnsworth	Danl Hickey	John Barry	
	Chas Gowin	Thos M Baker	Robt Ames	
	Ambrose Homan	Spafford Amer	Jona. Patch	
CT	Ehphalet Easton			
VT	Richd Fairbrother			
N Y	Peter D Demarest	John Devoe		
N J	Saml Dowdney	Benoni Hathaway	S Ogden	Wm Rebeck
VA	Chas M Thruston	Thos Coverly		
KY	Francis L Staughter	Benj Kendrick	John King	Jas Dysart

[Act of Apr 10, 1806]

Applied for increase in pension:,

N H	Jos Morrill	Wm Neley	Matthew Chambers	Seth Wyman
	Jonathan Holton	Jonathan Willard	Jos Huntoon	
MA	Gustavus Aldrich	John Maynard	Danl Nutting	Asa Ward
	Ebenezer Bancroft	Moses Wing	Thos Avery	
R I	Geo Bradford	Chas Scott		
CT	Ebenezer Coe	David Hawley	Abel Turner	
VT	Abel Woods			
N Y	Wm Worthington	Elisha Frizzle	Benj Smith	Wm Burritt
N J	Jabez Pembleton			
MD	Jacob Bernitz	Richd Hardin		
KY	Thos Pearson			

-H Dearborn, War Dept, Jan 12.

Caesar A Rodney is appt'd Atty Genr'l of U S.

Stray cow came to my plantation nr Eastern Branch. -Richd Eno.

WED JAN 28, 1807
Pblc sale of Saml Jones, late of PG Co, Md, dec'd; at hse of Chas Robinson; horse & 2 negro men. -Chas Robinson, Elisha Jones, excs, PG Co, Md. [Per last will & testament]

Orphans Crt of Wash Co, D C. Jan 28, 1807. Prsnl est of John Wight, late of said Co,dec'd. -Wash Boyd & Geo Moore, excs.

Montg Co, Md. Richd James brought a stray horse before me. -Thos Simpson.

Deposition of Wm Eaton, esq, of Mass: rgrdng Col Aaron Burr & his proposed overthrow of the U S Gov't. -Jan 26, 1807, Wash City. -Wm Brent, clk.

Deposition of Jas Lowry Donaldson: Genrl Jas Wilkinson had info ab't a treasonable design formed by Aaron Burr & others to dismember the Union, by separation of western states & territories from the Atlantic States. Jan 26, -Wm Brent, clk.

Depositions also of Wm Wilson & Ensign W C Mead-Jan 27. Jas Wilkinson, Brig Genr'l & Cmder in Chief of U S Army has warrants for Saml Swartwout, Jas Alexander & Peter V Ogden, on a charge of treason, misprison of treason. -Jan 26.

FRI JAN 30, 1807
Creditors of Alex'r Robinson, late dec'd, are to hand in their accounts to David Watterston & Jas Maitland; order of Orphans Crt of Wash Co, D C. -David Watterston, Jas Maitland, Geo Blagden, excs.

Pblc sale-5 tracts, namely-*Riley's Chance, Appenine Hills, Harrison's Delight, Addition to Hicks, & Let No Man Deceive You*, late prop of Kinsey Gillings of Benj; at suit of Nicholas Brewer use of Leonard H Johns. -John Fleming, shrf, Montg Co.

Ranaway: Joe, negro, from Leonard Soper living in PG Co, Md.

MON FEB 2, 1807
Edw Livingston of New Orleans City, swears he is utterly ignorant of schemes on part of Aaron Burr as hostile to the Union. Sworn, Dec 26, 1806, before Dom. A Hall, Dist Judge.

Genr'l Winlock, at Falls of Ohio, arrested Messrs Thos M Winn & Saml N Luckett, both of Jefferson Co, on suspicion of being concerned in Col Burr's expedition. -Frankfort, Jan 8.

Died: Mrs Anne Burnes, age 67 yrs, wid/o late David Burnes, of Wash, on Jan 28; Rev Mr Sayre of Episc Chr in Gtwn conferenced with her shortly before her death.

Meriwether Lewis, Capt 1st U S Reg Infty, Wash, Jan 15, 1807, persons who supported him with patience & fortitude on his tour to Pacific Ocean:

Peter Wiser	John Ordnay	John Newman
Nathl Pryor	Chas Floyd	Patrick Gass
Wm Bratton	John Collins	John Celter
Pier Cruzatte	Jos & Reuben Field	Robt Frazier
Silas Goodrich	Geo Gibson	Thos P Howard
Hugh Hall	Francis Labuicke	Hugh McNeal
John Shields	Geo Shannon	John Potts
John Bapteist La Page	John B Thompson	Richd Warsington
Wm Werner	Richd Windsor	Touisant Charbono
Alex Willard	Jos Whitehouse	Geo Drulyard

-Meriwether Lewis, Capt.

Mr Jas Alex'r, under the charge of Lt Savier, reached Annapolis, Jan 30, on board the schn'r *Bro & Sister*-Mr A was delivered to the Cmder of Ft McHenry. -Balt, Jan 31. [Aaron Burr case]

WED FEB 4, 1807

Jas Anderson appt'd agent for seamen & commerce at Havanna, & agent for Navy Dept in island of Cuba.

Hse of Reps: petition of Eliz Broadhead, wid of Luke Broadhead, pensioner of U S, praying for relief. -Referred to committee.

Trespassing bay mare came to my plantation, nr Bladensburg. -Saml Shekles.

John Dempsie thanks his fellow ctzns for extinguishing the fire which broke out in his hse, Sat. Wash City.

To be sold at the hse of Owen McCue at the Navy Yd: kegs, scales, benches & hsehld furn. -N L Queen, auct.

Ranaway: Moll, negro woman, d/o Rose who was freed by Mr Thos Marshall of Va. -Cornelius Robinson, Charlotte Hall, St Mary's Co, Md.

Died: Genr'l Levi Casey, Feb 1, of S C, mbr of Hse o/Reps. age 59 yrs, of pulmonick disease, in Wash; burial in *Rock Creek*, Wash.

FRI FEB 6, 1807

Runaway negroes committed to Wash Co, Md, jail: Geo, mulatto, says he belongs to Benj Fayton, of King Geo Co, Va; & Fanny & child, says she is wife of Geo & belongs to Col Taylor next to King Geo Co, Va. -Isaac S White, shrf-Hagerstown, Md.

Lands for sale in Fairfax Co, Va-900 acs; 857 acs on Turnpike Rd where I reside; tract of 337 acs; also a moiety of the farm where Bazil Williams resides; tract in Shenandoah Co, 280 acs; 6,000 acs in Ky. -Aug. J Smith, nr Alexandria.

Reward-$50 for Richd Gotier who broke jail; confessed to passing counterfeit cks. [Gotier was a sailor in U S svc] -Danl C Brent, mrsh'l-D C.

MON FEB 9, 1807

Died: Dr Calvin Taylor, of U S A, at Ft Pickering, Dec 4.

Basil D Beall has just opened a groc-liquor store next door to Mr Saml H Smith's printing ofc. Wash City.

Ctzns meet at Griffin Yeatman's Hotel, Cincinnati: David Zeigler, Isaac G Burnet, Dr John Sellman, Mr Andrew Burt & Dr Edw H Stall. Subj:-Hon John Smith resignation; his seat in U S Sen has been procured by erroneous impressions.

WED FEB 11, 1807

Act-relief of Seth Harding, late a Capt in U S N; so disabled in line of duty he is unable to support himself by labor; entitled to half his monthly pay beginning Jan 1, 1804. -Nathl Macon, spkr of Hse of Reps. Geo Clinton, VP. Approved-Thos Jefferson, Pres.

Directors for ofc of Disc & Deposit at Wash, Feb 11, 1807:

John P Van Ness	Wm Steuart	Thos Tingey
Wm Brent	Caleb Swan	Jos Carleton
Jos Nourse	Jas D Barry	Thos Munroe
Lewis Deblois	David Peter	Benj Shreve jr
Phineas Janney.		

Ltr to Maj Genr'l Andrew Jackson;-Aged & infirmed as we may be we offer our svcs to our country:

	Genrl Jas Robertson, Capt
Jas Hennen, Surg	*Genrl Thos Overton
*Maj Howel Tatum	*Maj Clem Hall
*Capt Jas Tatum	*Maj Wm T Lewis
*Col Joel Lewis	*Col Robt Hays
*Capt Wm Rich'd	*Capt Stephen Cantrell
*Capt Robt Edmonson	*Maj Wm Walton
*Capt Wm Lytle Sr	*Capt Joshua Hadley
*Capt John Beck	*Capt John Park
Capt Jos Coleman, Mayor-Nashville	Wm Tait
Thos Talbot	Geo Poyzer
Thos Dillon	Wm Whorton
Geo Whorton.	Ofcrs in Rev War, all over age 50 yrs.

Orphans Crt of Wash Co, D C. Ordered that Gerard Gibson, adm of Jane Kissick, dec'd, sell prsnl prop of dec'd. -J Hewitt, Reg.

FRI FEB 13, 1807
Act of relief for Edmund Briggs, owner of schn'r, *Phebe*; to be pd by collector for Newport Dist; for bounty-1802.

Wm Hearn, confined in Wash Co, D C prison; Hearn is to convey to Sec of U S all his estate; if no estate then proof that same has not been transferred to avoid payment of sum for which he is imprisoned. -Hse o/Reps.

In 1769-Dr Franklin, Mr Rittenhouse, Mr Gilpin & Mr Hollingsworth were appt'd to examine the ground bet the Delaware & Chesapeake Bays.

Claims against the est of Seth Carter, dec'd, late a Lt in U S N, are desired. -Jekiel Crossfield, adm, Wash.

Orphans Crt of Wash Co, D C. Feb 13, 1807; prsnl est of Thos Washington, late of Wash Co, dec'd. -Sarah Washington, excx.

MON FEB 16, 1807
For sale-valuable seats for iron works, bet 5 & 6,000 acs, in Amherst Co, Va. Proprietor, Nathan Lufborough, lvg in Gtwn.

Ranaway-John Thompson, negro; from Wm Glaze living in Clarksburg, Montg Co, Md. Reward-$8.

WED FEB 18, 1807
Orphans Crt of PG Co, Md. Ltrs of adm on prsnl est of Richd Cramphin, late of said Co, dec'd-obtained by Thos Bowie, adm. Pblc sale at farm lately occupied by Mr Richd Cramphin & at his late dwlg in Bladensburg-all prsnl est; likewise the unexpired term in a lease for 120 acs granted May 31, 1714 for 90 yrs; land contiguous to Wm D Diggs prop. -Thos Bowie, adm.

Orphans Crt of PG Co, Md. Sale at resid of subscriber, all prsnl est of Wilkinson Brashears, late of PG Co, dec'd; stock & plantation utensils. -John Brashears, adm.

FRI FEB 20, 1807
Funeral sermon will be preached by Rev Mr Sayr at Epis Chr in Gtwn, upon the occasion of the late Mrs Burns' death.

Crt Martial cld in Eng to try Capt Whitby for murder of Pierce. Capt Brewster, of our Revenue Cutter, Jonathan L Brewster, his bro, Robt Mitchell, branch pilot, & John White, will sail in the *Latona* for Liverpool whence to London as witnesses. -Ctzn.

Ltr from Cowles Mead, Sec of Miss Terr, acting as Gov, informs that Aaron Burr had surrendered himself to civil authority. -Thos Jefferson, Feb 19,'07.

MON FEB 23, 1807

Robt Welford is now opening, in Bridge St, a store with Sheffield Hrdw, cutlery, Japanned goods, etc. -Gtwn.

Stolen-grey horse. -Lawrence Hays, N J Ave, Wash.

WED FEB 25, 1807

Ltr rec'd that Aaron Burr was liberated on bail for sum of $10,000 and has returned to his boats.

Wash Co Crt: sale of rl est of Richd Cromwell, esq, of said Co, dec'd; land nr Hagerstown, total ab't 1300 acs; his late resid-450 acs; tract of 340 acs now occupied by Oliver Cromwell; tract of 250 acs now occupied by Richd Cromwell; tract of 250 acs. -Walter Boyd,

Martin Kershner, Henry Ankony & Josiah Price are com'rs. -Wash Co, Md.

Mr Generes advertises a practicing dancing ball at Mr Myer's Hotel, Wash.

FRI FEB 27, 1807

Deed of trust from Rev Geo Ralph to Saml Tyler, dec'd, & Mary Pottinger; sale of land cld *Hulston*, in vicinity of Charlotte Hall Acad in St Mary's Co, 150 acs & 5 negroes. -Mary Pottinger, survivor of Saml Tyler.

Deed of trust from Jas Wigfield-sale of 10 acs on rd leading to Marlbro. -Benson L McCormick, trust.

For sale at late resid of Mrs Parsons, dec'd, nr Mr Boothe's windmill; furn & animals. -Israel Little, auct.

Auct sale on Anthony Reintzell's wharf;-cargo of schnr *Laurel,* Capt Doyle, from Martinique. -J Travers, auct. [sugar & coffee]

MON MAR 2, 1807

Decree of High Crt of Chancery-auction at Piscataway, PG Co, Md; all rl est of Randolph B Latimer, dec'd: *Latimers Addition, Latimer's 2nd Addition, Latimer's Forest, Widow's Hardship, Baggot's Boot, Smallwood's Good Bargain,* part *of Daniel's Conclusion,* part of *Steuart's Oversight,* part of *Roby's Help,* & tract which said Latimer purch'd of Henry Hagan. -Nicholas Brewer, trustee.
Land for sale, virtue of last will of Josias Harrison, late of Montg Co, dec'd: 150 acs in Montg Co with large frame hse; adj this tract ab't 10-12 acs; & 133+ acs adj same. Apply to Mr Jas Hawkins or Mr John Purdam, both of Clarksburg, Md, or to Jas Day, exc.

Auction sale at hse of Dr John Bullus, living nr the Marine Barracks, all his furniture. -Saml Speake, auct.

WED MAR 4, 1807

Appt'd: Meriwether Lewis, Govn'r of Upper La. Thos Todd, of Ky, justice of Sup Crt of U S for new crct recently established.

FRI MAR 6, 1807

Sec of State requests proof of ctznship for: Jos Smith

Jas Forest	Richd Weaver	David Johnston
Jeremiah Culver	Saml Bond	Peter Rivers
Henry Wright	Aaron Young	John Twelves
John Green	Enos Dickson	Ebenezer Berry
Jos Mariner	John Morris	John Cappit
John Marks	Jos Jones	Saml Brown
John Hutt	Wm Gould	John Marshall
John Bolton		

[Impressed into the British svc & detained.]
-Dept of State, Feb 28, 1807.

Transported to the forts at Baco Chica, at entrance of the Harbor of Carthagena, for 8 yrs hard labor:

Benj Nicholson	Saml Price	Robt Stevenson
Wm Long	Henry King	Wm Praix
Geo Furguson	Joaquim Hoyt	Abraham Head
Wm Burnside	Wm Coante Wight	Benj Davis
Danl Newbury	Saml Techer	Henry Sperry
Pompey Grand		

Transported to Omoa for 10 yrs:

John O Sullivan	David Herclete	Henry Ingersel
John Birch	Robt Saunders	John Etssell
Paul Nangur	Jeremiah Powell	John Sherman
Danl Mackey	John Hays	John Elliot
Thos Gill	John Moore	Bradley Negus

Transported to Porto Rico for 10 yrs:

Moses Smith	Jas Grant	Alex. Behanen
Matthew Buchanan	David Winton	Jos Bernet
John Vancel	Fred'k Riesers	Finias Raymen
Eden Burhugman	John Scott	Stephen Bantis
Wm Lippincott		

Boys confined at Boca Chica until determination of the King: _____ Reng; Jos Hedelie & Jos Smith. The foregoing judgments have been regularly executed. -Philadelphia, Feb 28.

Died: Saml Hamilton, of Wash, Mar 3.

Died: Abraham Baldwin, mbr of Senate of U S, Mar 4. [Mar 11-paper: Baldwin, born in Conn in Nov 1754; never mrd; 6 orphans, his half bros & sisters were left to his care by the fr's death in 1787; 5 out of the six are still living; only his bro-in-law, Joel Barlow, was able to attend the funeral; procession from Capitol to Rock Creek Chr; burial next to his old friend, Genr'l Jackson.]

MON MAR 9, 1807

Evan Evans hse bet 6 bldgs & Potomac Rvr, Wash City. The improved tobacco, cider or flower press & straw cutter may be seen with Oliver Evans at Man's Works in Phil. Andrew Ellicott, Lancaster, Pa, has examined same.

WED MAR 11, 1807

Lost or mislaid-3 Navy 6% certificates. -Wm Patterson, Wash.

Act of relief of Daniel S Dexter, of Providence, R I; be dschgd from prison; he shall assign & convey all est, rl & prsnl for use & benefit of the U S. -Hse o/Reps.

Act issuing 320 acs ea; on public lands west of Miss. & each to receive double pay for time srvd in late enterprize to the Pacific Ocean to:

Wm Bratton	John Collins	John Colter
Pier Cruzatte	Jos Field	Reuben Field
Robt Frazier	Silas Goodrich	Geo Gibson
Thos P Howard	Hugh Hall	John Newman
Hugh O'Neal	John Sheilds	Geo Shannon
John Potts	John Baptiste Le Page	Wm Werner
John B Thompson	Richd Windsor	Peter Wiser
Alex Willard	Jos Whitehouse	Geo Diulyar
Tousaint Charbone	Richd Worsengton	John Ordway
Nathl Pryor	Francis Labruche	Patrick Gass

Heirs or legal reps of Chas Floyd, dec'd,. -Hse o/Reps.

Act issuing land warrants to Meriwether Lewis & Wm Clark, for 1,600 acs ea. -Hse o/Reps.

Levi Pellitt, adm of Jos Bounce, Shomerset Co, Md, hath obtained from Orphans Crt of Worcester Co, Md, ltrs of adm on prsnl est of Jos Bounce, late of Worcester Co, Md, dec'd.

FRI MAR 13, 1807

An Act for relief of John Chester, former supervisor of int revs & direct tax, for Dist of Connecticut-$317.90 + $233.34. -Nathl Macon, spkr of Hse o/Reps.

Orphans Crt of Montg Co, Md. Feb 18, 1807. Prsnl est of Robt B Crafford, late of said Co, dec'd. -Edw Owen, adm.

To let-possession immediately: dwlg hse & store nr the Navy yd lately occupied by Mr Adam Lindsay. Terms apply to Mr Matthew Wright, nr the premises. -Wm Emack, atty for Adam Lindsay, East Capitol St, Wash City.

Deposition of Hooke & Davidson. New-Orleans, Dec 23, 1806. Signed M Hooke & B Davidson; sworn before Jas Carrick, J P of this county. [Rgrd: Aaron Burr]

Deposition of John Nicholson, of the City of New Orleans, Dec 26, 1806, sworn before Eliphalet Fitch, justice of peace. [Rgrd: Aaron Burr]

MON MAR 16, 1807

Bk for sale at D Rapine's bk-store on Capitol Hill- *The Trial of Thos O Selfridge* , atty at law, before the Hon Isaac Parker, for killing Chas Austin, on public exchange, Boston, Aug 4, 1806. Taken in short hand by Thos Lloyd & Geo Caines-$1.

WED MAR 18, 1807

Supreme Crt held for Mississippi Terr, at town of Washington, Feb 3, 1807. Grand jury are of opinion that Aaron Burr has not been guilty of any crime or misdemeanor against the law of the U S. P Smith-foreman; jurors: Ebenezer Rees, Jas Andrews, Love Baker, Geo Overakse, John Rabb, E Newman, John Wood, Lewis Evans, Jas Spain, John Brooks, J Guion, H Turnep, Nathl Hoggatt, Jas Dunbar.

My name has been offered to the public thru the *Aurora* as one concerned in the expedition by Mr Burr; have witnessed the spirit of persecution in the U S, not to have anticipated surmises of every kind against the son-in-law of that gentleman...suit to be instituted against the editor of that paper. -J W Prevost, New Orleans, Jan 6, 1807. [Briefs of the ltr]

FRI MAR 20, 1807

Act-authorising the discharge of Gilbert Drake from his imprisonment. The mrsh'l of Dist of N Y, to discharge Drake, late coll of the direct tax, on warrant of distress issued against him; he shall assign & convey all rl & prsnl est to U S

Orphans Crt of PG Co, Md. Prsnl est of Thos Ducket, late of said Co, dec'd. -Allen B Duckett, adm, City of Wash.

Orphans Crt of St Mary's Co, Md; ordered that Jas Biscoe, exc of Deborah Wolstenholme, dec'd, give notice for creditors to exhibit their claims. -Jas Forrest, Reg wills, St M Co, Md. [Jas Biscoe, exc, of city of Balt, Md.]

Hon Geo Poindexter appt'd to Cong of U S by legislature of Miss Terr.

MON MAR 23, 1807

Died: Miss Nancy Crauford, 2nd d/o Nathl Craufurd, esq, of Green Wood, PG Co, Md, age 18 yrs, Mar 19; burial Mar 21, discourse delivered by Rev Mr Scott.

Appt'd by Pres of U S as justices of the peace for Wash Co, D C:

Robt Brent	Thos Peter	Wm Thornton
Jos Sprigg Belt	Thos Corcoran	John Ott
Saml N Smallwood	Robt Alex'r	Richd Parrott
Thos Fenwick	John B Kirby	Saml H Smith
Danl Rapine	Nicholas Young	John Threlkeld

WED MAR 25, 1807

Died: Genr'l Pascal Paoli, Corsican patriot & Godfr of Bonaparte, in Eng, Feb 5.

Wishing to leave the city, I offer 2 lots in sq 88-where I live, for sale. -John Stephen

Natchez, Feb 16. Duel bet Cowles Mead & Capt Robt Sample, of Wilkinson Co, fought nr the city of Mississippi, Feb 13, resulted in Mr Mead being wounded in the right thigh. He is fast recovering.

Act-invalid pensioners. Pursuant to law passed Apr 10, 1806.

Name	Amount/month	Commence Date
Richd Fairbrother	$3.00	May 25, 1806
John De Voe	$2.50	Aug 1, 1806
Peter Demarest	$3.75	Aug 1, 1806
Stephen Ogden	$2.50	Aug 1, 1806
John Berry	$5.00	Sep 2, 1806
John King	$4.00	Oct 18, 1806
Robt Ames	$5.00	Oct 18, 1806
Chas Gowin	$2.50	Oct 31, 1806
Francis L Slaughter	$3.00	Nov 15, 1806
Wm Rebeck	$4.00	Nov 22, 1806
Stafford Ames	$5.00	Dec 11, 1806
Josiah Jones	$4.00	Dec 22, 1806
Saml Dawndney	$2.50	Dec 27, 1806
Eliphalet Easton	$5.00	Dec 31, 1806
Jos Ligon	$3.00	Jan 8, 1807
John Hubbart	$3.00	Jan 8 1807
Danl Guard	$2.50	Jan 23, 1807
Elisha Forbes	$3.00	Jan 24, 1807
Alex'r Simonton	$3.00	Jan 9, 1807
Noah Robinson	$10.00	Oct 23, 1806
Chas Mynn Thruston	$20.00	Jul 14, 1806
Jonas Farnsworth	$10.00	Sep 2, 1806
Benoni Hathaway	$10.00	Sep 6, 1806
Thos Mrsh'l Baker	$10.00	Sep 29, 1806
Jas Dysart	$10.00	Dec 18, 1806
Henry Teneyck	$10.00	Jan 8, 1807
Jon Little	$20.00	Jan 13, 1807
Thos Harris	$15.00	Oct 3, 1806
Danl Ball	$10.00	Feb 17, 1807

-Hse o/Reps.

The following are already on pension list; receive increase in pension:

Seth Wyman	$4.00	Jun 16, 1806
Geo Bradford	$5.00	Aug 15, 1806
Abel Furney	$5.00	Aug 29, 1806
Chas Scott	$5.00	Sep 1, 1806

Ephraim Baily	$5.00	Sep 4, 1806
Asa Ware	$5.00	Sep 9, 1806
Danl Hickey	$5.00	Sep 24, 1806
Danl Nutting	$2.00	Oct 7, 1806
Abel Woods	$5.00	Oct 10, 1806
Jos Meiril	$5.00	Oct 24, 1806
Wm Neley	$5.00	Oct 24, 1806
Elisha Frizzle	$3.00	Nov 3, 1806
Wm Burritt	$5.00	Nov 3, 1806
Benj Smith	$5.00	Nov 3, 1806
Geo Pittman	$5.00	Feb 1, 1807
Gustavus Alrick	$3.33	Nov 21, 1806
Jabes Pembleton	$2.50	Dec 27, 1806
Wiat Hinkley	$5.00	Dec 28, 1806
Edw Evans	$5.00	Jan 15, 1807
Moses Wing	$5.00	Dec 24, 1806
John Cavenough	$3.00	Jan 17, 1807
Richd Hardin	$5.00	Sep 11, 1806
Jonathan Holton	$10.00	Sep 8, 1806
Jonathan Willard	$5.00	Sep 8, 1806
Thos Pearson	$13.33	Jul 28, 1806
John Maynard	$6.00	Jul 25, 1806
Thos Avery	$16.66	Oct 3, 1806
Ebenezer Coe	$20.00	Jul 31, 1806
Ebenezer Bancroft	$6.00	Oct 31, 1806
Wm Worthington	$15.00	Nov 19, 1806
David Hawley	$10.00	Dec 8, 1806

The pension of Benj Bartlett of Mass, employed in svc of U S as escort, spy, & guide, at pay of $1 per day during hostilities with indian tribes in 1794, disabled by wound, increase to $5 per mo. -Hse o/Reps.

Orphans Crt of St Mary's Co, Md; prsnl est of Walter Leigh, late of St M Co, dec'd. -Arnold L Leigh & Benj Williams-excs.

Ltr from Matthew & Alex'r Buchanan, of *Miranda* expedition, to relations in this city, dt'd-Carthagena prison, Dec 30, 1806. We are still kept in close confinement, loaded with chains & death staring us in the face. Benj Davis & Wm Long, of your city, are well & pass our prison window in chains. John Scott has lost his hearing, cannot live many days. -New York, Mar 20.

In Chancery. Wm O'Neale, vs Richd Wootton, Lewis Beall & Wm Pritchell. decree to correct error in 2 deeds conveying part of *The Cuckold's Delight* in Montg Co; on deed from Arthur Nelson to Thos Pritchell, dt'd Jun 2, 1741; the other from Wm Pritchell to Wm O'Neale, cmplnt, dt'd Jun 31, 1798. Wm Pritchell resides out of Md. -Sam H Howard, Reg.

FRI MAR 27, 1807

Orphans Crt of PG Co, Md, Mar 24, 1807. Prsnl est of Saml Hepburn, late of PG

Co, dec'd. Exhibit claims to Trueman Tyler, of Upper Marlborough. -Saml Judson Coolidge, adm.

MON MAR 30, 1807
To rent-Nov 19, brick hse on crnr of F & 11th Sts; now occupied by Mr Andrew Way. -Thos Herty

U S Crt, 5th Crct & Va Dist-term 1806-in Chancery. John McIlver, assignee of Josiah Watson, plntf, vs, Bird, Savage & Bird, Jas Watson, John Watson jr, Jas Taylor & Richd M Scott, dfndnts. Bill answers suit bet Robt Bird against Josiah Watson & John Love; sale of land cld *Buckland.* Srvyr of Fauquier Co to decide division; dfndnts, trustees for Mrs Watson be permitted to reap & carry off the now growing crop. -Wm Marshall, clk. [Buckland lies in Fauquier & Pr Wm cos]. Also under decree of said crt-sale of Chantilly, Westmoreland Co, Va. -Benj Mosby, D M for Jos Scott-M V D't.

Crct Crt o/Wash Co, D C. John Litle, cmplnt, vs Robt Sutton & Cath his wife, dfndnts. Dfndnts, who are non resids of Wash, are warned to appear in crt, Jun next. -Wm Brent, clk. [Copy to be published in Lancaster Intell, Pa.]

WED APR 1, 1807
Auction sale at dwlg hse of John Lowry Sr, *Greenleaf's Point*, all gun-smith utensils belonging to the late Mathias Hart, dec'd. -Israel Little, auct. -Abigail Hart, admx

Crct Crt of Wash Co, D C. Dec term 1806. John Hoye, adm d b n of Wm Deakins, & with Leonard M Deakins, exc of last will of Francis Deakins who was exc & devisee of said Wm Deakins, cmplnt, vs Adam Murray Stewart, Deborah Stewart, excx of Walter Stewart, late dec'd, & Wm Stewart, Robt Stewart, Ann Stewart, Walter Stewart, Henry Stewart, & Mary Anne Stewart-heirs & devisees of Walter Stewart dec'd-dfndnts. Bill is to establish a debt due to cmplnts & sum to be pd out of the rl & prsnl est of dec'd Walter Stewart. Print same in some paper in city of Phil. -Wm Brent, clk.

Ranaway: Daniel, negro, ab't 30 yrs of age; purch'd him last fall of Mr Robt Gunnell of Va, who bght him some yrs ago of Capt John Turbeville. -H Gunnell jr, Fairfax Co, Va.

Orphans Crt of Wash Co, D C. Mar 29, 1807. Prsnl est of Mathias Hart, late of Wash, dec'd. -Abigail Hart, admx.

FRI APR 3, 1807
Caution-ab't Nov 8, 1806, I passed my note to Thos Crowley, of Wash City, for $100. Payments have been made but not receipted on the back of said note. -Nicholas Whelan

Strayed cow -Cornelius De Krafft, Wash, D C.

Ladies with ltrs in Wash, P O:

Maria Butler	Mrs Liddy Birtch	
Mrs Mary Bowland	Miss Jane Barnhouse	Miss Eliz Beall
Miss Jane Farr	Mrs Crawford c/o Richd Forrest	
Miss Gatewood	Miss Milly Horkins	Miss Hannah Hopkins
Mrs Eliz Innes	Mrs Lyme	Miss Montgomerie
Miss Susannah Ronchor	Mrs Agostino Sera	Miss Fanny Shorter
Mrs Ann Strong	Mrs Cecelia Van Allen	Mrs Sarah Wilson

MON APR 6, 1807

Notice: Archibald Chesmer has taken up a stray cow.

Died: Mrs Anne Wilkinson, w/o Gen Wilkinson, Feb 23, at hse of Bernard Marigny, Hdqrtrs of the Army. -New Orleans, Feb 27.

Orphans Crt of PG Co, Md; prsnl est of Richd Wells Brashears, late of PG Co, dec'd. -Mary Brashears, admx.

Robt Cherry will rent his hse, sq 799 nr the Navy Yard, reserving the store & half the cellar to himself.

Wanted: a ship's steward. -Robt W Goldsborough, Wash.

WED APR 8, 1807

Mrd: Nicholas B Van Zandt of Wash, to Miss Maria Wood Southall, of Richmond, Mar 30, by Rev J Buchanan.

Orphans Crt of Wash Co, D C. Apr 7, 1807. Prsnl est of Rezin Beck, late of said Co, dec'd. Sale of groc, furn, 3 negroes, horse & coach, of said Beck. -Richd Beck, adm, Gtwn

Just published-ltr giving short account of south side of Lake Erie. Price 25 cents. -Jas Tongue, M D & of Md.

My negro man Fidelio left my svc. Reward $1. -Alice Dermott, Wash City.

FRI APR 10, 1807

Died: J W Pratt, Apr 5, in Wash, late deputy mrsh'll of D C.

Died: John Beckley, age 50 yrs, Apr 8, clk of Hse o/Reps; born in Gr Britain; came under protection of his uncle to this country when he was 11 yrs of age.

Appointments: Brockholst Livingston, of N Y, Assoc justice of Sup Crt vice-Wm Paterson, dec'd.
Wm Hull, Gov of Mich, com'r with indian tribes in vicinity of Detroit.
Wm Henry Harrison, of Indiana, Gov of Ind.
Eli Williams, of Md, com'r for rd from Cumberland to Ohio.
Joshua Lewis, of Ky, a judge of Terr of Orleans, vice John B Prevost-rsgn'd.

Walter Leake, of Va, a judge of U S for Miss Terr.
John Coburn, of Ky, a judge of U S for Terr of Mich.
Michl McClary, of N H, mrsh'l of N H.
Peter Curtenius, of N Y, mrsh'l of N Y.
Peter A Schenck, of N Y, now srvyr of Port of N Y, inspec of rev for same.
John Barnes, of Terr of Columbia, coll & inspec for Dist of Gtwn.
Willis W Parker, of Va, now coll of Port of So Quay, inspec for same.
John Page, of Va, com'r of loans for Va.
Jas Taylor, of N C, coll & inspec for Ocracock.
Wm Dunham, of Ga, srvyr & inspec of Darien, Ga.
Edwin Mounger, of Ga, coll for Savanna Dist.
Jeremiah Clarke, of Mass, coll for Dist & inspec of rev for York, Maine port.
John Lovell, of Orleans, srvyr of Port of New Orleans, inspec for same.
Thos Nicholson, of Md, coll of Chester town, Md, inspec of rev for same.
John Linton, of Va, coll for Dist, & inspec of rev for port of Dumfries, Va.
Julien Poydrass, of Orleans, mbr of Legislative Cncl of Orleans.
Seth Pease, of Terr of Columbia, srvyr of public lands of U S south of Tenn.
Edmund Blount, of N C, mrsh'l of Dist of N C.
Fred'k Bates, of Terr of Mich, sec for Terr of La, recorder of land titles in same.
Pierre Foucher & Jas Mather Sr, of Terr of Orleans, mbrs of Leg Cncl of Orleans, to supply places of Messrs Detrehan & Sauve-resigned.
Geo Johnson, of N Y, cnsl for U S at Glasgow, Gr Britain.
Thos Gamble, of Pa, cnsl for U S in island of Santa Cruz.
Maurice Rogers, of Pa, cnsl for U S at St Jago De Cuba.
John B Dabney, of Mass, cnsl for U S at Fayal.
Edw Carrington, of Conn, cnsl of U S at Canton in China.

MON APR 13, 1807

Alex'r Dade & Stephen French, chosen delegates to Genr'l Assembly. -Alexandria, Apr 8.

Stolen out of stable of Mrs Eliz Wells nr Queen Ann, PG Co, Md, a black horse. -Geo W Wells.

WED APR 15, 1807

Henry Hiort, atty at law, ofc in Mr Ingle's brick hse, on Capitol Hill, Wash City.

Jas Mullekin brght before me a stray mare. -Thos Fenwick, Wash City.

FRI APR 17, 1807

Miss Reagan has opened a young ladies acad in Wash City, hse next to one lately occupied by Mr Elliott on Capitol Hill. Mrs Reagan continues her acad on F St nr Mr Semme's tavern.

MON APR 20, 1807

Persons indebted to late firm of Crow, Wright & Co, Gtwn; accounts in hands of Thos Merty, atty. -Thos C Wright.

Died: Abraham Baldwin, Mar 25, Senator of Ga; ltr written by John Millege-Louisville, Mar 26, 1807. Attest-Jas Boozeman, sec. -Exec Dept-Ga.

Orphans Crt of Montg Co, Md. Prsnl est of Richd Thomas, late of said Co, dec'd. Apr 15, 1807. -Richd Thomas, Wm Thomas, excs.

Ben Higgins, adm, obtained ltrs of adm on prsnl est of Benj Becraft, late of Montg Co, Md, dec'd. Apr 20, 1807.

High Crt of Chancery-sale of rl est of Henry Addison, late of PG Co, Md, dec'd; 500 acs subject to dower of widow; two thirds will be sold free of incumbrances. -Thos G Addison, trust.

WED APR 22, 1807

Pblc sale of lot 100 in *Threlkeld's Addition to Gtwn* with improvements; all right & title of Jacob Gross, Bernard French & John Threlkeld. -Dan'l Bussard, trust.

Died: Lewis Harvie, esq, at Norfolk, of Richmond, Apr 15. Mbr of the Privy Cncl. -Richmond, Apr 18.

FRI APR 24, 1807

Orphans Crt of St Mary's Co, Md. Apr 14, 1807. Petition of Wm T Lee, adm, of Henry Lee, late o/said Co, dec'd. -Jas Forrest, Rg wills.

Orphans Crt of Wash Co, D C. Apr 23, 1807. Prsnl est of Saml Hamilton, late of said Co, dec'd. -Christina Hamilton, admx.

Life of Wilkes: John Wilkes, born Oct 23, 1727 in St John St, Clarkenwell, s/o Nathl, a distiller; in 1749 he mrd Miss Mead, heiress of the Meads of Buckinghamshire; in 1757 elected Burgess for Aylesbury-same for 1761.

Orphans Crt of St Mary's Co, Md. Apr 15, 1807. Petition of Wm Hebb, adm of Wm Somerville, late of said Co, dec'd. -Jas Forrest, Rg o/wills.

MON APR 27, 1807

Alex'r Cochand, jr, determined on going to Ireland as soon as he can offers prop in Wash for sale, groceries & dry goods.

WED APR 29, 1807

Orphans Crt of Wash Co, D C. Apr 23, 1807; prsnl est of John Wilks Pratt, late of said Co, dec'd. -Rachel Pratt, admx.

For sale: hse at I & 7th St, presently occupied by Dr McWilliams, nr the Navy Yd. -Wm Bunyie, Pa Ave, Wash.

Crct Crt o/Wash Co, D C. Chas Wadsworth, cmplnt, vs Owen Roberts & Jane his wife, Geo N Lyles, Jno Harper & Jas Keith, dfndnts. Pblc auction of lot 18 sq 168, Wash, with brick hse. -Lewis Ford, trustee.

Died: Mrs Tingey, w/o Thos Tingey, esq, Apr 25.

Ranaway: Watts, blackman, says he belongs to Wm Penn of Montg Co, Md. -Cartwright Tippett, kpr of jail, D C.

Land for sale on *Bullskin Run*, Jefferson Co, Va-400 acs. -John Gantt, Sr, on the premises.

FRI MAY 1, 1807

Life of John Wilkes-cont'd from Apr 24. Tablet written by himself: born at London, Oct 17, 1727, O S. Died in this parish. [Died age 70, interred in Grosvenor Chapel]

Orphans Crt of Wash Co, D C. Prsnl est of John Beckley, dec'd; will annexed. -Mary Prince, Maria Beckley, excxs.

MON MAY 4, 1807

Orphans Crt of St Mary's Co, Md; pblc sale at late resid of Deborah Wolstenholme, of said Co, dec'd. All prsnl prop, except negroes of Deborah Wolstenholme, dec'd, Geo Campbell, dec'd, & Ann Campbell, dec'd-furn & stock, etc. -J Biscoe, adm.

WED MAY 6, 1807

Ranaway: Wm Mason, negro, hired by me from Dr Jas H Blake of Fairfax Co, nr Alexandria, Va. -Pat Farrell-Navy Yd-Wash.

For sale: Union Tvrn, late the prop of Chas McLaughlin, dec'd, now occupied by Wm Crawford; creditors against said McLaughlin are to bring in their claims. -Dan'l Bussard, trust.

Col Burr arrived in Wash on May 2.

FRI MAY 8, 1807

Sealed proposals for erecting an infirmary in Wash City; bricklayers & carpenters wanted. -John Davidson, F St, Wash.

Orphans Crt of Montg Co, Md. Apr 21, 1807. Prsnl est of Ninian Willett, late of said Co, dec'd. -Burgess Willett, adm.

Orphans Crt of Montg Co, Md. Apr 21, 1807. Prsnl est of Wm Jones, late of said Co, dec'd. -Burgess Willett, adm.

Wm H P Tuckfield has rec'd an assortment of shoes from Phil & Balt. Shop nr the Navy Yd, Wash.

Genr'l Jas Wilkinson is lauded by his recent arrest of Aaron Burr.

MON MAY 11, 1807

Witnesses to lashing of a small black boy, at Matanzas, Jan 29, 1807-ship *Charlotte* lying in Port: Capt-Benj Jennings jr mstr of ship; Carolus Pelham-Capt assist; Wm Aymier, Isaac Atkinson, Jas Gibson, Alx Darbany, Jas Carter-seamen; Jas Moody & P Isardy, mates.

Va election of Rep in Cong; Danl Sheffey elected in room of Abraham Trigg.

Proof of Lee & Son's genuine medicine. John Kelly, Pitt St, Balt, Md, Nov 12, 1806-my 10 yr old son cured. John Kennedy, Potter Forest, Balt, Md, Jan 4, 1807-my 5 yr old son cured. Redmond Minchen, Peter's Brewery, Balt, Md, Feb 9, 1807-invaluable medicine. -Richd Lee & son.

WED MAY 13, 1807

Ltr written by Henry Ingersoll, s/o Jonathan Ingersoll, of Stockbridge, to his bro-in-law the late Thos Allen, dt'd Cathagena Oct 26, 1806 rec'd from N Y-deprived of liberty, I am under the galling chains of slavery for 10 yrs. From the Berkshire reporter.

For sale: 474 acs in Allegany Co, Md, or exchanged for improved prop in Wash City. -Wm Waters.

Orphans Crt of Wash Co, D C. May 11, 1807. Prsnl est of Jos Calvert, late of said Co, dec'd. -Ann Calvert, adm.

Sale of some furn, carpenter's tools, & interest in his late dwlg hse on F St, Wash City. -Ann Calvert, adm.

Pblc sale; all right & int of John Coles in lots 3 & 4 in sq 9 with large stone warehse, wharf, & brick dwlg hse; suit of John Hay against John Coles. -Danl Bussard for D C Brent, mrsh'l.

FRI MAY 15, 1807

Suicide: John C Love, late a Lt in Marine Corps, put an end to his existence, May 13, at the Marine Barracks. Burial at his bro's farm in Salisbury, Va, May 14.

MON MAY 18, 1807

Col John Mayo, of Richmond, has offered to furnish the granite stone to build the comtemplated pyramid at James town in commemoration of the first settlement in Virginia.

Cornelius Willis, insolvent debtor, confined in Alexandria Co jail, at suit of Alex'r Cochran. -G DeNeale, clk.

Jas Fenner, Rpblcn, elected Gov of R I.

John Morrow is re-elected a Rep of Va, without opposition.

WED MAY 20, 1807

Ranaway: Frank, negro, from John D Bell living in Pr Wm Co, 5 miles from Landon Carter's Mill, Va. -John D Bell.

Orphans Crt of Wash Co, D C. May 15, 1807. Prsnl est of Wm Swinton, late of Wash, dec'd. -Geo Blagden.

Runaways committed to Cecil Co jail-Robt Ensley, negro, says he was born free in N J & his wife who says she was born free in Phil. -Jos Baxter, shrf, Elkton, Md.

Wm Dyer, insolvent debtor, confined to Wash Co prison for debt. -Wm Brent-clk.

FRI MAY 22, 1807

Wanted: woman svt for a small family. -Joshua Dawson, oppo West City Mkt.

Ranaway: Jas, negro, on board the sloop *George*. -Tristrim Butler, Norfolk, Va.

MON MAY 25, 1807

Jedediah T Turner of Cazenovia Co of Madison, N Y, did on Oct 20, 1803 grant David Polock o/Wash City, power to vend the right to my patent threshing mach; informed he has done nothing for the business & remv'd from Va to Ga; in his rm I have appt'd Jas Linsey, of N Y, my lawful atty for selling said rights in Va.

Desirous of removing from this state in the fall, I have land I now occupy in Montg Co, 246 acs, for sale; & 2000 acs in Allegany Co, Md. -John Orme, Montg Co, Md.

WED MAY 27, 1807

Aaron Burr trial-sworn on the grand jury:
John Randolph-foreman

Jos Eggleston	Littleton Waller Tazewell	Robt Taylor
Wm Daniel jr	John Mercer	Jas M Garnett
Edw Pegram	Mumford Beverly	John Ambler
Jos C Cabell	Jas Pleasants jr	Alex Shepherd
John Breckenbrough	Jas Barbour	Thos Harrison

[Withdrawn-Wm B Giles & Wilson Carey Nicholas]-Va Argus.

FRI MAY 29, 1807

Aaron Burr trial-John Mrsh'l, Chf justice of U S; Cyrus Griffin, Judge of Dist of Va, Richmond, May 23. Witnesses summoned in behalf of the U S:

John G Henderson	Ambers Smith	Hugh Philips
Wm Eaton	Erick Bollman	Wm C Mead
Saml Swartwout	Jas Reid	Wm Duane
Geo Morgan	Leanor Domain	Wm Spence
Thos Petekins	Elias Glove	Saml Fairlamb
Jas L Donaldson	Wm Wilson	

Inspection of tobacco, Mr Smallwood's warehse, Wash City. -Michl Lowe, inspec.

Ranaway: Jesse, mulatto fellow, from Geo Sweeny, living in Brentown, Fauquier Co, Va. Reward-$40.

Orphans Crt of Wash Co, D C. May 23, 1807. Prsnl est of Richd Nelson, late of said Co, dec'd. -Sarah Thompson, admx.

MON JUN 1, 1807

Died: Thos Hamilton, esq, a judge of the Orphan's Crt of Somerset Co, after a lingering illness, Wicomico Creek, Apr 1807.

R C Wrightman, printer & bkseller, Pa Ave, Wash City, has purchased the establishment of Wm Duane.

To let-hse next west of Rhodes' Hotel, where Mr McLaughlin carries on boot & shoemaking business. -Jas Hoban

David Boudon, limner from Geneva, giving lessons in drawing; directions from Chas Avisse, merchant perfumer, 34 North Howard St, or Geo Hill, Balt, Md.

WED JUN 3, 1807

Job Haigh to undertake the sweeping of chimnies in Wash City.

Died: Mr Saml Dalton, age 115 yrs, in N Carolina; mrd but once; 600 of his offspring now living.

To be let-hse now occupied by Mr Geo Collard, nr the Bank of U S, F St, Wash City. -Walter Hellen

Honore Julien has a large quantity of ice for sale-F St. Wash ad.

Mbrs of City Cncl elected Jun 1 for Wash City:
First Chamber: Jeremiah Booth, John Dempsie, Gustavus Higden, Fred'k May, E B Caldwell, Jas S Stephenson, John McGowen, Phineas Bradley, C W Goldsborough.
2d Chamber: Saml Elliott, Henry Ingle, Alex'r McWilliams, Alex'r McCormick, Matthew Wright, Chas Minifie, Jos Bromly, Peter Lenox, Richd Forrest.

FRI JUN 5, 1807

Thos Thorpe has fitted up his hse on F St for travelers. Wash ad.

The editor of the Nat'l intell, having, from a regard to his health, determined to exchange his present profession for one less laborious, offers to dispose of his establishment, consisting of the Nat'l Intell & the Union Gazette.

MON JUN 8, 1807

Mrd: Thos Johnson, esq, to Miss Susan Buchanan, d/o late Andrew Buchanan, esq, of Balt, May 26 at Balt, Md.

Jas Sullivan elected Gov of Mass over Caleb Strong. Levi Lincoln elected Lt Gov In the Senate, Saml Dana elected Pres in Hse o/Reps; Perez Moreton elected spkr.

WED JUN 10, 1807

Crct Crt of Wash Co, D C. Jun term, 1807. In Chancery, Jun 6. John Threlkeld, vs Jacob Gross & Bernard French. Ratify report of Dan'l Bussard, trust; prop sold for $205 to Isaac Dawes. -Wm Brent, clk.

Notice to creditors of Zadock Baldwin, insolvent debtor; Silas Condit, assignee, will attend at hse of Johnson Tutle, innkpr in Newark, to ascertain debts due. Dt'd Neward, N J, Jun 1.

Orphans Crt of PG Co, Md. Jun 10, 1807. Prsnl est of John Hughes, of said Co, dec'd. -Wm Weems, Anne Arundel Co, Md.

FRI JUN 12, 1807

Board of comr's of Wash Co, will meet at Stelle's Hotel, Wash City, & at Semme's Tavern, Gtwn, for purpose of hearing appeals under the late assessments. -John Mountz jr, clk.

For sale-2 hses, 8th & L Sts nr the Navy Yd; frame hse is occupied by David Bates; other is brick. Apply to Mr Wm Prout, nr the premises, who is authorized to rent the brick bldg 'til sold.

MON JUN 15, 1807

Deed of trust from Uriah Forrest, dec'd, dt'd Jun 19, 1801, recorded in Wash Co, D C;-sale of 2 brick hses & ground in sq 118; one occupied under rent to Gen Tureau & the other to Mr Wm Kerr. -Jas M Lingan.

Notice: I shall apply to Chas Co Crt at Aug term for benefit of laws passed in favor of insolvent debtors. -John B Hanson

WED JUN 17, 1807

Impressed into British svc for want of documents to prove their U S ctznship:

Saml Stevens	John Herbert	Henry Jennings
Abraham Lacy	Jas Lin	John Sebastion
John Young	Mitchell Dennis	Jas Beans
John White	Jacob Bradberry	Wm Gibson
Stephen Hurley	Wm Hall	Thos Stevens

John Driver [call themselves ctzns of U S.]-Dept of State Jun 13.

To architects being appt'd to erect a commodious brick chr with steeple & clock in Wash, I offer $100 for plan & estimate of said bldg. -John Murray

FRI JUN 19, 1807

Runaway: Jim, reward-$40 for negro boy, ab't 13 yrs of age. Elkridge, Anne Arundel Co, Md. -Basil Simpson

MON JUN 22, 1807

Ranaway: Jim, reward-$300 for negro, ab't 35 yrs of age; has a wife at Mr Lawrence O'Neil's in Montg Co, Md. -John Hughes, Fred'k town, Md.

Auction-prop of Danl McNeall, seized for boarding & lodging by Mrs Thompson. -Saml Speake, auct.

Runaway-Frank Dutcher, mulatto, confined to Fred'k Co, Md, jail; says he belongs to Mrs Priscilla Coats o/Chas Co, Md, on Mattiomen Creek. -Geo Creager, jr, shrf.

Weiskopff & Keller, confectioners, High St, Gtwn. [Ad]

WED JUN 24, 1807

Runaway committed to Wash Co, D C, jail-Wm Butler, black fellow, says his right name is Prince & he belongs to Dan'l McCarty of Md; but he eloped from John Bennaw of Stafford Co, Va. -Cartwright Tippett, kpr of prison

Runaway committed to Kent Co jail, Bob, negro; says he belongs to Mr Furlow, Green Co, Ga. -Rasin Gale, shrf-Kent Co.

Orphans Crt of Wash Co, D C; est of Saml Baker, late of said Co, dec'd. Payments to Henry Burford. -Jane Baker adm.

For sale: land in Montg Co, Md, 217 acs. -Jas H Blake-Alexandria.

FRI JUN 26, 1807

Thos Ewell, living nr Cmdor Tingey's at the Navy Yd, will practice physic in private families of Wash.

Ranaway-Tom, negro slave; he left me at Mr Chas Carroll's nr Hagerstown, Md. Osborn Sprigg jr, in Hampshire Co, Va, nr Oldtown, Md; or to Jos Sprigg's, Wash Co, Md. -O Sprigg jr.

Six cents reward for apprentice boy, Naas Downs, age 18 yrs. -Robt Dillon, lvg nr the Navy Yd.

MON JUN 29, 1807

Died: on Jun 20, Mrs Elvertie Van Ness, wid of late Hon Peter Van Ness, of N Y, aged 64 yrs, at Lebanon Springs; remains are on their way to Kinderhook for burial with her hsbnd at their late residence. Columbia Co, N Y, Jun 21.

Gun & pistol manufactory, crnr of Ling & Water Sts, Alexandria. -R Nash.

Orphans Crt of St Mary's Co, Md, Jun term, 1807. Ordered that Wm Mills, exc of Jos Hargis, late of St Mary's Co, dec'd, give notice for creditors. -Jas Forrest-Reg wills-St Mary's Co. [Wm Mills, ex'r, follows with said notice]

Crt of Chancery, Jun 16, 1807. Jas Waring against Tab & Alethea his wife, formerly Alethea Turner, Noble & Eliz his wife, formerly Eliz Turner, Evans & Mary his wife, formerly Mary Turner, Walter Turner & Ary Turner. Bill to obtain a decree for sale of rl est of John Turner, dec'd, fr of said Alethea, Eliz, Mary, Walter & Ary, to satisfy debt which Waring as security for said dec'd pd to Chas Carroll of Carollton. [Dfndnts not residents of Md] -Nichs Brewer, R C C

WED JUL 1, 1807

U S frig *Chesapeake* arv'd in Hampton Rds Jun 22.

3 killed:

Jos Arnold-city of Wash
John Sharkley of Phil.
John Laurence of Pa

13 wounded:

Midshipman Mr Brook
Thos Short-Va
Francis Coenhoven-N Y
Cotton Brown-Candia, N H
Wm Hendrick-Albany, N Y
John Haydon-Balt
Wm Moody-Dela.
Robt McDonald-Wash City
Geo Perceval-Phil
Jos Eppes-Petersburg, Va
Peter Simmons-Prussia
Peter Ellison-Denmark
John Parker-N Y

Richmond Enquirer-Wanton attack upon one of our armed vessels by a British frig., *Norfolk.*

Ltr from Robt Thompson, chaplain on board the *Chesapeake*, to gentleman in Norfolk, dt'd Hampton, Jun 24. Jun 23 the *Chesapeake,* Capt Jas Baron, was fired on by the British ship, *Leopard*, Capt Humphreys.

Meeting held of the ctzns of Norfolk & Portsmouth on Jun 24, 1807. Genr'l Thos Matthews, chrmn; Saml Moseley, sec. Subj: firing on the *Chespeake* by the *Leopard;* [see above]. Commitee:

Thos Matthews
Theo Armistead
Wm Pennock
Dan'l Bedinger
Richd Blow
Thos Newton jr
Richd E Lee
Wm Newsum
Seth Foster
Francis S Taylor
Luke Wheeler
Moses Myers
Thos Blanchard
J W Murdaugh
-Test, Saml Moseley

Orphans Crt of Montg Co, Md. Ltrs of adm d b n, on prsnl est of John Holmes, esq, also ltrs of adm on prsnl est of Mary Holmes, both of said Co, dec'd. -Mesheck Browning, adm; Clarksburg.

Request that an order be issued for the arrest of Cmdor Jas Barren on charges that the surrender of the ship *Chesapeake* was premature & feel a terrible sense of disgrace. Signed: Ben Smith-1st Lt; Wm Crane-2d Lt; W H Allen-3d Lt; S Orde Creighton-4th Lt; Sidney Smith-5th Lt; Saml Brooks-S M. Ltr sent to Hon Robt Smith, Sec of U S N, Wash.

FRI JUL 3, 1807

Ltrs rec'd by collector of this port, from following men on board the British ship *Bellona,* Capt Douglas, stating that they are Americ ctzns:

*John Holdridge,	Wm Roberts	Jno Barnes
Jeremiah Holmes	*John Hartsman	Jas Farrell
*Jas Craig	Emery Griffin	Stephen Pindel
Conrad Smith	John Henry	John Hayton
Peter White	Geo Beams	Chas Washington

Wm Mears, born in Accomac Co, has a fmly there
Wm Ware, ntv of Balt Co, Scott's Fields, Md.
Description from register of seamen, Norfolk-*Hartsman-born in Balt-age 14; *Holdridge-born in Germantown, Pa-age 28 yrs; *Craig-born in Cumberland Co, Pa-age 21 yrs.

Grand inquest of U S for Dist of Va, upon its oath presents, that Jonathan Dayton, late a Senator in Cong of U S from N J; John Smith, Senator in Cong of U S from Ohio; Comfort Tyler, late of N Y State; David Floyd, late of Indiana Terr, are guilty of treason against the U S in levying war against the same, to wit: at Blannerhassett's Island, County of Wood, Va, Dec 13, 1806. Upon info of:

Wm Eaton,	Erick Bollman	Peter Taylor	John Morgan
Jacob Allbright	Chas Willie	Saml Swartwout	Geo Morgan
Thos Morgan	Elias Glover	David Fish	Jas Wilkinson
D Woodbridge jr	David C Wallace	Edmund B Dana	Alex Henderson
John G Henderson	Jacob Dunbaugh	Saml Mozley	Hugh Phelps
John Monholland	Chandler Lindsley	Jas Knox	John Graham
Wm Love	Thos Hartly	Stephen Welch	Benj H Latrobe.
Jas Kinney	[-John Randolph]		

Died: Robt McDonald, mariner wounded on the ship *Chesapeake;* Norfolk committee made arrangements for his public burial.

WED JUL 8, 1807

Died: Robt MacDonald, seaman wounded on board the frig, *Chesapeake*, on Jul 4, at the Marine Hospital. -Norfolk, Va.

Jacob H Geiger, insolvent debtor, confined to Wash Co prison, for debt. -Wm Brent, clk.

Ladies with ltrs in Wash P O-Jul 1, 1807:

Nancy Belt	Mrs Mary Sands	Sarah Wilson.
Mrs Susannah Collins	Mrs Charles	Mrs Cushing
Mrs Jane Fan	Miss Hepburn	Harriet Peden
Miss Eliz Shannon	Mrs Mgt Scott	

Saml Mozley deserted from U S ships of War; & Richd Brown, negro, age ab't 22 yrs. -John Cassin, Navy Yd, Wash.

For sale-order of Calvert Co Crt [Md]. Rl est of late Mr Jas Weems; land on which he resided-640 acs; tract nr the crt hse-450 1/2 acs, now in possession of Mrs Weems, the widow of aforesaid Jas Weems; 2 other tracts nrby-100 acs & 162 acs. Apply to Dr Nathaniel T Weems who lives adjacent to 1st tract. -Fred'k Skinner, Jas Duke, Parker Bowen, comrs.

In Chancery-ratify sale made by Bushrod Washington, trustee for sale of rl est of Geo Washington, dec'd; 519 acs in Montg Co, Md sold for $6446.37 & 511acs in Chas Co for $5.50 per ac. -Nichs Brewer, R C C

Strayed or stolen-bay horse. Reward-$15 to be pd by Horace H Edwards at Mrs Kearney's on F St, Wash City.

MON JUL 13, 1807

Meeting of ctzns of Fredericksburg, Va & its vicinity: Wm Smock, Mayor; John Stanard, sec; committee-Jas Brown, Geo French, Thos Goodwin, Chas L Carter, Robt Hening, John Tayloe Lomax, Robt Patton, John Mercer, John W Green, Hugh Mercer, Thos R Rootes Sr, Dr John Taliaferro, Wm Brooke & Carter L Stevenson. Subj: British-*Leopard* attack on frig-U S *Chesapeake*. See Jul 1, 1807.

Meeting of ctzns of Annapolis, Md, Jun 29, 1807. Robt Wright, chrmn; John Johnson, sec; committee-Jeremiah T Chase, Wm Kilty, John Kilty, Nicholas Carroll, John Muir, Burton Whetcroft, John T Shaaff, Reverdy Ghiselin, John Gassaway, Richd H Harwood, Lewis Duvall, Nicholas Brewer. [Attack of *Leopard* on *Chesapeake*]

Meeting of ctzns of Wilmington, Del, Jul 5. Chrmn-John Dickinson; sec-Outerbrige Horsey; cmtee-Dr Jas Tilton, Saml White, John Warner, Edw Rouche, Jacob Broom, Dr Ebenzer A Smith & Jas Lea. Subj: British-*Leopard* attack on frig-*Chesapeake*. See Jul 1, 1807.

WED JUL 15, 1807

Ltr from Mr G Pindell to editor of Federal Gazette, dt'd Pig Point, Ann Arundel Co, Jul 3. His son's name Stephen Pindell is mispelled [Findell]-Gassaway Pindell. Jun 15, 1807, on board the *Bellona*. Honored fr...I shipped at Capt Tenant's request, was captured a few hrs after the pilot left her. Schn'r sent to Halifax & all her crew put on the *Melampus* frig; month later sent to the Bellona, I despair of getting clear....your dutiful son, Stephen Pindell.

Church on F St will be opened next sabbath; pews remain undisposed; apply to John McGowan, Michl Nourse or Toppan Webster. Wash.

FRI JUL 17, 1807

Richmond Light infnty Blues, commanded by Capt Wm Richardson; Manchester [Va Cvlry]-commanded by Capt Harry Heth; Robt Anderson, of Co of riflemen, formed in Wmsburgh; Capt John Burk, of Rpblcn rifle Corps of Petersburg; Capt Byrd C Willis, Vol Co of Light infantry at Fredericksburgh; offer their svcs to Pres of U S.

MON JUL 20, 1807

Meeting at Fairfax Co, Va, at the Crt Hse, Jul 11, 1807. Thomson Mason-chrmn; Hugh West Minor-sec; committee: Genr'l Thomson Mason, Geo Graham, Chas Little, Jas H Blake, Wm Payne, John Chapman Hunter, Geo Minor, Edw Washington, Hancock Lee, Geo Summers, John Thos Rickets, Newton Keene & Dodridge Pitt Chichester. [Attack of *Leopard* on *Chesapeake*]

Boston meeting, Jul 10, 1807-Elbridge Gerry, moderator; Perez Morton, sec; committee: Barnabas Bidwell, John Quincy Adams, Dr Chas Jarvis, Benj Austin, Thompson J Skinner, Geo Blake & Perez Morton. [Attack of British *Leopard* on frig *Chesapeake*]

WED JUL 22, 1807

Died: Uriah Tracy, age 54 yrs, Jul 19, Senator of U S from Conn.

FRI JUL 24, 1807

Meeting held at Salem, Jul 10 regarding attack of British *Leopard* on U S frig *Chesapeake*. Moderator-Col Wm R Lee; committee: Hon Wm Gray, Jos Story, Jacob Crowninshield, Benj Pickman jr & Wm Cleveland, by order of: Wm Gray-chrmn, John Punchard, town clk.

Meeting at Hartford, Jul 10. Chrmn-Thos Seymour; sec-Eli Todd; cmtee: Alex Wolcott, Sylvester Wells, Daniel Olcott, Luther Loomis & Lemuel Whitman.

Meeting at Marblehead-Joshua Prentiss, moderator; John Sparhawk, clk; cmtee: John Prince, Jos Barker, John Baley, B Martin, Benj Knight, Nath'l Hooper & Henry Gallison. By order of John Prince, chrmn.

Meeting at St Mary's Co, Md, at Leonard-town, Jul 18, 1807. Chrmn-Capt Jos Ford; sec-Jos Harris; committee: John R Plater, Wm H Brown, Wm Hebb, John Leigh, John Ralph, Edmund Key, Athanasius Fenwick, Jos Ford, Dr Henry Ashton, Col Henry Neale, Col Mathias Clarke, Enoch J Millard & Chas Chilton-appt'd committee of correspondence. Jos Ford, chrmn; Jos Harris, sec.

Long boat taken up adrift; apply to Wm Pursel nr Peter Miller's, Jersey Ave, Wash.

MON JUL 27, 1807

Meeting at Culpepper Co, Va, Jul 16. [See meetings above] Philip Slaughter-chrmn; John Shackelford-sec. Meeting at Albemarle, Va: H Nelson-chrmn; John Carr-sec; cmte: Thos M Randolph, John Harris, Chas Everit, Chas Yancey, Benj Brown, Saml Dyer, Peter Carr, Wm D Meriwether, Joel Harris, Nimrod Branham, Reuben Lindsay, Wisham Wood, Dabney Carr, Edw Garland, Thos Garth Sr, Christopher Hudson, Rice Garland, Hugh Nelson, Wilson C Nicholas & John Coles Sr.

Mariners of Balt, Md, Port offer their svcs to avenge murder of our seafaring brethren. Thorndick Chase-chrmn; Timothy Gardner-sec.

WED JUL 29, 1807
Seamen pressed by the British: Wm Ware, ntv American, born on *Pipe Creek*, Fred'k Co, Md. Daniel Martin, ntv of West Port, Mass. John Strachn, born on Eastern Shore of Md, Queen Anns Co. John Little, alias Francis, & Ambrose Watts escaped from the melampus.

Taken up a stray cow & calf. -Thos Sandiford, F St Lear's Wharf, Wash.

FRI JUL 31, 1807
Meeting held at ChaptiCo, St Mary's Co, Md. [British *Leopard* attack on U S frig *Chesapeake*] Hon Wm Thomas-chrmn; Jas Egerton-sec; committee: Col Thos Barber, Philip Key, Capt John Chaplain, Dr Henry Ashton & Dr Jas Thomas.

MON AUG 3, 1807
Crct Crt o/Wash Co, D C. Wm Hawkins, cmplnt, vs Benj Stoddert, Danl Reintzell & Ann his wife, late Ann Robertson, Saml Robertson, Henry Robertson, Thos Robertson, & Sarah Robertson an infant under age of 21 yrs, which said Ann, Henry, Thos & Sarah, are the heirs of Wm Robertson, dec'd, dfndnts. Wm Robertson, dec'd, rec'd conveyance of ground & premises in Wash from Benj Stoddert-same was not recorded & lost; Wm Robertson, before his death, conveyed same to Wm Budden; Budden conveyed same to complainant-not recorded; legal title now vested in Benj Stoddert; bill is to get a legal title. Saml Robertson does not reside in Wash & his resid is unknown; Henry Robertson & Sarah Robertson, infant, reside in MontgCo, Md. -Uriah Forrest, clk.

Strayed or stolen-sorrel horse from plantation of Geo Calvert, esq, nr Bladensburg. Reward-$10; Richd Barry nr the Centre Mkt, Wash City.

WED AUG 5, 1807
Savannah, Jul 7-meeting cld by John Y Noel, mayor. Subj: attack of British *Leopard* against U S *Chesapeake*. Edw Telfair, chrmn; Thos U P Charlton, sec; committee: Wm Stephens, Geo James, Chas Harris, Jos Habersham, Edw Telfair, John M Berrien, P H Morel, W B Bulloch, John Y Noel, Thos U P Charleton, Archibald S Bulloch, & John Cumming.

Rev Andrew T McCormick-divine worship, Aug 9, in new church nr the Navy Yd.

FRI AUG 7, 1807
Elected trustees of institution for Education of Youth in Wash City: Robt Brent, Gabriel Duvall, Saml H Smith, Jas Davidson, Elias S Caldwell & John Dempsie.

MON AUG 10, 1807
Died: Gen De Rochambeau, age 82, in France, formerly a Marshal of France, Cmnder of French Troops in U S during Rev

Petit jurors for May Crct term, 1807, summoned from body of Dist of Va, for trial of Col A Burr.

Wm Pope	*Powhatan*	Peyton Randolph	*Richmond*
John Bowe	*Hanover*	John Roberts	*Culpepper*
Joshua Chaffin	*Amelia*	Jarvis Storrs	*Henrico*
Miles Selden	*Henrico*	Lewis Truehart	*Hanover*
Wm Yancey	*Pittsylvania*	Thos Prosser	*Henrico*
John Staples	*Albemarle*	Edw C Stanard	*Ablemarle*
Richd B Goode	*Chesterfield*	Nathl Selden	*Henrico*
Esme Smock	*Henrico*	Wm Wardlaw	*Richmond*
David Lambert	*Richmond*	Richd E Parker	*Westmoreland*
John W Ellis	*Hanover*	Thos Stark	*Hanover*
Wm White	*Hanover*	Wm B Chamberlaine	*Henrico*
Randolph Harrison	*Cumberland*	Jerman Baker	*Cumberland*
Wm Hoomes	*Caroline*	Overton Anderson	*Richmond*
David Bullock	*Richmond*	*Edw Carrington	*Richmond*
Geo W Smith	*Richmond*	Hugh Mercer	*Spottsylvania*
Wm R Fleming	*Goochland*	Robt Haskins	*Chesterfield*
Armistead T Mason	*Loudon*	Dabney Minor	*Albemarle*
Wm McDaniel	*Stafford*	John Horace Upshaw	*Essex*

[*Absent] -Jos Scott, mrsh'l V D.

Jurors summoned from Wood Co, for 5th Crct in Va Dist, Aug 3, 1807, for trial of Col A Burr: Hazekiah Bucky, Jas G Laidley, Jas Henderson, Jas Compton, Hamilton Morrison, Yates S Conwell, Jacob Beeson, Wm Prince, Nimrod Saunders, Thos Creek, Anthony Buckner, David Creel. -Jos Scott, mrsh'l.

WED AUG 12, 1807

Died: on Aug 9, suddenly, Gen Nicholas, age 84 yrs, long a respectable inhabitant of Alexandria. Irishman by birth, by profession a patriot soldier. Alex; Aug 10.

Order of Orphans Crt of Wash Co, D C. Pblc auction at Mr Orlando Cook's, Pa Ave, all prsnl prop of Wm Swinton, dec'd. -Geo Blagden, exc, Wash.

Land for sale: 300 acs, adj *Swan Point*, where I reside. -Edw Digges, Cobrach, Chas Co, Md

In Chancery, Jul 28, 1807. Abraham Umstattd, vs Chas Howard, Alex'r Howard & others. Bill to obtain a decree for conveyance from dfndnt, heirs of Jacob Howard to cmplnt, of parcel in Montg Co, nr Edmund Jenings; Chas & Alex Howard are non-residents of Md. -Nichs Brewer, R C C

FRI AUG 14, 1807

Died: Mr Edw Welsh, Aug 9, late of Charleston. -Americ Consulate, St Jago De Cuba. -Maurice Rogers, Jul 19, 1807.

Hugh Maguirk, late professor o/St John's College, Md, his late resid in PG Co, Md; having obtained Mr Simon Cantwell as his assistant; informs the public that his academy is now open; hopes 23 yrs of teaching in Md, 11 at St John's, will procure him a share of public confidence & patronage. -Wash City, nr the Seven Bldgs.

MON AUG 17, 1807

Died: Mrs J March, age 57 yrs, Aug 11, of Gtwn, relict of late Mr J March, stationer, of that place.

Reward-$100 for Oliver, Harry, Lina, & Sarah. Lina & Harry purch'd from est of Mr Benj Grimes of PG Co, Md in 1800; all are negroes. -Thos Graves, Thos Graves jr, Madison Co, Va.

For sale or rent-hotel on Capitol nr the Capitol, presently occupied by Mr P D Stelle. -Dan'l Carroll of Dud'n.

WED AUG 19, 1807

Trial of Col A Burr, Mon Aug 10. In crt: Herman Blannerhasset; Return J Meigs; Maurice P Bellnap, Chas Duval, Jas Taylor, Tunis Dills, Bennet Cock, Hezekiah Lewis & G B Vanhoree. Dr Wardlaw was discharged-his wife was in extreme danger & required a sea voyage. Mr Randolph Harrison whose extreme disposition was attested to by Dr Adams-dischg'd. Blannerhasset was arraigned for high treason. Mr Jas Henderson is sick with bilious fever. Hezekiah Bucky was summoned. *Jury: John Horace Upshaw had opinions hostile to the prisoner; same for Jas G Laidley, David Creel, Jas Hamilton, Hamilton Morrison, Yates Y Conwell, Wm Pope, Jacob Beeson, Wm Prince, John Bowe, Gervas Storrs, Miles Selden, Lewis Truehart, Wm Yancey, Thos Prosser, John Staples, Edw C Stannard, Richd B Goode, Nathl Selden, Esme Smock, Richd E Parker, John W Ellis, Thos Starke, Wm White, Nimrod Saunders & David Lambert. Wm Hoomes, Wm B Chamberlyne & Overton Anderson-set aside. Thos Creel-no opinion. Peyton Randolph, atty, set aside. [*Jury selection]

Patrick Lyddau, insolvent debtor of Montg Co, Md; trustee to be appt'd. -Upton Beall, clk, Montg Co, Md.

Lost-certificate no. 10766 for $5,400, to credit of Francis Beauchampon. -Jas Davidson, jr. [Treas of U S]

FRI AUG 21, 1807

Meetings on the attack of British *Leopard* on U S frig *Chesapeake*. Vansville-Aug 15: Gen Rezin Beall-chrmn; Gabriel P Van Hornsec; committee-John C Herbert, Henry Culver, Josiah Jones, Thos Richardson, Nicholas Snowden, Richd S Jones. Cleveland, Ohio-Jul 22, 1807: Saml Huntington-chrmn; Amos Spafford-clk; committee: Saml Baldwin, John Walworth, Lorenzo Carter & Saml Huntington. Prince Wm Co, Va, -Slatey Run Chr, Aug 8: Richd Brent-chrmn; Jas Kempe-sec; committee: Dr Fitzhugh, Richd Foote, Philip Alex'r, Stephen French, Walter Lindsay, Gerrard Alex'r jr, Thos Harrison jr, Bernard Hooe jr, Dr Geo Graham & Wm Grant.

Jury selection-Aaron Burr Trial: set aside-Jerman Baker. Suspended-Geo W Smith, Armistead T Mason, Dabney Minor. Selected-Edw Carrington, Richd E Parker, David Lambert, Hugh Mercer, Christopher Anthony, Jas Sheppard, Reuben Blakey, Benj Graves, Miles Bott, Henry Coleman, John M Sheppard & Richd Curd. [Petit Jury]

MON AUG 24, 1807

Impressed into British svc-call themselves ctzns of U S & need proof of same sent to Dept of State:

Jas Carr	John Bolton	John Johnson
Jas Johnston	John Devis	Thos Bravo
Matthew Myles	John Gray	Thos Real
Levy Brown	Geo Roberts	Wm Cammamile
Geo or Jos Nicholls	John Blackwood	John Chapman
Dennis Megavey	Benj Dennings	John Veil
John Lindsay	Martin Powers	Isaac Hunter
Wm Simmons	Wm Mockhall	Nathl M Warren
Geo Bround	Aug 21, 1807	-Dept of State

WED AUG 26, 1807

Comr's o/Wash City appt'd by the Mayor: Mich'l Nourse-1st Ward; Thos H Gillis-2d Ward; Dan'l Rapine-3d Ward; Geo Collard, 4th Ward.

Orphans Crt of PG Co, Md. Pblc sale at dwlg hse of Ann Greenwell; hsehld furn, horses, negroes.

FRI AUG 28, 1807

Orphans Crt of PG Co, Md. Aug 24, 1807. Prsnl est of Leonard Waring, late of PG Co, dec'd. -Clement Holyday, adm.

Trial of Aaron Burr-evidence given by Wm Eaton; Col Geo Morgan, Gen John Morgan & Mr Thos Morgan-[fr & 2 sons] from Pittsburg, Pa neighborhood, were introduced. Examined: Jacob Allbright, Wm Love, Dudly Woodbridge, Simeon Poole, Maurice Bellnap & Edmund P Dana. [another Morgan bro is Geo-Aug 31]

Orphans Crt of St Mary's Co, Md. Aug 5, 1807. Prsnl est of Rev Chas Smoot, late of said Co, dec'd. -Jas Egerton, adm.

MON AUG 31, 1807

Orphans Crt of PG Co, Md. Pblc sale of prsnl est of John Beans;-horses, furn, etc. -Geo N Thomas, adm.

Aaron Burr trial: examination of Cmdor Thos Truxton & Peter Taylor.

WED SEP 2, 1807

Mrs: Mr Geo Washington to Miss Eliza Beall, d/o Thos Beall, Sep 1, by Rev Mr Balch.

Mr John Minchin wants 20 journeymen-shoemkrs & 5 or 6 apprentices, for boot & shoemkg business. N J Ave, Wash.

Died: Cmdor Edw Preble, U S N; info rec'd at Navy Yd-Sep 1. [Sep 4 info: Died Aug 25, age 46 yrs, hsbnd & fr -Wash City]

FRI SEP 4, 1807

Jas Leander Cathcart, Cnsl & Navy agt for U S at Madeira, writes his unfeigned thanks to Capt John McNamara, of brig *Louisa* of Alexandria, for his attention to himself & family during their passage from thence to Madeira, likewise their property whilst on board said brig.

John Muir has 20,000 ft of mahogany for sale & 2000 ft of walnut. Shop opposite Daily Advertiser, Royal St, Alexandria.

Orphans Crt of PG Co, Md, Sep 1, 1807; prsnl est of Thos Stalling, late of PG Co, dec'd. -Wm Stalling, exc.

Orphans Crt of St Mary's Co, Md. Aug 4, 1807. Jas Cooke, adm of Rich'd Jordan, late of said Co, dec'd. -Jas Forrest, Reg W. -Jas Cooke, adm.

Aaron Burr Trial. Examination of Wm Love, Dudley Woodbridge, Simeon Poole, Edmond P Dana, Israel Miller & Purley Howe. Sep 1-jury in 25 mins found Burr not guilty. Jonathan Dayton appeared & was admitted to bail-sum $10,000.

Mr Duncan of New Orleans, cnslr at law, was almost poisoned by his svt, Frank, who was promised $700, a horse & his freedom; Laudanam was put in Mr Duncan's porter, which he detected just before drinking it.

Orphans Crt of PG Co, Md; pblc sale of part of prsnl est of John Beans. -Geo N Thomas, adm.

MON SEP 7, 1807

Schn'r *Volunteer*, owner Mr Jas Calwell, volunteered same to take the pirate lately molesting the commerce of the Chesapeake; Capt Porter of Americ
Navy volunteers: [all of Balt.]

Chas Wirgman	Wm Davidson	Geo Lee
Wm Richardson	Jas Vinson	Jas Towers
Thos Ring	Wm Macey	Tobias Belt
John Miller	Wm Deahins	Jas Brien
Jas Dunnahoe	Claudius Besse	John Davis
John Ferns	Wm Murdoch	Overton Hardy

Wm Cooper of Norfolk

Piracy plan was broken up & 12 are in confinement. Ltr of thanks was signed by: Saml Sterett, Capt-Independent Co; Jos Sterett, Capt-of Balt United Volunteers; Col John Stricker-5th Md Regt; Jas Calhoun jr-Lt independent Co, 5th Regt Md Militia.

Mr Jos Gales jr, able stenographer, has been hired by Mr Saml Harrison Smith, printer of Nat'l intell & Wash Advertiser.

Runaway: Cornelius, negro, says he belongs to Wm Barry of Ga. -Jos McCeney, shrf, A A Co, Md.

WED SEP 9, 1807

For sale-farm where I now live; 280 acs in Montg Co, Md; adj Evan Thomas' Mill. -Nathl Wilson.

Meeting at Detroit, Mich on attack of British man of war, *Leopard,* against U S frig *Chesapeake.* Stanley Griswold-chrmn; Jas Abbott-sec. [Meeting at hse of Wm M Scott, Jul 26, 1807]

FRI SEP 11, 1807

No person whatever can be admitted into the so wing of the Capitol excepting those actually engaged in the work. -B H Latrobe, srvyr of public bldgs of U S.

Pblc sale-order of Orphans Crt of Montg Co, Md; at plantation of Volinda Beatty; est of Volinda Beatty & Dr Ozias Offutt, both of Montg Co, dec'd; furn, negroes & stock. -Jas Offutt of Wm, adm of Volinda Beatty & Dr Ozias Offutt.

David Gelston is collector at the Custom Hse, N Y.

MON SEP 14, 1807 NOT PUBLISHED

[Failure of regular supply of paper to arrive from Balt]

WED SEP 16, 1807

Depositions of three seamen taken from the *Chesapeake*-Alleghany Co, Md. Upton Bruce swore that his fr, Normand Bruce, had a female slave named Phillis, she bec mthr of 2 chldrn by a white man named Andrew Ware, one was a boy raised on my fr's farm on Pipe Creek, Fred'k Co, his mthr is living, his fr is dead, his name is Romulus, age ab't 28 or 30. -Upton Bruce-sworn before Thos Thistle, Alleghany Co, Jul 18, 1807. John Lynn, clk, Alleg Co, Md. Wm *MacNeer swore the same as above before Andrew Bruce, Jul 17, 1807, J. P for Allegany Co, Md; Signed Wm *McNair. Sarah Lewis swore on Jul 17, 1807 the same as above & lived in the neighborhood of Normand Bruce's family. [X-her mark]. Wm Bruce swore on Jul 18, 1807, same as above; at age 12 yrs he went to live with his Uncle, Normand Bruce; sworn before Geo Rizer, J of Peace-Alleg Co, Md. Deposition of Greenbury Griffin, of Talbot Co, Md, age ab't 37 yrs, taken before Wm Lindsey, J. P. for Queen Ann's Co, Md, Aug 4, 1807, saith that John Strahan or Strawhan, s/o Saml Strawhan, of said Co, was bound to him to sea svc ab't 1802; left him at Norfolk ab't 1804; J Strawhan was 17 yrs 10 mos on Mar 20, 1802, date of indenture. Witness: John Merchant, Thos Lambdin, & John McDaniel. Rec'd Mar 21, 1802. -J Price, Reg o/wills, Talbot Co, Md. Jas Roe Pratt, of Queen Anne's Co, Md, aged ab't 45 yrs, swore before Wm Lindsey on Aug 4, 1807-same as above for John Strahan. John Price, of Kent island, Queen Anne's Co, Md, aged ab't 41 yrs, swore before Wm Lindsey, Aug 4, 1807, same as above for John Strahan. Thos Lynch, of Queen Anne Co, Md, aged ab't 47 yrs, says that Saml Strahan lived at the tan-yd of Mr Wm Tilghman, bet Centreville & Queen's town & John, the son, was born there. Saml Strahan or Strawhan, of Caroline Co, Md, aged ab't 56 yrs, saith that his son John was born ab't Apr 14, 1784; has not seen him for svrl yrs. [*2 splgs]

Deposition on seaman taken from the *Chesapeake* by the British. Benj Davis of Westport, Bristol, Mass, Yeoman, says that Wm Howland, late of same place, mariner, dec'd, brought to Westport a colored boy then ab't 6 yrs of age, this was 14 yrs ago; his name was Dan'l Martin; at 14 yrs of age he was appr or svt of Nancy Howland, widow & relict of said Wm Howland; he has not seen him for ab't 7 yrs. Signed-Benj Davis before Eli Haskell, notary public, of New Bedford. Nancy Howland, of New Bedford, adds to the above statement, that Dan'l was brought from Buenos Ayres by her hsbnd. She appeared before Eli Haskel, Notary Pblc, Jul 13, 1807. U S, Commonwealth of Mass, Bristol, SS.

FRI SEP 18, 1807

Orphans Crt of Montg Co, Md. Sep 7, 1807; prsnl est of Absalom Beddo, late of said Co, dec'd. -Jas Beddo, exc.

Court Martial held on board his Majesty's ship, *Belleisle*; John Wilson alias Jenkin Ratford, lately taken from Americ frig, *Chesapeake;* charges of desertion, mutiny & contempt. -Halifax, Aug 28. [Wilson born in London-Trial Aug 26] The death sentence of execution was carried out on Aug 31.

For sale-*Westbury*, 1,464 acs, in Anne Arundel Co, Md; shown by Mr John Shew, residing thereon. Terms apply to Wm Cooke, Balt, John Galloway, West Rvr or Henry L Waddell, Phil.

Orphans Crt of St Mary's Co, Md. Jos Edwards, adm of Stourton Edwards, late of St M Co, dec'd, is to give notice for creditors to exhibit their claims. [Jos Edwards, adm, follows with said notice. Jun 9, 1807] -Jas Forrest, Reg wills.

Pblc auction of 100 acs on Oxen Run in Wash, cld *Burches*. Mr Philip Evans will show the boundary lines. -Saml & Jesse Burch.

Died: Thos Newton Sr, esq, Sep 11, coll of this port. -Norfolk, Va.

MON SEP 21, 1807

John Long, insolvent debtor, confined in Wash prison, for debt. -Wm Brent, clk.

Ofcrs chosen for Anacostia Library Co: Dirs-Alex'r McWilliams, Buller Cocke, Gustavus Higdon, Robt Bunvie, Benj More, Jas Boddington, John Davis of Abel, John Dempsie, Edw Fitzgerald. Jas S Stevenson, lib; Jos Cassin, treas. -Wash.

WED SEP 23, 1807

Crt of inquiry to be held at Norfolk in case of Cmdor Jas Barron. Capt Alex'r

Murray-Pres; Capt Isaac Hull & Capt Isaac Channcey will preside.

FRI SEP 25, 1807

Jos Calhoon elected mbr of Hse o/Reps of U S for S C, vice Levi Casey, dec'd.

Thos Stockdale, born in Harford Co, Md arv'd in Alexandria, having made his escape from British ship *Tamar*. Capt Robison, from Lynn Haven Bay, some 8 or 9 days since, was on board said vessel for 3 yrs. -Alexandria, Sep 22.

Caution against trespassing. -Anne Soper, PG Co, Md.

Tenn Co will meet at Mechanic's Hall, N Y. -E Jackson, surviving trustee.

Died: Mr Jas Toomy, late teacher of Latin at Charlotte Hall School, Sep 3; survived by his widow. -Ferdinand S Campbell, clk. Charlotte Hall, St Mary's Co, Md, Sep 20, 1807.

MON SEP 28, 1807

Died: Victor Hughes, Govn'r of Cayenne.

VP Geo Clinton took passage with his youngest dght on the N Y Rev Cutter; same was fired at by the British ship-*Leopard*.

Orphans Crt of Wash Co, D C. Sep 26, 1807; prsnl est of Saml Kirkpatrick, late of said Co, dec'd. -Geo Kirkpatrick, adm.

Decree of U S Crct Crt, Dist of Col, for Alexandria Co: sale of *Abingdon*, formerly the resid of Mr Robt Alexander; 553 acs. -Thos Swann, G Deneale, Edmund I Lee, comrs.

Wash Jockey Club Races. -Saml Boots, sec.

Plating manufactory, 19 North St, Balt, Md. -Geo Sharp

WED SEP 30, 1807

The Grave Yard on sq 100, nr Mr Holmead's, will be inclosed; limit is 6 sites per person or family, at $2 per site; sale Oct 10. -Thos Herty, esq, Rg o/Wash.

Mrd: on Sep 29, Mr Toppan Webster to Miss Martha Osborne, both of Wash, by Rev Mr Laurie.

Stolen or strayed from the Commons of Wash-brownish horse. North F St nr St Patrick's Chr, Wash City. -Thady Hogan

Persons holding lots in Cumberland, Alleghany Co, Md-ground rents due by Jan 1 next; unpaid-same will be sold at public sale. -Thos Beall of Saml.

Dry Goods just rec'd, 14th St, Wash. -H Aborn

FRI OCT 2, 1807

Runaway: Beatty, negro woman; says she belongs to Fred'k Slate, living in Dutch settlement, Loudon Co, Va. -John Fleming, shrf, Montg. Co, Md.

MON OCT 5, 1807

Ranaway: Hampshire, negro man, from Wm Goodall, Orange Co, Va, nr Stannardsville.

Died: Genr'l Peter Muhlenburg, Sep 30, coll of Port of Phil.

Israel Smith, Rpblcn, elected Gov of Vt over Mr Tichenor.

Auction-all the furn of Jos M Semmes. -Saml Speake-auct, Wash.

WED OCT 7, 1807

In Chancery-Jun term 1807. Peggy McLaughlin & others, vs Wm Evans & Jas S Morsell. Ratify report of Dan'l Bussard, trustee; prop sold for $14,600.
-Wm Brent, clk.

Ranaway: Andrew, negro, prop of Sarah Foughee, of Pr Wm Co, Va. -John Stone, Pr Wm Co,Va.

Ezekial Bacon elected Rep o/U S for Mass, vice Barnabas Bidwell, rsgn'd.

Orphans Crt of Wash Co, D C. Oct 1, 1807. Prsnl est of Saml Whann, late of said Co, dec'd. -Thos Hunter, adm.

Decree of Co Crt of Pr Wm, Va. Sale at Benj Bronaugh's Tavern at Hay-Mkt, Va. Tracts of land belonging to est of Henry Dade Hooe, lately dec'd; 100 acs in Fauquier Co; 200 acs, dwlg hse & merchant mill of said Co; per will of said H D Hooe. -John H Peyton & Wm Wade, com'rs.

Ladies with ltrs in Wash P O:

Mary Barnhold	Mrs M Buchan	Rebecca Conner
Jean Gate	Eleanor Johnson	Eliz Jackson
Mrs Lee	Mrs Phenix	Eliz Shorter
Eliz Smith		

Ranaway: Laurance Buttler, negro; from Geo Huguley, nr *Little Falls* of Potomac, Fairfax Co, Va. Reward-$20.

FRI OCT 9, 1807

Under mortgage from Henry Schively to Mich'l Hivener, lot 12 sq 1 in Wash will be sold. -S Speake, auct.

Pittsburg, Sep 29. Last wk Mr Wm B Irish, deputy mrsh'l, left for Beaver Co, to execute writs for Dist of Pa; Sep 23 Mr Irish proceeded to hse of Wm Foulkes against whom judgment had been obtained in company with Enion William & Jas Hamilton. Entering the Foulkes' lane shots were fired & Mr Hamilton fell from his horse & expired.

Orphans Crt of Wash Co, D C. Oct 8, 1807. Prsnl est of John Haydock, late of said Co, dec'd. -Jos Huddleston.

For sale: lot 1 on Loudon St & lot 2 on Back St, Leesburg, Va; also 369 acs nr *Short Hill*, Loudon Co, Va. Apply to Saml Murray-Leesburg or Stephen Donaldson-living on premise.

MON OCT 12, 1807

Ranaway: Francis Boyd [Frank], mulatto man; from Wm Holmes, living in lower part of Montg Co, Md.

Crct Crt o/Wash Co, D C: sale on premises, all right int & claim of John Crookshank, dec'd; prop held by him & Geo Thompson, to wit, lot 5, part of lot 4 sq 461 with the three story brick bldgs, now occupied by Saml H Smith & Miss Finnigan; lot 6 sq 347 & lot 25 sq 533. -Chas Glover, trust.

WED OCT 14, 1807

Appointments: Genr'l John Shee, of Pa, super of Indian affairs, to be coll of Port of Phil, vice Genr'l Muhlenberg, dec'd. Genr'l John Mason, of D C, to be super of Indian affairs.

Thorn hedges for sale at my nursery nr Little Falls of Potomac. -Thos Main.

Lessons in drawing & painting at my hse on 8th St, nr the Navy Yd. [Thos Bell jr also now teaches] -John Bell

John Borrows, insolvent debtor, confined in Wash Co prison for debt. -Wm Brent, clk. Same for Thos Le Tellier, insolvent debtor.

FRI OCT 16, 1807

Mr Hugh Maguire was appt'd principal teacher for Western School vice Mr Richd White, rsgn'd. [Wash City]

Died: Robt Hanson Harrison, Oct 2, at Nanjemoy, place of his nativity; a young man. -Benj C Ridgate, clk, Charlotte Hall.

Order of Orphans Crt of PG Co, Md. Sale at hse of late Zepheniah Prather, hsehld furn & stock. -Zepheniah Prather jr., adm.

MON OCT 19, 1807

Will sell or hire, a second hand piano; also for sale: violins, bows & strings; svcs in tuning. -F A Wagler, Wash.

Pa election-Edw Heston elected Sen for Dist of Phil City & Co; Wm T Donaldson, shrf for same area.

Saml W Dana elected Sen of Conn, in rm of Uria Tracy, dec'd.

Geo W Lindsay has taken the well calculated hse on Capitol Hill, late occupied by Mr Frost formerly by Mr Stelle; he intends to open a tavern on Oct 24.

Strayed or stolen-bay mare. -G Docker, Capitol Hill.

WED OCT 21, 1807

Geo Truit elected Gov of Dela; Nicholas Van Dyke, Rep in Cong, in room of James M Broom, esq, rsgn'd.

FRI OCT 23, 1807

Strayed or stolen-sorrel horse from plantation of Geo Calvert, esq, nr Bladensburg. Reward-$10. -Richd Barry nr Centre Mkt, Wash.

Elizabeth town, Oct 13. Cornelius Hatfield, came from Eng to possess estate left him by his fr, was conveyed to Newark goal on charge of brutal murder of Stephen Ball, ctzn of this state, on Jan 25, 1781 at Bergen Point. Hatfield was discharged by spirit of Treaty of 1783. Those in on the act were: Cornelius Hatfield, John Smith Hatfield, Job Hatfield, Jas Hatfield Sr, Jas Hatfield jr, Elias Mann & Saml Mann, all late inhabitants of Eliz town & Job Smith, late of Bergen. [Tragic events are detailed in paper]

MON OCT 26, 1807

Teacher wanted for school ab't 5 miles from Bladensburg in neighborhood of Jonathan Beall, Humph'y Williams, Oliver Barron & others.

Orphans Crt of Wash Co, D C. Pblc sale at hse of Ralph Charlton, nr the Navy Yd, prsnl prop of Saml Whann, dec'd. -Thos Hunter, adm.

Geo Collard appt'd trustee of John Borrows, insolvent debtor.

W Waters appt'd trustee of Thos Le Tellier, insolvent debtor.

Runaway: Ned, negro; says he belongs to Wm Casson, of Spotsylvania, Va, nr Fredericksburg. -Cartwright Tippett, kpr of the jail for Daniel C Brent, mrsh'l, Wash Co, D C.

Saml W Dana having declined; the Leg of Conn chose Chauncy Goodrich as Sen in Cong of U S vice, Uriah Tracy, dec'd.

Runaway: Lewis, negro; says he belongs to Henry Davidson of Chas Co, Md. Cartwright Tippett, kpr of jail, Wash.

TUE OCT 27, 1807
Orphans Crt of PG Co, Md-public sale at his dwlg hse, part of Philips Nicholl's prsnl prop; furn, horses & cattle. -John Riddle

Tenth Congress-Senate:

Conn	Jas Hillhouse	Chauncey Goodrich
Ga	John Milledge	Geo Jones
Ky	Buckner Thruston	John Pope
Mass	Timothy Pickering	John Q Adams
Md	Philip Reed	Saml Smith
N C	Jesse Franklin	Jas Turner
N H	Nahum Parker	Nicholas Gilman
N J	John Condit	Aaron Kitchell
N Y	S L Mitchill	John Smith
Ohio	John Smith	Edw Tiffin
Pa	Saml Maclay	Andrew Gregg
R I	Benj Howland	1 vacancy
S C	John Gaillard	Thos Sumpter
Tenn	Dan'l Smith	Jos Anderson
Va	Andrew Moore	Wm B Giles
Vt	S R Bradley	Jonathan Robinson

FRI OCT 30, 1807
Wm O'Neale's brdg hse can accomodate 6 or 7 gentlemen. Wood & coal for sale at his coal yard. -Wm O'Neale, Wash City.

MON NOV 2, 1807
Mrd: on Oct 11, by Rev Mr Brook, Lewis Ford, formerly of Wash, to Miss Eliz Plowden, of St Mary's Co, Md.

WED NOV 4, 1807
Orphans Crt of Chas Co, Md. Sale of all prsnl est of Matthias Redmond, late of Chas Co, dec'd. -Terecy C Redmond, adm.

Thos Bruff, dentist, Six Bldgs, Wash City, has a machine for washing windows, patented, for sale.

Impressed into British svc. Proof of ctznship of U S requested by sec of State for:

John Duston	Jas Danniels	Thos Fenwick
John Harvey	John Ryan	Fred'k Porter

Hse o/Reps-Petitions referred to committee: 1-Jos Knox, sldr of Rev, comp for svcs. 2-Nathan Babbitt, of N H, srvd as physician in Military Hosp at Providence, comp for svcs. 3-Petition of Mary F Hills, of Pa, referred to committee of claims. 4-Paul & J M Revere, of Boston, pray that a duty be laid on imported copper in sheets. [Agreed]

FRI NOV 6, 1807

Hse o/Reps-1-Petition of Danl Buck, of Vt, praying for increase of pension. 2-Pet of John Carteret, of Boston, comp for his svcs as cooper during Rev War. 3-Pet of H Doolittle, comp for svcs in Rev War. 4-Pet of Reuben Colburn, allowance of a sum of money due him for svcs in Rev War. 5-Pet of Philip Turner, late of Conn but now of N Y, for his svcs as physician & surg in Rev Army. All referred to committee.

Jos Bloomfield has been re-elected Gov of N J.

Money found by Adam King, Gtwn.

MON NOV 9, 1807

Hse o/Reps-1-Petition of Ludwick Kuhn of Phil, comp for supplies furnished during Rev. 2-Pet of Wm Hanna, of Schenectady, manufacturer of leather, act prohibiting export of green hides & skins. 3-Pet of John Evans, of Monangahela, stating that David Scott, to whom a pension had been granted entered into the Army in spring of 1777, the following yr he was broke by a crt martial, praying that the circumstances of the case may be enquired into. All referred to committee.

Jos M Semmes, insolvent debtor, confined to Wash Co jail, for debt. -Wm Brent, clk.

WED NOV 11, 1807

Sale of inn, presently occupied by Capt Brooks, in Upper Marlborough, Md, with 10 acs. -Thos C Bowie.

Ltr from Havanna to Wash City, dt'd Oct 2, 1807. Yellow fever has continued to rage. List of victims:

Young Mr Stoughton, s/o his Cath Majesty's Cnsl at N Y; Amos Picket, Moses Prince & Edw Hoyt of ship *Hope*, Bryam Lovett mstr, of Salem; Benj Wood, Moses Tucker, of ship *Hampden & Sidney,* Kennard jr mstr, of Portsmouth;
John Shadwick, John Hoffman, of brig *Geo Wash,* Jeremiah Blanchard of Newbury Port; Geo C Naglee, supercargo from Phil; son of Capt Patrick Hays of Phil;
John Jackson, Michl Thompson, Nathl Cole & Ebenezer Richard of brig *Rpblcn,* Noah Emery, mstr of Salem; Jas B Collins of ship *Minerva* of Phil, Wm Bainbridge, mstr; Wm Lamb & Thos Wildes, of brig *Superior*, Patrick Hays, mstr, of Phil; Mr Erastus Huntington, merchant; Capt Calven Gardner, of schn'r *Regulator* of N Y; John Lin, of brig *Susan*, Anthony Moffeth, mstr of N Y; Wm Rees, of sloop *Fly,* of Phil, John Dove, mstr; Jas Mason & Jos Bowdish, of brig *Love & Unity* of Warren, R I, Cabel Eddy, mstr; Capt Jos Sevier of brig *Industry*, of Newbury Port; his bro died on his passage; Jos Williams of schn'r *Harmony* of Boston, Barnabas Hopkins, mstr; Isaac King, of ship *Golden Age*, Thos Rennick, mstr of Plymouth; Casper Bowers, of schn'r *Sally*, of Boston, Thos Vickery, mstr;
Capt Robt Rogers, mstr of brig *Eunice* of N Y.

Henry O Dyer has opened his new brick store in Bridge St, bet Elisha & Remulus Riggs' stores, 2d doors from John Cox-fall & winter goods. -Gtwn.

FRI NOV 13, 1807

Strayed from the Commons o/Wash City, a red cow. Reward-$2. -Cath Lardner, living nr the jail.

Crt Martial on board U S ketch *Aetna* on Jun 8 last: Wm Rogers, surgeon, for disobedience of orders & unofcr like conduct. Decreed he shd be dismissed from svc & rendered incapable of ever srvng therein. Sentence confirmed by Pres of U S. - Oleans, Oct 5.

Orphans Crt of St Mary's Co, Md. Mary Eleanor Ford & Philip Ford, adms of Philip Ford, late of said Co, dec'd; to give notice required by law for creditors. -Jas Forrest, rg o/wills; Philip Ford, surviving adm.

MON NOV 16, 1807

Wm Scott brought before me a stray mare. -S N Smallwood, Wash.

Jos Wheaton, broker & commission merchant, has opened an ofc in his own hse in F St, Wash City.

Subscriptions for Richmond Enquirer will be rec'd by D Wiley in Gtwn or Wash City.

Orphans Crt of Wash Co, D C. Prsnl est of Hugh Somerville, late of said Co, dec'd. -David Somerville, Alex'r Reid, adms. Prop will be sold at hse of Mrs Somerville.

WED NOV 18, 1807

Hse o/Reps: 1-Petition of Martha Wyatt, admx of Pitman Wyatt, for arrearages of her hsbnd's pension. 2-Jacob Ritten jr, praying for a drawback. 3-Gideon Edwards-to be on pension list. 4-Joel Chase, of Vt, comp for svcs-Rev War. 5-Saml Doak, praying for same. 6-Isaac Claxon, of N Y C, praying for a drawback. 7-Pet of Wm Fontaine for value of horse taken by indians in 1790. 8-Pet of Constant Taber et al of Newbury-capture of ship *Wm* & cargo. All referred to committees.

Return of dead & wounded from frig *Chesapeake,* Cmdor Jas Barron, Jun 23, 1807.

Killed:	John Lawrence	Jas Arnold	John Shukly.
Badly wounded:	John Haden	Cotton Brown	Jas Eppes.
	John Parker	Robt McDonald	Geo Percival
	Peter Simmons	Francis Cownoven	
Slightly wounded:	Cmdor Jas Barron	Mid Jas Broom	John Wilson
	Peter Ellison	Wm Hendricks	Thos Short
	Wm Moody	David Creighton	John Master
	Emanuel Fernandes		

-J G Hunt, Surg, to the *Chesapeake*.

In Chancery-Jun term 1807. Chas Wadsworth vs Owen Roberts & Jane his wife, Geo N Lyles, Jno Harper & Jas Keith. Report of Lewis Ford, trustee: ratify sale of mortgaged prop, sum of $800. -Wm Brent, clk.

Mrd: on Nov 12, by Rev Mr Pitt, Mr Wm Varden to Miss Maria Maul, eldest d/o Mr John Maul.

FRI NOV 20, 1807
Alex'r Suter, at store lately occupied by Mr Edgar Patterson, High & Bridge Sts-Gtwn, has books & fancy articles for sale; a lot in Gtwn on Wash & Gay Sts; & tract-1003 acs in Monongalia Co, Va. -Alex'r Suter

Saml Lowdermilk, determined to decline the mercantile business in Wash, has stock of goods for sale. -S Speake, auct.

Mrd: on Nov 5, by Rev Wm Steers, at Milford, Capt Wm Weems of Anne Arundel Co, Md, to Miss Sally E Taylor of Pr Wm Co, Va.

Montg Co crt-sale of farm whereon Zachariah MacCubbin lives, 544 acs with large dwlg hse, late prop of said MacCubbin, taken at suit of Nicholas Pegno & wife, adms of Wm Benson. -John Fleming, shrf.

New store, dry goods & groceries, nr the Navy Yd. -Lewis Zimmer

MON NOV 23, 1807
Hse o/Reps: 1-Petition of Israel Isaacs, sldr in Rev War, praying for comp. 2-Pet of John McKinney, srvyr of Port of Alexandria, increase in salary. Both referred to committees.

WED NOV 25, 1807
Middleburg Grammar School has been remv'd to my farm, *Green Hill*, Loudon Co, Va, nr Middleburg; teacher for over 20 yrs. -Wm Williamson, V D M

For sale: lot 15 sq 377 in Wash. For terms apply to Thos Patterson, Wash City; or Alex'r Porterfield, Berkeley Co, Va.

Hse o/Reps: 1-Petition of John Pitchlym, interpreter to Choctaw Indians-praying for money due him for svcs. 2-Pet of John Whitney. 3-Pet of Peter Landais-bal of comp due him. All referred to committees.

St Andrews Soc to meet Nov 30. -J Murdoch, sec. [Local]

FRI NOV 27, 1807
Mrd: on Nov 15, by Rev Mr Malvey, Jeremiah Boothe, merchant of Wash, to Miss Ann Walker, of St Mary's Co, Md.

Taken up-a stray brown horse. -Jos Hardisty, nr Bladensburg, Md.

Saml Baxter, insolvent debtor, asks Chas Co, Md, crt for relief. -John Barnes, clk.

Died: Dr Chas Jarvis, Rpblcn of Mass. [No date-appears recent]

MON NOV 30, 1807

Pblc sale: hse now occupied by Mr Geo McCaully, also hses nrly oppo school of Mr Van Zandt; lot nr Mr Robt Cherry's sq 799. -Alex'r Cochran, Wash City.

WED DEC 2, 1807

Notice-wanted a gentleman, unencumbered with a wife or family, to teach in capacity of priv tutor. Apply to Rev David Wiley, Gtwn; or to Armistead T Mason, Loudon, Va.

Pblc sale at Mrs Master's dwlg plantation on east side of Eastern Branch Bridge-furn, stock, & negroes.

Benj Williams is elected Gov of North Carolina.

FRI DEC 4, 1807

For sale-family of blacks. Enquire of Mr Saml Speake or G B Bitouzey, both in PG Co, Md, nr the forks of Patuxent Rvr. The man wishes to live in Montg Co, Md. An offer from that quarter will be preferred.

In Chancery. U S, Wash Co, D C. Oct 9, 1807. Benj Stoddert & John Mason, vs Thos Waters Griffith, John R Livingston, Jonathan Burreli, Gabault & Dodrey, Jas C Montflorence, I I Picaud & Jas Davidson. Rg: debt of $35,675 liquidated by La Convention; transfer of bills to various dfndnts; Griffith now & for sevr'l yrs has resided in Balt; dfndnts reside out of Wash Co, D C. -Wm Brent, clk.

To let, store in occupation of Edw Davis, stationer, on Bridge St, Gtwn. -E Davis.

Madam Du Cherray, French lady, lately arrv'd from Moscow, intends forming an academy in Wash City.

MON DEC 7, 1807

Died: Oliver Elsworth, Nov 6, at Windsor, Conn.

In Chancery, Wmsburg, Va-Nov 5, 1807. Alex'r Love, plntf, against, Wm Crammand, John Lemay & Hugh Holmes, excs of David Cay surviving partner of Clow & Co, Messrs Hugh Holmes & Robt Rainey, Arthur Jones, Houlder Hudgin & Sarah his wife, excx of John Moor, dec'd, Miles King, Geo Lang, John Darby, Robt Andrew Armistead & Worlieh Westwood, dfndnts. Extractions: debates as to the dfndnt Robt Rainey, by his death; dfndnts insist that assets in hand are not equal to debts; present the bks of Clow & Co. -Anty Robinson, clk, Williamsburg. -Wm Coleman, M C. Accounts of dec'd, Messrs Andrew Clow, & Co, & that of

Messrs Holmes & Rainey from their bks for Jan, Feb, & May, 1793, will furnish evidence in the controversy bet parties. Alex Love

WED DEC 9, 1807

Died: on Dec 5, in Wash, Mrs Mary Haraden, consort of Lt Haraden late of, Boston, Mass.

Mrd: Mr Geo French, of Gtwn, to Miss Mgt Hall Weems of PG Co, Md, Dec 1, by Rev Thos Scott. [No date-recent]

For sale: negroes at dwlg plantation of Miss Hoods, nr Annapolis City. -Wm Worthington, sr; actg for Miss Hoods.

Pblc sale by order of Orphans Crt of Montgomery Co, Md; at my dwlg plantation, all prsnl est of late Jas Beall of Robt; & all prsnl est of Mgt Beall. -Dan'l Beall, adm d b n of Jas Beall of Robt & adm of Mgt Beall. Montg Co, Md.

Stray cow, nr the Great Hotel, Wash City. -Geo Thompson

FRI DEC 11, 1807

Orphans Crt of St Mary's Co, Md. Nov 9, 1807. Prsnl est of Bennet Mattingly, late of said Co, dec'd. -Jas Cooke, Aloys Mattingly, excs.

MON DEC 14, 1807

I wish to sell ab't 20 acs of land adj Gtwn with new framed dwlg; I wish to improve nr the Rope Walk, I would sell this place low.-Richd Parrott, Gtwn.

Having sold my goods & declined business in Gtwn, I am now preparing to leave the District. -John Maffit.

Taxes due on property in Wash City:

Adamault's heirs	Capt Adlington	John B Anderson
Richd Brashears	John Barnet	Chas a Beatty
Redmond & Garrett Barry	Benj Bacon	Ignatius Boone
Leonard Cook	John Cale	Bishop Clagget
Chas Cook's heirs	Benj Coombs	Eliz Detterly
Jas Calder	John Carter	Jas Dant
Wm M Duncanson	Alex Davidson	Lewis Deblois
Jasper De Carnap's heirs	Jos Dove	Tristram Dalton
John Duh	Martin Dawns	Edw Fallon
Evan Evans	Jos Estep	John Gowen
Wm Francis	Gardiner & Greenfield	Richd Gudley
Jas Gannon	Joshua Gregg	Alex Hand
Merto Garretty	Timothy Garretty	Geo Jacobs
Wm Herron	Danl Hurley	Thos M Kirk
Jones & Kean	Absolom Joy	Wm Lowry
Jas Kennedy	Jas King	Chas Lovering

Henry Luddington	Jas M Lingan	Jas Larner
Geo Lyles	Abraham Lindo	Ephraim Mills
Moses Liverpool	Andrew McDonald	Henry Mascrop
Archibald McDonald	John McIntire	Chas McDonald
John Minor	Jas McCormick	David Pollock
John McCarthy's heirs	Peter Murray	John Phillips
Susanna Osborne's heirs	Jas O'Brien	Mary Rose
Wm Prentice Philips	Grant & West	Robt Right
Pratt & Francis	Isaac Reed	Philip Selby
Mary Reynolds	Shaw & Birth	Wm M Smith
Thos Stenman's heirs	John Stevens	John Swank
Robt Sewell	John Story	Chas Shorter
Geo St Clair	Ann Shaw	Theatre Co
Geo & Sarah Sweeney	Mr Stewart-painter	Wm Thompson
Jas Thompson	Henry Thompson	Geo Thompson
Patrick Tool	Mich'l Tool	Thos Wilson
Mr Taylor	Jas Varden	Geo Wheatly
Saml Wilson	Doct Willis	Joshua Ward
Luke Whealan	Thos Webb	Jas Waugh
Colin Williamson's heirs	John Wallace	Augustus Woodward

[Yrs range from 1802 thru 1806. Am't due ranges from .25 to $166.33 due by Jan 8, 1808.] -Wash. Boyd, Treas o/Wash City.

Auction sale of sundry articles of Thos Letellier, insolvent debtor. -S Speake, auct.

WED DEC 16, 1807

Orphans Crt of Balt City, Md. Nov 3, 1807. Prsnl est of Wm Evans, late of Balt, dec'd. -Jas Stewart, Wm Lorman, Wm Gwynn, excs. [Gwynn's ofc is on Chatham St, Balt City]

FRI DEC 18, 1807

Mr John Banks o/Wash Co, D C, made assignment of his est & effects to Thos Herty, in trust for benefit of his creditors; those indebted to make immediate payment. -Thos Herty, Wash.

For sale: 2 story brick hse in sq 930, Wash City, now occupied by Mr Tunis Craven as a retail store. -Wm Brent

MON DEC 21, 1807

Weekly Register of Politics and News -issued at seat of the Gov't. -John P Colvin, post ofc at Wash.

Orphans Crt of Wash Co, D C. Dec 15, 1807. Prsnl est of Thos Jenkins, late of said Co, dec'd. -Francis Jenkins.

Partnership of Jos Cassin & Co being dissolved by mutual agreement. Business in future carried on my Jos Cassin at his store nr the Navy yrd, groc & wines, etc.

No. 1 of *The American Military Library* , 50 cents, book store, Pa Ave, Wash. -R C Weightman.

Stray bay mare came to my plantation. -Zach Crawford, living nr Beaver Dam.

WED DEC 23, 1807

District of Biddeford & Pepperelborough, Mass, shall now be called the District of SaCo. -J B Varnum, spkr of Hse o/Reps.

Orphans Crt of PG Co, Md. Prsnl est of Thos H Harson, late of PG Co, dec'd. -Thos G Addison, adm.

Order of Orphans Crt of PG Co, Md. Sale at dwlg hse of late Henry Addison, all prsnl prop of dec'd. -Dennis Magruder & Thos G Addison

FRI DEC 25, 1807

Wanted: negroes by the yr to work in timber business on *McCarty's island,* ab't 20 miles above Gtwn. Apply to Jas Middleton, mgr on the island or John W Bronaugh, in Gtwn, opposite the Roman Chapel.

Runaway: Two negro fellows; deliver to Nathan Chaffin jr or Joshua Beeson Sr, Surry Co, No Car. Reward-$50.

Tuition at *Charlotte Hall* School after Jan 1808 shall be $28 per annum. -Neale H Shaw, Reg, Charlote.

MON DEC 28, 1807

Americ ship the *Horizon* belonging to John & Alex'r McClure, bros of Charleston, cleared out in Sep 1804 under command of Alex'r for Zanzibar, Africa; arv'd at Montevideo giving up Zanzibar destination; ship was injured by bad weather & put into Lisbon; Eng frig the *Diana* captured him in Jun 1805 & carried him to Eng; later released & in May 1807 *Horizon* set sail & on May 30 was wrecked on coast of Clouan, nr Morlaix. Rgrd: decision from Imperial Cncl of Prizes; bros asking to receive proceeds from sale of wreck.

Archibald Van Horne, residing nr Bladensburg, brought before me a stray sorrel mare. -Gabriel P Van Horne.

WED DEC 30, 1807

Hse o/Reps: 1-Petition of Andries Van Patten of Shenectady, payment of claim against U S. 2-Pet of J Cooper jr, of Phil, remission of certain duties. 3-Pet of Ebenezer Brown, comp for Military svcs. 4-Pet of Wm Rice, sldr of Rev War. All referred to committee.

Runaway: Francis Thomas, alias Peter, committed to Wash Co, D C jail; says he belongs to Jacob Bare of Wash Co, Md, nr Hagerstown. -C Tippett, kpr of the jail for D C

1808

FRI JAN 1, 1808
I certify that Richd Fenwick brought before me a stray bay mare. -Danl Rapine, J P of Wash Co.

MON JAN 4, 1808
Hse of Reps: Petition of White Knaggs, praying for certain grants or confirmations of titles to certain lands.

Committed to jail, Edgar, negro; says he belongs to John Love, living at old Crt Hse, Fairfax Co, Va. John Fleming, shrf of Montg Co, Md.

Ranaway: Wm Chase, negro, formerly prop of Wilkerson Brashears, dec'd, who manumitted Him. -Richd Duvall, PG Co, Md.

WED JAN 6, 1808
Dr Lancaster has commenced prac of medicine on Pa av, Wash.

Intending as soon as possible to remove to Tenn, I will sell the estate *Abbington*, known for 50 yrs past, on Potomac Rvr opposite Wash City, 460 acs; now leased to Messrs Wises for $360 per annum; she has other lands nr Gtwn. Apply to Baldwin Dade, esq, Alexandria, for Cath F Alexander.

For sale: Frame hse nr the Navy Yard. -Wm Prout

FRI JAN 8, 1808
Ladies with ltrs in Wash Post ofc:

Mrs Baker	Sarah Burnett	Mildrid Dixon
Miss Lesey Davis	Eliz Finch	Eliz Foyles
Mrs Fitzhugh	Rebecca Falor	Ann Glover
Rachael Grove	Mary Hersey	Mary Lane
Susannah Lynch	Mary Madrick	Grace McDaniel
Mrs Myers	Miss M Wilson	Eliza Wilson
Eliz Williams		

Mrd: on Dec 27, by Rev Parson Compton, Andrew Coyle, esq, of Wash, to Miss Eliza Cheisholm, of Anne Arundel Co, Md.

Died: on Dec 28, John Gale, esq, mbr of Hse of Delegates for Kent Co, at Annapolis; remains interred Dec 30 in Kent Co; he leaves 2 dghts.

MON JAN 11, 1808
We agree to sell bread per weight pblshd by the Mayor. -Peter Miller, Geo Burns, Jas Friend. Wash City.

WED JAN 13, 1808

For sale-35 negroes, stock, plantation utensils, etc, at Hezekiah Wood's hse in Wash, D C. -Thos Peter & others, excs of Robt Peter, dec'd. Also 150 negroes, stock, utensils at Anthony Tracey's hse, in Montg, within 2 miles of Messrs Bowie & *Hersey's Mill*, Seneca.

Stray horse taken up nr Mrs Anne Greenwell's in PG Co, Md. -Joshua Farr.

Runaway: Geo, negro, formerly the prop of Wm Alexander, of Va, by him sold to Mr Robertson of Ohio, from whom he escaped. -Notley Maddox, shrf, PG Co, Md.

FRI JAN 15, 1808

Pblc sale:-decree of High Crt of Chancery of Md; all rl est of Dr Wm Lansdale, dec'd, lying in St Mary's Co, Md: *The Ramble*, *Haunslow*, & *The Strand,* adj ea other, 1,000 acs with dwlg hse. -Jos Harris, trust, Leonard Twn, Md.

MON JAN 18, 1808

Orphans Crt of PG Co, Md. Ltrs of adm on est of Francis Clement Dyer, late of said Co, dec'd. -Anne Dyer, excx.

Died: Mr Geo Mitchell, ntv of Scotland, age 75 yrs, in Wash, on Jan 11.

WED JAN 20, 1808

Committed to Allegany Co jail, runaway, Rueben, negro. -Wm Bruce, shrf, Allegany Co, Md.

FRI JAN 22, 1808

Phila Grand lottery for encouragement of useful arts. Tkts $1.50-

Jas Oellers, 1 So 3rd St;
Thos Peters, 22 N 2d St
Silas Willson, 341 N Front St
Chas Bitters, 11 3d St
Dan'l Miller, 427 N 2d St.
Leonard Kechmle, 79 N 3d St
Thos Bedwell, 178 N 3d St
John Shaw, 232 N 2d St
Isaac Carpenter, 245 So 2d St

MON JAN 25, 1808

Died: on Jan 7, Jas Barry, esq, age 53 yrs, of a lingering illness; Cnsl-Genr'l from Prince Regent of Portugal to eastern states.

Persons recommended to citizens of U S to fill ofc of Pres & VP-Jas Madison of Va 99 for Pres; Geo Clinton of N Y for VP. John Milledge & Jos B Varnum were appt'd tellers of the proceedings. [Term-4 yrs beginning Mar 4, 1809.] Wash City.

WED JAN 27, 1808

Orphans Crt of Montg Co, Md. Prsnl est of Hilary L Fisher, late of said Co, dec'd. [Jan 18, 1808.] -Artaxerxes Fisher, adm

FRI JAN 29, 1808
Died: Mr Ezra Darby, late a mbr of the Hse from N J, Jan 28, of consumptive complaint; tender hsbnd, leaves a tender consort. Funeral on Jan 29 with interment in burial ground on the Eastern Branch.

Meeting of the U S Military Philosophical Soc in the War ofc. -Jona Williams, Pres.

Pblc sale-deed of trust dt'd Jun 17, 1803 from Isodore Hardey of PG Co, Md, to John Francis Hardey; tracts in PG Co, Md, cld *Gardinor's Meadows & Tylers Advantage*, 330 acs; encumbered with right of dower. Tracts are 5 miles from Piscataway. -Richd B Gardinor, adm of John F Hardey.

MON FEB 1, 1808
Order of Orphans Crt of PG Co, Md. Sale at his late dwlg, part of the prsnl est of Zachariah Baldwin, dec'd. -Henry Culver, adm.

Order of Orphans Crt of PG Co, Md; public sale at dwlg hse of late Capt Hezekiah Wheeler; prsnl prop. -Hezekiah Wheeler, exc.

WED FEB 3, 1808
Committed to Cecil Co jail-Philip, negro; says he was sold by John Tyler, nr Fred'k Town to Mr Crown. -Jo Baxter, shrf.

In Chancery-Thos Beall of Sam, Thos, John, Benj, Jos & Richd Foster, & Isaac Van Meter, vs Geo, Wm, Richd, Ann & Sarah Mason, & Jared Hooe & Eliz his wife. Rgrd: conveyance of land in Allegany Co, cld the *Welshman's Conquest*, which Thos Beall of Saml, as atty in fact for Geo Mason, dec'd, contracted to sell to John Foster, by bond of conveyance, dt'd Feb 24, 1787. Dfndnts reside out of State. -Nichs Brewer, R C C

FRI FEB 5, 1808
Strayed-black horse. Apply to Mr Erskine, British Mnstr. Reward-$5.

MON FEB 8, 1808
Elected directors of ofc of Discount & Deposit at Wash:

John P Van Ness	Wm Stewart	Thos Tingey
Caleb Swan	Jos Nourse	Jas D Barry
Thos Munroe	Lewis Deblois	David Peter
Benj Shreve jr	Phineas Janney	Wm Brent
John Taylor.		

WED FEB 10, 1808
Orphans Crt of Wash Co, D C. Feb 8, 1808. Prsnl est of Geo Mitchell, late of said city, dec'd. John McGowan, Mich'l Nourse, excs. Prsnl prop will be sold at public vendue.

Reward $40: stolen-bay horse, John Hall living nr head of South Rvr, A A Co, Md.

FRI FEB 12, 1808

In Chancery, Jan 26, 1808. Issachar & Malon Scholfield, vs McCarty, Theodorick & Dan'l Fitzhugh, Mary Brent, Henry Lee & Nath'l Pendleton. Bill to obtain decree to foreclose mortgage executed by Philip Fitzhugh to cmplnts for undivided moiety of mills in PG Co, Md, cld the *Adelphi Mills*, sale for payment of the debt; also sale of rl est of said Fitzhugh for payment of his debts. Cmplnts sold said prop to Fitzhugh for $9,800; Fitzhugh executed a bond for conveyance of said prop to Pendleton, & has since died, leaving dfndnts the Fitzhughs & Mary Brent his heirs at law or devisees of his est. Henry Lee, dfndnt, is his exec. All dfndnts reside out of State. -Nichs Brewer, R C C

MON FEB 15, 1808

Runaway: Stephen Lockerman, black man, committed to Wash Co jail; says he belongs to John McFadden of Balt. -Cartwright Tippet, kpr of jail

Strayed or stolen-2 horses. -Francis Jenkins, Wash City.

Reward-$20 for Leo Taborgan, ab't 19 yrs of age, engaged as overseer for ensuing yr; raised in Ohio; left last evening wearing apparel belonging to Mr Saml C Jones. -John Welch, St Mary's Co, Ridge Post ofc, Md.

Proof of U S ctznship requested for the following who were impressed into British svc: John Porter, Wm Callicut, Clement Rivers, John Troup, Jos Mead, Wm Sloane, Wm Bartlet, Jos Pew, Jonathan Stuart, Geo A Cope., Geo Wagnere, John Moore, Peter Jones, Wm Wagemen

-Dept of State, Feb 9, 1808.

WED FEB 17, 1808

De Witt Clinton is appt'd Mayor of N Y C.

FRI FEB 19, 1808

Meeting of students of Western Acad in Wash; regarding death of their fellow student, Alex'r Kerr. -Valentine Welch, chrm'n. John Eversfield, sec.

Reward-$50 for Harry, mulatto man. -Jacob Jenkins, living in Hampshire Co, 18 miles from Winchester, Va.

Com'rs appt'd under act of Cong of U S, authorising erection of a bridge over the Rvr Potomac, within the District of Col: Robt Brent, Dan'l Carroll of Dud'n, Thos Munroe, Jas D Barry, Fred'k May, Saml H Smith, Jonah Thompson, Jonathan Swift, Thos Vowell, Cuthbert Powell, Elisha Janney, & Chas Alexander.

Wanted-a school mstr. Thos H Lyles, Richd Ireland jr, Theodore Hodgkin, Mordecai Smith, Calvert Co, Md.

MON FEB 22, 1808

Power of atty from Geo N Thomas, I will offer for sale, 3 negro men. -Richd B Gardiner, Wash.

Died: John Dickenson, Rev Patriot at a good old age. [No date-recent]

Orphans Crt of PG Co, Md. Ltrs of admin on est of Chas Hodges, late of PG Co, dec'd. -Alex'r Boteter, adm, Upper Marlboro

WED FEB 24, 1808

Notice-persons having demands against Peter Foorhis, insolvent debtor; Wm A De Peyster, assignee of said Peter, will attend at hse of John Baird, innkpr in Hackensack, N J, Aug 1.

FRI FEB 27, 1808

Pblc sale-decree of High Crt of Chancery of Md. Rl est of Gustavus Scott, dec'd, at Van Wyck & Dorsey's auction rm in Balt city, following tracts of land lying in Allegany Co, Md: *Governor's Neglect*-1031 acs; *Robey's Delight*-421 acs; *Bome's Attention*-684 acs; *Chesnut Grove*-461acs; *Now or Never*-600 acs; *Hard Struggle*-1554 acs; lot No. 2487-50 acs; *Western Connection*-15,484 acs. -Roger Perry, trustee, Cumberland.

Phil city meeting. Thos Leiper, chrmn; Geo Bartram, sec; candidates to attend a conf at Lancaster: Mich'l Bright, Wm Duane, Jonas Simonds, Callender Irvine & Thos Leiper.

Order of Orphans Crt-public sale of all prsnl est of Mgt Roberts, late of Montg Co, Md, dec'd. -Henry Roberts & Jos Roberts, adms.

MON FEB 29, 1808

Pblc sale-decree of Crct Crt Wash Co, D C. John Roberts & Saml G Griffith, cmplnts, against Benj Bryan, dfndnt. Sale of lot in said city-sq north of sq numbered 743-N J av. -John G McDonald, trustee.

WED MAR 2, 1808

Promotions & appointments in Corps of Engrs made Feb 23, 1808.

Lt Col Jonathan Williams to Col	Maj Jared Mansfield to Lt Col
Capt Alex'r Macomb to Major	Capt Jos G Swift to Maj
1st Lt Wm McCee to Capt	1st Lt Geo Baneford to Capt
2d Lt Chas Gratiot to Capt	2d Lt Eleazer D Wood to 1st Lt
2d Lt Wm Partridge to 1st Lt	2d Lt Prentice Willard to 1st Lt

Jos G Totten, Cadet Saml Babcock, Cadet Dan'l A A Buck & Cadet Sylvanus Thayer-all to 2d Lts.

Setting out in 7 or 8 days for Tenn-offer my svcs to transact business in that country. -W Ball [Enquire of printer]

Private sale-lot in Gtwn, No. 1, with good frame hse; 2 warehses; one occupied by Mr Casper Jackson as a store, the other by Mr John Lutz as a saddler's shop. Terms apply to Mr Seth Clarke, Fredericktown, Mr John Lutz on the premises, or to Adam Link or Geo Link, Shepherd's town, Va.

For sale-coal-2,200 bshls just arv'd. -Anthony Reintzel-Gtwn.

FRI MAR 4, 1808

Meeting took place Mar 2 bet Mr Gardenier of N Y & Mr Geo W Campbell of Tenn; Mr G was wounded but the surgs say it was a flesh wound. -Wash Item.

MON MAR 7, 1808

We protest the nomination of Jas Madison to fill ofc of Pres:

Jos Clay	Abram Trigg	Jno Russell
Josiah Masters	Geo Clinton jr	Gurdon S Mumford
John Thompson	Peter Swart	Edwin Gray
W Hoge	Saml Smith	Dan'l Montgomery
John Harris	Saml Maclay	David R Williams
Jas M Garnett	John Randolph.	-Wash City, Feb 17, 1808.

WED MAR 9, 1808

Genr'l Moreau arrv'd at New Orleans on Jan 22; his lady was detained at Bordeaux, not permitted to proceed to Paris to make arrangements which her mthr's death rendered nec; she will settle her affairs at Bordeaux & then to N Y.

Reward-$100 for Wm Randle, alias Wm Riddle, deserted svc in Phil; says he was born in Sussex Co nr Easton in Northamton; age ab't 27 or 30 yrs. -Nichs Neligh, Allen's Twnshp, Northampton Co.

The purchasers of prop at sale of the late Mr Rich'd Cramphin's effects, are notified that the creditors of the dec'd are becoming urgent. -Thos Bowie, adm of R Cramphin.

Ranaway-Ozwell, negro; was employed by Mr Henry Studer as a boatman in Berleley Co in 1807. -Jesse M Shurburn, Pecawaren, Chas Co, Md.

Persons with claims against est of Saml D Beck jr, late of PG Co, Md, dec'd, are to exhibit same. -Andrew Hamilton, adm.

FRI MAR 11, 1808

Died: on Mar 7, in Wash, Mrs Cath Sanford, age 66 yrs, many yrs an inhabitant of Alexandria; leaves mourning chldrn & relatives.

Jos Ricks, insolvent debtor, confined in Wash Co, D C, prison for debt. -Wm Brent, clk.

Greatly improved family physician bk-just published. *The Planter's & Mariner's Medical Companion,* by Jas Ewell, physician at Savannah. Testimony by: W Shippen, M D, Phil, Dec 31, 1807, Prof of anatomy;
John Crawford, M D, Balt, Mar 7, 1808;
B S Barton, M D, Phil, Dec 31, 1807, Prof of Med;
Jas Woodhouse, M D, Prof of Chem, Penn U, Dec 28, 1807;
John Shaw, A M, Prof of Chem, Col of Med of Md;
Chas S Caldwell, M D, Phil, Dec 26, 1807;
John B Davidge, M D, coll of Med of Md, Balt, Feb 19, 1808;
John Weems, M D, Gtwn, Columbia, Mar 3, 1808;
N Chapman, M D, Lecturers on Midwifery & Disease of women & chldrn, Phil, Dec 29, 1807.

MON MAR 14, 1808

John McGuire, age ab't 20 yrs, murdereded Jas Coyle in Cecil Co. Reward-$150. -Robt Wright, Gov of Md.

From the *Aurora*, Lancaster, Mar 7, 1808. Democratic Conf. Thos Leiper, chrmn; Gen Wm Reed & Wm Leib, secs. Tkt for electors of Pres & VP:

Chas Thomson	Wm Montgomery	Thos Leiper
Mich Leib	Jos Engle	Wm Rodman
Archibald Darrah	Jacob Weygand	John Steele
Gabriel Heister jr	Geo Hartman	Jas Cowden
Wm Wilson	Robt Giffin	Jacob Hortetter
David Fullerton	Peter Kimmel	Jos Huston
John McDowell	Adamson Tannehill	

WED Mar 16, 1808

Died: Mrs Eliz Prather, age 24 yrs, w/o Dr Prather, & d/o Chas Tompkins, of Balt, on Feb 20, at Clarksburgh, Md; wife & mthr, illness of 3 wks.

Pblc sale: hse of Mr Sarah; one carpenter's chest with tools, bk of architecture, drawing instruments, nr Navy Yd.

Mr Elisha Riggs has sold his entire stock to Mr John Peter, both of Gtwn. Mr Riggs' bks are remv'd to counting hse of his bro, Romulus Riggs; settlement by his assistant, Mr Saml C Offuttt, Gtwn.

Pblc sale: High Crt of Chancery of Md; at store of Thos Duvall, 187 acs cld *Brashears Pacson*, prop of John Turner, dec'd, in PG Co, Md. -Geo Page, trust.

Lots with ground rents due with no improvements-Cumberland, Md, to be sold at hse of Mr John Rine, Apr 22, in said town. -Thos Beall of Saml.

FRI Mar 18, 1808

Wishing to decline the hrdware business-entire stock for sale. -Henry Ingle.

Mr Joshua B Bond's running horse, *First Consul*, will stand in PG Co, Md, this season, Bladensburg & Upper Marlborough. -Isaac Duckett. Pedigree-Joshua B Bond, Phil.

Orphans Crt of St Mary's Co, Md. Prsnl est of Mary Jenkins, late of said Co, dec'd. -Athanasius Fenwick, exc.

Reward-$30 for Moses, black; alias John Lucas Ronds. -John Payne, Black Walnut Run, Orange Co, Va.

MON MAR 21, 1808
Jas Cheatham of N Y, in his paper *Republican Watch Tower* , published false libel against reports of trial of A Burr. -David Robertson, of Petersburg, Va, writes the Nat'l Intell & his ltr is supported by Geo Hay, Wm Wirt, Benj Bolts & Edmund Randolph; also ltrs by John Wickham & Alex Macrae.

Chancery-Md. Henry H Lowe vs Lloyd M Lowe, Jas R M Lowe, Barbary & Eliz Lowe. Bill is to record a deed executed to cmplnt by dfndnts, Lloyd, Barbary & Eliz; 2 tracts in PG Co, Md, cld *Landhim's Delight* & *Soper's Rest Enlarged* for conveyance of said land by Jas R M Lowe, or to vacate a deed by dfndnt, Lloyd M Lowe, to him for said land. All dfndnts except Lloyd reside out of Md. -Nichs Brewer, Reg Cur Can.

WED MAR 23, 1808
Navy Yd Rifle Vols-meet at hse of Lt Dobbin. -John Davis o/Abel, 1st Sgt.

For sale: brick hse nr the Navy Yd, in Wash, occupied by Mr John Jolly.
-Philip Spalding, Saml Speake.

Robt Glenn, insolvent debtor, confined to Wash Co prison for debt.
-Wm Brent, clk.

Jos Pollard, Thornsburg, Va, will attend the public sale of lands at Jeffersonville, Indiana Terr on Apr 21; will transact business there on commission.

Decree of High Crt of Chancery, Md. sale of all right, title & int of Thos Clark, dec'd in sundry lots in Gtwn, purch'd of John M Gantt; sale at Brooks's Tavern, Upper Marlbro-tract lying in PG Co, Md, purch'd by Clark of Brock Mockey, 150 acs. -Jas S Morsell, trustee.

Buffalo cow strayed to my place nr the hotel in Wash. -Arthur Thompson.

FRI MAR 25, 1808
Died: Capt Russell Bissell, of 1st U S Regt of infty; Dec 18, 1807, at Cantonment Belle Fontain, nr St Louis in Upper La, of inflammatory bilious disorder.

Creditors of Andrew Kaldenbach, with claims against him or his est, to meet at Mr Wm Rhodes Htl, Pa av. -Andrew Kaldenbach.

Orphans Crt of St Mary's Co, Md. Mar 20, 1808. Prsnl est of Wilfred Neale, late of said Co, dec'd. -Henry Neale, exc.

Orphans Crt of PG Co, Md. Sale of prsnl est of John Rustin, late of said Co, dec'd, at his late dwlg in PG Co, Md. -John H Hall, adm.

MON MAR 28, 1808

For sale-at dwlg hse of Mrs Ann Smith in High St, her hsehold furn, piano, shower bath, negro woman & boy. -Gtwn.

Orphans Crt of St Mary's Co, Md. Ltrs test on prsnl est of Comund Plowden, late of said Co, dec'd. -Henry Neale-exc.

WED MAR 30, 1808

Orphans Crt of Wash Co, D C. Sale of part of prsnl est of John Wight, dec'd; stock etc. -Wash Boyd, Geo Moore, excs.

Jas Hancock with John Stockwell the elder, & Geo Johnston & Jane his wife of Co of Tyrone, Ire, executed a Power of Atty, Apr 9, 1806, authorising John Stockwell jr, to receive, sell, convey all rl & prsnl est which we were entitled as heirs at law of Mark Stockwell, late of Wash City, or of Henry Stockwell, late of Phil; lots in Wash City & lands in Greenbrier & Kenaway Cos, Va. We do hereby revoke & annul said ltr of atty. -Jas Hancock, Mar 28, 1808.

FRI APR 1, 1808

In Chancery. Robt H Smith vs Eliz C Smith. Cmplnt as exc of John H Smith, he overpaid the prsnl est to a considerable amount. John H devised rl est in Calvert Co to his 2 dghts, Eliz Chew Smith & Mary Smith, who is since dead intestate & w/o issue; Eliz is sole heir of her sister; Eliz is under 21 & resides in Ky nr Gtwn in Scot Co. Robt H prays to sell the rl est for reimbursement of money he has advanced. Wm Kilty, Chancellor. -Nichs Brewer, Reg C C.

Land holders in Ohio-Th S Hinde & Ch A Stuart, agents for non-residents. Chillicothe, Mar 10, 1808.

Ranaway-Sam Jointer, negro. -Mareen Duvall, PG Co, Md, nr Govn'r Bridge.

MON APR 4, 1808

Crape to be worn to memory of Nath'l C Weems, esq, of PG Co, Md, late an honorary mbr of Wash Soc. -Robt Murphy, sec. Charlotte Hall, Mar 27, 1808.

WED APR 6, 1808

Orphans Crt of Wash Co, D C. Prsnl est of Addison Murdock, dec'd, late of said Co. Apr 2, 1808. -Mariamne C Murdock, Geo French, adms.

FRI APR 8, 1808

Applying for act of insolvent debtors. -Robt McKoy, PG Co, Md.

MON APR 11, 1808

Ladies with ltrs in Wash Post ofc; Apr 1, 1808:

Miss Sally Alexander	Miss Betsey Bill
Eliz Bowen	Mrs Anne Butler
Agness Cook	Mrs Sarah Crawford
Marg Davis	Mrs Dyson
Mrs Rebecca Edward	Miss R B Edwards
Nancy Freeman	Miss Eliza B Finch
Mrs Susanna B Finch	Miss Hannah L Gibbs
Miss Lettice Hall	Mrs Prudence Jones
Mrs Anny Marshall	Miss Mgt G Nicholas
Miss Mary Oliver	Susan Seutorious
Mrs Dorcus Talbeck	Miss Rusha Ann Wilson

WED APR 13, 1808

Decree of High Crt of Chancery, Md. Sale of all right, title & int of Thos Clark, dec'd in tract, *Brock Hall*, 120 acs & part of *Beall's Hunting Quarters*, ab't 70 acs, in PG Co, Md. -Jas S Morsel, trustee.

Stray calf came home with my cow. -Wm Bowhay, Navy Yd, Wash.

Seamen impressed into British svc in need of proof of U S ctznship:

Nathan Thompson	Thos Williams	Benj Bagnell
Jos Setta	Jos Cox	Chas Redding
Saml Henshaw	A Girdon	Saml Clapson
Wm Thompson	John Brant	Thos Webben
Mathew Soderborn	F Race	Geo Smith
Wm Brown	Minor Smith	Wm Bender
Robt McCord	Wm Price	Henry Muller
David Porter	Benj Young	Chas Anderson
Isaac Gaines	Thos Cook	Wm Jones
John Gallaway	Peter Lewis	Thos Marcumber
John Melville	Dan'l M Hagan	Jas Boggs
Wm Tiel	John Jason	Jas Carney
John Lemont	Wm Lindsey	Nichs Miller
John Porter	Peter Murphy	Jas Peterson
John Skinner	Thos Allen	Christopher Styon
J C Brecker	John Swaine	John Jarvis
Wm A Jennings	Theodore Young	Jas Hoyt
Jos Rosey	John Tul	Jos Haswell
John Williams.		

-Dept of State Apr 13, 1808

U S Navy Hosp, nr Marine Brcks, will be open Sat & Wed for physicians & students of Med to observe cases. -John Kearny, Dresser U S N H.

MON APR 18, 1808
Died: on Sat, Jacob Crowninshield. The remains were attended from the hse of Mr Machin by mbrs of the two hses; body to be carried to Salem. -Wash City Item.

WED APR 20, 1808
Oscar, thorough bred running horse, will stand at Christopher's, adj *Belle-Air*, seat of Benj Ogle, jr, esq, in PG Co, Md. -Apply to mgr at Christopher's..

FRI APR 22, 1808
Wanted-40 or 50 shares of Wash Bridge stock. -A Lindo, broker, Alexandria.

MON APR 25, 1808
Wash Co, D C-In Chancery, Crct Crt-Dec term 1807. John Robertson & Saml G Griffith, cmplnts, vs Benj Bryan, dfndnt. Ratify report of Jno G McDonald, trustee, for sale of mortgaged prop for $405. -Wm Brent, clk.

Orphans Crt of PG Co, Md. Pblc sale in Piscataway, Md, all prsnl prop of Electius Edelen, dec'd; horses, dry goods & groceries. -W Edelen, exc.

WED APR 27, 1808
To let-brick hse, lately the prop of Mr Wm Woodward, Pa av, Solomon Myers's lease for 3 yrs, at $250 per annum, will expire on Jun 20 next. Apply to Robt Underwood, Wash City.

Jas Bowdoin, late Mnstr at Crt of his Cath Maj, Envoy at Paris, his lady & niece, Miss Sarah B Winthrop, & Geo Sullivan, Priv sec to Mr B, arv'd at Boston, ship-*Sally*, from Liverpool. -New York, Apr 22.

Ranaway-Oliver & David, negroes; from Thos Graves jr, & Theophilus Eddins, living in Madison Co, Va.

Beck, negro girl slave, was purch'd from Walter Wilcoxen Summers, then of PG Co, Md, now of Montg Co, Md, for $200-some time since. Said Summers not being of age at the time, his Uncle Thos Wilcoxen, entered into bond of indemnity; said Summers being now of age, refuses confirming said sale. -Orlando Cook.

Alex'r Kedgley, insolvent debtor, confined to Wash Co, D C, prison, for debt.
-Wm Brent, clk.

Runaway-Stephen, negro, says he belongs to Letty Claxton of Montg Co, Md.
-C Tippet, kpr of jail for Wash.

Pblc sale-at dwlg hse of late John Beckley, esq, prsnl est of dec'd. -Maria Beckley, Mary Prince, excrs.

Goods stolen from my store on F St. -Wm Ward, Wash City.

FRI APR 29, 1808
Edw Graham Handy, cabinet & chair maker; north G St next to Dr Elzey has commenced business; 2 apprentices wanted.

Runaway-Lenn, negro man, says he belongs to Ralph Bowman, of Chas Co, Md. -John Fleming, shrf of Montg Co, Md.

MON MAY 2, 1808
Act-Concerning invalid pensioners; enacted by Senate & Hse of Reps; per law passed Apr 10, 1806. Added to pension list of invalid pensioners: [am't per mo]
Thos Lamar Davis, $2.50 per mo, to commence Dec 29, 1807
Albert Chapman, $10, Oct 17, 1807
Ambrose Homan, $2.50, Dec 15, 1806
Francis Blood, $5, Dec 16, 1806;
Jonas Green, $5, Oct 8, 1807;
Wm Green, $8, Feb 7, 1807;
Seth Weed, $6, Oct 7, 1807;
Saml Lathrop, $5, Sep 22, 1807;
Peter Smith, $4, Jul 16, 1806;
Wm Johnson, $2.50, Apr 1, 1807;
Jas Houston, $15, Jul 13, 1807;
Jedediah Hyde, $15, Aug 3, 1807;
Saml Nesbit, $5, Oct 18, 1807;
Shepherd Packard, $3, Feb 7, 1807;
Rich'd Kisby, $4, Mar 24, 1807;
Jonathan Wilkins, $2.50, Mar 26, 1807;
Waterman Baldwin, $5, Oct 25, 1807;
John Clark, $8, Dec 15, 1807;
John Venus, $2.50, Dec 11, 1807;
John Holcombe, $15, Dec 1, 1807;
Rich'd Steads, $4, Dec 9, 1807;
Alex'r Jones, $3.33 1/3, Jun 19, 1784;
Benj Saddler, $3, Jan 1, 1803;
Benj Jenkins, $2.50, Sep 16, 1807;
Wm Scott, $25, Mar 12, 1807;
Jas Bruff, $25, Aug 17, 1807;
Nathan Taylor, $10, Feb 19, 1808;
Aaron Stevens, $10, Feb 24, 1808;
Simon Morgan, $20, Mar 2, 1808;
Jonathan Patch, $5, Jul 11, 1806;
Ebenezer Rowe, $5, Jan 16, 1807;
Benj Kendrick, $3.33 1/3, Jan 1, 1786;
Nicholas Hoff, $5 Feb 22, 1808;
Saml Shaw, $8, Feb 13, 1808;
Nicholas Lott, $2.50, Jan 23, 1808;
Humphrey Becket, $2.50, Jan 8, 1808;
Silas Parrott, $6, Feb 10, 1808;
Jared Hinkley jr, $2.50, Jan 19, 1808;

Francis Davidson, $4, Jan 16, 1808;
Andrew Waggoner, $20, Nov 2, 1807;
Geo Richardson, $4, Feb 10, 1808;
Wm Wallace, $8, Jan 13, 1808;
Jos Bird, $4, Jan 29, 1808;
John St John, $5, Jan 29, 1808;
Abner Snow, $3.75, Jan 27, 1808;
Aaron Crane, $2.50, Nov 3, 1807;
Jas Hawkley, $5, Jan 6, 1808;
Elijah Morse, $4, Jan 6, 1808;
John Van Anglen, $15, Nov 3, 1807;
Jas Boden, $2.50, Mar 28, 1808
Isaac Burnham, $4, Jan 1, 1803;
Benj Hillman, $10, Mar 14, 1808;
Silas Pierce, $10, Mar 7, 1808;
Randel McAllister, $5, Mar 7, 1808;
John Durnal, $3, Apr 7, 1808;
Jabez Church, $2.50, Feb 22, 1808;
Thos Machin, $10, Mar 19, 1808;
David Richey, $2.50, Apr 2, 1808.

Persons already on pension list of U S-increase of pension.
Jas Campbell, $4 per mo, Sep 25, 1807;
Thos Bristol, $5, Oct 22, 1807;
Isaac Higgins, $3.33 1/3, Sep 29, 1807;
Josiah Smith, $5, Dec 29, 1807;
Jos Wace, $5, Dec 29, 1807;
Dan'l Buck, $5, Dec 17, 1807;
Lemuel King, $5, Dec 23 1807;
Wm Wallace, $5, Nov 17, 1807;
Reuben Dow, $15, Feb 19, 1807;
Jos Saunders, $5, Feb 7, 1807;
Wm Hastings, $5, Feb 11, 1807;
Joshua Lovejoy, $5, Jun 5, 1807;
John Beardsley jr, $5, Nov 13, 1807;
Jos Harrup, $5, Sep 15, 1807;
David Ranney, $5, Nov 5, 1807;
John Whitehorn, $5, Sep 30, 1807;
Rich'd Sherman, $5, Oct 8, 1807;
Noah Sinclair, $3.75, Oct 8, 1807;
Nath'l Church, $5, Oct 8, 1807;
Gershom Clark, $5, Jan 1, 1808;
John McKinstrey, $12, Dec 7, 1807;
Ebenezer Perkins, $5, Sep 15, 1807;
Henry Ten Eyck, $15, Nov 21, 1807;
Thos Simpson, $13.33 1/3, Dec 24, 1806;
John Rybecker, $4, Apr 18, 1807;
Lemuel Dean, $5, Oct 8, 1807;

Thos Johnson, $5, Apr 17, 1807;
Levi Chubbuck, $3.75, Jun 20, 1807;
Geo Walter, $2.50, Feb 24, 1808;
Saml Rossetter, $5, Jan 30, 1808;
Jeremiah Pritchard, $13.33 1/3, Jan 6, 1808;
Abner Gage, $5, Jan 26, 1808;
John Devoe, $5, Jan 30, 1808;
Nathl Bradley, $5, Jan 26, 1808;
Thaddeus Seely, $2.50, Jan 9, 1808;
John Herron, $2.50, Jan 26, 1808;
Peter Nevius, $4, Feb 17, 1808;
John Hampton, $6, Feb 17, 1808;
Roswell Woodworth, $5, Mar 23, 1808;
David Hullbell, $5, Mar 19, 1808;
John McCoy, $5, Mar 15, 1808;
Caleb Hunt, $5, Mar 5, 1808
Henry Gates, $5, Mar 9, 1808;
David Hall, $5, Feb 12, 1808;
Jonah Cook, $5, Apr 4, 1808;
Wm Nelson, $5, Jan 22, 1808.

Ltrs of adm de bonis non have been obtained from Orphans Crt of Montg Co, Md on prsnl est of Wm Chambers, also ltrs of adm on prsnl est of Sarah & Ann Chambers, dec'd, all of Montg Co, Md. -Dennis Lackland, adm.

Orphans Crt of Montg Co, Md; ltrs of adm on prsnl est of Stephen Adams, late of said Co, dec'd. -Hennaritta Adams-excx.

WED MAY 4, 1808

Orphans Crt of PG Co, Md. Apr 22, 1808. Prsnl est of Wm Bowie, late of PG Co, dec'd. -John B Bowie, Wm M Bowie.

Ranaway, Henry, black man, in 1805, from Rich'd Straughan, in Westmoreland Co, nr Kinsale, Va; formerly prop of Jas A Thompson, dec'd. Henry formerly waited on Jo Thompson, Jas A Thompson, Chas Thompson & Wm S Thompson, in Alexandria, when said Thompson was merchant in Alexandria. Henry, born in St Mary's Co, Md, waited on Messrs Thompsons in all parts including Alex & Gtwn; bought from Mr Rich'd Jackson. -Richd Straughan.

FRI MAY 6, 1808

Meeting of Rpblcns in Somerset Co, Md, held at Princess Ann, Apr 13, 1808. committee appt'd: Robt Lemmon, Geo James, Thos Williams, Henry King & Jas Miller. Tkt for Genr'l Assembly: Chas Nutter, Arthur Dashiell, Martin L Haynie & Peter Dashiell. Committee appt'd: Jas Bennett, Levin Ferrington, Wm Williams, Josiah Polk jr & Josiah Wilson Health. Order of Martin L Hanie,chrmn. Peter Dashiell, sec. [2 splgs for Haynie, Hanie]

Benj Tabbs, application to Judges of St Mary's Co, Md, praying benefit of act for relief of sundry insolvent debtors. -Jos Harris, clk.

Annual sheep shearing instituted by Geo Wash Parke Custis, esq, held recently at his seat at Arlington. Maj Lawrence Lewis of *Woodlawn*, John Tayloe, esq, of *Mt Airy*, Hayward Foote, of *Hayfield*, & Wm Alexander, of *Preston*, contended as breeders, were present. Judges of the day: Thos Digges, esq, of *Warburton*, Genr'l John Mason of *Analostan Island*, Wm Lee, esq, of *Burgandy Farm*, & Jonathan Swift, esq, of Alexandria. Col Deneale appt'd judge of weights. Mrs Denison, Mrs Ball, & Miss Peggy Fields, all of Fairfax Co, Va, produced each a piece of cotton cloth of their own home manufacture.

MON MAY 9, 1808
Strayed from Commons in Wash City, grey horse. -Chas H Varden, Capitol Hill, Wash City.

In Chancery, Wash Co, D C. Crct Crt, Dec term 1807. Gideon Snow, cmplnt, vs Abigail Perkins widow & admx & Hanah Perkins, sister & heir of Jos Perkins, dec'd & Nathan bond, dfndnts. Jos Perkins, formerly of Boston, dec'd, indebted to U S for duties-$757.50; cmplnt became his security; bonds came due & Perkins failed to pay same; Abigail & Hanah reside in Boston; lots in Wash City were conveyed to said Jos Perkins by Nathan Bond, of Boston, same pd for; pray for sale of said lots. -Wm Brent, clk.

WED MAY 11, 1808
Orphans Crt of Wash Co, D C. May 9, 1808. Prsnl est of Geo Mitchell, late of said Co, dec'd. -John McGowan, Michl Nourse.

Auction at Myer's Hotel: furn, horse, cart, carriage etc. Settlement to those who remain in my debt. -Solomon Myer.

Trial of Capt Jas Barron, Capt in U S N, attack of British-*Leopard* on U S ship-*Chesapeake*. Guilty of the charge- *for neglecting on the probability of an engagement to clear his ship for action;* sentence-suspended from all command for 5 yrs in U S N, without pay; from Feb 18, 1808. Present at Crt-Martial on U S ship, *Chesapeake,* in Norfolk, Va, Harbor, Jan 4, 1808: Capt John Rodgers-Pres; Capts: Wm Bainbridge, Hugh G Campbell, Stephen Decatur jr & John Shaw. Mstrs Commandant: John Smith & David Porter. Lts Jos Tarbell, Jacob Jones, Jas Lawrence & Chas Ludlow-mbrs. Littn W Tazewell, Judge advocate. Sentence confirmed by Pres of U S.

Luke Kent, clock & watch mkr, from Phil, has taken the shop occupied by the late Mr Suter, F St, Wash, nr the Treasury.

Jas A Porter, atty at law, just settled in Wash City & opened his ofc in hse of Thos Herty, Pa av

FRI MAY 13, 1808
Mgr wanted-at the woodyard. -Rd W West, on premise, Wash.

Runaway-John Roman, negro, committed to Fred'k Co, Md, jail; says he belongs to Bennet Taylor of Jefferson Co, Va. -Geo Creager jr, shrf, Fred'k Co, Md.

Ranaway-Bob or Robt Thomas, mulatto man. Deliver to Dr Rich'd Duckett in PG Co, Md or Allen B Duckett.

MON MAY 16, 1808

Ranaway-Joe Key, negro, from Hon Marmaduke Williams, mbr of Cong for N C; formerly belonged to Dr Thornton of Wash.

Wm Conner, insolvent debtor confined in Wash Co, D C, prison, for debt. -Wm Brent, clk.

Orphans Crt of St Mary's Co, Md. May 15, 1808. Prsnl est of Dr John Reeder, late of said Co, dec'd. -Jos Harris, adm.

Decree of High Crt of Chancery of Md-public sale in Chaptico of valuable plantation whereon John Eden, Sen, formerly lived, St Mary's Co, Md, 277 acs. Mr Enoch Hammett lives on the land & will show same. -Wm Mills, trustee.

Pblc sale-furn, prop of Jas Dougherty, lately dec'd.

WED MAY 18, 1808

Sons of St Tammany or Columbian Order, of the city of Wash. Grand Sachem-Wm Patterson Gardner; Fr of the Cncl-Rich'd Dinmore; sec-Bernard Smith; Treas-Joshua John Moore; Sachems:

Cornelius Conyngham	Benj Moore	Francis P Hamilton
Benj Burch	Saml Hamilton	R C Weightman
Jas W Bryson	Chas Jones	John Sessford
Ezra Varden	Henry Aborn	Bernard Smith
Rich'd Dinmore	Wm R Cozens	Saml McIntire
Henry Herford	Joshua John Moore.	

Anniv of 316th yr of discovery.

Wanted-100 workmen to hew, haul, saw, raft, timber for Wash bridge. Apply to Andrew Scholfield in Alex, John Muncure at Aquia or Wm Hoe jr, King Geo Co, or to Joan & M Scholfield.

St Andrew's Soc will meet at hse of David Waterstone. -John Murdoch, sec.

For sale-400 acs, land of Saml Aurant, Beaver Twnshp, Northumberland Co, Pa. -Jos Wheaton, Wash City.

Need 150 cords of hickory wood for Hse o/Reps. -Patrick Magruder, clk. Clk's ofc, H R May.

Runaway-committed to Calvert Co, Md, jail; Jim, negro; says he belongs to Balden Lee of King Geo Co, Va. -John Ledwick, shrf of Calvert Co, Md.

FRI MAY 20, 1808
Miss Sinnott, lately from Balt, has opened her English acad, north G St. Terms of tuition at acad or of Mr Francis Clark & Mr Jas Hoban.

MON MAY 23, 1808
Orphans Crt of Wash Co, D C. Ordered that Dan'l Brent, adm of Edw Killen, dec'd, give notice to creditors. -John Hewitt, Reg.
Followed by-prsnl est of Edw Killen, late a Mariner of U S schn'r *Enterprise*, dec'd. -Dan'l Brent, adm, with will annexed of E Killen.

WED MAY 25, 1808
Runaway-Cornelius, blackman; says he belongs to John Cross of Anne Arundel Co, Md. -Cartwright Tippet, shrf, Wash jail.

For sale-hse nr Navy Yd. Andrew Armstrong on the premises.

FRI MAY 27, 1808
Crt Martial, Norfolk: Cases of Capt John Hall of Marines & Wm Hook, gunner of *Chesapeake*. Hall to be privately reprimanded. Hook to be dismissed from svc of U S.

MON MAY 30, 1808
Notes of the Bank of the U S were enclosed by Wm Kenis, coll of Customs at Wash, N C, Jun 1, 1807, & put in the Post Ofc there addressed to Thos Tudor Tucker, Treas of U S; same not rec'd. Notes were issued to Adam Gilchrist or bearer at Charleston, dt'd Jul 20, 1808 thru Feb 27, 1807; Jos Habersham, Savannah, Mar 23, 1804 thru Nov 18, 1806; W Warner at Bank of U S, Apr 2, 1806; Cornelius Ray, N Y, Jan 22, 1805 thru Apr 16, 1805. -Albert Gallatin, sec o/Treas.

Waggon screw was left last April with Sam Collingwood, oppo the Fish Wharf in Gtwn. Owner may have it by proving prop & paying charges of this advertisement.

WED JUN 1, 1808
Robt Brent named paymaster of the army vice Maj Swan who resigns on Aug 1.
-Wash City Item

Jos Forrest elected Pres of the Commercial Co. -Wash City

Appointments made during last session of Cong:
Wm Pinckney of Md, Mnstr Pleni at Crt of London;
Robt Williams, Gov of Miss Terr;
Moreau De Lisle, Judge of Terr of Orleans;
Wm Hull of Mich Terr, re-appt'd Gov;

Reuben Atwater of Vt, sec of Mich Terr, coll of Dist of Detroit & inspec of Rev-Port of Detroit;
Wash Boyd, mrsh'l of D C;
Jonathan Laurence of S C, coll of Beaufort, S C & inspec of Rev for same Port
Venables Bond of Ga, coll of Dist & inspec of Rev for Port of Hardwick, Ga;
Wm Gazzam of Pa, srvyr of Port of Pittsburg;
Thos H Storm of N Y, Commercial agent of U S at Genoa;
Philip Grymes of Va, atty for U S in Terr of Orleans;
Jas Prince of Mass, mrsh'l of Dist of Mass;
Lemuel Trescott of Mass, coll & inspec of Dist & Port of Machias;
Jonathan Bull of Conn, com'r of Loans for Conn;
John Vernor of N Y, srvyr & inspec of Rev for Port of Albany;
Oliver Wayne Ogden of N J, Mrshl of Dist of N J;
John Shee of Pa, coll & Phil Dist;
Lewis Ford of Md, srvyr & inspec of Rev for Port of Lewillingsburg;
Lemuel T Spence of Md, coll o/Dist & inspec o/Rev for Snowhill Port;
Alex'r Moore of Columbia, Reg of wills for Alexandria Co, in Col;
John McKinny of Col., srvyr & inspec of Rev for Port of Alexandria;
Larkin Smith of Va, coll of Norfolk & Portsmouth Dist;
Thos Nelson of Va, coll of the Dist & inspec of Rev for Port of Yorktown;
Jacob Decamp of Va, srvyr of Port of Charleston in Dist of Miss;
John S West of N C, Mrshl of Dist of N C;
Robt Cochrane of N C, coll of Dist of Wilmington, N C;
Wm H Ruffin of N C, srvyr & inspec of Rev for Port of Windsor;
Abraham Bissent of Ga, coll for Dist of St Mary's;
Geo M Bibb of Ky, atty of U S for Dist of Ky;
Jas W Moss of Ky, Srvyr of Port of Limestone;
Rich'd Ferguson of Ky, srvyr & inspec for Port of Louisville;
Jos Buell of Ohio, srvyr of Port of Marietta;
Thos Boling Robertson of Va, sec of Terr of Orleans;
Saml Croudson of Orleans, Naval ofcr for Port of New Orleans;
Thos H Williams of Miss Terr, sec of same;
Jonathan Davis of Miss Terr, srvyr of Port of Natchez;
Lemuel Henry of Miss Terr, Rec of pblc monies for U S lands East of Pearl Rvr;
John Coburn of Ky, a Judge of Terr of Louisiana;
Gideon D Cobb of Indiana Terr, srvyr of Port of Massac;
Jas Abbot of Mich, Receiver of pblc monies for lands of U S at Detroit;
John McClellan of Md, Consul for U S at Port of Batavia.

N Y Congressional election: 1st Dist: Ebenezer Sage, 2-Gurdon S Mumford, Wm Denning, 3-Jonathan Fisk, 4-Jas Emott, 5-Barent Gardenier, 6-Robt Leroy Livingston, Herman Knickerbacker, 7-Killian K Van Rensselaer, 8-John Thompson, 9-John Herkimer, 10-John Nicholson, 11-Thos R Gold, 12-Erastus Root, 13-Uri Tracy, 14-Vincent Mathews, 15-Peter B Porter.

Election of city Cncl for Wash: 1st Ward at Mr Calwell's new hse; 2d Ward at Tvrn of Lewis Morin-Pa av; 3d Ward at Mr Stelle's Hotel; 4th Ward at Hugh Drummond's Tvrn-7 St.

FRI JUN 3, 1808
Sale of frame hse, lot 1 sq 104, 20th St. -Chas Jones, trust.

For sale: *Buzzard's Island*, where I reside, Calvert Co, Md, nrly opposite Benedict, 800 acs. -Richd W Harwood.

Henry T Compton of PG Co, Md, applied for benefit of act for relief of sundry insolvent debtors. -John Read Magruder jr, clk, PG Co Crt, Apr term 1808.

Orphans Crt of PG Co, Md; est of Thos Upton, dec'd. -John R Bussard, exc.

Barbarous duel lately fought nr Christianburg, Va, bet Mr Thos Lewis & Mr John McHenry; dispute over election in Montg; McHenry elected del to the legislature; fought with rifles at 15 steps; both fell, Mr L with ball thru the heart & Mr McH just below it.

Mrd: on Jun 4, Jesse Talbott of Alexandria to Hannah Litle jr of Wash, at Friends meeting hse, being the first marriage solemnized by that Society in city of Wash.

For sale-dwlng hse-possession immediately if required. -Jos Forrest. [resides there]

MON JUN 6, 1808
Buffaloe Bull will be let to cows this season on Col Tayloe's farm, cld *Petworth*, nr Wash City; $1 ea.

WED JUN 8, 1808
Leg of Ga elected Robt Walker, esq, Judge of the State Superior Crt for Middle Dist & John Forsythe, esq, atty Genr'l.

Meeting in Richmond, Va-Jun 1. Purpose of promoting domestic manufactures; Gvn'r cld to the chair; Thos Ritchie-sec; committee:

Jas Monroe	Edw Carrington	Alex McRea
David Bullock	Creed Taylor	Wm Foushee Sr
Abraham Venable	Robt Gamble	Jas Brown
Norborne Nicholas	Geo Hay	Thos Ladd
Jno Brockenbrough	Peyton Randolph	Wm Wirt
Benj Tate	Saml Adams	Jos Gallego
John Cunningham	John Clark	Wm H Cabell

Claims against est of Eliz Philpot, late of Chas Co, dec'd, exhibit by Dec 8; payments to Mr Laurence Perry is authorised. -P B Smoot, exc, Millersburg, Bourbon Co, Ky.

Nathan Orme, insolvent debtor, confined to Wash Co, D C, prison for debt.
-Wm Brent, clk.

FRI JUN 10, 1808
Died: Mr Henry Kreemer, Jun 9, late a clk in Treas Dept. Funeral from hse of Mr Wm Rhodes.

Oath of insolvent debtor will be administered to John Alexander on Jun 20th. He is now confined in Wash Co, D C, prison for debt. -Wm Brent, clk.

MON JUN 13, 1808
Orphans Crt of Wash Co, D C. Jun 11, 1808. Wm Rhodes applied for ltrs of adm on prsnl est of Henry Kreemer, late of Wash Co, dec'd. -Jno Hewitt, Reg of wills.

For sale: 300 acs in St Mary's Co, Md: 1 mile within Chaptico; plantation whereon I now reside, 560 acs cld *Queen Tree*; also my dwlg place, negroes, stock, furn, etc. -Josiah B Grindall.

WED JUN 15, 1808
Pblc auction of brick hse & lots 10 & 11, on sq 925; hse lately inhabited by Lt Col Wharton, now by Mr Thos Carberry.

Stolen-sorrel horse. -Gerard Gibson, nr Eastern Branch bridge in city of Wash.

David Woods, insolvent debtor, confined to Wash Co, D C prison for debt.
-Wm Brent, clk.

FRI JUN 17, 1808
Col Burr was passenger on British pkt which sailed on Thu last. -N Y, Jun 11.

Walter Mitchell, manager at farm of Robt Brent, brought before me a stray bay horse. -Dan'l Rapine, a justice of Wash Co, D C.

MON JUN 20, 1808
Certificates of Christian Alexander & Jane Alexander, of London or of Bath in Gr Britain, lost in ship *Bristol Packet*, Capt Burns, captured & burnt by the French; certificates dt'd Dec 5, 1792 thru Dec 17, 1799. [Christian or Christine is noted as same person & credits refer to both as her credit, i e, Christopher-$19,999.99 & Jane-$25,891.05]

Jas Theker, insolvent debtor, confined in Wash Co, D C, prison for debt.
-Wm Brent, clk.

WED JUN 22, 1808
Orphans Crt of Montg Co, Md. Tabitha Richards, adm, has ltrs of adm on prsnl est of Wm Richards, late of said Co, dec'd.

Wm B Chappell, insolvent debtor, confined in Wash Co, D C, prison for debt.
-Wm Brent, clk.

FRI JUN 24, 1808
Dr Chas Hutten, of Somerset Co, Md, nominated as candidate for Cong; Joshua Prideau, esq, of Worcester Co, as candidate for the trust of elector of Pres & VP. -John Cropper-chrmn Josiah Polk jr-sec.

Orphans Crt of Calvert Co, Md. Pblc sale at late resid of Gilbert Smith, of said Co; all prsnl prop, furn, negroes, etc. -Mordecai Smith, adm.

MON JUN 27, 1808
Died: Mr Michl Dougherty, age 135 yrs, at his plantation on *Horse Creek*, Scriven Co; one of the 1st settlers of this State. Day before he died he walked 2 miles; day he died he ate a hearty dinner, smoked his pipe, & in 2 hrs after expired, which was on May 29, 1808.

Mrd: Thos L Smith, of Louisa Co, to Miss Sarah G Clay, eldest d/o Matthew Clay of Pittsylvania Co, all of Va, on Jun 16, 1808, by Rev Mr John Atkinson.

WED JUN 29, 1808
Died: Hon Nehemiah Knight, esq, one of the Reps in Cong of U S from R I; died at his seat in Cranston, age 63 yrs, Jun 13. -Providence Phenix, Jun 18.

Dr Jas H Blake offers his svcs to inhabitants of Wash City; his resid is on 13th bet Pa & F St.

FRI JUL 1, 1808
Raleigh Register-Messrs Franklin, Holland & M Williams, Reps from N C, have declined re-election to Congress.

St Mary's Co, Orphans Crt, Jun term 1808. Ordered that Monica Jones, admx of Solomon Jones, dec'd, sell at pblc auction, the whole of the dec'd prsnl est. -Jas Forrest, Reg of wills for St Mary's Co. Followed by: sale at late dwlg of dec'd, nr *Great Mill* in St Mary's Co, all his prsnl est: negroes, stock, furn, utensils. -Monica Jones, admx.

Died: Mrs Ann Warren, consort of Mr Wm Warren, Mgr of Phil & Balt theatres, on Jun 25, at Alexandria, after a short but severe illness.

Died: Wm Brown, Jun 24, respectable inhabitant of Annapolis; at the seat of his son in St Mary's Co.

MON JUL 4, 1808
In Chancery-Jun 24, 1808. Jas Egerton, vs Jas Eden & Wm Mills. Sale by Wm Mills, the trustee, in this case be confirmed. Report states that the land in the bill whereon John Eden the grfr of the dfndnt, Jas Eden, formerly lived, 277 acs, was sold to Wm Thomas of St Mary's Co for $3,111. -Nichs Brewer, R C C.

For sale-decree of High Crt of Chancery of Md. Pblc sale in Port TobacCo, Chas Co, Md: land late the prop of John D Scott, dec'd, part of tract cld *Foynton Manor*, 300 acs. -F S Key-trustee.

WED JUL 6, 1808
Dr Greenfield has remv'd from Md to city of Wash, F St, next to Mr Colvin.

<u>Ladies with ltrs in Wash Post ofc Jul 1, 1808:</u>

Priscilla Allen	Mrs Bayley	
Amelia D & J G Brashears		Mary Bramble
Mrs Baker	Mrs J S Blount	Mrs Boss
Eliz Ditterly	Deborah Essex	Mrs Jane Eastburn
Betsey Fletcher	Martha Hall	Mrs S Hamilton
Mary Lane	Rosanna McKenney	Mrs Marriott
Mrs Oliver	Mrs E Oliver	Ann Smith
Miss S Seutorius	Miss P Spunaugle	Nelly Y Thomas
Ann Wade	Mrs M Wilson	Mary Young.

FRI JUL 8, 1808
Ranaway-apprentice boy, Thos A Austin, taylor by trade. -Jos S Clarke.

Mr Henry Whetcroft is appt'd ofc of Treasurer of Wash City.

MON JUL 11, 1808
Orphans Crt of PG Co, Md. Ltrs of adm with will annexed, on prsnl est of Zachariah Baldwin, late of PG Co, dec'd. -Henry Culver, adm.

Solomon Stenger has his Wash & Alexandria packet ready for passengers; sails from 17th St wharf to Alexandria.

In Chancery, Md, Jul 2, 1808. Alex'r Clagett & Rich'd Henderson, vs, Margery Beall & others. Bill to obtain sale of two tracts, *Azadia & Gleaning* for payment due from Isaac Beall, dec'd, to Saml Beall, dec'd. Bill states that Isaac was indebted to David Ross, Richd Henderson & Saml Beall. To secure payment of same, Isaac on Jan 9, 1775 executed a bond to them for conveyance of said land. Isaac died w/o paying the debt & his will devised land to his chldrn, Anne, Alex'r & Margery Beall as tenants in common after death of Margery his wife; Ann & Alex'r have since died intestate, under age, & w/o issue; Margery mrd Chas Vance & resides in Va. Saml Beall also died intestate. -Nichs Brewer, R C C.

Ltr carrier wanted-I shall quit the carriage of ltrs in city of Wash on Oct 10 & give public notice. -Z Farrell.

WED JUL 13, 1808
Died: lately, Fisher Ames, at Dedham, Mass. Funeral honors paid him at Boston.

John Achman has constructed a fire engine which is fully complete. Given under our hands-Jun 24, 1808: Henry Bantz, Jacob Medtert, Francis Manz, Peter Buckhart, Henry Steiner, Geo Creager Sr, Lewis Weltheimer. Fredericktown, Md.

Died: John Shee, coll of the Port of Phil. [Retraction-Jul 20-death of Genr'l Shee is incorrect]

In Chancery, Jul 9, 1808. Chas Neale vs Leonard Neale, Francis Ignatius Neale, & others. Bill to obtain a decree for 2 tracts of land in Chas Co, Md, devised by the cmplnt's fr, Raphael Neale, to dfndnts & others during their lives; to be released to cmplnt when he arrived at age; Leonard & Francis Neale reside out of Md. -Nichs Brewer, R C C.

FRI JUL 15, 1808
Wm McCreery, Rep in Cong for Balt City, declined re-election.

Mungo Parke, traveller in interior of Africa, is no more. British Parliament granted his widow 3236l. 10s sterling, & to Mr Anderson, f/o Mr Anderson who was with him, 1085l.

Aaron Burr was in Halifax on Jun 21st & assumed the name of Edwards, name of his mthr. Judge Edwards, of Conn, is his rel.

Ranaway-Robt Graves, apprentice boy, plaister by trade. -John Kedgle.

Ranaway-Baptist negro man. -Obid Beall, nr Bladensburg.

MON JUL 18, 1808
Ranaway-Baptist & Lydia, negroes; from John Tippet, living in St Mary's Co, on Patuxent Rvr, in Halfpone Neck, Md.

Ranaway-Stephen & Ralph, negroes; from Benedict Boarman, living nr Bryan town, Chas Co, Md.

WED JUL 20, 1808
Reward-$30 for Theoderick Lyles, Englishman by birth, ab't 25 to 30 yrs of age; rode away on my horse Jul 1 & not heard from since. -Thomson Mason, the *Retreat*, nr Leesburg, Loudon Co, Va.

Found-gold mourning locket. -Francis Clark, F St, Wash City.

FRI JUL 22, 1808
Died: Mr John Barber, lately, at Albany, pblshr of *Albany Reg.*

Meeting at Cedar Ward, Phil, at hse of Michl Hickey, Jul 13; Jas Stuart, chrmn; Tench Coxe, sec; cmtee: Chas Johnson, Geo Summers, Benj Lyndall, Alphonso C Ireland, John Cooper. [Rg: Jas Madison for Pres & Geo Clinton for VP-election]

MON JUL 25, 1808
David R Williams declines re-election as Rep in next Cong; Robt Witherspoon will, if chosen, serve. -So Carolina.

Pres appt'd Robt H Jones, of Warrenton, atty of U S for Dist of N C, in place of B Woods, dec'd.

Ranaway-Luke, negro; purch'd him of Mr Theophilus Hughs to take to my resid in Ky; has a wife-prop of Mr Isaac Barrett nr Bladensburg. Mr Everard Gary of Gtwn is my agent. -Saml McLean, Ky.

Runaway for sale-John, black man; says he belonged to John Clarekis, of Alexandria; since confessed he belongs to John P Woodbeck, of Neshiuva, nr Albany, N Y. -C Tippett, kpr o/jail.

Runaway committed to Wash Co jail, Ellick, black man, says he belongs to David R Williams, esq, Cheraw Dist, S C. -C Tippett, kpr of jail.

Democratic ctzns of Adams Co, Pa-meeting held at Mr Lashell's on Jul 4. John Agnew, esq, chrmn; Dr Dan'l Sheffer, sec.

Rpblcn ctzns of 10th ward, N Y-meeting at hse of Dan'l Tier, Bowery, Jul 15; Mangle Minthorn, chrmn; Reuben Munson, sec.

Pres appt'd Mr Chas Minifie a Justice of Peace for Wash Co.

WED JUL 27, 1808
Robt Fulton has commenced a second boat with additional accomodations; to run bet N Y to Albany, 160 miles in 29 hrs.

FRI JUL 29, 1808
Runaway-Alfred, negro; says he belongs to Jas Bowling nr Middleburg, Loudon Co, Va. -Isaac S White, shrf, Wash Co, Md.

Ltr to Clement Dorsey, esq, Port TobacCo, dt'd: Chas Co, Md, Pomonkey, Jul 25, 1808, by Jas Fenwick. Copy in newspaper.

MON AUG 1, 1808
In Chancery-Jun term 1808-Wash Co, D C. John Hoye & Leonard M Deakins, excs & devisees of Francis Deakins, dec'd, which John Hoye is acting exc & devisee, & Pres, Dirs, & Co of Bank of Columbia, cmplnts, vs *Chas F Brodhag, Wm Steuart & *Aquilla Beall, Philip B Key & Benj Stoddert, dfndnts. Bill states that Francis Deakins sold to Chas F Brodhag rl prop in Gtwn-never pd for or cnvyd; said prop is under rent to Steuart & Beall as tenants of said Brodhag; Brodhag has assigned same with other prop in trust to P B Key; Benj Stoddert as the cmplnts have been informed, sets up some claim to same. Bill to obtain a decree for sale of said prop. [*reside outside of D C] -Wm Brent, clk.

Mr Irvine, editor o/Whig, printed in Balt, guilty of libel on Edw J Coale, rgstr of the city; sentenced to $200 fine & 60 days imprisonment.

WED AUG 3, 1808
Pblc sale-order of Orphans Crt of St Mary's Co, Md. All prsnl prop of Betty Ann Eden, late of said Co, dec'd; consisting of negroes, horses, cattle & furn, at hse of Ann T Eden & Cath M Eden, admxs d b n of Betty Ann Eden. Jun 24.

Maj Jas Fenwick, of Chas Co, an inflexible Rpblcn, is candidate as Rep to Congress from District composed of Chas, St Mary's & Calvert Cos, Md.

FRI AUG 5, 1808
Runaway-Fanny, negro woman, says she belongs to Richd Owing of Anne Arundel Co, Md. -John Fleming, shrf, Montg Co, Md.

<u>Appointments made previous to this day-Act of Apr 12 last.</u>
<u>Regt of Light artl</u>: Capts-Abraham Eustis, Jos Chandler, N Easterbrooks, Solomon D Townsend, M N Ervine, Geo Peter, Winfield Scott, Josiah Tellfair, Saml Gano, *John R Spann.
<u>1st Lts</u>: Alex'r S Brooks, Jno H T Estis, Thos Pitts, Saml Watson, *Thos S McKilvey.
<u>2d Lts</u>: Wm Campbell, Killian N Van Rensselaer, R H McPherson, Jas Gibson, *Geo Walton, *Saml Haskins, Andrew McDowell.
<u>Regt of Light Dragoons-Capts</u>: Alex'r F Rose, David Brearly, Clement C Biddle, *Wm Wilson, *Presley N O'Bannon, Jacint Lavall, Noah Lester, *Jas Thomas.
<u>1st Lts:</u> Bille Williams jr, Thos A Helmes, Jas I Bowie, *Alex'r S Lyle, Arthur P Haynie, Asa Morgan, John M Barclay, Sellick Osborn.
<u>2d Lts:</u> J W Van Vechten, Silas Halsey jr, Alex'r Cummings, Saml M Lee, Geo Nichols, Wm Littlejohn, Jonas Munroe.
<u>Cornets:</u> *Jas Wiltsie, Levi Hickill, *Wm R Davis, Elijah Boardman, John Hollingshed, Jos Kean.
<u>Regt of Rifleman</u>-Col Alex'r Smyth; Lt Col Wm Duane;
<u>Capts:</u> Thos A Smith, Elijah Craig, Thos Anderson, Geo W Sevier, John Ragan jr, Jas McDonald, David Findley, *Alex S Walker, *Benj Forsyth, Moses Whitney.
<u>1st Lts:</u> Thos Spencer, *Geo Morrison, Abraham A Massias, Chas Porterfield, Fielder Ridgeway, Michl Hays, Dill Armor, *Nathl Williams.
<u>2d Lts:</u> Elzey L James, Matthew Cannan, John Mays, Lodowick Morgan, *Edw Rector, Joshua Hamilton, *Lewis Toomer.
<u>Ensigns:</u> Elias Stallings, *Smith Pepper, Arthur W Thornton, Francis Stribling, John Stroud, *Richd F Alexander, Angus Langham, Jno Logan.
<u>3d Regt of Infantry.</u> Col Edw Pasteur; Maj Homer V Milton;
<u>Capts:</u> Mossman Houston, *Ch Crawford, John Darrington, Abner Pasteur, *Ross Bird, *J J Faust, Prentiss Law, *Henry Atkinson, John Nicks, *John McClelland.
<u>1st Lts:</u> Robt McDougall, Wm Butler, Robt B Moore, Jas Cooper, Cadwallader Jones, *Jas E Denking, *Chas Christmas, Wm S Hamilton, *Hays G White, Duncan L Clinch.
<u>2d Lts:</u> Saml W Butler, Henry Chotard, *Alex Silliman, Wm Johnson jr, *Timothy Spann, *Benj D Herriot, *Stephen B Daniel, Benj M Jackson, *Chas C McKenzie.

Ensigns: *John N McIntosh, Stephen Rose, *Thos Hesell, *Joel Lyon, *Andrew Hesell, *Saml C Mabson, *John Burnett, *Robt Watson, *Sterling Anderson.
4th Regt of infantry: Lt Col John Whiting; Maj *Jas Miller;
Capts-Paul Wentworth, Learned Lamb, Wm C Baen, Wm Hutchins, David Byers, Stephen Ranney, Joel Cook, Geo W Prescott, Isaiah Doane, Chas Coffin.
1st Lts-Robt C Barton, Josiah Snelling, Alden G Cushman, Nicoll Fosdick, Wm Welch, Nathl F Adams, Saml Haines, Saml Page, Oliver G Burton, Ch Fuller.
2d Lts-Eben Way, Chas Larabe, Jackson Durant, Silas W C Chase, Eleazer B Billings, Minor Huntingdon, Saml Borden, Lewis Harrington.
Ensigns-Timothy Gerrish, Fred'k Conklin, Abram Hawkins, John Smith, Geo P Peters, Jonathan Simonds, Howard, *Thos H Clark, Milo Mason.
5th Regt of infantry:
Col Alex'r S Parker; Capts-Thos Strode, Nimrod Long, Edw Dillard, Nathan N Wright, Rich'd C Dale, Geo Hanrmill, Geo Gibson, Benj Wallace, Jas Bankhead, Colin Buckner.
1st Lts-Henry Saunders, Roger A Jones, Townsend Stith, *Wm Brook, Jas Fonerdon, Mordecai Griffith, Rich'd Whartenby, Talbot Chambers, Alex'r McIlheny, Jas Dorman.
2d Lts-Rich H Bell, Leroy Opie, *Robt Crutcher, *Thos Randolph, Wm Henshaw, Wm King, Jacob Hiadman, Wash Lee, *Silas Amberson, *Robt Alexander.
Ensigns-Elias Edmonds, *Will Skipwith, *Frazer Otey, Robt Carson, David Gallagher, Owen Alston, Nicholas Ulerick, Jas Saunders, John Jamieson jr.
6th Regt of infantry: Col Jonas Simonds; Maj Zebulon M Pike; Capts-Saml Cherry, Ebenezer Cross, Wm P Bennett, John T Bentley, Chas F Lott, Benj Walton, *Thos Davis, Jona Brooks jr, Wm Cock.
1st Lts-Ebenezer Becbe, Gad Humphrey, Wm Lake, Geo Nelson, John Christie, John Machesney, John T Arrowsmith, Jas Chambers, Christopher Snyder.
2d Lts-Jas E A Masters, Abel Morse, Clement Sadlier jr, Chauncey Pettibone, Robt Sterry, Wm Nicholas, Wm Fergrave, John I Plume, Jas I Voorhis, Henry Philips.
Ensigns-Jacob Heet, Edw Webb, Chas H Gardner, Neil Shaw, Wm Gamble, *Ephraim Pentland, Jacob Sinn, Henry Shell, Asa Grimes.
7th Regt of infantry: Col *Wm Russell; Capts-Geo R C Floyd, Thornton Posey, *Edw Hord, Robt C Nicholas, Jervis Cutler, Gilbert C Russell, Thos Vandyke, *Arthur Morgan.
1st Lts-Rich'd Oldham, Zach Taylor, Uriah Blue, Carey Nicholas, Enos Cutler, Jas Doherty, Wm McClellan, Walter H Overton, *_ Durald, *Minor R Sturges.
2d Lts-Elisha Edwards, *Lowry Bishop, Thos S Jessup, Alex'r White, *Jos Tricou.
Ensigns-Wm S Allen, John Hughes jr, Saml Vail, *Henry M Gilman, Saml McCormick, *Jas S Wade, *Narcissus Brutin.
1st & 2d Regts are now in svc on the frontier.
*Ltrs of acceptance have not as yet been rec'd.

In Chancery, Jul 23, 1808. Ratify sale made by Geo Page, trustee, for rl est of John Turner, dec'd; tract of land in PG Co cld *Third Rsrvy on Brashears Pocoson*, 180 acs, sold for $900. -Nichs Brewer, Reg Cur Can.

MON AUG 8, 1808
Removal by the Pres of Edw Pope, coll & inspec of Port of New Bedford, Mass, for not using due diligence in execution of the embargo laws. Isaiah Weston appt'd in his place.

Ltr to Col Jas Taylor of New-Port, Ky, from Andrew F Price, Lexington, Ky, May 28, 1808. Rg: Meeting in Oct 1806 in Cincinnati, Ohio, at Yeatman's Tavern; present were Gen Findley, Col Jas Taylor, Mr John Smith & others. [J Smith's family consisted of his wife, dght, & several sons] To determine association with Aaron Burr-if any. -Senate-Wash.

Pblc sale-Order of Orphans Crt of Wash Co, D C. Prsnl est of Henry Kramer, dec'd; wearing apparel, bks, horse & chair, 2 gold watches, bedstedding, prints. -Wm Rhodes, adm. Saml Speake, auct.

Premiums for the Phil Premium Soc will be rec'd by: John Dorsey, Pres; John Goodman, V P; Hugh Henry, Treas; Geo Bartram, Sec. Mgrs: W Y Birch, Jas Ronaldson, Thos Wood, Jos Garlick, Saml Carswell, Abm Small, John Lang, John Connell & Saml Smith. Phil, Jul 25, 1808.

Died: Gen John Shee, coll of Port of Phil, it is now true. [Corr:-Died Aug 4, ntv of Ire, in circle of his fmly-Aug 12 nwspr.]

WED AUG 10, 1808
Rev Gideon Blackburn, Super of Indian Schools, Cherokee Indians, writes to a friend in Elizabeth-town, N J-dt'd, Maysville, Tenn, Jun 10, 1808. Rg:-life in the area.

2d Ward-Wash mbrs of the Union Fire Co are to meet. -Jas Kearney, sec'y U S Co. Wash City.

Gtwn College: Ceremony of distributing the premiums & dramatical performances of the students to take place Aug 11. Tkts-$1, may be purch'd at Mr Geo Fenwick's, Mr Milligan's bk store, both Gtwn; Mr Rhodes Hotel, St Patrick's Chr, both Wash. Robt Molyneux, Pr.

Order of Crct Crt of Wash Co, D C. Rl & prsnl prop of John Banks; some valuable lots in Wash. -Jos Porter, trust.

Persons indebted unto J Banks as also unto Lowdermilk & Co, late of the city of Wash, to make payments to Jas Porter.

Pblc sale at tavern of Capt Henry Ruth, Gtwn, a moiety of lot 215 in *Beatty & Hawkins Add to Gtwn*, on 6th St & Fred'k St, with frame hse. -Saml Brooke.

Jas McCutchen, insolvent debtor, confined to Wash Co prison for debt. -Wm Brent, clk.

FRI AUG 12, 1808
Mrsh'l's sale: all rght, title & int of Thos T Gantt, [lots in Wash City] at suit of Saml Crowden & others for use of Wm Brent against Thos T Gantt. -Wash Boyd, Mrshl of D C.

Chas Henry Willingmann, Annapolis, Md, has taken the inn cld the *Union Tvrn,* formerly in possession of Mr Geo Mann.

Orphans Crt of Wash Co, D C. Aug 11, 1808. Prsnl est of Abraham Young late of Wash Co, dec'd. -Gerard Gibson, adm.

MON AUG 15, 1808
Wm Cobbett was expelled by the Pa Democrats by the coercion of the laws, from Phil in 1800.

Gov of Commonwealth of Va. $100 reward-by inquisition in Northumberland Co, Sep 21, 1806, before John H Fallin, esq, coroner for said Co, that on Sep 2, 1806, Geo Gordon, late of said Co, stands chrgd with murder of slave, Bartley. Gordon immediately doth still fly from justice. -Wm H Cabell

WED AUG 17, 1808
Charlotte Hall school-exam of pupils was held Jul 26-27; examiners were: Dr John Parnham, Mr Fred'k Campbell, late of Wm & Mary College, Va & Mr John Ralph, late of Princeton College, N J. -Neale H Shaw, Reg. *Cool Springs.* [Md]

FRI AUG 19, 1808
Burlington, Vt-Aug 15. Rev *Cutter* commanded by Lt Farrington was in pursuit of batteau cld the *Black Snake*, known smugglers; cutter took possession of same; cutter was fired on from shore & killed were: Elias Drake, Asa Marsh, of the cutter and Jonathan Ormsby, inhabitant returning from work. Capt Peas of the *Black Snake* was apprehended on Hogg island. [deaths occurred Aug 10]

For sale-3 brick hses belonging to Wash bldg Co. Apply to Messrs Michl Nourse & Alex'r Cochran. Messrs Hadfield, Wilson, Evans & Gray, present occupants. -Wash City.

Crct Crt of Wash Co, D C. Solomon Davis, exc of Solomon Simpson, dec'd, cmplnt, vs Abiel Jenners & Deborah his wife & Ferdinando Fairfax, dfndnts. Oct 1799, S Simpson loaned Abiel $2,650, & for securing repayment thereof to Simpson with int by Nov 1, 1801, Abiel Jenners & Deborah by deed-same dte, mortgaged to Simpson, one part of tract cld *Knock* in Wash City; money & int never pd to Simpson nor to Davis the exc; lots in Wash were conveyed to Jenners & wife who on Jan 2, 1802 cnvyd same to F Fairfax. Bill to fore-close mort & obtain decree for sale of said lots. Abiel, Deb & Fairfax do not reside in D C. -Wm Brent, clk.

Prop & tenants of hses in Wash City are to have their fire buckets complete by Sep next. -J C Shindle, inspec.

Pblc sale-intending to break up my present establishment; hsehld furn, plate, linen etc. -Henry Hiort, Capt Hill

Auction sale-hsehld furn of Timothy Caldwell, about to remove to Ohio. -S Speake, auct.

Orphans Crt of PG Co, Md. Robt McGill, adm of Benj Gaither, late of said Co, dec'd; absence of decds' reps from Md, & doubts if they are in existence; McGill cannot make distribution w/o the Crt. -Trueman Tyler, Rg of wills-PG Co, Md.

MON AUG 22, 1808

Appt'd by the Pres-Gen John Steel of Lancaster, Coll of Customs, for Port of Phil, vice Gen Shee, dec'd. -Phil Paper.

Appt'd-Philip Grymes of Va, atty for U S in Terr of Orleans. Saml Croudson of Orleans, Naval ofcr for Port of New Orleans. John Coburn of Ky, one of the Judges of Terr of La.

Act for relief of John C Shindel, Wash City; reimbursing any expences incurred in his capacity as Sealer of Weights & Measures, $12.37.

Persons having claims against John B Medley, dec'd, are to exhibit same. -Peter Bouic, exc.

Auction sale at hse of Rich'd Harrison nr Gtwn, Frederic Rd: hsehld furn & carriage. -John Travers, auct.

Orphans Crt of Wash Co, D C. Prsnl est of Henry Kreemer, late of said Co, dec'd. -Wm Rhodes, adm.

Ltr ab't proceedings of Boston signed: Chas Bulfinch, Wm Porter, Ebenezer Oliver, Jona Hunewell, John May, Francis Wright, Jona Chapman. Boston, Aug 10, 1808.

Mrsh'l's sale-all rght, title & int of Benj Perkins to lot 1 sq 75 in Wash City with small frame workshop; at suit of Timothy Caldwell, & at suit of Alex Cochrane use of Hugh Smith, against said Perkins. -Wash Boyd, Mrshl of D C.

Strayed or stolen-sorrel horse. -P Purcell, Wash City.

WED AUG 24, 1808

For sale-hse & 308 acs of land on St Clement's Bay & nrly bet Chaptico & Leonardtown. -John Bond, St Mary's Co, Md.

Mrd: Mr Ezekiel McDaniel to Miss Ann Moore, both of Wash, on Aug 23, by Rev Mr Balch.

Partnership bet Philip Hines & Wm Defields is dissolved by mutual consent. Payments to Hines, Wash City.

Uncertain state of my health, I am declining the practice of law. -Henry Hiort, Capt Hill, Wash City.

Benj Finnicum, insolvent debtor, confined to Wash Co prison, for debt. -Robt Brent, clk.

Port Tobacco Jockey Club Races. -Wm D Harrison, sec. [Md]

FRI AUG 26, 1808

Col Ignatius Fenwick is f/o Jas Fenwick, present candidate, & a rev vet. [Ltr to Roman Catholics of Chas, St Mary's & Calvert Co, Md.] Names: Athanasius Ford, Maj Jas Fenwick, & Sir John Fenwick [was murdered by law-Hume.] -Theophilus.

Auction sale: at Andrew Armstrong's nr Navy Yd, hsehld furn. -Israel Little, auct.

Sale by Order of St Mary's Co Crt, at resid of Benj Tabbs; prsnl est; his right to 1/5th part of tracts: *Guythers Grove*-202 acs; *Flowers of the Forest*-263 acs; *Chas Park*-137 acs; *Hickory Bottom*-100 acs. Part of *Brick-Kiln & Park's Addition,* joined with addition on which *Great Mill* stands. -Jos Stone-trust.

Thos Y Sprogell, insolvent debtor, confined in Wash Co, D C, prison, for debt. -Wm Brent, clk.

For sale-brick hse F St, Wash City. Enquire of Wm Cocking, owner & occupier.

Fire in N Y took life of Mrs Watkies & her dght; w/o Mr Watkies, tallow-chandler, Nassau St, Aug 25. -New York

Meeting of voters in Nottingham Dist, PG Co, Md; Robt Young, esq, chrmn; Rinaldo Johnson, sec.

Spanish Royal family: Chas III died, crown fell on Dec 13, 1738 on Chas IV, born Nov 11, 1748, mrd Sep 4, 1760 to Louisa-Maria-Theresa, d/o Duke of Parma, who was born Dec 9, 1751. Bro to Chas IV, 3d s/o Chas III, Ferdinand-Antoine, born Jan 12, 1751, proclaimed King of both Sicilies, Oct 6, 1759. Chldrn of Chas IV: 1-Charlotte-Joachim-Theresa, born Apr 25, 1777, mrd Jan 9, 1790 to Johan-Maria-Joseph, Prince of Brazil, who took reign of Portugal, Jul 15, 1799. 2-Maria-Louisa-Josephine, born Jul 6, 1782, mrd Sep 25, 1795 to Ludwig, L'infant of Spain, who died May 27, 1803. 3-Ferdinand, Prince of Austurias, born Oct 14, 1784, mrd Aug 26, 1802 to Maria-Anthonietta-Theresa-Amelia, Princess of Sicily, born Dec 15, 1784. Ferdinand is now King; his wife died a short time since. 4-Caroline Isabella-Isidor, born Mar 29, 1788. 5-Maria Isabella, born Jul 6, 1789, mrd Jul 6, 1802 to Francis-Januar-Joseph, heir to Kingdom of Sicily & infantado of Spain. 6-Francis-De-Paula-Antoine-Maria, born Mar 10, 1794. Hse of Sicily, who have pretensions to Spanish Throne: King of Sicily, Ferdinand IV.

L'infantado of Spain, s/o King Chas III, mrd to Maria Caroline Ludowick Joseph, d/o Roman Emperor, born Aug 13, 1752, wedded May 12, 1768. their issue:
1-Maria Theresa-Caroline, born Jun 6, 1772, mrd Sep 19, 1790 to Francis II Emperor of Romans & King of Hungary.
2-Francis-Januar-Joseph, born Aug 19, 1777, mrd Maria Isabella, 5th child of Chas IV; this person is denominated L'infantado of Spain.
3-Maria Christiana-Theresa, born Jan 17, 1779.
4-Maria-Amelia, born Apr 26, 1782.
5-Maria-Antonietta Theresa-Amelia, mrd to Prince of Asturias.
6-Leopold Johan-Joseph Michl, born Jul 2, 1790, Grand Prior of Messina. Genealogy of the hses of Spain & Sicily; most of the Spanish family Napolean has in his power.

Act of relief for Saml N Smallwood, enacted by Wash City Cncl; $56.50 for warehse rent. -Robt Brent, clk.

Wm Kain, insolvent debtor, confined in Wash Co, D C, prison for debt. -Wm Brent, clk.

Henry Addison Callis, PG Co, Md: petition in writing for benefit of act for relief of insolvent debtors. -John M Gantt.

MON AUG 29, 1808

Rich'd W Belt, insolvent debtor, confined in Wash Co, D C, prison for debt. -Wm Brent, clk.

In Chancery-Jul 22, 1808. Bailey Erles Clark vs Thos Rhoades. Bill to obtain a decree to record deed dt'd Apr 3, 1806, from T Rhoades, late of Montg Co, to B E Clark, for land cld *Rhoades's Good Luck & Any Thing*, in said Co; deed duly executed, but not recorded. -Nichs Brewer, Reg C C.

Mrsh'l's sale-all rght, title & int of Wm Esenbeck to lots 2 & 3 in sq 257 in Wash City; suit of John C Severman against said Esenbeck; Crct Crt of Wash Co, D C. -Wash Boyd

WED AUG 31, 1808

Meeting at the Masonic Hall o/mbrs of the Wash Polemic Soc. -Saml Spots, sec.

I will rent for the next yr svr'l large farms on the Potomac in Va. Apply to Mr Jas Middleton who resides at *McCarty's Island* nr them, or John W Bronaugh, Gtwn.

MON SEP 5, 1808

Orphans Crt of PG Co, Md. Sep 3, 1808. Prsnl est of Geo Lee, late of Wash Co, D C. -John Reed Magruder jr, exc.

To holders of non-resid lands within Ohio. I reside with the auditor of Ohio & have access to his bks; offer my svcs as agent to superintend payment of taxes etc. -Cadwallader Wallace, Chillicothe, Ohio. Aug 15.

Store now opening in Bridge St. -Edw L Smith, Gtwn.

WED SEP 7, 1808

Bennington, Vt-Aug 23. Burlington, Aug 5, 1808. Murder of Ormsby, Drake, & Marsh. Crt of Enquiry-testimony by: Sgt David B Johnson, Jas H Hays, Stephen P Lathrop, Jas Mead, Mr Ledyard. Saml I Mott killed Ormsby & Marsh. [See Aug 19, 1808 account]

Second time I advertise an unfortunate, dissipated woman, my wife-Mable Farrell. First time I retracted the words on account of 4 female chldrn, thought she wld better her conduct, but all to no purpose. Will not pay her debts. -Pat Farrell

FRI SEP 9, 1808

Rpblcns meet-St Mary's Co, Md, held Aug 13, 1808, at ChaptiCo. Hon Wm Thomas, chrmn; Henry Ashton, sec; committee: Athanasius Fenwick, Col Thos Barber, Philip Key, esq, Hon Edmund Key, Dr Barton Tabbs & Dr Jas Thomas.

Meeting of Rpblcns of Montg Co, Md, Sep 3, 1808. Col Edw Tillard, chrmn; J Elgar jr, sec. Resolved to support election of Col John Wampler as Rep in next Cong of U S for 3d Dist of Md, & Messrs Howard Griffith, Elijah Viere, Rich'd West & Benj Higgins, as Dels to next Genr'l assembly. Cmtee: Honore Martin, Dr Jas Anderson, Thos Linstid, Jos Elgar jr & Robt Wallace.

Hezekiah Berry, insolvent debtor, confined to Wash Co prison for debt.
-Wm Brent, clk.

Orphans Crt of Wash Co, D C. Sep 9, 1808. Ltrs on will & prsnl est of Capt John Mitchell, late of Gtwn, in said Co, dec'd. -Mary Mitchell, excx.

For sale-furn & sundry items at my dwlg hse on Jersey Ave, Wash City.
-John Coyle.

MON SEP 12, 1808

Electors of Va:

Jos Godwin Sr-Nansemond;
Edw Pegram Sr-Dinwiddie;
Col Thos Read-Charlotte;
Hugh Nelson-Albemarle;
Philip Norborne Nicholas-Richmond City;
John Roane-King Wm;
Gustavus B Horner-Fauquier;
Mann Page-Gloucester;
John T Brooke-Stafford;
Osborn Sprigg-Hampshire;
Archibald Stuart-Augusta;
Gen John Preston-Montgomery;
Benj Harrison-P Geo;
Rich'd Field-Brunswick;
Jos Eggleston-Amelia;
Col Geo Penn-Patrick;
Spencer Roane-Hanover;
Robt Taylor-Orange;
Robt Nelson-York;
Richd Barnes-Richmond City
Hugh Holmes-Fred'k;
Jas Allen-Shenandoah;
Andrew Russell-Wash;
Wm McKinley-Ohio.

WED SEP 14, 1808

Auction sale at hse formerly occupied by Jas Webb; variety of hsehld furn & items. -Henry Weaver.

Shrf's sale, on farm whereon Ignatius West now lives, 300 acs; late the prop of said West taken at suit of Cornelia Lansdale, assignee of John Hodges of Thos, who was assignee of Benj Oden, use of Wm B Beans. -John Fleming, shrf-Montg Co, Md.

Dr Wm Grayson has taken the hse lately occupied by Mr John Templeman on Bridge St, Gtwn; offers his professional svcs.

Mr John Rust, your not being a resid of this State-notifying you of injunction pending in Chancery crt, Williamsburg, Va; I am plntiff & you are dfndnt. -Peter Rust, Richmond Co, Va. Sep 14.

Orphans Crt of PG Co, Md. Sep 13, 1808. Prsnl est of Isaac Magruder, late of PG Co, dec'd. -Ann Magruder, Thos Magruder, adms.

FRI SEP 16, 1808

Pblc sale at hse of Jacob Chandler, Navy Yd Hill; window & door frames, grindstone, scales; prop of Dan'l Bailey late of Wash City. -Israel Little, auct.

Taken up a stray cow & calf. -Adolpheus F Plate.

MON SEP 19, 1808

Rpblcn voters of Calvert Co, Md, convened at Hunting Town on Sep 1; Capt Fred'k Skinner, chrmn; Mordecai Smith, sec. Resolved that Rich'd Ireland, Wm Holland, Thos H Wilkinson & Suttin J Weems are proper persons to rep them in next Genr'l Assembly of Md; Gen Robt Bowie of PG Co, as elector for Pres & VP; support Maj Jas Fenwick as mbr of Congress; Genr'l Jos Wilkinson, Dr Wm Somerville, Geo F Janny, Dan'l Kent & Wm S Morsell, be committee to correspond.

Taken up a stray cow. -Walter Mullikin living nr forks of rd on *Piney Branch*.

WED SEP 21, 1808

Accident at the Capitol Sep 19: the vault of the Court Rm in the north wing fell down; Mr John Lenthall was buried under many tons of bricks & deprived of sensation & life.

Rich'd T Spalding, my appr, absconded on Sep 11. -Robt Clarke.

Meeting of Rpblcns of N Y C on Sep 15, 1808 at Abraham B Martling's: Col Wm Few, chrmn; Ichabald Prall, sec. Cmtee: Tunis Wortman, Nathan Sanford, Augustus Wright, Abraham Bloodgood, Adrian Hegeman, Jonas Humbert, Saml Lawrence, Jas Townsend & John Mills.

Fred'k Aug Muhlenberg, Spkr of Hse o/Reps; Ralph Izard, Pres of Sen, Pro Tempore, Geo Washington, Pres; Jun 4, 1794.

FRI SEP 23, 1808
Meeting of Rpblcns in Chas Co, convened at Port Tobacco, Sep 3, 1808. Francis Digges, esq, chrmn; Jos I Merrick, sec. Cmtee: Gen Caleb Hawkins, Francis Newman, Luke F Matthews & John Digges, esqs. Resolved to support Jas Fenwick's election to Hse o/Reps for U S. [Md]

Died: on Sep 19, Mr John Lenthall; born in Chesterfield, County of Derby in Eng; carpenter by trade; superior draughtsman; resided in America the last 15 or 16 yrs; leaves a widow & 3 small chldrn; his age ab't 45 yrs. -B Henry Latrobe.

Burlington, Vt, Sep 2. Chief Justice Tyler presided at trial of Saml I Mott, W Noaks, Slocum Clark, Truman Mudget, Cyrus B Dean, Josiah Peas, David Sheffield & Francis Ledgard; in killing Ormsby & Marsh; verdict-guilty. Prosecution: Col Harrington & David Fay, esq. Cncl for accused: Bates Turner & Amos Marsh.

Strayed or stolen from Commons of Wash City, a sorrel horse. -Mary Nevitt, Wash City-Navy Yard. Reward-$5.

MON SEP 26, 1808
Sailing for New Orleans-brig *President*, from Eastern Branch. Apply to Rich'd Parrott, Gtwn, or J Cassin, nr Navy Yd-Wash.

Notley Maddox of PG Co, Md, brought before me a stray gelding. -Henry A Callis, J P, PG Co, Md. [Maddox living Nr Eastern Branch Bridge, PG Co, Md.]

Runaway-Mich'l Thomas, negro; says he belongs to Robt Locher, living bet Winchester & Romney, Frederic Co, Va, was committed to Wash Co, Md, jail.
-Isaac S White, shrf.

WED SEP 28, 1808
For sale-125 acs in Montg Co, Md, with dwlg hse & grist & saw mill; will barter for prop in Wash City or Gtwn. -Rich'd Lansdale.

FRI SEP 30, 1808
Alexandria Co, D C. Case of Robt Brown Jameson, insolvent debtor, late of said Dist. Claims to be brought to Colin Auld, trustee. -G Deneale, C C .

Pblc sale-negro Sally & her child, prop of heirs of Jas R Dermot, for taxes due Wash City. -Henry Whetcroft, Treas.

MON OCT 3, 1808
John W Hollingsworth, merchant taylor from Balt, nr the Navy Yd in 8th St, has quantity of ready made goods for sale.

Trenton, N J, Sep 21. Meeting on election: Jas Linn, Pres; Abrm Brown, sec to be. Supported for mbrs of Congress: Adam Boyd, Henry Southard, Wm Helms, Jas Cox, Thos Newbold, Jacob Hufty. Electors for Pres & VP: Jas Mott, Jas Morgan, Amos Harrison, David Welch, Benj Egbert, Thos Hendry, Geo Burgin, & Abijah Smith.

Reward-$10 for Daniel Hargin, age 31 yrs, born in Ire, blacksmith; deserted on Sep 29, recruit belonging to this rendezvous. -Robt Cherry, Commanding Recruiting Rendez. -Wash City.

To let-dwlg hse now occupied by Rev Mr Laurie. Possession on Oct 17. -Pierce Purcell, Wash City.

Pblc sale-hack carriage & 2 horses. -Lund Washington, Capt Hill, Wash.

WED OCT 5, 1808

Meeting of Rpblcns of city & Co of Phil, *White Horse Tvrn*, Mkt St, Sep 24. Capt Wm Jones, chrmn; Mahlon Dickerson, sec. Cmtee: Rich'd Bache, Blair McClennachan, John Sergeant, Guy Bryan, Jacob Sommer, Manuel Eyre, & Saml Wetherill jr. Electors: Chales Thompson, Wm Montgomery, Thos Leiper, Isaac Worrell, Jos Engle Wm Rodman, Archibald Darrah, Jacob Weygandt, Jos Lefever, Gabriel Hiester jr, Geo Hartman, Adamson Tannehill, Jas Cowden, Wm Wilson, Robt Giffin, Jacob Hostetter, David Fullerton, Peter Kimmell, Jos Huston, John McDowell.

Mrd: on Oct 4, Mr Jos Clark to Miss Nancy Thompson, both of Wash, by Rev Mr Mathews.

Mrd: Harvey Bestor, esq, clk in Dept of Genr'l Post ofc, to Miss Matilda Owen, lately in Westfield, Mass.

Lost-ck on Branch Bank in Wash dt'd Oct 3 for $250 in favor of Robt King, at Treas Dept. Reasonable reward.

Pblc auction-frame hse on N J ave. -Thos Oliver, Wash.

FRI OCT 7, 1808

High Crt of Chancery, Md. Sale of part of rl est of Jas Beall, s/o Robt, dec'd; at pblc auct at Mr Daniel Beall's, lvng on premises; tract or parcels lying in Montg Co & adj the late Allen Bowie: *Part Euster*-142 acs; *First Vacancy*-41acs; -33 acs; *Rsrvy on Batchelor's Purchase*-49 acs. -Solomon Holland, trustee, Rockville, Md.

Ladies with ltrs in Wash Post Ofc-Oct 1, 1808:

Lucy Austin	Anne Crone	Ann Cooper
Mrs Elizabeth	Mary Fox	Mrs Fletcher
Eliz B Finch	Hannah L Gibbs	Peggy Jones
Mary Jones	Sarah King	Mary Mathews
Miss Mile	Mrs Simon	Susan Sotorious

Eliz Tucker Miss Cath M Wood Mrs Cloe Young.

Orphans Crt of PG Co, Md. Oct 6, 1808. Prsnl est of Cassandra Hilleary, late of said Co, dec'd. -Geo Hilleary, adm.

Died: Miss Lucretia Dashiell, d/o Mrs Sarah Wilson of Wash, age 16 yrs, Sep 29, after a long & distressing illness.

MON OCT 10, 1808

Meeting of Rpblcn freeholders of Fairfax Co, Va, held at tvrn of Resin Wilcoxen, Oct 3, 1808. Genr'l Thomson Mason, chrmn; John C Hunter, sec. Cmttee: Geo Graham, Geo Summers, Humphrey Peake, Henry Rose, Wm Moss, Jas Waugh, Francis Coffer, Geo Minor & Lewis Summers.

Reward-$50 for horse stolen from my stable. -Fred'k May, Wash City.

WED OCT 12, 1808

Mrd: Daniel Carroll, esq, of Duddington, to Miss Ann Boyce, at *Sweet Air*, resid of Mrs Carroll, Oct 6, by Rev Mr Beeston.

Pblc sale-Order of Orphans Crt of Calvert Co, Md; at *God Graces Levels* in Calv Co, late resid of Mrs Rebecca Mackall, dec'd; hsehld furn, stock etc, of said R Mackall; & law bks. -Rich'd Potts, adm. Calvert Co, Md.

Patent granted by Pres of U S for improved life buoy or sea-man's friend. -Wm Flower, Genr'l Com agent, 58 Walnut St, Phil, Pa.

FRI OCT 14, 1808

Appts by the Pres of U S. Wade Hampton of S C, Col of Light Dragoons. John C Boyd, Col of 4th Reg of infantry. Jos Constant of N Y, Lt Col of 6th Ref of infantry. Electus Backus of N Y, Maj of Light Dragoons.

Sale-nr Leonard Town at late dwlg of Philip Ford, dec'd, all prsnl prop, except negroes. -Philip Ford, surviving adm.

Benj Halsey of Wash Co, D C, brought before me a stray horse. -Saml H Smith.

MON OCT 17, 1808

Died: Col Thos Hunt, of 1st Regt U S infantry, at Belle Fontaine Cantonment, on the Mizami, Terr of La, Aug 18, 1808; leaves his wife & numerous & infantile offspring.

Pblc sale of lots in city of Wash. Decree of High Crt of Chancery of Md, passed in Oct 1806; suit instituted therein, [Prior to separation of D C from Md,] by excs of Mordecai Lewis & by Edw Burd, against Morris, Nicholson, & others. Sale of 739 lots. -John Kilty, Josias W King, trustees.

Mrd: Mr Geo Hay, of Richmond, to Miss Eliza Monroe, eldest d/o Jas Monroe, late Mnstr to Gr Britain, in Albemarle Co, Va. -Date not given-appears recent.

Sale-young negro woman. -John Woodward, nr Vansville.

Died: on Oct 9, Dr John Claiborne, lately a mbr of Congress from Va, at Mr Drummond's in Brunswick Co, Va; of consumption.

WED OCT 19, 1808

Orphans Crt of Wash Co, D C. Oct 17, 1808. Prsnl est of Robt Tilley, late of said city, dec'd. -Ann Tilley, admx.

Died: on Oct 12, John Page, of *Rosewell*, Glocester Co, Va, age 65 yrs, late Govn'r of this Commonwealth.

Columbian Dragoons will meet Sat. -Saml Burch, 1st Ser.

Union Light infantry will parade on Sat. -John Davidson, Capt.

Reward-$200 for four ltrs put into the post ofc; one to Jas Dall & Co; one to Luke Tiernan & Co; one to Francis J Mitchell; & one to Labes & Co, all of Balt, Md. Zepaniah & John Turner, Woodville, Culpepper Co, Va. Oct 8, 1808.

Info wanted-of John Bateby Dobbins, came from Eng some yrs ago & resided at Wash [not certain in what State] for some time; he will hear something much to his advantage. Need info as to whether he is alive or not. -Saml Spackman, No. 1 Bank Alley, Phil, Pa.

FRI OCT 21, 1808

Orphans Crt of Wash Co, D C. Oct 17, 1808. Prsnl est of John Lenthall, late of said city, dec'd. -Jane Lenthall, admx.

For sale: residing next door to Mr Latrobe, bet the Capt & Navy Yd; sale-the whole of my hse, kitchen & ofc furn, sundry items. -Wm O Sprigg.

Drs Jas H Blake & Gerard T Greenfield have entered in copartnership.

MON OCT 24, 1808

Ranaway-Giles, negro boy; last heard of he was carried into Alexandria by Wm A Adams. -Chas Tyler jr, *Sudly Mills*, P Wm Co, ab't 8 miles from either Hay-Mkt or Centerville, Va.

WED OCT 26, 1808

Pres of U S has appt'd Benj Harrison, esq, of Chas city, Com'r of Loans for State of Va.

John Harris, insolvent debtor, confined in Wash Co, D C prison, for debt.
-Wm Brent, clk.

Saml Stettinius, Pa av nr the Centre Mkt, Wash City, has just rec'd assortment of fall goods.

FRI OCT 28, 1808
Nat'l Intellgncr will henceforth be conducted by Saml H Smith & Jos Gales jr.

Runaway-Philip, negro man; says he belongs to Mgt Rucket of Orange Co, Va; was committed to Wash Co, Md, jail. Also, Jerry, negro, says he belongs to Elijah Edwards of Orange Co, Va. -Isaac S White, shrf.

Proclamation by Gov Robt Wright, esq, of Md. Kitty Brawner, age 10 yrs, d/o Wm & Cath Brawner, was raped by Thos Burk of Fred'k Co; oath certified by Thos Bond, esq, Justice of Peace of Fred'k Co, Md. Reward-$150.

Mbrs to Rep Cong from Md: 1st Dist-John Campbell, esq; 2d Dist-Archibald Van Horn, esq; 3d Dist-Philip Barton Key, esq; 4th Dist-Roger Nelson; 5th Dist-Nicholas Ruxton Moore & Alex'r McKin, esqs; 6th Dist-John Montgomery, esq; 7th Dist-John Brown of Nathan, esq; 8th Dist-Chas Goldsborough, esq. -Robt Wright, Gov Ninian Pinkney, clk of Cncl.

MON OCT 31, 1808
Impowered by Judge Findley, inventor of the chain bridge, to superintend & build said bridges. -John Templeman.

Pblc sale-Orphans Crt of Montg Co, Md. Prsnl est of John Fletchall, dec'd.
-Darcus Fletchall, adm.

New store, Wash City, groceries; late Thos Thorpe's store opposite the Centre Mkt.
-Bacon & Moore.

For sale-Madeira wine, 4 yrs old. -Toppan Webster, Wash.

WED NOV 2, 1808
Pblc sale of all prop of Jacob Edelen, of PG Co, Md; & all prop said Jacob Edelen is entitled to by last will of Jos Edelen. Sale at dwlg hse of Jacob Edelen nr Piscataway. Terms will be cash. -Alexius Boone.

Lost-Benj Contees' note for $1,500 negotiated last May & payable to Ludwell Lee; same now annulled. -H Lee

Horses, 15 to 20, may be wintered at my farm 2 1/2 miles from Gtwn. -Nathan Lufborough, Gtwn.

Wanted-nursery for hedge plants, 10 acs, in Wash. -Thos Main.

Anastius Dial, insolvent debtor, confined to Wash Co, D C, prison, for debt.
-Wm Brent, clk.

FRI NOV 4, 1808
Wm Warren, of Wash Co, D C, brought before me a stray horse. -Sam H Smith.

Merino sheep for sale at my farm nr Phil. -Jas Mease.

Wash City Cncl awarded $14 to Henry Johnson for his svcs as sec to Brd of appeals from Dec 19 to 30th, 1805; $20 to Wm Hewitt, for same svcs from Jun 14 to 24th, 1808.

Reward-$50, for runaway Jack, negro. Mgt Offutt living in Montg Co, Md, nr the Great Falls of Potomac.

MON NOV 7, 1808
Electors from Va:

John Nevison-Norfold Borough
Rich'd F Taylor-Petersburg
Paul Carrington Sr, esq-Charlotte
Wm Cabell-Amherst
Col Edw Carrington-Richmond City
Gen Henry Young-King & Queen
Leven Powell-Loudon
John D Watkins-New Kent
Raily Washington-Stafford
Col Elisha Boyd-Berkley
Gen Robt Porterfield-Augusta
Col John Stuart-Greenbrier
Geo K Taylor-Pr Geo
Maj John Nelson-Mecklenburg
Wm Berkeley, esq-Powhatan
Col John Watts-Bedford
Chas Dabney-Hanover
Gen Edw Stephens-Culpepper
Dr Corbin Griffin-York
John Campbell-Westmoreland
Robt Page-Fred'k
Robt Grattan-Rockingham
Gen Wm Tate-Wash
Philip Doddridge-Brooke
[-Richmond Argus].

Reps for next Cong elected in Pa: *New mbrs.

*Benj Say John Porter
Wm Milnor
Robt Jenkins
Wm Findley
David Bard
*David Crawford
*Wm Anderson
*John Ross
*Dan'l Heister
John Rea
*Aaron Lysle
*Geo Smith
Matthias Richards
Robt Brown
John Smilie
Robt Whitehill
Saml Smith

Died: Lewis Hallam, age 75 yrs, at Phil; the father of the American theatre

Dark red cow came to the farm of Robt Brent, nr Wash City ab't 2 mos since; apply to Walter Mitchel, mgr of the farm.

Wm H P Tuckfield has opened a boot & shoe store on N J av, nr the factory of Gilbert Docker, Capitol Hill, Wash.

WED NOV 9, 1808
Dennis M Burgess of PG Co, Md, has written said Crt for benefit-act of insolvent debtor; he is now confined. -John Read Magruder jr, clk.

Electors from Conn: Jonathan Trumbull, John Treadwell, David Daggett, Roger Griswold, Saml H Johnson, Jesse Root, John C Smith, Stephen T Hosmer & Frederic Wolcott.

Dennis M Burgess of PG Co, Md, has written said Crt for benefit-act of insolvent debtor; he is now confined. -John Read Magruder jr, clk.

Leg of N J elected John Lambert, Senator in place of John Condit, whose term expires on Mar 3, next.

Dennis M Burgess of PG Co, Md, has written said crt for benefit-act of insolvent debtor; he is now confined. -John Read Magruder jr, clk.

FRI NOV 11, 1808
Died: on Nov 10, Dr John Weems of Gtwn. Funeral at 3 P M on Nov 11.

Rich'd Beck, Gtwn, has just rec'd fashionable goods.

MON NOV 14, 1808
Wm King, late of Abingdon, Va, has bequeathed $10,000 to the acad of that town.

I warn all persons from advancing money on my acc't. -Patrick Magruder, Wash City.

John Cox of Gtwn, offers for sale: tracts of land in Alleghany Co, Md: *Governor's Neglect*-108 acs; *Ormes Attention*-684 acs; *Chestnut Grove*-461 acs; *Hard Struggle*-1554 acs & 1057 acs; *Western Connexion*-1691acs & 6180 acs; lot No. 2487-50 acs; lying bet Cumberland & Simkin's Tavern. Also 2038 acs in Shenandoah Co, Va.

Jos Milligan, Gtwn, wishes to open a union circulating library.

WED NOV 16, 1808
Electors of New York:

Ambrose Spencer	Henry Huntington	John W Seaman
Henry Rutgers	John Garratson	Ebenezer White
Thos Lawrence	Jas Tallmadge	Jonathan Rouse
Michajah Pettit	Henry Lates jr	Benj Mooers
Adam B Yrooman	Thos Shankl	Wm Hallock
Russel Atwater	Jos Simonds	Hugh Jamison
Matthew Carpenter.	-All Rpblcns.	

Wm O'Neale-boarding hse; nr the West Mkt hse, Wash City. Coal & wood available-also keeps a coal yard. -Wm O'Neale.

Orphans Crt of PG Co, Md. Nov 11, 1808. Prsnl est of John Lovejoy, of said Co, dec'd. -Wm Nevitt.

Orphans Crt of PG Co, Md. Sale at plantation of late Geo Hatton, nr Piscataway, PG Co, Md. -Basil Hatton, adm.

Mrd: Nicholas J Roosevelt, esq, of N Y C, to Miss Latrobe, d/o B H Latrobe, esq, srvyr of public bldgs of U S, on Nov 15, by Rev Mr McCormick.

Wash Artl Co to meet on Fri. -John Burns, sec.

FRI NOV 18, 1808
Independent Wash Vols Co of Infantry to meet on Sat. -John Sessford, sec.

Died: Capt Stephen Decatur, Nov 14, at Frankford.

Pblc sale at Rhodes's Tavern: negro woman & 2 chldrn. -Ann Tilley, Wash.

Reward-$5 for strayed horse. -Thos Young, Wash City.

MON NOV 21, 1808
Vincennes, Oct 8. Gov Harrison rec'd a ltr from Geo Holsman, coll of Dist of Michilimackinac, & Saml Abbott, assist Judge; appears that on Aug 12, John Campbell, esq, indian agent for U S at Prairie Des Chiens & Mr Radford Crawford, of the British Mackinac Co, met nr the British fort to decide an affair of honor, the former was mortally wounded & died on the evening of the next day.

Miss H Dargen has commenced business in millinary & mantua-making line; Pa Ave, Wash City.

WED NOV 23, 1808
New ship, *Missouri,* Robt Hast-mstr, will sail from Balt for N Orleans; apply in Balt to Capt on brd or Rezin D Shepherd.

FRI NOV 25, 1808
Died: Mrs Simmons, w/o Wm Simmons, accountant of War Dep, on Nov 19.

Ranaway-John, negro; may have remv'd to neighborhood of Mr Wm Carroll's in Montg Co, Md. -Nathan Soper, PG Co, Md. $50 Rwd.

Notice-Renewal of certificate 12329, issued by Jos Nourse, esq, dt'd Jun 16, 1798, in favor of Wm Wolland, of London, for $5,000. -John Davidson.

For sale-4 young saddle horses, at Rhodes Htl. -Enos Noland

MON NOV 28, 1808
For rent-dwlg hse, ware hse & wharf on Eastern Branch, lately occupied by Mrs Barry-immediate possession. -Garrett Barry.

Electors for R I: Thos P Jones, Jas Rhodes & Thos Noyes.

WED NOV 30, 1808
Pblc sale-decree of High Crt of Chancery of Md; rl est of late Saml Hepburn, esq, of PG Co, Md; part of rl est of dec'd being part of two tracts cld *Maiden's Dowry & Grey Eagle,* 392 acs. -Trueman Tyler, trustee.

Orphans Crt of PG Co, Md. Nov 20, 1808. Prsnl est of Nathl C Weems, late of said Co, dec'd. -Violetta Weems, admx.

Runaway-Dick, mulatto man, says he belongs to Wm Dent, of Chas Co, Md, nr Port TobacCo. -John Fleming, shrf, of Montg Co, Md.

FRI DEC 2, 1808
Mrd: Jos Ferdinand Wingate, esq, to Miss Mgt Gay Tingey, d/o Thos Tingey, esq, Commandant of Navy Yd, Nov 29, by Rev Mr McCormick.

MON DEC 5, 1808
Electors of Ga:

John Rutherford	John Twiggs	Henry Graybill
David Merriwether	Christopher Clark	J E Houston

Mrd: Mr Jacob Boss, of Leesburg, to Miss Rebecca Matilda Scott, of Wash, on Dec 1, by Rev Mr McCormick.

Notice-I intend to petition the next Co Crt of Chas, for benefit of an act of insolvency. -Geo Boarman, Chas Co, Md.

Orphans Crt of Chas Co, Md. Dec 2, 1808. Prsnl est of Benj Benson, late of said Co, dec'd. -Wilson Smoot, exc.

Having rented my farm on rd leading to Marlborough; have for sale, stock, waggon, ploughs, etc. -Wm O Sprigg.

WED DEC 7, 1808
Pblc auction-prop in Wash City, formerly the prop of Messrs Lear & Co; also 6 lots in Holmeads addition to Gtwn. -John Davidson or Walter Hellen.

Shrf's sale-the farm whereon John Orme now lives, 238 acs, horses, cows, cart; late the prop of said Orme, at suit of John Hoy, adm d b n of Wm Deakins, jr. -John Fleming, shrf of Montg Co, Md.

To let, blacksmith's shop, newly built, Pa av. -John C Shindle, Wash City.

John Achman, coppersmith, tinner & fire engine mkr, commenced business in High St, Gtwn.

Ranaway-Lyd, negro girl. -John Threlkeld, Gtwn. Rwrd-$20.

FRI DEC 9, 1808
Runaway-Kitty Thomas, black woman; says she belongs to Domindigo Gambera, of Chas Co, Md; committed to Wash Co, D C, jail. -C Tippett, kpr of jail for Wash
Boyd, mrshl.

Partnership of Collard & Moore is dissolved by mutual consent-business in future will be transacted by Geo Collard.

MON DEC 12, 1808
Strayed-bay horse, from Commons of Wash City. -Chester Bailey, Wash.

Runaway committed to Wash Co, D C jail-Dick, black boy; says he belongs to Gerard B Causeen of Chas Co, Md. -C Tippett, kpr of the jail for Wash.

WED DEC 14, 1808
For sale-5,000 acs in Monroe Co, 12 mi from *Sweet Springs*, Va; apply to Alex'r Hutchinson who lives on plantation nr the furnace, or Maj John Handley nrby, or Mr Robt Bland-lives on part of plantation. -John Cabell, Buckingham Co, Va.

FRI DEC 16, 1808
For sale-valuable family of negroes. -Benj Oden, PG Co, Md.

Died: Jas Sullivan, late Govn'r of State of Mass.

MON DEC 19, 1808
Notice-caution: no trespassing on my plantation, no hunting. -Benj Harwood, PG Co, Md.

Geo W Willett, of PG Co, petitions for benefit of insolvent debtor; now confined for debt. -Danl Clarke, assoc Judge of First Judicial Dist of Md.

So Carolina has elected John Drayton, Rpblcn, Governor.

WED DEC 21, 1808
Mr Jos Story, elected from Mass, vice J Crowninshield, dec'd.

Romulus Riggs intending to close his business in Gtwn.

FRI DEC 23, 1808
Italian marble for sale; intended for base of monument in memory of Americ ofcrs who fell before Tripoli; severity of our winters render it improper for use.
-B Henry Latrobe.

MON DEC 26, 1808
Pblc sale, rl est of Allen Quynn, dec'd, in Annapolis city, brick hse where Capt John Kilty now resides, brick hse in possession of Capt John Gassaway, frame hse-

Mr Thos Wilmar now resides with adj frame hse; lot formerly cld *Swan's Tan Yd*; decree of Crt of Chancery. -John Johnson, trust,

Died: Rev Robt Molyneus, Dec 9, age 72 yrs, late Pres of Gtwn College; ntv of Eng; came to Americ several yrs prior to Americ Rev

Robt McKoy, of PG Co, Md, petitions for act of insolvent debtor; now confined in prison. -John R Magruder jr, clk PG Co..

Ranaway-Geo Dyer, mulatto slave. -John Rowe, Pomonky, Chas Co, Md.

WED DEC 28, 1808

Mrd: Mr Ralph Charlton, of Wash, to Miss Abigail Stillwell, of Bedford Co, Pa, on Dec 11.

Sale of negroes, prop of Dan'l Carroll of *Duddington*, esq, to satisfy taxes due city of Wash. -Henry Whetcroft, Treas.

J J Shaaff, Gisbourough, having suffered much from trespasses committed on his farm at *Gisborough Point*; will prosecute all offenders in the future.

Lottery in Pa: prizes pd by Thos Alibone, esq, Treas of Phil; Tkts-Geo Taylor jr, 85 So 2d St, Phil; John Davidson-Wash.

FRI DEC 30, 1808

Senate-in the absence of the VP due to indisposition, Senate chose Stephen R Bradley, President Pro Tempore.

1809

MON JAN 2, 1809
For sale-35 shares of Wash Bridge stock. -Apply to Saml Elliott.

WED JAN 4, 1809
Nathl Hagen, of PG Co, Md, prays for-act of insolvent debtor; now confined in prison. -Dan'l Clarke.

In Chancery, Dec 27, 1808. Alex'r Greer & wife, vs, Rebecca Bond, Caroline Cecelia Bond, Martha Vanswearingen, Eliz Mary Vanswearingen, Peter Campbell, Rich'd Llewellen, Nicholas Peerse, Eleanor his wife, Ann Jordan, Henry Jordan, Chas Jordan, David Easton & Sarah his wife, & others, heirs of John Jordan, dec'd. Bill to obtain sale of land which John Jordan, died, seized & possessed in fee simple, to pay debt due from said Jordan to Alex Greer & Sally his wife, excx of last will of Wm Trueman Stoddert, dec'd. Above named dfndnts reside out of state. -Nichs Brewer, Reg C C.

Geo Gordon, of Va, a fugitive from justice, alleged to be at large in Md; Gordon chgd with shooting & killing, Bently, negro; coroner's inquest Sep 21, 1806 in Cumberland Co, Va.

Saml Maclay has rsgn'd his seat in the U S Sen & appt'd srvyr Genr'l of Pa.

Return J Meigs jr is appt'd Sen of U S for Ohio, vice John Smith who rsgn'd.

FRI JAN 6, 1809
Mrd: Mr Robt Getty, merchant of Gtwn, to [illegible] of Annapolis, by Rev Mr Judd, Dec 27, at Annapolis.

MON JAN 9, 1809
Mrd: Wm J Burwell, esq, Rep in Cong from Va, to Miss Letitia MacCreery, in vicinity of Balt. [Wash City item-Jan 9] No date given for marriage.

WED JAN 11, 1809
Bank notes found on John Moss lately convicted of having stolen bank notes out of ltrs in Petersburg P O, while clk therein; now in possession of Jas Byrne, mayor of Petersburg. [First name is by whom drawn-2d, in whose favor,-3d bank.]
Abr'm B Venable-Robt Birchett-Petersburg-1805;
D Lenox-John Swan-Balt-1807;
J Poydror-Jas Carrick-La-1806;
D Lenox-J Habersham-Savannah-1807;
Thos Willing-Robt Taylor-Norfolk-1804;
Thos Willing-not known-Balt-1807;
G Clymer-D Fortune—Phil-1808;

John G Wright-Thos F Davis-1806;
Abr'm R Venable-Jas Muir-Richmond-1805;
Venable-Rich'd E Lee-Norfolk-1807;
J Poydror-Paul L Musse-La-1806;   [others not legible].

Mr Wm Girod, friend of Mr Dennis O'Neal & Mrs Shylock, is informed that upon application to Nat'l intell ofc in Wash, he will hear something very interesting to his happiness. Info needed of this gentleman's address.

U S Crt, 5th Crct, Va Dist, Nov Term, 1808. U S against John Moss. Bank notes which Jas Byrne, a witness, examined on the trial of the indictment spoke, & he declared himself to be in possession of, taken from John Moss, be retained by said Byrne until further order of Crt. -Wm Marshal, clk.

FRI JAN 13, 1809
Rich'd Brent chosen Senator in Cong for Va, vice Mr Moore who declined a re-election.

Act of relief for Andrew Jos Villard, sum of $1000 for his extra svcs & expense in mounting heavy cannon for batteries.

Pblc auction, Jehiel Crossfield, having retired from groc business will sell stock on hand. Store nr Pa av, Wash.

MON JAN 16, 1809
Michl Leib chosen Senator of U S for Pa, vice, Saml Maclay, rsgn'd.

To lease-lot where soap & candle manufactory is established in Fredericksburg, Va; proprietor desirous of retiring. Geo W R Spooner, Fredericksburg, Va.

WED JAN 18, 1809
Sweepstakes are open to be run for at Warwick, Md, in Oct 1809. -Wm Frazer, White Hall, Dela.

All persons to whom Jas Duddle is indebted are to produce their accounts.
-Buller Cocke, Matthew Wright.

FRI JAN 20, 1809
David Brower, black man, committed to Wash Co, D C jail; says he belongs to Ralph Boarman of Chas Co, Md. -C Tippett-kpr of the jail.

For sale-valuable mulatto ladd. -John Tayloe, Wash City.

MON JAN 23, 1809
Lt Jos Cross writes to Hon sec at War; from Artl Cantonment, Sackel's Harbor, Oct 21, 1808. Contains events regarding villainous attempt to assassinate him; a need to enforce the bargo. -Jos Cross.

WED JAN 25, 1809
Subscription dancing assembly-at Mr Long's Hotel; mgrs: Robt Brent, Dan'l Carroll of D, Lt John Johnson & John Law.

Pblc auction-lot 6 sq 253; half of lot 10 sq 225, both on F St. Mary M'Nemara, excx of Cornelius M'Dermott Roc. Saml Speake, auct.

Notice-we, in spring of 1808, did execute a Power of Atty to Col John Ballenger, of Knox Co, Ky, to collect monies which we were to receive for damages sustained by the military under Capt Ball, on Yellow Creek, Knox Co, Ky; said Power has been revoked. -John [X] Brown, Edw [X] Gideons, John Corden, Saml Mosly, Robt Ballon.

Orphans Crt of Wash Co, D C. Jan 25, 1809. Prsnl est of Maurice Cribbin, late of said Dist, dec'd. -Nichs Callan.

FRI JAN 27, 1809
Purnel Carty, fugitive from justice, alleged to be at large in Talbot Co, Md; chged with felony in kidnapping Hester Craig & her 2 chldrn. Exec of Delaware hath demanded of exec of Md, to arrest & commit said Purnel Carty to the jail of the county in which he may be found & to give notice to exec of Delaware.

MON JAN 30, 1809
Solomon Stenger, brought up to the glass manufacturing business, offers his svcs to those who may require such person.

New book just rec'd: *Sketch of Plan & Method of Educating* founded on an analysis of the human faculties & natural reason; by Jos Neef, formerly a coadjutor of Pestalozi, at his school nr Berne, Switzerland. Price 75 cents.

WED FEB 1, 1809
Ranaway-Pompey & Basil, 2 negroes. Reward-$100. -Jacob Ducket, Piscataway, PG Co, Md.

Persons interested in receiving their dividend in est of Henry Lee, dec'd; attend at ofc of Jas Forrest, esq, Leonardtown, Md. -Wm T Lee, adm.

Just published-T*he Exile of Erin;* a novel by Mrs Plunket, late Miss Gunning. Price one dollar.

For sale-a light coachee. -Armstrong Charlton, Wash.

FRI FEB 3, 1809
Jos Reed, inspec & srvyr of revenue at Thomastown, Maine, rsgn'd his ofc.

Orphans Crt of Wash Co, D C. Est of Absalom Joy, late of said Dist, dec'd. Exhibit claims to Dr John Ott or Saml Brook.

MON FEB 6, 1809
Hse of Reps. act of relief for Edmund Beamont, imprisoned in Conn, shall be released & dischgd from all claim of U S, judgment for $400, at their suit before Dist Crt of Conn, at New Haven, Aug 1806. -J B Varnum, Spkr of Hse o/Reps.

WED FEB 8, 1809
Dissolution of partnership of Wm T Reed & Co. Business will be carried on at same place by Francis Clark. Wash.

FRI FEB 10, 1809
Recapitulation of the votes of electors for Pres of U S. Jas Madison-122 votes; Chas Cotesworth Pinckney-47; Geo Clinton-6. For VP: Geo Clinton-113; Rufus King-47; John Langdon-9; Jas Madison-3; Jas Monroe-3. Term of 4 yrs to begin Mar 4, 1809.

Appt'd by the Pres:-John Cox, Brigade-Maj & inspec of the Militia of the District of Columbia.

Orphans Crt of Wash City, D C. Prsnl est of Henry Howes, late of said city, dec'd. Feb 10. 1809. -Ignatius Howe, exc.

For sale-80 acs in Dist of Columbia, at present occupied by Mrs Halsey. Apply to Mr Thos Claxton at the Capitol.

MON FEB 13, 1809
Proposals will be rec'd for a contract to supply the Navy in ordinary with fresh beef. -Thos Tingey, Superintendant.

An act dividing Indiana Terr into 2 separate Governments; constituting a separate Territory cld, Illinois. -J B Varnum, Spkr of Hse of Reps. Feb 3, 1809. Approved, Th Jefferson.

Edw Gantt, insolvent debtor, confined in Wash Co, D C, prison, for debt.
-Wm Brent, clk.

WED FEB 15, 1809
Case of Robt Brown Jameson, insolvent debtor; time limited for production of claims expires Feb 22. -Colin Auld, Trustee, Alex.

FRI FEB 17, 1809
Mgrs for Gen Washington nativity commemoration: John Tayloe, Lt Col Franklin Wharton, Lt A Henderson, Jas Eakin.

For sale or rent: 2 story hse & lot; 13th St West. Possession of Wm Yeates jr who will occupy same until Apr 1.

Tan yard to be rented nr the Navy Yd in Wash City. Enquire of Robt Underwood, Pa av

Mrd: Mr Thos Johnson to Miss T Dixon, Feb 16, by Rev Mr Matthews.

MON FEB 20, 1809
For sale at hse of Solomon Stenger, nr the Glass Hse, Wash City: furniture & sloop, *Rising Sun*. -Saml Speake, auct.

WED FEB 22, 1809
State of Md, in Chancery, Feb 4, 1809. Ordered, sale of lots in Wash City, reported by Edw S Burd as trustee in suit by excs of M Lewis & Edw Burd, against Morris, Nicholson & others, be ratified; sold for $13,000. -Nichs Brewer, Rg C C.

Stockholders of manufacturing Co, observed that John Gardner has offered himself as sec; he presently holds 2 ofcs; wish to recommend Thos Carpenter to fill said ofc of sec.

FRI FEB 24, 1809
Meeting of Rpblcns of Loudoun Co, Va, at Leesburg, Feb 13, 1809. Col Wm Ellzey, chrmn; Armistead T Mason, sec.

In Chancery, Feb 1809. Solomon Holland vs Hezekiah M Ford. Bill is to have a deed recorded, granted from H M Ford to said Holland, dt'd Aug 6, 1800, for land cld *Exchange & New Exchange Enlarged*, in Williamsburgh, Montg Co. Ford has remv'd to of Ky. -Nichs Brewer, R C C.

Died: Saml Turner, age 84 yrs, on Feb 8, at his seat in Montg Co, Md; 30 yrs reg of wills for said Co.

Partnership of Spiden & Cook, stone cutters, is dissolved. Orlando Cook will continue the business.

MON FEB 27, 1809
Order of Orphans Crt of PG Co, Md. Sale at late resid of Jos Ramsey Hodges Sr, dec'd, nr Baldwin's Tavern, PG Co, Md-all prsnl est of said dec'd: negroes, stock, furn. At resid of Jos Ramsey Hodges jr, nr the brick chr, PG Co, prsnl est of said dec'd: negroes, stock, furn. -Benj Hodges, adm.

WED MAR 1, 1809
A new work-*The Private Life of Washington*, by M L Weems, rector of Mt Vernon Parish; for 15 yrs, the intimate of the grey-hair'd vets of last century. H H Brackenridge, Judge, dated Carlisle, Jan 19, 1809, recommends the bk.

Order of Orphans Crt-sale at dwlg hse of David Somerville, Pa av, silver watch, wearing apparel & tools of the late Andrew M'Lean, stone-cutter, dec'd. -Jas Laurie, David Somerville, excs. Saml Speake, auct.

Runaway, John, black man, committed to Wash Co, D C, jail; says he belongs to Ignatius Dennis, of York Co, Va. -C Tippett, kpr o/jail.

To rent: brick hse on Va Ave nr the Navy Yd, lately occupied by Mr Josiah Fox. Enquire of Fred'k May.

Pblc auction on plantation where I now live: stock, farming utensils, hsehld & kitchen furn. -Jos L Scholfield.

FRI MAR 3, 1809

Thos Jefferson retired from the Supreme Magistracy amidst the blessings & regrets of millions. Fri, Mar 3, 1809.

Orphans Crt of St Mary's Co, Md. Jan 13, 1809. Prsnl est of Rich'd Bond, late of said Co, dec'd. -Rebecca White Ford-excx.

Ltr to Capt John Rust-Your not being a resid of Va, I shall proceed to take the depositions of Messrs Dan'l Lawson Sr & Wm Palmuir jr at Richmond Crt Hse, in tvrn occupied by John Howe; also of Mr Thos Spence & others in his tvrn at West-Moreland Crt Hse, also of Geo Moore in Crt Hse in Urbanna, Middlesex Co, also of Col Alex'r Parker in Eagle Tvrn in Norfolk Borough. Yours, Peter Rust, Richmond Co, Va. [dates for said meetings are thru March]

SAT MAR 4, 1809 extra

This day at 12 o'clock, Jas Madison took the oath of ofc as Pres of the U S; oath administered by Chief Justice Marshall. Copy of speech followed

MON MAR 6, 1809

Ranaway-Cuddy, negro man, from plantation of Thos Blake, living nr Lower Marlbro in Calvert Co, Md. Rwd-$20.

Ltr by Mr Macall Medford, Phil, Jan 28, 1809, [witness-Geo Rundle]: Regrets being instrumental to the injury of the feelings & character of Mr John Lisle, of Phil. Ltr by John Lisle, late John Lisle jr, Phil, Mar 6: agrees to discontinue prosecuting him for libel. Macall & Lisle were prtnrs.

Case unsettled-Gideon Olmstead commanded an Americ armed vessel during Rev; captured & carried into Jamaica, he was incarcerated in a dungeon for svr'l mos; put on board a vessel for N Y & seized same; brought her into Del; vessel was condemned & prop hung up for 30 yrs in law suits; crts in his favor; money has not been pd to Olmstead who has grown old in yrs. Gov of Pa: rec'd info that Sup Crt of U S ordered a peremptory mandamus to be issued to suit of Gideon Olmstead, vs Eliz Sergeant & Esther Waters, excxs of late Mr David Rittenhouse; they are to pay a sum of money from sale of British ship, *Active;* money is in Penn Treas; Simon Snyder is protecting the int of said excxs. -Lancaster, Feb 27, 1809.

WED MAR 8, 1809

Dissolution of partnership bet Jacob Duckett & Hannibal Clagett. Business will be cont'd by Jacob Duckett.

Appt'd by the Pres of the U S:
Robt Smith of Md, sec of State;
Wm Eustis of Mass, sec of war;
Paul Hamilton of S C, sec of Navy;
Thos Sumter jr of S C, Mnstr Pleni to Rio Janeiro;
Henry Hill, cnsl at St Salvador, Brazil;
David Holmes of Va, Gov of Miss Terr;
John Boyle of Ky, Gov of Illinois Terr;
Nath'l Pope, sec of Illinois Terr.

FRI MAR 10, 1809

Appt'd by Pres Madison: Francis Xavier Martin of N C, Judge of Miss Terr vice Peter Bryan Bruin rsgn'd.

Judges of Ill Terr:
Obadiah Jones of Ga, Jesse B Thomas of Ill Terr & Alex'r Stuart of Va.
Thos Nelson, coll & inspec of York, Va.

Navy agnts:
Saml Storer-Portland, Maine
Francis Johonnot-Boston, Mass
John Bullus-N Y
John Stricker-Balt
Jas Morrison-Lexington, Ky
Archd S Bullock-Savannah, Ga
Nath'l Ingraham & son-Charleston, S C
Henry S Landgon-Portsmouth, N H
Jos Hull-Middletown, Conn
Geo Harrison-Phil
Theodorick Armistead-Norfolk
Keith Spence-N Orleans
Dan'l Carmick, from Capt to Maj of Marines
Jas Thompson, Edw Halt & Mich'l Reynolds, from 1st Lt of Marines to Capts of Marines.
Saml C Miller, from 2d to 1st Lt of Marines.
Jasher Hand of Pa-Surg in Navy of U S.
Saml Blair & Saml Horseley of Va-Surgs mates in U S N.

Military appointments made previous to Mar 4:
Brig Gen-Wade Hampton & Peter Gansevoort.
Regt of Light Artl-Lt Col-vacant, Maj-John Saunders.
Light Dragoons-Col Wade Hampton, Lt Col Leonard Covington & Maj Electus Backus.
Riflemen: Col Alex'r Smith, Lt Col Wm Duane & Maj John Fuller.
3d Regt of Infty: Col Edw Pasteur, Lt Col John Smithe & Maj Homer V Milton.
4th Regt of Infty: Col John P Boud, Lt Col John Whiting & Maj Jas Miller.
5th Regt of Infty: Col Alex'r Parker, Lt Col Wm D Beall & Maj Tully Robinson.
6th Regt of Infty: Col Jonas Simonds, Lt Col Jos Constant & Maj Zebulon M Pike.
7th Regt of Infty: Col Wm Russell, Lt Col Robt Purdy & Maj Elijah Strong.

Mrs Greentree has opened a ladies boarding & day school in Gtwn, in hse lately occupied by Maj Beall.

Ranaway-Helon, mulatto girl; from Wm Holmes, west Wash City.

Act of relief for Dan'l Cotton; allowance for detention of his ship, *Anna Maria*, from Dec 23 1800 'til May 23, 1801, when she was arrested by Bey of Tunis; sum of $5,000 was pd by Wm Eaton, then cnsl for U S at Tunis to the mstr of said ship; bal with int to be pd Dan'l Cotton. -J B Varnum-Hse o/Reps.

Treaty bet U S & Chippewa, Ottawa, Pottawatamie, Tyandot & Shawanoese Nations of Indians concluded at Brownstone, Mich Terr on Nov 25, 1808. Ratified by Pres of U S on Mar 1, 1809. Witnessed by: Reuben Attwater, sec of Mich Terr; Jas Witherill, Judge of Mich Terr; Jacob Kisger, Judge of Dist Crt; Jas Watson, sec L M T; Wm Brown; B Campau; Lewis Bond; A Lyons; interpreters-Wm Knaggs, Wm Walker, F Dughonquet, Saml Saundeks. Attest-Harris Hampden Hickman-sec to commission. -Wm Hull-L S.

Mill Wrights wanted, at Occoquan & Ellicott's Lower Mills, nr Balt. -Robt Welsh.

MON MAR 13, 1809

Ranaway-Wm Hutchingson, appr in baking business, age ab't 16 yrs. -Esias Travers. Reward-$5.

WED MAR 15, 1809

Naval appointments made by Pres Jefferson:

Henry Caldwell of Mass-to Capt in Marine Corps vice Robt Rankin, rsgn'd.

To 1st Lts:

Robt D Wainwright of S C	Wm Anderson of N J
Nelson Luckett of Va	Thos H Pinckney of S C
Thos R Swift of Pa	Lee Massey jr of Va
John Brooks jr of Mass	Andrew Hasel of S C.

Marine Corps prmtd from 2d Lts to 1st Lt: Wm Winthrope, v Lt Johnson, rsgnd.

To be 2d Lts in Marine Corps:

Mathew Boyle of Ky	Ichabad B Crane of N Y
Lewis C A Armistead of Va	Roger Jones of Va
Edw P Wilmer of Md	Henry M Parker of S C
Wm D Wilson of S C	John Crabbe of Pa
Henry H Ford of Pa	Jas Ragland of Va
Robt Gardner of Mass	

Humphrey Magrath, now sailing mstr

Mdshpmn to be Lts in U S N:

Chas C B Thompson	Jas P Wilmer
Francis Mitchell	Robt B Gamble
John Nevit	Jaquelin B Harvey

Surg's mates: Nicholas Harwood, Robt D Thorn, John Brown;

Surgs in U S N: Saml R Trevett jr of Mass & Stephen C Blyden of Mass.

Surgs' Mates in U S N:

Gustavus R Brown of Md	Grafden D Hanson of Md
Thos Lawson jr of Va	Henry Fackler of Pa
John Reynolds of Pa	J H Hampton of N J
Jos Trevett of Mass	Theodorus C Van Wyck of N Y

Jas R Owen of N Y
John Maxwell of Md
Stith Lewis of Va
Saml R Trevett of Mass
John A Kearney of Dist of Col
Saml Davis of Va
Wm Barr of Pa
Thos J H Cushing of Mass.

Act of relief for Jacob Barnitz formerly an ensign in Capt Christian Stoke's Co in Col Mich'l Swope's btln of Pa Flying Camp: $1000 sufferings & costs for med & surg aid from wounds rec'd in Rev War. -J B Varnum, Hse of Reps.

Stop the swindlers. $1000 reward-for John Thomas, age ab't 35 yrs; resided many yrs in Union St-had a brdg hse & groc store; & Honore Monpoey, Creole man from St Domingo, resided at Wentworth & King Sts-had a groc store. Cmtee on behalf of the creditors: Wash Potter, Wm Potter, Dan'l Latham, Philip Cohen, Joshua Brown. -Charleston.

Gov Drayton issued orders for mortar battery to be erected at White Point; same completed under direction of Col Dan'l Stevens of the Artl. -Charleston, Mar 2.

Died: Mrs Mgt Daniel, consort of Dr John M Daniel, & eldest d/o late Hon Thos Stone, esq, of Md; on Mar 9 at her resid in Falmouth, Va; leaves her hsbnd & 6 small chldrn.

Forewarn all persons from hiring my man, Monday, without applying to me.
-Mary Brumly, Wash.

To let: large brick bldg, lately occupied by Gen Tureau, East end of the 7 bldgs.
-Jos Harbaugh, Capitol Hill, Wash.

Pblc sale at Drummonds Tavern, Navy Yd; all right, title of John Vintt in part of lot in sq 930, 8th st, with brick hse, prop now occupied by Mr John Dobbins; at suit of Lewis Clephan in Crct Crt of Dist of Col. -Wash Boyd, mrshl.

FRI MAR 7, 1809

State of Md-in Chancery. Nathan Gregg vs Sarah Awl Gregg, Mgt Ferguson Gregg, & Robt Awl Gregg. Bill to obtain cnvync from dfndnt to cmplnt for part of land, cld *The Re-Srvy on Indian Fields*, in Alleghany Co, formerly sold by Thos Cresap, dec'd, to fr of cmplnt. Cmplnt prchsd of his fr, Robt Gregg, in 1791, amongst other lands, the above said land for 1000l; money pd & all land except the above were conveyed; Robt Gregg died intestate, leaving amongst other chldrn, Thos Gregg who also died intestate, leaving the dfndnts his heirs at law; they are minors & reside out of state. The other chldrn of Robt Gregg have cnvyd or are willing to cnvy. -Nichs Brewer, Rg

State of Md-In Chancery. Nathan Gregg, vs Thos Parsons & Eliz his wife, Virgil M'Crackin & Mary his wife. Bill to record a deed executed by dfndnts to cmplnt for land cld *The Re-Srvy on Indian Fields*, in Allegany Co. -Nichs Brewer, R C C

MON MAR 20, 1809

Committed to Frederic Co, Md, jail-Phil Blake, negro man; says he belongs to Dr Wm P Matthews, on Elk Ridge, 5 miles of Elk Ridge landing. -Geo Creager, shrf, Fred'k Co.

Reward-$30 for Stephen, Ambrows & Rafe, negroes; left my plantation nr Bryan town, Chas Co, Md. -Benedict Boarman.

WED MAR 22, 1809

Info wanted of heirs of Robie Hohrein, ntv of Wurtemberg, Ger; is said he died at Fred'k town, Md, in 1773; will receive info to their advantage. -Dept of State.

Pblc sale-order of Orphans Crt of PG Co, Md; at Upper Marlborough, prsnl prop of late Dr Saml Hepburn, dec'd; negro boy, saddle horse, med & surg instruments, med library. -Gabriel Peterson Van Horn, adm.

Persons who claim title to certain lots in Gtwn are notified their titles are defective; apply to Mr Abner Ritchie or F S Key, Gtwn. -Anne Maria Davidson, excx of Gen John Davidson.

FRI MAR 24, 1809

Meeting held at Kent Co, at hse of Thos Peacock, Chester, Md, of Democratic ctzns, Mar 4. Dr John Thomas, chrmn; Cornelius Comegys, esq, sec; Dr John T Rees, Dr Robt G Maxwell, Benj Massey, Jos Thomson, Wm Ferrel, Jas Brook & Geo Palmer, esqs, were duly elected.

For sale-300 acs within 3 miles of Gtwn. Apply to Jas Morsell, esq, of Gtwn or to Edw Hall, of West Rvr.

MON MAR 27, 1809

Sale-being about to leave the city, I offer my hse on Pa Ave; sundry articles of furn. -Rebecca Scott.

WED MAR 29, 1809

Ranaway-Johnson Crawford, apprentice boy, age nrly 14 yrs. Dinmore & Cooper. Reward-one cent.

New Dry Goods store opened in Gtwn by John Laub.

Appointments made by Pres Jefferson:

Jas Chas Jewett of Mass-srvyr for Portland & Falmouth & inspec of Rev for Ports with-in;
Isaiah Weston, coll of Dist & inspec of New Bedford Port;
John Steele of Pa, coll of Phil;
John Ennals of Md, coll & inspec for Vienna;
Athanasius Fenwick of Md, coll for Dist of St Mary's;
Wm Jackson of Md, srvyr & inspec for Nanjemoy Port;
Eugene Sullivan of Va, srvyr & inspec for West Point Port;

Robt H Jones of N C, atty of U S for Dist of N C;
Levi Bounts of N C, coll & inspec, Port of Plymouth, N C;
John Pooler of Ga, com'r of loans in Ga;
Rich'd Wall of Ga, coll for Savannah;
Peter Wilson of Ohio, receiver of public monies at Steubenville;
Chas Minifie, Justice of Peace for Wash Co, D C;
Rich'd S Briscoe, Justice of Peace for same Co;
Wm Orr of N C, coll & inspec for port of Wash, N C.
Appts made with advice & consent of the Senate:
John Thompson of Orleans Terr, Judge of same;
Gen Henry Dearborn of Mass-coll for Boston & Charlestown;
Peter Sailly of N Y-coll & inspec for Champlain;
Thos Coles of R I-coll for Providence;
Jos Marguand of Mass-srvyr of Newburyport;
Nath'l Williams of Mass-coll & inspec for Dighton;
Wm Otis of Mass-coll & inspec for Barnstable;
Isaac Carter of Mass, srvyr & inspec for port of Augusta;
Alex'r M'Intire of Mass-coll & inspec for York;
Jos Storer of Mass-coll & inspec for Kennebunk;
Dan'l Grainger of Mass-coll & inspec for Saco;
Wm M Daws of Mass-srvyr & inspec for Thomaston;
Peter Freneau of S C-com'r of loans for S C;
Philip Grymes now Dist atty of Orleans, to be Reg of land ofc of U S for eastern part of that territory.

Mrd: John Florentius Cox, esq, of N Y, to Miss Eliza R Lansdale, d/o late Maj Thos L Lansdale of PG Co, on Mar 28 by Rev Mr Addison.

FRI MAR 31, 1809

Sec of war is directed to place the following named persons on the pension list of invalid pensioners of U S:

[name-rate per month-effective date]

Oxford Tash-$2.50-Jun 1, 1807;
Hezekiah Sawfell-$2.50-Sep 28, 1808;
Amos Spafford-$3.33 1/3-Oct 23, 1808;
Josiah Temple-$2-Apr 15, 1808;
Isaac Abbott-$8-Nov 19-1808;
Thadeus Waugh-$5-May 31, 1808;
Joel Hinman-$5-Jun 8, 1808;
David Pendleton-$5-May 20-1808;
Eliphalet Sherwood-$2.50-May 20, 1808;
Dan'l Treadwell-$4-May 20, 1808;
Obadiah Perkens-$8-Nov 18, 1808;
John Daboll-62 ½ cents-Nov 18, 1808;
Gideon Edwards-$5-Dec 17, 1808;
Elijah Sheldon-$2.50-Dec 19, 1808;
Nath'l Church-$2.50-Dec 30, 1808;
Rich'd Mellon-$5-Nov 9, 1808;

Elisha Prior-$3.75-Dec 13, 1808;
John Cramer-$2.50-Apr 25, 1808;
Jas Philips-$2.50-Apr 19, 1808;
John Walsh-$2.50-Sep 8, 1808;
Saml Lindsley-$3.75-Oct 31, 1808;
John Fergus-$2-Oct 20, 1808;
Jos Elliot-$3.33 1/3-Apr 21, 1808;
Jas Correar-$2.50-Nov 25, 1808;
John Smith-$2.50-Jan 27, 1808;
JosWhite-$3.75-Feb 22, 1808;
Edw Tack-$3-Jan 2, 1808;
Evan Ragland-$3-Jan 7, 1808;
John Crute-$13-Sep 28, 1808;
Wm Evans-$8-Nov 21, 1808;
John Carmichael-$5-Dec 1, 1808;
Benj Vickery-$3-Jun 14, 1808;
Joshua Hawkins-$3-Mar 25, 1808;
Jos M'Junkin-$12-Oct 18, 1808;
Saml Otterson-$8-Oct 6, 1808;
Wm Carr-$2.50-Mar 28, 1808;
Jonathan Tinsley-$5-Sep 23, 1808;
Jas Gallespie-$4-Jun 18, 1808;
Christian Smith-$5-Nov 5, 1808;
Bartholomew Berry-$5-Nov 7, 1808;
John Robt Shaw-$5-Oct 12, 1808;
Saml Burton-$2.50-Dec 29, 1808;
Nath'l Hewitt-$3.75-Jan 5, 1809;
Jacob Redenour-$5-Apr 10, 1806;
Wm Keough-$5-Jan 23, 1809;
Isaiah Corben-$2.50-Oct 31, 1808;
Jos Richardson-$2.50-Jan 20, 1809;
Wm Johnson-$2.50-Jan 18, 1809;
Henry Overly-$5-Dec 1, 1808;
Abraham Gamble-$5-Jan 18, 1809;
Wm M'Clannahan-$2.50-Oct 27, 1808;
Wm M'Laland-$5-Feb 4, 1809.
<u>List of pensioners already on pension list of U S; increase in pension.</u>
[name-rate per mo-effective date]
Wm Curtiss-$5-Sep 1, 1808;
Saml Potter-$3.33 1/3-Sep 6, 1808;
Thos Haines-$5-Jan 17, 1807;
Dan'l Bussell-$5-Oct 3, 1808;
Wm Wood-$3.33 1/3-Sep 14, 1808;
Thos Pratt-$3.33 1/3-Oct 24, 1808;
Ebenezer Tinkham-$2.50-Nov 8, 1808;
Jos Brown-$5-Jun 3, 1808;
Benj Merrill-$3.33 1/3-Sep 28, 1808;
Wm Leach-$5-May 2, 1808;

Constant Webb-$3-May 30, 1808;
Jonathan Bowers-$5-Jul 23, 1808;
Abner Andrews-$5-Sep 1, 1808;
Josiah Merriman-$5-Sep 17, 1808;
Saml Burdwin-$5-Sep 23, 1808;
Oliver Bostwich-$10-Oct 3, 1808;
Edw Bassett-$2.50-Apr 28, 1808;
Jeremiah Markham-$3.75-Jun 3, 1808;
Saml Andrus-$3.75-Sep 23, 1808;
Elisha Clark-$2.50-Sep 28, 1808;
Aaron Tuttle-$3.33 1/3-Oct 25, 1808;
Benj Sturges-$4-Oct 25, 1808;
Burr Gilbert-$5-Jul 28, 1808;
Jehuel Judd-$4-Apr 16, 1808;
Ashbel Hosmer-$5-Oct 6, 1808;
Andrew M'Guire-$5-Aug 1, 1808;
John Lowry-$3.33 1/3-Apr 19, 1808;
Jas Blever-$5-Apr 8, 1808;
Saml B White-$5 -Apr 8, 1808;
Judah Levy-$5-Apr 12, 1808;
Enoch Turner-$5-Nov 14, 1808;
Edw Stanton-$5-Nov 19, 1808;
Elisha Lee-$20-Nov 30, 1808;
Wm Starr-$3.75-Nov 18, 1808;
John Morgan-$3.33 1/3-Nov 18, 1808;
Andrew Gallup-$3.33 1/3-Nov 18, 1808;
Jos Woodmancy-$5-Nov 18, 1808;
Solomon Perkins-$5-Nov 18, 1808;
Walter Burdick-$2.50-Nov 18, 1808;
Park Avery-$5-Nov 18, 1808;
Amos Avery-$2.50-Nov 18, 1808;
Ebenezer Avery-$2.50-Nov 18, 1808;
Benj Denslow-$5-Dec 7, 1808;
Amos Skeele-$3.33 1/3-Nov 28, 1808;
Wm Burrows-$5-Dec 12, 1808;
Elisha Frizzle-$5-Jan 1, 1809;
John M'Kinstrey-$20-Jan 1, 1809;
Saml Gibbs-$13.33 1/3-Oct 8, 1808;
John Barbarick-$5-Dec 15, 1808;
Jas Morgan-$2.50-Jan 5, 1809;
Jos Moxley-$2.50-Jan 5, 1809;
Daniel Bill-$5-Jan 5, 1809;
Christopher Latham-$3.75-Jan 5, 1809.
Approved, Th Jefferson, Mar 3, 1809.

Christ Church will put up svr'l pews to public sale. -Henry Ingle, Reg/W P.

In Chancery-Mar 2, 1809. Alex'r Greer & wife against Benoni Wheat & Mary his wife, & others, heirs of John Jordon, late of Chas Co, dec'd. Bill to obtain sale of land John Jordon died seized, for purpose of paying a debt due from said Jordon to Alex Greer & Sally his wife, excx of last will of Wm Trueman Stoddert, dec'd. Dfndnts have remv'd out of state. -Nichs Brewer, Rg C C. [Md]

MON APR 3, 1809

In Chancery-State of Md, Mar 20, 1809. Wm Deakins & others against the heirs of Peter Casanave. Francis Deakins against Thos S Lee, Peter Casanave & others. Ordered that claims filed in said suits will be determined after Jul 4; claims objected to by the auditor are those of Uriah Forest & Wm Deakins & of David Lynn. -Nichs Brewer, Reg C Cr.

Pblc auction at hse of Jas Deaver, cabinet mkr on High St, Gtwn. -John Travers

John Condit appt'd to Senate of U S by Gov Bloomfield, of N J, vice Aaron Kitchell having rsgn'd.

WED APR 5, 1809

Eliz Burnill, my wife, has eloped from my bed & board, & living an adultress with another man; I will pay none of her debts; mean to apply to next Genr'l assembly of Md for an act of divorce. -John Burnill, PG Co, Md.

Pblc sale-deed of trust executed by John Stephen; lots 4 & 5 sq 88; lots 4 & 5 sq 89; Wash City. -John Mountz jr, trust.

FRI APR 6, 1809

Ladies with ltrs in Wash Post ofc, April 1, 1809:

Miss Mary B Addison	Cassandra Brevitt	Ann Cooper
Eleanor Conner	Agnes Cook	Cath Casey
Charlotte Coyeres	Miss Tracy Dixon	Mrs Doyne
Miss Frances Few	Sarah E Goodwin	Mrs Ann Green
Hannah L Gibbs	Mrs Mary Ann Gregory	Deborah Gardiner
Helen H Leiper	Eliz C Leiper	Madame Lavendel
Mrs Mary Lane	Miss Milly Perry	Cath Spunaugle
Mrs M Shaw c/o John Shaw	Sarah Sheppard	Charlotte Taylor
Eliz Thrift	Eliz Tucker	Mrs S Thompson
Mgt Williams		

Mrd: on Mar 27, John Montgomery, esq, Rep in Cong for Md, to Miss Maria Nicholson of N Y, by Rev Dr Abeel.

Elected Vestrymen of Christ Chr: Messrs Thos Tingey, Tunis Craven, Peter Miller, Geo Blagden, Fred'k May, John Coyle, Griffith Coombe, Henry Ingle. Chr wardens: Geo M'Cauley & Jas Owner.

Wm Eustis has accepted his appointment as Sec of War.

U S Navy [ship's-& Commanding ofcr]:

Constitution, Com Rodgers
U States, Capt Decatur
Essex, Capt Smith
John Adams, Capt Evans
Siren, Capt Gordon
**Vixen*, Lt Dent
President, Capt Bainbridge
Chesapeake, Capt Hull
Wasp, Capt Robinson
Hornet, Capt Dent
Argus, Lt Jones
Enterprize, Lt Trippe

[*Apr 17 Corr: *Vixen*-Lt Lawrence not Lt Dent.]

MON APR 10, 1809

Bordenton Acad, for young gentlemen; on Dela Rvr in State of N J; recently purch'd by Andrew Hunter, Princeton, N J.

WED APR 12, 1809

U S, Wash Co, D C-in Chancery, Mar 28, 1809. John P Van Ness, cmplnt, against Wm H Dorsey, dfndnt. In 1805 dfndnt being indebted to cmplnt for $4,974.34, payable Jan 10, 1809 with int from that day, if not then pd; Apr 19, 1805 mortgaged ground in Wash to said cmplnt-ground leased to Cornelius M'Clan; to Edw Frithy, to Geo Blount, to Thos Herty, to Alexr Joncherez, to Peter Murray, to Wm Woodward & to John M'Gowan; dfndnt hath failed to pay to said cmplnt sum of money or part thereof. Wm H Dorsey has remv'd from D C. -Wm Brent, clk.

Meeting at Crt Hse in Pittsburg, Allegany Co, Pa: Maj Wm M'Candless, chrmn & Wm B Irish, sec; cmtee: Zadock Cramer, Thos Enochs & Jos M'Clurg. [Corr cmtee: Gen Thos Baird, Geo Cochrane of Rich'd, E Pentland. Feb 20, 1809.]

Declining boarding hse kpg, Henry Tims has hsehld furn & a riding chair & harness for sale. Local item.

FRI APR 14, 1809

For rent-brick dwlg nr Lower Bridge, Rock Creek. Enquire nr the premises of -Leonard Harbaugh jr.

Marine Corps of U S: Lt Col Commandant-Franklin Wharton;
Maj-Dan'l Carmick;

Capts-

John Hall
Henry Caldwell
Edw Hall
Anthony Gale
Jas Thompson
Mich'l Reynolds

1st Lts:

John R Fenwick
John Williams-qrtrmstr
Archibald Henderson-[Adjut]
Robt D Wainwright
Thos H Pinckney
Lee Massey
Andrew Hasell
Saml Miller
Robt Greenleaf-paymaster
Chas D Coxe
Rich'd Smith
Wm Anderson
Thos R Swift
John Brooks
Peter W Winthrop

2d Lts:

Lawrence Cruise
Roger Jones
H M Parker
John Crabb
Jas Ragland
Ichabod B Crane
Edw P Wilmer
Wm D Wilson
Henry G Ford

Pblc sale-Order of Chancery Dist Crt of Williamsburg; at Westmoreland Crt Hse; farm on Nomony Rvr, said Co, prop of John Matthews, late of Westmoreland Co, Va, 643 acs.

Ranaway-George, negro man; may pursue a woman he calls his wife who was bght & carried from St Mary's Co, Md to Rockingham Co, Va, by Dan'l Smoote, of said Co. -Jos Bennett, Ridge, St Mary's Co, Md.

MON APR 17, 1809

Pblc auction-lots 16 & 17 in sq 101, Wash City, with bldgs; oppo Mr Wm O'Neale's hses nr West Mkt; being est formerly owned by Mr Saml Wilson, dec'd.

Pblc auction-lot 3 sq 161, Wash City, with dwlg hse & slaughter-hse thereon; formerly owned by Dan'l Guyer.

Pblc sale-Order of Orphans Crt of Anne Arundel Co, Md: farm of John Gwinn, esq, dec'd, on *Deep Creek*, A A Co, & all prsnl est. -Th Harris jr, adm.

Edw Tiffin, of Ohio, has rsgn'd his seat in Senate of U S.

WED APR 19, 1809

Wash Navy Yd Rifle Vols to meet at Lt Dobbin's hse on Sat. Order of Capt Ed Fitzgerald. Wash City.

Jas Shaw brought before me a stray bay mare. -Geo Page, a J P, PG Co, Md.

Cash sale-at hse of Benj Burch, valuable furn; under distrain for hse rent due Dan'l Carroll of Dud. -David Bates, cnstbl.

FRI APR 21, 1809

Birthday of Genr'l Washington, Feb 11, 1732 O S, last century was celebrated on Feb 22; in consequence of the reformation of the Julian Calender by Pope Gregory XIII in 1582; 10 days were struck out of the month of Oct in that yr; in 1752 Gr Britain adopted the Gregorian Reformation.

MON APR 24, 1809

Runaway-Geo Jones alias Geo Evans, negro, committed to Wash Co, Md, jail; says he belongs to Jos Penticost of Wash Co, Pa. -Isaac S White, shrf.

Runaways-committed to Wash Co, D C jail: Giles, negro, says he is prop of Dr Stephen Cook, of Loudon Co, Va; John, negro, says he is the prop of Enoch Mason of Stafford Co, Va. -C Tippet, kpr of the jail for Wash. Boyd, mrsh'l.

Pblc sale-decree of Crct Crt of Wash Co, D C, passed in case of Godfrey Haga against the heirs of Chas Cist, dec'd. Three brick & one frame hse on E St, Wash. -Phineas Bradley-trust.

Orphans Crt of Fred'k Co, Md. Apr 15, 1809. Prsnl est of Lt Alex'r Contee Harrison, late of U S N, dec'd. -Kitty Harrison, admx.

In Chancery-Crct Crt of Wash Co, D C. Benj Young, Nicholas Young & Robt Brent, exc of Notley Young, cmplnts, vs Jas Greenleaf, Standish Ford, Jos Ball, Geo Harrison, Saml Sterret, Paul Bustie, Thos Fitzsimmons, Matthew Pearce, Dan'l Ludlow, Jas Crawford jr, Jas Crawford, Jasper Moylan, Wm Read, Chas G Paleskio, John Gardner jr, Edw Fox, Henry Pratt, Thos W Francis, John Miller jr, John Ashley, Jacob Baker, Hannah Nicholson wid of John Nicholson, Wm Nicholson, Anna Nicholson, Seth Nicholson, John Nicholson, Jas Nicholson, Saml Nicholson, Sarah Nicholson & Louiet Nicholson, heirs at law of John Nicholson, John Millar, Mary Morris wid of Robt Morris, Robt Morris, Thos Morris, Henry Morris, Jas Marshall & Hester his wife, & Henry Nixon & Maria his wife, dfndnts. Rg: Jas Greenleaf, dfndnt, on or ab't Sep 25, 1793 purch'd of Notley Young numerous lots in city of Wash; dfndnts were concerned in the purchase & sale of the greater part of said prop. -Wm Brent, clk.

Lost-brown mare in Commons of Wash City. -Wm Thornton-Wash.

WED APR 26, 1809

Longevity: now living in So Carolina:
Mrs Jackson, widow, High Hills of Santee-110;
Peter Carson, nr Greenville Crt Hse-107;
Fred'k Hooner, nr Orangeburg-102;
Wm Atwood, Abbeville-100;
Mrs Lane, nr Statesburg, walks 10 miles to chr on Sun with her descendants to 5th generation-95;
Mrs Walker nr Dorchester-92;
Amos Tims age 83 & his wife-91, mrd 66 yrs, nr Dorchester.
Following persons have died in S C since 1800:
Mrs Newby, Laurence-112;
Mrs Minnick, nr Edisto Rvr-108;
Mgt Dickson-Abbeville-104;
Rev Jeremiah Ream, Sumter Dist-100;
In Charleston: Abraham Jones-94;
Mrs Hopton-90; Thos Syles-90;
Mrs Ann Anderson-90; Miss Mary Bacot-89;
Peer Buyck-87 David Risdel-87;
Mrs Haynesworth, High Hills of Santee-87;
Mrs M'Kewn, Dorchester-87;

Following, svr'l above 80, but all had reached 80:

Ralph Atmar	Theodore Trezevant	Eliz Rivers
Mgt Buckle	Christiana Damson	Emanuel Abrahams
Ann Gray	Mary Tucker	Cath Cordes
Sarah Jones	Sarah Butler	Ann Morgan
Mgt Young	Mgt Woolf	Rachel Caw

From the times -David Ramsay.

Pblc sale-cargo of schn'r *Fame*, just arv'd from St Bartholomews-coffee, rum, sugar. -Philip G Marstellor, Alexandria.

Mrd: Hon John W Eppes, mbr of Congress from Va, & Miss Martha Jones, d/o late Willie Jones, esq, at Halifax, Apr 15.

FRI APR 28, 1809

Mrd: Mr John M'Daniel jr to Miss Mary Osborne, Apr 25, by Rev Mr Balch.

St Mary's Co, Md, Crt. Petition of Francis Howard, of St Mary's Co, for act for relief of insolvent debtor. -Jo Harris, clk.

MON MAY 1, 1809

Order of Crct Crt of Wash Co, D C. Pblc vendue at hse of Mr Wm Rhodes, innkpr, May 13: lot 6 sq 224 with lge 3 story brick hse, now occupied by Mrs Suter as brdg hse & part by Mr Edgar Patterson, as a store, crnr of 15th & N F Sts, oppo Treas Dept;-lots 15 & 16 sq 407, with wooden frame hse, 9th & E Sts. Lots 26 & 27 on 13th St W. small wooden hse; all sold subject to dower of Mrs Mary Ann Fenwick, wid of Bennet Fenwick, dec'd. Apply Jas A Porter, esq, atty. -Comr's: Edgar Patterson, Alex'r Cochrane Sr, Francis Clarke, Jas H Blake & Pierce Purcell.

WED MAY 3, 1809

Crct Crt of Wash Co, D C, as Crt of Chancery. Thompson & Hyde vs the heirs of John Crookshank, dec'd. Pblc auction of lot 5 & part of lot 4 in sq 461 with 3 three story brick hses on Pa av, one in occupation of S H Smith, esq; also lot 6 sq 347 & lot 25 sq 533, all Wash City. -D Bussard-trustee.

Crct Crt of Wash Co, D C as Crt of Chancery: Wm Lowman vs Peggy M'Laughlin & heirs of Chas M'Laughlin, dec'd. Sale of all interest of Chas M'Laughlin, dec'd, in lot 171, Gtwn, & part of lot 175. Dan'l Bussard, trustee.

Dr Robt French has began the practice of physic & surgery in Gtwn; keeps his shop in hse lately occupied by Dr John Weems, dec'd.

FRI MAY 5, 1809

Phil, Pa, May 1. U S against Gen Bright & others for resisting the mrsh'l of this Dist. Jury found all guilty: Gen Mich'l Bright, 3 mos imprisonment-$200 fine; Jas Atkinson, Chas Westfall, Abrm Ogden, Chas Hong, Wm Cole, Saml Wilkins,

Dan'l Phyle, John Knipe, 1 mo imprisonment-$50 fine. [See Gideon Olmstead-Mar 6, 1809 paper & below]

Elected to the next Congress from Va:

		John W Eppes
Dan'l Sheffey	Wilson C Nicholas	John Randolph
Peterson Goodwyn	John Clopton	John Smith
Thos Gholston jr	Thos Newton	Burwell Basset
Wm A Burwell	Walter Jones	Jacob Swoope
J Breckenridge	John Dawson	John T Roane
John Love	John G Jackson	Jos Lewis
Mathew Clay	Edwin Gray	J Stephenson

Reward-$10 for person who shot my horse on the Commons in Wash City. -Robt King.

MON MAY 8, 1809

Phil, Pa, May 1, 1809. Jurors in case of U S vs Gen Bright-[See above] Wm Sharswood, Benj Thaw, Mathias Corless, John Gallagher, John Philips, Conrad Seybert, Liberty Brown, John Jennings, John White jr, Chas Barrington, Thos Algeo, Geo A Wray. [See Gideon Olmstead-Mar 6, 1809 paper] [May 12, 1809 has detailed account which led up to this trial]

Wash Co, D C. Creditors of Henry Harshman, insolvent debtor confined in Wash Co prison for debt; to appear May 15th, at crt rm in Long's Hotel. Same info for Cornelius Williss, insolvent debtor. -Wm Brent, clk.

Crct Crt, Wash Co, D C-In Chancery, Apr 11, 1809. Gideon Snow, cmplnt, vs Abigail Perkins & others, dfndnts. Report of John G M'Donald, trustee, be ratified; lots & premises sold for $562. -Wm Brent, clk.

WED MAY 10, 1809

Lost certificates: issued by Jos Nourse, Reg of Treasury, in favor of John Barnes; dt'd Oct 7, 1800 & Aug 8, 1801. -John Barnes, Gtwn, D C.

FRI MAY 12, 1809

Act passed to divide the city of Washington into 4 wards: west of 14th St-Ward 1; bet 14th west & 2d west-Ward 2; bet 2d St west & 4th St east-Ward 3; east of 4th St east-Ward 4. Geo Andrews, Pres of First Chamber. Rich'd Forrest, Pres of 2d Chamber. Apprv'd, May 8, 1809. Robt Brent, Mayor.

In Chancery, May 15, 1809. Eleanor Hungerford, vs Eliz Bourne, Dorcas Bourne, Thos Reynolds, Jos Blake, Jas Heigh, & Wm E Hungerford & Saml Chew. Bill is to make the rl est of Thos Bourne liable for payment of his debts, in lieu of prsnl prop which was left to cmplnt; to recover money due from S Chew for land in Ky sold him by the dec'd. Eleanor H is Thos' sister; Eliz & Dorcas, his nieces. -N Brewer-R C C.

Jas Butcher, now Govn'r o/Md, vice, Robt Wright, who rsgn'd May 6, 1809.

Died: John Fitzhugh, May 11, at his seat in Stafford Co, Va, age 82 yrs; ntv of Va.

Ranaway-Charles, negro man; has a wife living at Capt Henry Garnet's in Essex, Va; his mthr belongs to Mrs Blair in Fredericksburg. -James Roy, Essex, Tappahannock, Va.

Reward-$20 for Thos Burnett, appr to sail mkg bus., ab't 19 yrs of age; his mthr keeps hse for Mr Clark up Rock Creek, Montg Co, Md. -Danl M'Dougall.

MON MAY 15, 1809
Supposed to be stolen-Milly-negro girl ab't 14 yrs of age; formerly the prop of Mr John Sanders of Pr Wm Co, Va; & his prop when sold by shrf of said Co, which girl I purch'd at said sale. -Jeremiah Sandford jr.

Died: Count Louis De Cobenzel, Mar 22, at Vienna, after a lingering illness, at his hse in Clipstone-St, age 61 yrs, leaves his wife & 6 chldrn, the oldest 9 yrs; he also left 2 dghts by his first wife.

WED MAY 17, 1809
History of Virginia- 4th Vol, left unfinished by death of John D Burk, is now in the hands of author, Skelton Jones. -Petersburg Paper.

Died: on May 9, Mr Benj Patterson, ntv of Delaware, at his residence in Balt Co, Md, formerly a resid of Gtwn, D C; leaves his widow & 6 infant chldrn.

Runaway-Osmond, negro man; svr'l yrs past in possession of Mr W Robinson, late of Fred'k City; he has a wife at Mr Humphries at *Harper's Ferry*. -Thos Richards, Orange Co, Va.

For sale-farm & lots in PG Co, Md, cld *St Osyth*, 750 acs; est of O Carr, dec'd. Apply to Col Sam Hanson of Wash, or Dr Wm Baker, Gtwn. -Jona B Carr, exc, lvng on the premises.

Pblc sale of furn, etc, at John P Moles, F St. -S Speake-auct.

FRI MAY 19, 1809
Geo III King of Britain will be 72 next Jun; Francis II Emperor of Germany & King of Austria was 42 in Feb; Napoleon I Emp of France will be 41 in Aug; Fred'k Wm III King of Prussia will be 40 in Aug; Alex'r I Emp of Russia was 33 in Dec.

John P Lherbette, 81 Maiden La, N Y, obtained a patent from the U S for an improved knapsack.

Mrd: on May 15, Mr Andrew Way jr, of Wash, to Mrs Mary Matilda Pawson, of Balt, by Rev Mr Roberts.

MON MAY 22, 1809
New grocery store, Saml Burch, N J Ave, oppo sec of State.

Orphans Crt of PG Co, Md. May 19, 1809. Prsnl est of Nath'l Clagett, late of PG Co, dec'd. Wm Marshall, Nicholas Young, Wm R Glagett, Hannibal Clagett.

WED MAY 24, 1809
A W Preuss, broker & commission agent at Alexandria, buys & sells merchandize of every description.

Runaway-Rose, black girl, confined in Wash Co, D C, goal; says she belongs to Miss Fanny Fitzjerield of Alexandria. -C Tippett, kpr of jail.

FRI MAY 26, 1809
John Condit, appt'd a Senator by State of N J, vice, Aaron Kitchell, rsgn'd.

MON MAY 29, 1809
Purchasers of prop at public sale of Mrs Rebecca Mackall's prsnl est in Calvert Co, Md in Nov last are reminded their obligations bec due May 23. Alex'r Contee Magruder, esq, at Annapolis, for collection. -Wm Potts, adm d b n of Rebecca Mackall. Fred'k Co, May 29.

Ranaway-Jacob Vails, young negro man, from Wm Fulks, living in Montg Co, Md,
nr the Court Hse.

Wash Co, D C. Edw Langley, insolvent debtor, confined in Wash Co prison, for debt. -Wm Brent, clk.

Nicholas L Queen & Henry M Queen have obtained a license to sell merchandize at vendue in Wash City.

WED MAY 31, 1809
Orphans Crt of Calvert Co, Md. May 10, 1809. Prsnl est of Gilbert Smith, late of said Co, dec'd. -Mordecai Smith, adm.

Hse o/Reps: Petition of Mrs Hamilton, wid of late Gen Alex. Hamilton; hsbnd was Col during Rev war & as such entitled to half-pay; he relinquished his claim because he was a mbr of Congress; prays to be allowed his claim. Referred to comm.

FRI JUN 2, 1809
Mrd: Mr John Smith to Miss Cath Way, both of the town of Alexandria, by Rev A T M'Cormick. [No date given-recent]

MON JUN 5, 1809
Robt Ellis, nr the Navy Yd, has commenced the profession of conveyancer in all its branches; writing is prepared with neatness, correctness & on moderate terms.

Died: Francis Malbone, esq, Senator from R I; he dropped down Jun 4 on his way to divine svc at the Capitol, sudden death.

Runaway, Dick, negro man, committed to my custody; says he formerly belonged to John Watson of Chas Co by whom he was sold to a negro man from Ga. -N Maddox, shrf-PG Co, Md.

For sale or lease: manufacturing mill on Neabsco Run; apply to my agent, Thos T Page, at Neabsco nr Dumfires, Va. -John Tayloe.

Trustees for the town of Bath, Berkley Co, Va:

Rawleigh Colston
Henry St Geo Tucker
Hugh Holmes
John Baker
Henry S Turner
David Hunter
Alfred H Powell
Elisha Boyd
Philip C Pendleton
Adam S Bandridge

Rl est auction-entire rl est yet unsold of Col Chas Beatty, dec'd. John M Beatty, Chas A Beatty, Gtwn.

FRI JUN 9, 1809

John Stephen, insolvent debtor, confined in Wash Co, D C, prison for debt. -Wm Brent, clk.

For sale-the ship, *Allegany,* laying at mouth of Eastern Branch. -Andrew Smith.

Mbrs of Wash City Cncl:

S N Smallwood
A Lindsay
John Law
Alex M'Cormick
J M'Clelland
John Dobbin
Elec Middleton
J S Stevenson
D Rapine
Wm Prout
Jos Parson
P Bradley
Jos Cassin
John Sinclair
N L Queen
A Kerr
G Higdon
T Craven

Pblc auction, at Northumberland Crt Hse, in said Co, Va; 5 contiguous plantations, ab't 2,700 acs; estates formerly belonged to Presley Thornton, & are the same on which he lived. Apply to Col Jas Moore, who lives on them, or Saml Blackwell, esq, lives nr them. -Thos Robinson, nr Chester, Dela; or to W Lewis, at Phil.

Died: Dr Jas Woodhouse, Prof of Chemistry in Univ of Pa.

Edw Lloyd is elected Gov of Md for remainder of current yr.

MON JUN 12, 1809
Died: the celebrated Thos Paine, at New York, Jun 8.

Jas Boddington-determined to pay no debts contracted by any person but myself after this day.

WED JUN 14, 1809
Reward-$10 for return of Rosetta, mulatto girl, prop of Rachel Gantt; her mthr is at the farm of Mr Stoddert's nr Bladensburg. -Edw Gantt.

FRI JUN 16 1809
Crct Crt of Wash Co, D C-In Chancery. Rich'd Soderstrom, vs Saml Goodman, Geo Little & Josiah Quincy. Bill is to compel S Goodman to pay Soderstrom sum of money alleged to be due for Judgment obtained in island of St Thomas; decree in Sup Crt of U S rendered in favor of said Goodman against said Little for lge sum of money bec of capture of brig *Flying Fish* & her cargo, prop of said Goodman, a Danish Burgher of said island, by the said Little, Cmder of U S ship of war, the *Boston;* Josiah Quincey-atty of Little, has the money. Little & Goodman reside out of Wash, D C. -Wm Brent, clk.

In Chancery: ratify sale made by Solomon Holland of rl est of Jas Beall; 270 ½ acs. for $3,246. -Nichl Brewer, Reg C C.

Reward-$100 for negro men, prop of Jas Cassin, residing at Wash City; David bought of Maj Calvert, Mt Airy; & Jim, bought of Mr Saml G Griffith of Balt. -Jas Cassin

MON JUN 19, 1809
Dr I J Comnyn, operating dentiss-practice in Wash & Gtwn.

Ranaway-Jim, mulatto lad; his fr lives in Wash City nr the Navy Yd, by name of Geo Beall, who srv'd his time with Mr John Addison jr; & a mthr, Sophy, who I sold to her hsbnd a few yrs past, has rltvs in Balt. -Rachel Pratt, PG Co, Md.

Decree of Chancellor of Md-sale on premises, all est of Nath'l Washington of St Mary's Co; tract cld *Trent Neck* in St M Co, to which N Washington is entitled in right of his wife Mgt Washington; also prsnl prop of said N Washington. -John Ralph, trustee, Charlotte-Hall, St Mary's Co, Md.

WED JUN 21, 1809
Henry Selby, insolvent debtor, confined in Wash Co, D C prison, for debt.
-Wm Brent, clk.

Sweet Springs, Va-open to those desirous of visiting those waters. -O Towles jr.

FRI JUN 23, 1809
Desirous to sell or exchange ab't 4,000 acs. of old military land, in Mason Co, Va. -John Fenton Mercer, Fredericksburg; [Ltrs directed to me at Gallapolis, Ohio, after Jul 15.]

In Chancery, Jun 16, 1809. Wm Tunnicliff, vs the heirs at law of Basil Warring & Jasper Wirt. Obtain a decree for recording a deed executed by Basil Warring & Jasper Wirt to *Erasmus Gantt, on May 19, 1794, for conveying to E Gantt land in PG Co, cld *Scotland,* also tract cld *Scotland Aforesaid,* cnvyd to Jasper Wirt, by Jacob Wirt; & land bght by Jasper Wirt, of person named Conn; Jasper made pymnt & receipt, no conveyance by Conn or his heirs. Basil Warring died leaving Thos Warring, Basil Warring, Edw Warring, Eleanor Warring, Jane Beall w/o Walter B Beall, *Mary Mitchell w/o Dr Spencer Mitchell, Sally Warring, *Priscilla Gantt w/o John Gantt, & Ann Warring, his heirs at law. Jasper Wirt died leaving *Henry Wirt, Barbara Tilley, Eliza Farrall w/o Thos Farral, a grdght Barbara Beckett w/o [blank] Beckett, Wm Crown, Elisha Wood & Susannah Wood, [space] Mummer w/o Christian Mummer, his heirs at law. [*reside out o/state] -Nich Brewer, RCC.

If Chas Hughes, age ab't 43 yrs, who left Eng in 1799 for Va, supposed to be at Fairfax in 1804-5, will make himself known to Chas Wirgman, merchant, Balt, he will hear something to his advantage. Chas is 5ft 5, red bushy hair, strong & athletic, & sings a good song; reported he keeps a tavern & is married to a widow.

MON JUN 26, 1809
St Mary's Co, Md, Orphans Crt, Jun 13, 1909 [must be typo error 1909] Decandia S Smith, excx of Henry A Smith, late of Chas Co dec'd; ordered to give notice to creditors. -Jas Forrest, Reg wills, St M Co, Md. -Notice followed.-D S Smith-excx.

WED JUN 28, 1809
St Mary's Co, Md, Mar term 1809. Edw T Carpenter praying to divide the rl est of John Carpenter, late of St M Co, dec'd; same wld not admit of division; Jas Carpenter & John H Carpenter, 2 of the reps, reside out of Md. -Jo Harriss, clk.

FRI JUN 30 1809
Notice-Sunday the 2d of Jul next, will be opened the new Roman Catholic Church of St Patrick. Ceremony will be performed by Rev Dr Carroll, Archbishop of Balt; Divine svc by Rt Rev Dr Neale, Bishop of Gortyna.

Reward-$20 for bay mare that strayed from Centreville, Fairfax Co, Va.
-Henry W Ball.

Ranaway-Geo M'Kelden, age ab't 11 yrs. -Wm W Vernon, Pa Ave, Wash City. Reward-one cent.

MON JUL 3, 1809
Died: Henry Drinker, ntv of Phil, age 76 yrs, Jun 26; formerly a merchant in very extensive business.

Died: Mr Jas Davison, age 72 yrs, on Jun 27th; late Professor in Univ of Pa. [Phil, Jun 28.]

WED JUL 5, 1809
Orphans Crt of Wash Co, D C. Jun term-1807. On application of Jas Clagett for ltrs of adm on prsnl est of Thos Shelton, late of Va, dec'd-claiming same as a creditor; ordered to give notice of his said application. -John Hewitt, Rg.

FRI JUL 7, 1809
Ladies with ltrs in Wash Post ofc-Jul 1, 1809:

Charity Austin	Miss Mary B Addison	Eliz G Berry
Mrs Mary Butler	Sarah Bryan	Jane Downs
Cath Daley	Miss Lucy Evans	Hetty W Hall
Susannah B Finch	Eliza Frobust	Mary Fiancon
Sarah Gahagan	Anne C Gregory	Maria Lukins
Kitty Lyons	Eliza Lansdale	Mrs Wm Lansdale
Miss Lansdale	Mrs Lindsey	Rachael Lane
Eliz Lowry	Eliz Lewis	Mrs R R M'Cormick
Mrs Manigault	Nelly Proctor	Miss Charlotte Rind
Betsey Reagan	Eliz Scott	Mary Skook
Mary Watson	Charlotte Williams	Mrs Nelly Williss

Mrs Webb-[Rock Creek]
Mrs Hunter-rep of Wm & Jas Hunter formerly merchants in St John's island

Died: on Jun 25, Mrs Cath Laidler, w/o Mr John Laidler, of *Rose Hall*, Chas Co, Md, age 40 yrs, after a long & painful illness.

MON JUL 10, 1809
Died: Lord Dunmore, lately in England, formerly Gov of Va.

Pblc auction-on premises, nr the Navy Yd gate, all prsnl prop of Jas Boddington, dec'd. -Robt Rose & Robt Brown, excs.

Crct Crt of Wash Co, D C. Godfrey Haga vs Chas Cist's reps. Ratify sale made by Phineas Bradley, trust; brick hse on lot 6 sq 377-sum $1,005. -Wm Brent, clk.

Newport, R I-Christopher Grant Champlin elected Senator to U S Congress, vice, Francis Malbone, dec'd.

Auction sale-furniture in front of Mr Geo Miller's hse on F St.

WED JUL 12, 1809
To let-hse in occupation of J M Baker in F St. Also hse on Pa av, occupied by Mr Wm Cooper. -Wm Cocking-19th St W.

Ranaway-negro Sam, from Walter Waters lvng nr Clarksburg, Montg Co, Md.

For sale-furniture at my hse on Capitol Hill -Henry Tims.

FRI JUL 14, 1809
Pblc auction on Aug 7 of 39 lots of ground in Wash City. -Sam Elliot jr, trustee.

Crct Crt of Wash Co, D C. Suit of Solomon Davis against Abiel Jenners & Deborah Jenners his wife, & Ferdinand Fairfax.

Order of Orphans Crt of PG Co, Md. Sale of remaining prsnl est of the late Mr John Campbell. -Wm Bruce, adm.

MON JUL 17, 1809
For sale or rent-plantation where I now live, ab't 10 miles from Alexandria. -Michl Broad, Accotink.

Reward-$10 for Ally, negro woman, who absconded from me; I purch'd her from Mr Custis. -Mary Ressler, Alexandria.

For sale, by Lewis Deblois, his store nr the Navy Yd-fine spirits, coffee, etc, in Wash.

Mrd: on Jun 19, Horace H Edwards, esq, of Wash, to Miss Maria G Butler, of New Haven, Conn, at New Haven.

Ran away-2 apprentices to the shoe-making trade: John Long, ab't 16 yrs of age, & Geo W Brooks, ab't 15 yrs of age. -John Minchin.

WED JUL 19, 1809
Wm Emack,in the mercantile line, is remv'g his store to Fredericksburg, Va; his hse & store on E Capt st are for rent; apply after 10 days to Mr Adam Lindsay, nr the Navy Yd.

For sale-lands in Ohio & Ky. Per last will of Robt Means, dec'd. Apply to Mr Walter Dun, residing in or nr Chillicothe, Ohio. -Dan'l Call, exc, Richmond.

FRI JUL 21, 1809
Act discharging John Heard from his imprisonment; late collector of Port of Amboy, N J; he must first convey all his estate for use of U S. -J B Varnum, spkr of Hse of Reps.

Reward-$100 for Tom, mulatto fellow; & Isaac, black fellow; purch'd latter of Mr Diggs in Chas Co nr Brian's town. -Rich'd Snowden, PG Co, Md.

Ranaway-Debby, mulatto woman; did belong to est of Mr John Bunbury, dec'd, Boyd's Hole, Va. -Clement Kennedy, o/Wash; was of *Sandy Point*, Chas Co, Md.

MON JUL 24, 1809
Mrd: Mr Erastus Roberts, printer of Hudson, N Y, to Miss Eliz Jenkins, of Alexandria, Columbia, Jul 18, in Wash, by Rev Mr M'Cormack.

Caleb Hessey has opened a shop oppo the West Mkt Hse: white smith, lock & gun smith business, cuttlery & bell-hanging.

For sale-700 acs o/land for $14,000, in Calvert Co, Md with 2 story brick mansion hse. -Henry Gardiner, St Leonard's, Calv Co, Md.

WED JUL 26, 1809
Died: Allen Bowie Duckett, esq, age 35 yrs, Jul 19, at his seat in PG Co, Md, Assoc Judge of Crct Crt of D C.

Notice-She will not pay any debts contracted by Wm Prime, heretofore.
-Zipporah Corning.

Horatio Moore of Chas Co, Md, has by his deed of trust, assigned all his prop rl & prsnl, to pay all his creditors. -Peter Hoffman jr, 103 Balt St, Balt, Md.

FRI JUL 28, 1809
Died: on Jul 27, Mr John Dempsey, late chf clk to U S Sen; funeral from his late dwlg.

Mrd: on Jul 26, Chas Lee, esq, of Alex to Mrs Mgt C Peyton, of Fauquier Co, Va, by Rev Jas Thompson.

Sale of farm in Montg Co, Md, late resid of Saml Turner, dec'd; ab't 700 acs.
-Tho Turner, Saml Turner, excs.

MON JUL 31, 1809
Runaway-Andrew, negro man, from Isaac Lake's farm, Fielding Lynn, living in Loudon Co, Va, nr Middleburg.

WED AUG 2, 1809
Orphans Crt of Wash Co, D C. Jul 28, 1809. Prsnl est of Edw L Smith, late of said Co, dec'd. -Mgt Smith, adm.

Calvert Co Crt-Md, May term, 1809. Application of Wm Spencer & wife-2 of the reps of John M'Dowell, dec'd; would est admit of division; stated it wld. Some of the reps, to wit: Ann Blackburn, Jas Ellis & Dolly his wife & Alice Blackburn, live out of Md. -Wm S Morsell, clk, C C.

Edw Lloyd, esq, Gov of Md: offers $300 reward for return of Thos Burk, lately sentenced to suffer death, for rape of Cath Maria Brawner, infant under age of 12 yrs; he escaped from jail on Jul 4.

FRI AUG 4, 1809
Died: on May 7, Rt Rev Beilby Porteus, age 79 yrs, at Episc Hse at Fulham; Lord Bshp of London, Dean of Chapel Royal.

The editor of the *Monitor*, having ascertained that his subscription was not sufficient to sustain the establishment, to relinquish same; printing materials for sale. -J B Colvin, his resid on F St at 11th, Wash City.

Orphans Crt of PG Co, Md. Aug 4, 1809. Prsnl est of Saml Lusby, late of PG Co, dec'd. -John Lusby, exc.

MON AUG 7, 1809
Sale-decree of Chancery Crt: *Partnership*, 934 acs, in Anne Arundel Co, Md; formerly owned by Wm Hammond, dec'd; nr Maj Philip Hammond's mill. apply to Mr Valentine Brown, living nr the premises. -Basil Brown, trustee.

Mrd: Count Rumford, recently, to wid/o M Vereecy, in Paris.

WED AUG 9, 1809
Absconded-negro Tom; purch'd of Capt J S Brooks ab't 5 yrs ago-may be in Upper Marlboro. -Henry Basford, mgr at farm of Mr Isaac Ducket, on South Rvr nr Annapolis.

FRI AUG 11, 1809
Rt Rev John Randolph, late Bshp of Bangor, translated to Metropolitan See of London, vice, Dr Bielby Porteous, dec'd.

Turpentine for sale-H Catlett's Drug store on F St, Wash.

MON AUG 14, 1809
Died: lately, Jonathan Trumbull, esq, Gov of Conn, age 66 yrs, at his seat in Lebanon.

Died: Mrs Frances Gwynn, age 71 yrs, Aug 5, in Gtwn.

WED AUG 16, 1809
Orphans Crt of Wash Co, D C; sale at late dwlg hse of Eliz Whitewood, dec'd, in Gtwn, all prsnl prop. -Ann B Powell-adm.

Absconded-my hse svt, Anthony, mulatto. -C W Goldsborough.

Lost-a Balt bill of $100, nr Barry's Wharf. -Jos Varden

FRI AUG 18, 1809
Crt of Chancery-sale of rl est of Solomon Jones, late of St Mary's Co, dec'd, whereon he lived, viz: *Plumb Point*-375 acs, & pasture ground-18 acs; Great Mill Post ofc within 1 ½ miles. -Enoch J Millard, trust. Leonardtwn, Md.

Runaways committed to Wash Co, D C, jail: negro John, says he belongs to John Roberts, Bond St, Balt, Md; Basil, says he was the prop of Jacob Smith, of Balt, Md. -C Tippett, kpr of jail.

MON AUG 21, 1809
Creditors of late Henry Addison are to attend at tavern of John Smith Brookes in Upper Marlborough, Sep 28. -Thos G Addison, Dennis Magruder, adms.

Orphans Crt of Montg Co, Md-excs of Saml Turner, late of said Co, dec'd, are to give notice for creditors. -Solomon Holland, Reg. Said notice followed-on prsnl est of Saml Turner. -Thos Turner, Saml Turner, excs, of Gtwn.

WED AUG 23, 1809
Timothy Pickering, Sen of U S from Mass, has an action for libel against Baptiste Irvine, editor of the Whig, printed at Balt; laid his damages at $10,000.

Caution-against purchasing articles belonging to partnership of Lewis Talbott & myself. -Clement Venable, Wash City.

For sale-at Long's Hotel, a negro man, woman & their dght. Family formerly belonged to John Boothe, dec'd & were willed by him to the chldrn of Wm Carpenter, dec'd. -John Cator.

FRI AUG 25, 1809
Fire broke out in Norfolk yesterday week which consumed 5 warehses; the warehse of Mr Thos Dickson, fire proof, stands.

MON AUG 28, 1809
Univ of Athens, Ga, conferred degree of Dr of Laws on Joel Barlow of Wash City.

For sale-1100 acs on N W Branch, Montg Co, Md with dwlg hse; 113 acs on *Paint Branch*, Montg Co, nr Peter Kemp's Mill; svr'l tracts in PG Co, adj the lands of Maj Williams & Messr Berry. -Josias E Beall, Jas A Beall.

WED AUG 30, 1809
Died: on Aug 6, Mrs Sarah M'Mahon, consort o/ Mr Wm M'Mahon, at Cumberland, Md, after a severe & painful indisposition.

Partnership bet Jos Bentley & Wm Wood; silver smiths & clock & watch mkrs, is dissolved by mutual consent. [-Wash City.]

FRI SEP 1, 1809
Longevity-died in Feb 1806 at Gloves, nr Athenry, Ire, Dennis Coorobee, of Ballendaugin, age 117 yrs; mrd 7 times, the first at age 21 yrs; his last wife of 26 yrs survived him. He mrd her at age 93; he had 48 chldrn, 236 grchldrn, 944 g grchldrn, & 25 g g grchldrn, oldest now 4 yrs. Of 1253 dscndts 487 survive him. His last wife had 6 sons-youngest is 18. [Taken from documents kept by Mr Coorobee]

Died: Saml Stearns, L L D, celebrated astronomer in U S; at Brattleboro, Vt.

Claims against prsnl est of Adderson Conaway, late of PG Co, dec'd; submit same A S A P. -Eleanor Conaway, admx.

Orphans Crt of Chas Co, Md. Aug 26, 1809. Ltrs of adm on prsnl est of John Neale, late of Chas Co, dec'd. -Jas Neale of Jas, exc.

Orphans Crt of St Mary's Co, Md-sale of 3 tracts of land formerly the prop of John Carpenter, late of St M Co, dec'd; on St Clement's Bay, 175 acs & 120 acs; also tract of 70 acs. -Jas Forrest, Ethelbert Cecil, Jas Morgan, com'rs of St M Co.

Ranaway-Harry, negro fellow. -John Jarbeo, living in lower end of Montg Co, Md, nr Vansville.

Died: Haydn, celebrated musical composer, at Vienna, May 31.

MON SEP 4, 1809
For sale-frame hse on Va av bet 7th & 8th. -Wm Sisterson.

WED SEP 6, 1809
Orphans Crt of Worcester Co, Md. Aug 22, 1809. Prsnl est of John Cutler, late of said Co, dec'd. -Rowland E Bevans-adm.

Rev W L Turner, Principal of Raleigh Acad & pastor of the city, intends to resign. -N Jones, Pres, Raleigh, N C.

Orphans Crt of PG Co, Md. Sep 4, 1809. Ltrs of adm on prsnl est of Nath'l Newton, late of PG Co, dec'd. -Wm Marbury, Jos N Burch-adms.

FRI SEP 8, 1809
Rev Walter D Addison, of Gtwn, will brd & instruct in Latin, Greek, reading, writing & arith, a few more young gentlemen.

Absconded-my apprentice, Geo Lathan, age bet 18 & 19 yrs. -Chas Varden, N J Ave, Wash City. -Reward, six cents.

Benj Adamson, cabinet mkr, has taken the 2d hse on Pa ave, formerly occupied by Mr Webb, to carry on business.

MON SEP 11, 1809
Seamen impressed now on board *L'Africaine*, [Americ ctzns]:

Edw Swaine	John Ferguson	Geo Wilson
*John Butler	*John Williams	*Ambrose Cross

[*Men of color; frig is now lying in Annapolis.]

Sheep breeder notice, Merino breed. -Jos Dougherty, Wash.

MON AUG 21, 1809
Mrs E Steward, of Chatham Co, Pittsburg, has 9 dghts; the dghts have 13, 12, 9, 15, 10, 13, 11 & 9 chldrn; chldn of 3d generation was 67, making an aggregate of 159 for 57 yrs-11 of this number has died. -S C paper.

Died: Field Mrsh'l Lt D'aspre, of his wounds on Jul 8 & was buried at Brunn. -From the Danube, Jul 10.

Committed to my custody as runaway-negro lad, Dick; says he is prop of Mr Furton of Alex, D C. -J M'Ceney-shrf-A A Co, Md.

To exchange for prop in Wash City, my hse on Prince St, Alexandria. -Dr Chas Douglas, Alexandria.

FRI SEP 15, 1809
For sale at my hse-hsehld & kitchen furn, milk cow & 5 hogs, flat bottomed boat. -Jacob Chandler.

Dirs of bank of Wash:	Dan'l Carroll of Dud'n	Geo Blagden
John Davidson	Joel Barlow	Robt Brent
Wm Cranch	Wash. Boyd	Robt Sewall
Fred'k May	Geo Calvert	Jos Forrest
Jas S Stevenson		

For sale-furn & library of late Allen B Duckett, esq, at hse of Mr Peter, nr lower bridge on Rock Crk where Mr D resided.

Henry Roberts has 2 stray horses at his plantation in Montg Co, Md, nr the Great Falls of Potomac.

MON SEP 18, 1809
For sale-farm & mill seat, 5 miles from Wash City, adj farm of Widow C Diggs; 137 acs. -Issachar Scholfield.

Died: Mr John Doyne, Sep 15, long a resident of Wash.

WED SEP 20, 1809
Info given to Messrs Thos & Geo E Fakes, or their reps if dead, that prop of considerable val nr Bath, Berkeley Co, Va, has fallen by will to them thru death of their Uncle Absolem M'cay. Messrs Fakes' parents, John & Anne Fake, formerly resided nr Mr Snowden's, , Bladensburg, Md. -John Dugan jr, nr Martinsburg Co, Va.

Dr Adam Seybert, nominated by Rpblcn ctzns of Phil, as candidate for seat in Congress, vice, Dr Say who rsgn'd.

Died: Geo Clinton jr, at N Y, formerly a Rep in Congress.

FRI SEP 22, 1809
Ranaway-Caesar, mulatto man, from Gerard Alexander Sr, living in Brenton, Pr Wm Co, Va.

Orphans Crt of Chas Co, Md. Sale at plantation of late dec'd, Dr Dan'l Jenifer, nr Port Tobacco; 21 negroes, 60 head of cattle, etc. -Dan of St Thos Jenifer-adm of Dr D J, dec'd.

Union bank of Gtwn -Subscriptions available at Union Tavern, Gwtn:

Robt Beverly	Thos Beal of Geo	Ninian Magruder
Elisha Riggs	Andrew Smith	John Peter
Francis Dodge	Saml Davidson	Thos Corcoran
Adam King	John Teakle	Thos Turner
Dan'l Renner	Chas J Nourse	Geo Magruder
Rich'd Parrott.		
Fredericktown-	Wm Campbell	John M'Pherson
Wm M Beall	Geo Creger jr	Lawrence Brengle.
Hagerstown-	Ely Williams	Dr Schnively
Saml Ringold	John Harry	Edw Tilghman.
At Rockville-	Dr John Bowie	Caleb Bentley
Thos Riggs	Thos Davis	Bern'd Gelpin
Upper Marlborough-	Gen Walter Bowie	Edw Calvert
Isaac Duckett	Dr W Hill	John Hodges
Libertytown-	Francis B Sappington	Abraham Crabster
Joshua Delaplane	Robt Cummings	Jeremiah Browning
Taneytown-	John M'Calip	John Ross Key
Jos Little	Thos Jones	Dr J S Smith
Port Tobacco-	John E Ford [P T]	Col Philip Stewart
Francis Digges	Gen Caleb Hawkins	Col Saml Chapman.

[Limit 1500 shares per person or corporation]

MON SEP 25, 1809
For sale-land nr Bladensburg, 100 acs; also female servants. -Mgt Adams.

WED SEP 27, 1809
Ofcrs of bank of Wash appt'd Sep 26: Overton Carr-teller; Wm Dupuy-bkkpr; Isaac K Hanson-disc clk; Henry Johnson-runner; Laurence Hays-porter; Henry Whetcroft-notary pblc.

Died: on Sep 21, Mr Alex'r Reinegle, age 62 yrs, one of the mgrs of the Balt & Phil theatres; musical composer.

Polly Ross, my wife, has eloped from my bed & board; I am not liable for any of her contracts. -Saml Ross.

Wash Co, D C-In Chancery. John McLeod, vs Alex'r Cochran jr & wife. McLeod purch'd of Cochran, jr, lot 29 sq 904, Wash City; May 16, 1808 dfndnts executed a deed to J McLeod; same has not been recorded. -Wm Brent, clk.

Died: Mr Harwood, comedian, in the neighborhood of Phil.

FRI SEP 29, 1809
Died: Nath'l Craufurd, esq, age 44 yrs, Sep 19, at Greenwood, PG Co, Md.

Partnership of Robt & Walter Clark [painters] is dissolved by mutual consent; Robt Clarke Randolph will continue bus. -Pa Ave

MON OCT 2, 1809
Orphans Crt of PG Co, Md. Prsnl est of John Marlow, dec'd. -Eliz Marlow, excx.

Fred'k Wm Brune, esq, has been temporarily appt'd Vice Cnsl of his Danish Majesty for Md; will reside in Balt.

Jas Claypole, tanner & currier of Chestertown, Kent Co, Md, had his bark mill hse destroyed by fire by a malicious person.

WED OCT 4, 1809
Rich'd D Boyd has opened a livery stable back of Carroll's Long Row, Wash.

John C Thompson & Co-leather manufactured & for sale, in High St, Gtwn, oppo Mr Milligan's bk-store.

Mr & Mrs Gray have mv'd their English school to G St-Wash.

FRI OCT 6, 1809
<u>Ladies with ltrs in Wash Post Ofc-Oct 1</u>:

		Mrs Delia Byus
Mary Butler	Mrs Brackenridge	Mrs Eliz Berry
Jemima Costen	Mrs Dames	Louisa Evans
Miss Mary Graham	Sally Galagan	Mrs A Grant
Cath Goldsborough	Eliz Lovell	Rebecca Morrow
Rebecca Russ	Rachel Snodden	Deborah Spooner
Rebecca Scott	Rosett or Matilda Smith	Mrs Thompson
Eliz Thomas	Mrs Maria Van-Zandt	Miss Verlinder

MON OCT 9, 1809

Ltr from Chancellor Livingston to Elkanah Watson, of Pittsfield, Mass; Lebanon Springs, Sep 12, 1809. Subj-Merino wool.

Mrd: on Aug 29, Mr Jas Murray jr, lately of Wash, to Miss Charlotte Racliffe, of Worcester Co, Md.

Leg of Tenn chose Jos McMinn-spkr of Senate & Gen Jos Dickson of Hse of Reps.

To rent-part of the Six Bldgs in Wash lately occupied by Mr Lansdale-possession immediately. John Heugh, Gtwn; Honore Martin, Rockville.

St Mary's Co Crt-Petition of John B Davis, that the rl est of Hezekiah Davis, late of St M Co dec'd, wld admit of division; same wld not admit to div; reps to appear. Judith Davis resides out of this state. -Jo Harris, clk.

Cabinet & chair manufactory, Pa av. -Wm Worthington, jr.

WED OCT 11, 1809

For sale-sq 464 in Wash, with improvements of David Hepburn, dec'd, & lease of 14 yrs. -Alice Hepburn, Alex'r Hepburn.

Died: on Oct 6, Wm Claiborne, old resid of Richmond, & f/o W C C Claiborne, esq, Gov of Terr of Orleans, in Richmond.

Died: Maj W Armistead, Oct 7, old Rev ofcr.

<u>Commencement at Princeton, Sep 27, 1809, College of N J.</u>

Salutory-Mr Geo W Cook of N C; Jacob G McWhorter of S C.

Orations delivered by:
F Anderson of Md
Thos C Ryerson of N J
Wm A M'Dowell of N J
T T Stanley of N C
Wm Finney of Pa
Thos Skinner of N C
John Wiley o/Dist of Col
Ezek Forman of Md
Saml Eager of N Y
John S Wood of N J
Chas Brown of N Orleans
John De Witt of N Y.
<u>Valdictry</u>-Benj C Howard of Md

<u>Bach of Arts</u> conferred on:
Franklin Anderson of Md
Lewis P Bayard of Princeton, N J
Elias Boudinot of Newark, N J
Joshua G Brinckle of Wilmington, Dela
Chas F Brown of New Orleans Jacob
R Castner of Somerset, N J
John S Conger of Orange, N Y
Geo W Cook of Newbern, N C
John De Witt of Greene, N Y
Volckest P Douw of Albany, N Y
Jacob B Drake of Somerset, N J
Saml W Eager of Orange, N Y
Wm Finney of Chester, Pa
Esekiel Forman of Eastern Shore, Md
Chas D Hasbrouck, of Ulster, N Y
Chas W Henry of N Y
Lewis D Henry of N Y
John Hopkins of Lancaster, Pa
Benj C Howard of Balt, Md
Moses T Hunton of Martinsburg, Va
Robt M Livingston of N Y
Wm A M'Dowell of Elizabeth town, N J
Clymer Ross of Phil

Jacob G M'Whorter of Sumpter, S C
Jonathan Pimmer of Marietta, Ohio
Thos C Ryerson of Sussex, N J
Johnson P Scudder of Monmouth, N J
John G Sims of Phil
Wm R Weeks of Steuben, N Y
Geo Douglass Wise of Eastern Shore, Va
Thos B Salter of N Y
Nich G R Rhea of Trent, N J
Ch Thomas of Morris, N J
Chas Seely of Cumberland
Thos T Stanley of Newbern, N C
John Wiley of Dist of Col
John S Wood of Cumberland, N J.
Thos H Skinner & Wm Skinner of Edenton, N C
Abraham Voorhies of N Brunswick, N J
Mstr of Arts:

Lewis P Balch	Isaac Blackford	Enoch Burt
Jas T Clarke	Edw Colston	Jon Conover
Janathan Cook	Ely Cooly	John Cruse
Jacob F Field	John Howard	Robt S Green
Fred'k Frelinghuysen	Jas Iredell	Christopher Hughes
Arnold Naudian	Nath'l Wyekoff	Rich'd B Magruder
Thos L Woodruff		

& alumni of this college & on Rev Jonathan Freeman of Cumberland Co, N J.
Dr of Divinity on: Rev Theodore Dehon of R I; Rev John B Romeyn of N Y; Rev Aaron Woolworth of Long Island.

FRI OCT 13, 1809
Caution-I am determined not to pay any debts contracted by my wife, Nelly. -Geo Rice.

Geo Reynolds has opened school at Broad-Crk nr Piscataway, PG Co, Md.

For sale-the estate where I live in Montg Co, Md, 350 & 550 acs. -Benj G Orr, *Honeywood*

MON OCT 16, 1809
Orphans Crt of PG Co, Md: sale at late dwlg plantation of Wm Warman Berry, dec'd, in PG Co; all prsnl est. Ann Berry, admx; Archd Van Horn, adm.

Mrd: on Oct 10, Mr Jas Wilson, of U S N, to Miss Harriett Balch, d/o Rev S B Balch, of Gtwn, Columbia, by Rev David Wiley.

WED OCT 18, 1809
Ranaway-Isaac Dorsey, negro, from John Winemiller living in Montg Co, Md.

Sale-at hse of Wm Sanford on M St, nr the Navy Yd; furniture & sundry articles. -N L & H M Queen, auc.

Ranaway, Esme Richardson, appr to boot & shoemkg bus., age 19 yrs. -Jas Patterson, Wash.

Persons having demands against me, call on board the U S brig *Nautilus* at the Navy Yd-expect to sail soon. -Peter Joseph.

FRI OCT 20, 1809
Augusta, Maine, Sep 22, 1809. On Fri, Jabez Meiggs & others belonging to Malta, in Kennebec Co, were committed to jail, chgd with the murder of Paul Chadwick, assist srvyr.

MON OCT 23, 1809
Mrd: Mr Henry W Ball, of Fairfax Co, Va, to Miss Cath B Frost, of Wash, Oct 19, by Rev Mr M'Cormick.

Navy Yd Rifle Vols to meet at Lt Dobbins. -Edw Fitzgerald, sec. Jo Davis, of Abel, 1st Serj.

Copartnership of Drs J H Blake & G T Greenfield, is dissolved this day, by mutual consent.

For sale-200 acs of land, on which I now live, laying in Montg Co, Md. -Edw Willett.

In Chancery-Oct 18, 1809. Rich'd T Lowndes & Geo Calvert, excs of Benj Lowndes, vs Wm Dent Beall, Thos Hewett & Anne his wife, Theodore Beall, Basil Beall & Ariana his wife & Levi Beall. John Beall, Oct 5, 1799 executed a deed of trust of svr'l tracts of land & svr'l negroes to Benj Lowndes for payment of his debts; J Beall died intestate; Wm Dent Beall, Thos Hewett & Anne his wife & Levi reside out of state. -Nichs Brewer, Reg Cur Can. [Md]

WED OCT 25, 1809
Auction sale-hsehld furn, at hse of Thos Y Spregel, F St.

John Bridges, Baker, center of Bridge St, Gtwn. [Ad]

FRI OCT 27, 1809
I have declined the sale of my prsnl estate as advertised in this paper. -R W Harwood.

MON OCT 30, 1809
Trenton, Oct 23. On Tue last, the sale of the stock of the late Jos Capner, of Flemington, took place, attended by farmers from Pa; he was well known in improvement of sheep.

Treaty concluded at Ft Wayne on Sep 30th by W H Harrison, Gov of Indiana Terr & com'r on part of U S with Miamies, Potawatamies & Eel Rvr tribes of indians. -John Johnston, Indian agent.

Mrd: on Oct 29, Mr Fred'k A Wagler, merchant of Wash, to Miss Susana Hinton of PG Co, Md, by Rev Mr Addison.

Partnership of Honis Newton, Wash, & Jas Ward, Alexandria, Va; dissolved by mutual consent as of Sep 14.

Shrf's sale-farm whereon John Orme at present resides-238 acs, stock.at suit of Ninian Magruder use of Upton Beall, one do, at suit of Upton Beall, one do, at suit of Mgt Beall & Upton Beall, adms of Brook Beall, & one do at suit of Dennis Lackland & for ofcrs fees due subscriber. -John Fleming, shrf, Montg Co, Md.

WED NOV 1, 1809
Dr Davis, Surg of the 6th Regt who was arrested by Col Simonds, has been tried by a Genr'l Crt Martial at Ft Columbus and *honorably acquitted* .

Capt Wm P Bennett, of 6th Regt U S infantry, has had his sword restored to him by the decision of Genr'l Crt Martial at Ft Columbus, & rec'd command of his company.

FRI NOV 3, 1809
Prospectus of New Rpblcn nwspr to be established in Fredericktown, Md, *The Freeman of Frederic.* -Saml Magill, ntv Americ.

Runaway-Henaw, negro man, committed to Fred'k Co, Md jail; says he belongs to Mr John Ray of Bath Co, Va. -Ezra Mantz, shrf o/Fred'k Co, Md.

Strayed or stolen at Rinker's Tavern, nr Leesburg, horse & mare; deliver to Thos Lyttleton Moore in Leesburg, Loudon Co, Va or to Dan'l Eversoll, nr Key's Ferry. Reward-$50.

For sale: my tract of land on *Collington Branch*, adj Mr Walter Bowie's & Mr Benj Ogle's estates in PG Co, Md, 272 ½ acs. with dwlg hse. -Geo Hilleary, PG Co, Md.

Strayed-black horse; return to Robt M Key, Piscataway, Md.

MON NOV 6, 1809
Persons with claims against Col Luke Marbury, dec'd, late of PG Co-Md, to exhibit same. -John F Bowie, Colmore Beans, excs.

For sale-rl & prsnl prop of Robt D Reeder; *Workington Park*, land where he now lives: 700 acs, for his just debts. Jo Harriss, trustee, Leonard town, Md.

WED NOV 8, 1809
Died: Lt Genr'l Alex'r MacKenzie Fraser in England.

Assembly at hotel of Rich'd Smyth, Detroit, Michican Terr on Oct 10, 1809; to pick Gov't of said Terr. Augustus B Woodward, Chf Justice of said Terr-Pres; Geo Hoffman, esq, sec. Cmtee: Jas Henry, Jas May & Solomon Sibley.

Mr John Wormly of Cumberland Co, Pa, planted 2 pumpkin seeds which produced 12 pumpkins. Seth Hall of Fairfield, Conn, has a sgl stalk of indian corn that produced 51 ears upon it.

Died: Saml White, esq, at his lodgings this morning; Rep from Dela in Senate of U S. -Wilmington, Del, Nov 4.

FRI NOV 10, 1809
Ltr from gentleman in County of Barnstable to his friend in Boston, Oct 25, 1809. Trial of 2 embargo smuggling cases: David Scudder & Jos Gage vs John Freeman & John Chipman, inspecs of the revenue, for detaining the schn'r *Eliz* & her cargo. Timothy Crowell & others vs Mr Otis, collector, for detaining schn'r *Hornet* & cargo; cases argued by Messrs Sprout & Whitman for plntfs & by Mr Bidwell & Blake for dfndnts. Judge Thatcher presiding. Juries in both cases-verdict in favor of the defendants.

Mrs Jerome Patterson of Balt, first wife of Jerome Bonaparte, has been created a Duchess of hse of Napoleon, salary-50,000 crowns per annum; her son is created a Prince of the French Empire; Col Tousard, late of Americ Rev Army, appt'd Gov with rank of Genr'l. Balt, Md is to be their residence for present.

Orphans Crt of St Mary's Co, Md. Pblc sale at hse of Geo Cole, dec'd, of said Co-negroes, furn, stock, carpenters tools. -Thos Cole, adm, nr the Great Mills.

FRI NOV 13, 1809
Died: Meriwether Lewis, esq, Gov of La, by suicide; Oct 11th at hse of Mr Grinder, nr the Indian Line in Tenn.

Horace H Edwards advertises gin, cheese & window glass for sale. Wash City.

Nathan Prather, residing nr Vansville, brought a stray horse before me. -Gabriel T Vanhorne.

WED NOV 15, 1809
Mrd: on Nov 8, Geo M Troup, mbr of Hse o/Reps from Ga, to Miss Ann Carter, d/o late Geo Carter, by Rev Mr Gibson. Alexandria, Nov 11.

Lexington, Oct 28. Ltr dt'd Russelville, Oct 20, 1809. Meriwether Lewis was buried Oct 12 ab't 40 miles beyond Nashville on Natchez Rd. Gov Lewis had arrv'd weak from a recent illness at Natchez, showed marks of mental derangement; few hrs later he took a gun & shot himself twice & then cut his throat. Additional info says he also shot himself twice in the body & cut the arteries in his thighs & arms; he had drawn bills to a considerable amount on the Gov't of U S. No appropriations had been made for same & they came back protested. [Mrs Grinder was in her hse with her chldrn & svts, Mr Grinder was away, Lewis was on his way to Wash] Appears he leaves a widowed mthr.

Libel suit on Oct 27, case of John C Wright, edtr of *Troy Gazette*, vs Francis Adancourt, edtr of *Farmer's Reg*. Wright was accused of swearing falsely in affidavit to put off trial pending bet himself & Chas Seldon. Verdict-$800 damages & cost. -New York Paper.

The remains of Maj Genr'l Anthony Wayne, late Cmder in Chief of the armies of U S were raised from the U S Garrison on Lake Erie & transferred to Chester county, late resid & birth place of the Genr'l. Occasion was under command of Capt Abram Phillips of the Great Valley, Chester Co; met at Gen Wayne's Inn kept by Mr Campbell Harris; Field ofcrs-Col Wm Harris & Jos Pearce; Issaac Wayne, esq, the son, & Wm Ratlee, esq, son-in-law of the Genr'l followed; Mr Chas Fahnestock Spoke; interrment at St David's Chr Cem; Rev David Jones, Chaplain to the Genr'l delivered a discourse. -From Dela & Chester Co Federalist.

FRI NOV 17, 1809

Edw Lloyd, esq, was re-elected Gov of Md on Nov 13.

Ranaway-Saml Deedle, appr to cabinet mkg bus, age 20 yrs. -Benj Adamson, Alexandria.

To be sold-lots 16 & 17, sq 101 in Wash City; deed of trust dt'd Jan 16, 1805, bet Saml Wilson, of the one part, & the undersigned of the other part, to satisfy John P Van Ness of a debt of $76.77 with int, due from Wilson to Van Ness. -Jas Davidson, trustee.

Jenkin Whiteside, esq, was re-elected a Sen of U S from Tenn.

MON NOV 20, 1809

Meeting held on Nov 1, 1809 at Gtwn: attended by -Jos Kent of PG Co, Md; Thos Chramphin, of Montg Co, Md; Henry Manadier, of A A Co, Md; John Mason of Gtwn & Tench Ringgold of Wash Co, D C. Topics: Encouraging home manufactures & rearing of domestic animals.

Died: Matthew Bolton, esq, F R S, in England; funeral tk place Aug 24 & 600 workmen followed the corpse. [Date of death not included.]

WED NOV 22, 1809

Mrd: on Nov 19, Mr Simeon Matlock to Miss Sarah Y Dove, both of Wash, by Rev Mr Rozell.

Two stray cows may be found at the farm of A Bradley, jr, near Tenleytown.

Leg of Md have elected Messrs-Jas Butcher, Geo E Mitchell Thos W Hall, Reverdy Ghiselin & Lewis Duvall, Cncl to the Gvrnr.

Pblc auction-farm in PG Co, Md, cld *Mount Calvert*, late the prop of Mr John Brown, dec'd, being part of two tracts, cld *Mount Calvert Manor & Beall's Gift*-ab't 400 acs; bet Up Marlborough & Nottingham. -Trueman Tyler, trustee.

FRI NOV 24, 1809
Stolen or strayed from the Commons in Wash City-a horse. [mouse-colored] -Patrick Donaho, nr the Hotel, Wash.

Rich'd Ballad, taylor & habit maker; now a mstr taylor; commenced his business in apt adj the new store belonging to Jos Wheaton, on F St, Wash.

MON NOV 27, 1809
In Chancery, Nov 4, 1809. Isachar & Mahlon Scholfield, vs Theodorick M'Carty, & Dame Fitzhugh, Mary Brent, Henry Lee, & Nath'l Pendleton. Ratify sales by Jos L Scholfield, trustee; moiety of the *Adelphi Mills* & adj 30 acs sold for $5,000 & 27 acs sold for $310; prop was struck off to Wm A Scott, who, the report says was the cmplnt's agent, & the cmplnts are returned as the purchasers. -Nich Brewer-R C C.

For sale-brick hse, lately occupied as a tavern by Mr Hugh Drummond, Va av, So K & 7th st E. -Notley Maddox, John Law.

Mr Wm H Dorsey, merchant, Balt, Md is seeking a ltr sent to him from the Post Ofc in Wash, Aug 10, but not rec'd.

Jas Young has remv'd his store lately from Balt to Wash City, has opened in a store lately occupied by Capt Burch, N J Ave; liquors, groc, shoes & hdwre.

Died: Gen Wade Hampton-authority of the Whig of Baltimore. [Dec 25 paper-Gen Wade Hampton not dead]

WED NOV 29, 1809
The Spirit of Seventy Six, formerly printed in Richmond, Va will commence this wk in Wash City. -Edw C Stanard-Wash.

Orphans Crt of Wash Co, D C. Nov 1, 1809. Prsnl est of John Doyne, late of said City dec'd. -Mary Doyne, admx.

Died: Evan Alexander, suddenly on Oct 28, late a rep in Congress from N C.

St Andrew's Soc to meet at Lindsay's Htl, Wash. -John Murdoch, sec.

David B Mitchell, esq, chosen Govn'r of Ga, vice Jared Irvin.

FRI DEC 1, 1809
Orphans Crt of PG Co, Md, sale at late dwlg hse of Mrs Eleanor Beall, dec'd, nr Bladensburg; all prsnl prop. -Jas Shaw.

MON DEC 4, 1809
For sale-order of Orphans Crt of PG Co, Md, at late dwlg of Thos Woodward, dec'd: negroes & stock. -Abraham B Woodward & Wm R Woodward, adms.

Union College lottery, New York, mgrs: Wm W Gilbert, Benj DeWit, Geo Merchant, Isaac Denison, & Stephen Thorne. Judah & Lazarus, [late N Judah], 84 Maiden La, N Y, having purch'd half of the tkts, offer same for sale.

Ranaway-Pompey, negro man-from Saml Carr, living ab't 4 miles above Charlotteville, Albemarle Co, Va. -S Carr.

Orphans Crt of Wash Co, D C. Prsnl est of Rebecca Nalley, late of said Co, dec'd. [will & ltrs] -Saml N Smallwood, exc.

Died: Caleb Swan, Nov 29, in Wash, was Paymstr Genrl to U S.

State of Md-In Chancery. Nov 27, 1809. Fred'k Kemp, John Kemp, Philip Kemp, Sarah Kemp, Geo Kemp, Adam Mayne & Cath his wife, vs Mary, Eliz, Michl, Cath, Geo, Nicholas, Susannah, Mgt Whitmore, chldrn & heirs of Michl Whitmore. Convey to cmplnts 2 tracts of land in Fred'k Co; Jan 20, 1798 said Mich'l Whitmore, f/o dfndnts sold to Henry Kemp, f/o cmplnts, said land cld *The Rsrvy on Rocky Hill & Puzzelsome Corrected,* on same day executed his bond for cnvynce of same. Money was pd-no cnvynce has been made. Henry Kemp is dead lvg cmplnts his heirs at law; Michl Whitmore is dead lvg dfndnts his heirs at law; dfndnts reside in Loudon Co, Va. -Nichs Brewer, Reg Cur Can.

WED DEC 6, 1809

Wm O'Brian, merchant taylor from Phil, carries on his business on 7th St nr the Navy Yd.

Died: Mrs Eliz Galvan, age 65 yrs, at *White Chimnies*, Va; consort of Francis Galvan, Postmstr at that place. [No date-recent]

Saml Fitzhugh has just rec'd paper hangings at his new store in High St, Gtwn.

FRI DEC 8, 1809

Wilson Carey Nicholas, in consequence of a severe indisposition on his way to this city, has rsgn'd his seat in the Hse of Reps.

MON DEC 11, 1809

Nov 16, Elijah Barton, David Lerin, Jebez Meigs, Ansel Meigs, Nath'l Lewin, Prince Kain & Adam Pitts were arraigned before the Supreme Crt held at Augusta, for murder of Paul Chadwick, in town of Malta. Verdict of acquittal for ea prisoner. -State of Massachusetts, trial at Augusta; Judge Parker.

For sale-50 slaves, at plantation of the late Robt Peter in Sugar Lands, nr Seneca Mills, Md. -Thos Peter, exc.

WED DEC 13, 1809
Distribution of the est of John M'Carty, dec'd, Dec 23 at ofc of Reg of Wills, Wash City.

B Richmond took the hse lately occupied by Mr Henry Tims for a boarding hse.

FRI DEC 15, 1809
Died: Robt Ellis, Dec 4, at Phil, was bk-kpr in Dept of War.

Died: on Dec 13, Mr Edw Fennell, ntv of Ire, age 60 yrs, many yrs a resid of Wash.

Order of Orphans Crt of PG Co, Md. Sale at late dwlg of Mary Meck Duckett, dec'd, within 7 miles of Upper Marlboro & nr Mr Dennis Magruder; sale o/prsnl prop of dec'd, negroes, furn, stock. -Jacob Ducket, U Bruce, excs, PG Co, Md.

Cath Fliset, mantua maker, has left Mrs Mary Ann Pic & is now working for her own account, at her lodgings formerly occupied by Mr W Holmes.

Lost-Pointer dog, Mrs Dowson's, Capitol Hill, Wash.

MON DEC 18, 1809
Bruckner Thruston, esq, appt'd by Pres of U S as Assoc Judge for D C, vice A B Duckett, esq, dec'd.

Died: Barnabe Chiaramontz, Pope Pius VII, in isle of Santa Margaretta, nr the frontier of France, in Provence; born in Cesene, Romania, Apr 14, 1742, created Cardinal in Apr 1785; elected Pope at Venice, Mar 14, 1800; Spanish papers say he was poisoned & sucessor as head of the Church is to be Cardinal Fesch, Uncle of Bonaparte.

Orphans Crt of Wash Co, D C. Dec 15, 1809. Prsnl est of Edw Fennell, late of said city, dec'd. [with will] -Mgt Fennell, excx, Jas Hoban, Geo Andrews, excs.

Leather manufactory. -Daniel Miller, High St, Gtwn.

WED DEC 20, 1809
Reward-$10 for Judy & her 2 chldrn, John & Mary, harbored by John Herberd, yellow man, who has her for a wife; purch'd them from Benj Oden. -Jas White, Little Monococy, Montg Co, Md.

Orphans Crt of PG Co, Md. Sale of part of prsnl prop of Christoper Hyatt, dec'd. -Sarah Hyatt, admx.

Henry Shultze, High St, Gtwn, has an elegant grand piano forte for sale.

FRI DEC 22, 1809

Dr Alex'r Campbell, Rpblcn, elected a Senator of U S for Ohio, vice resignation of Mr Tiffin.

Orphans Crt of PG Co, Md. Sale on plantation which late Newman Harvey, dec'd, occupied, nr Bladensburg; stock & one black woman. -Thos Harvey, adm.

PG Co Crt, Sep term, 1809. Isaac Swain, of said Co, confined in prison as insolvent debtor. -John Read Magruder jr, clk.

Notice-John Scott, negro man, committed to Fred'k Co, Md jail as runaway; had a pass with the names John Goff, Rich'd Evans, Jeremiah Cooksey, dt'd Nov 10, 1809; says he belongs to Mr Jas Harvey, nr to Clem Baden's mill, Upper Marlborough, PG Co, Md. -Ezra Mantz, shrf of Fred'k Co, Md.

MON DEC 25, 1809

Proclamation by Edw Lloyd, esq, Gov of Md. Negro Perry, alias Peregrine, slave of Eliz Rochester, & negro John, alias John Armstrong, [free], lately sentenced to death for murder of negro Stephen, slave of Jos Sudler, made their escape from Queen Anne's Co jail-Reward $300. -Edw Lloyd.

WED DEC 27, 1809

Chas Bastian, insolvent debtor, confined to Wash Co prison for debt. -Wm Brent, clk.

Reward-$20 for thief who broke into & stole boxes of glass. -Way & Co.

FRI DEC 29, 1809

Mrd: on Dec 24, Saml Burch, esq, of Wash, to Miss Susan Maria Wilson, of PG Co, Md, by Rev Mr Breckenridge.

I have deposited in the pblc library a memorial to disprove the charge that I fired into the *Bonhomme Richard,* commanded by Capt Jones & killed many of her men; & to show that the capture of the *Serapis*, Capt Pearson, was attribued by him to my ship, *The Alliance*. Above memorial was presented in 1785 and never replied to. -Peter Landais.

Deed of trust from Mr Wm Hodgson, dt'd Nov 10, 1808, for purpose of indemnifying Mr John Hopkins; sale at Alex Crt-Hse, 3000 acs of land on Big Sandy Creek, Monongalia Co, Va; tracts were granted by State of Va to John Allison by 3 patents of 1000 acs ea, dt'd Oct 1, 1784, same duly conveyed to said Wm Hodgson, Aug 2, 1790. -Edmund J Lee, trustee.

Pblc sale of numerous lots in Wash City-at suit in Chancery [Chas Minifie & others vs Geo Walker]. -P B Key, Wm Brent, trustees.

Wm Henry Harrison re-appt'd Govn'r of the Terr of Indiana.

The National Intelligencer and Washington Advertiser
Washington, D C

1810

MON JAN 1, 1810
Lewis Zimmer has an assortment of dry goods & groceries for sale.

Liverpool coal just arv'd at Alexandria; apply to Wash Bowie or Andrew Smith.

John Dennis, now residing in Wilmington, Dela, within 6 yrs has made & sold ab't 90 carding machines. -Phil Paper.

Reily's Store on Pa av has assortment of liquors & groc.

WED JAN 3, 1810
Orphans Crt of Montg Co, Md. Dec 20, 1809. Prsnl est of Basil M Perry, late of said Co. dec'd. -Robt Edmondston, acting adm.

Died: Mr Benj Wilkinson, s/o Genr'l Jos Wilkinson, of Md, a few days ago on his passage from New Orleans to Balt; an active young man; had been absent from Md for svr'l yrs on business in the Western country.

Orphans Crt of PG Co, Md. Sale of negro boy, prop of Jesse *Helen, dec'd, to discharge his debts. -Thos Wall , adm, of Jesse *Hellen -[*2 Splgs] dec'd, living nr Bladensburg.

FRI JAN 5, 1810
Elected directors of Commerc Co of Wash: Buller Cocke, C W Goldsborough, Alex Kerr, Adam Lindsay, Peter Miller, Wm Prout, Saml N Smallwood, Thos Tingey, Matthew Wright, Moses Young, Thos Young, Jos Forrest -Pres.

Hse o/Reps-Act of relief for Wm & Elias Rector for surveys made for same, of claims in Kaskaskia Dist, or Ill Terr-$3 per mile. -J B Varnum, Spkr of Hse o/Reps.

Chancery Crt-Md: sale of all land devised to Alex Frazier & John Alex'r Frazier by their fr, viz-818 acs in Calvert Co with dwlg hse. -Rich'd H Harwood, trustee.

MON JAN 8, 1810
Partnership of Thos Young & Thos Foyles, butchers, dissolved by mutual consent. -Thos Foyles will continue the business.

Ladies with ltrs in Wash Post ofc-Jan 1, 1810:

Sarah Antrim	Sophia Alexander
Ruthy Allen	Mrs Jane Brown
Widow Bain	Miss Eliz Bennet
Sarah Boyce	Mrs Jane Bedford

Juliana Brittan
Sally Colbert at Jas Clerkleis
Mrs Eleanor Currin
Jane Downs
Mrs Mary Doyne
Charlotte Fenix
Ann Hana
Betty Jackson c/o Jas Clerkler
Mrs Mary Lee
Nancy Martin
Sarah Magore
Mary Shryock c/o Geo Miller
Cath Smith
Eliz Shannon
Miss Eliz L Thompson
Polly Watson
Rach'l Ebbs c/o Mr Waterston
Sam or Elinor Cloky
Cath Cassell
Mrs Dempsie
Miss Dixon c/o Jacob Alford
Mrs Mgt Ewell,
Mrs Mary Hankoet
Mrs Honour
Miss Ann Jeams c/o Ben King
Maria Hill c/o Rt Long
Mgt Moore
Cath Spunaugle
Anna Maria Smyth
Mrs Anna Shaw
Mrs Mary A Stewart
Rebeccah Tyler
Mary A Wethuell
Mrs M Walston c/o W Sanford

Decision on patent rghts in Crct Crt of U S, Judges Washington & Peters. Oliver Evans vs John Weiss. [dfndnt guilty only from time he rec'd notice of the law-Feb, 1809] Evans invented 2 wheels & 2 stones for manufacture of flour. Weis' Mill on Wissabiccon Creek, Phil Co, Pa. -Phil, Jan 8.

Partnership of Thos Young & Thos Foyles, butchers, dissolved by mutual consent. -Thos Foyles will continue the business.

Honoria Julien has groc for sale at his store on F St.

Directors meeting of Columbian Library. -Jos Milligan, lbrn.

WED JAN 10, 1810
Hse o/Reps: Petition of Col Daniel Boone for svcs for U S for which he asks compensation-referred to committee.

Treasurer's sale of lots 43, 44, 45 & 46, sq 503, prop of Pratt, Francis & others, for taxes due Corp of Wash. -H Whetcroft.

Sale of 5 negroes, prop of Col John P Van Ness, to satisfy taxes due the Corp of Wash. -Henry Whetcroft, Treasurer.

John B Colvin, insolvent debtor, confined in Wash Co, D C, prison, for debt; J Colvin follows this notice with a ltr to his creditors. Wash City.

Dr Jas Ewell has remv'd to Wash City & offers his svcs.

FRI JAN 12, 1810
Elisha King, insolvent debtor, confined in prison for debt, PG Co, Md, to be dschg'd from prison. -Dan'l Clarke.

Roger M'Namara, insolvent debtor, confined in Wash Co, D C prison, for debt.
-Wm Brent.

MON JAN 15, 1810
Treas sale-3 story brick hse now occupied by John Woodsides, prop of Rev Henry Moscrop, for taxes due Corp of Wash. -Henry Whetcroft, Treas, Wash City.

Orphans Crt of St Mary's Co, Md. Rich'd Clarke, exc of Chas Gough, late of said Co, dec'd, is ordered he give creditors notice to exhibit their claims. -Jas Forrest, Reg Wills. Said notice followed. -Richd Clarke, exc o/Chas Gough.

For sale-prsnl est of Joshua Pope, dec'd, stock, farming utensils at dwlg hse of Saml Marshall, exc, on rd leading from Eastern Branch Bridge to Up Marlb.

Runaway, Aaron alias Broctston, committed to Anne Arundel Co jail; says he is the prop of Wm Fitzhugh of Pr Wm Co, Va, ab't 10 miles from Dumfries.
-John Cord, shrf, of A A Co, Md.

WED JAN 17, 1810
Mrd: on Jan 4, Mr John Franks, printer of Wash, to Miss Mary Tuttle, of Gtwn, by Rev Mr Boswell.

Ranaway-3 negro lads: Gerrard, John Steward & Jerry Gerrard; Reward-$150.
-Turner Dixon, Saml Adams. Fauquier Co, Va, nr *Oak Hill.*

In Chancery, Jan 10, 1810. Philip B Key vs *Zachariah Beall & Saml Beall. Bill is to record a deed executed by dfndnts on Nov 23, 1796, for conveying to cmplnt tracts of land in Montg Co, cld *James's Gift & Resurvey on James's Gift* . [*Resides out of Md] -Nichs Brewer, Reg Cur Can.

FRI JAN 19, 1810
Sale of all prsnl est of late Geo Frasier Hawkins, of PG Co, Md at hse of Humphrey B Berry, Piscataway. -Basil Bowling, adm.

Lewis Beeler, confectioner, nr Wash Tavern, King St, Alexandria; practiced in most of the countries in Europe.

Mrd: on Jan 18, Mr Jacob Gideon, printer, to Miss Mary Coone, both of Wash, by Rev Mr Brown

Hse o/Reps-Petition of Peter Sternberg, of Montg Co, N Y; compensation for discovery of preventing smut in wheat; referred to committee.

MON JAN 21, 1810
Henry Clay, esq, appt'd Senator from Ky, vice Buckner Thruston, esq, resigned. Outerbridge Horsey, elected Atty-Genr'l of Dela, by Leg of Dela; vice Saml White, esq, dec'd.

Orphans Crt of Wash Co, D C. Jan 22, 1810. Prsnl est of John Kedglie, late of said city, dec'd. -Ann Kedglie, admx.

WED JAN 24, 1810
Wish to exch for stock in the Wash bridge, the following prop: hse & lot formerly occupied by me, Pa Ave, sq 1044, now occupied by Dr Harrison; bldg lot sq 461 bet hses of Saml H Smith, esq & Mr Peltz, Pa Ave; 10 to 100 acs of land I lately purch'd lying bet Wash Bridge & Alex. -W Cranch.

Walter & Clement Smith have just rec'd goods from N Y; for sale at their store in Gtwn.

FRI JAN 26, 1810
Mrd: on Jan 23, Mr Baptiste Maupin to Miss Cath Fliset, both inhabitants of Wash, by Rev Mr Balch. Cath Fliset, now Cath Maupin, informs that she will remove to Gtwn next week.

Ranaway-Bill Pane, negro slave, from Priscilla H Courts, lvg in Chas Co, Md.

Tan-Yard for sale or rent, sq E of sq 642, Wash City. Robt Underwood, Pa Ave, will show the premises.

Ranaway-Beverley, negro fellow, from Eleanor Wormeley, *Rosegill*, Midd Co, Va. Reward-$20.

MON JAN 29, 1810
Orphans Crt of PG Co, Md. Jan 23, 1810. Prsnl est of Mary Muk Duckett, of PG Co, Md, dec'd. -Jacob Duckett, U Bruce, excs. [excs note-one of PG Co, Md-other of Allegany Co.]

Orphans Crt of Wash Co, D C. Jan 26, 1810. Prsnl est of Maj Caleb Swan, late of said city, dec'd. -Maria H Swan, excx, Thos Patterson, exc.

WED JAN 31, 1810
Nath'l Gregory, insolvent debtor, confined to Wash Co, D C prison, for debt. -Wm Brent, clk.

Nichs B Van Zandt offers hdwr for sale at his new store nr Centre Mkt-Hse.

Hse for rent or lease on F St; formerly occupied by John Martin Baker. -Wm Cocking.

FRI FEB 2, 1810
Orphans Crt of St Mary's Co, Md. Oct term, 1809. Mgt Reeder & Rich'd Reeder, adms of Geo Reeder, late of said Co. dec'd, ordered they give notice for creditors. -Jas Forrest, Reg of wills for St M Co. [Said notice followed.]

MON FEB 5, 1810
I commenced the practice of law-Apr 1. I shall open an ofc nr the Navy Yd, oppo the hse in occupation of Dr Alex'r McWilliams. -Enoch M Lowe, Wash.

Individuals who deserted from the Army of the U S, & are desirous of returning to their duty-a full pardon is hereby granted to ea & all , within 4 mos of this date; surrender themselves to Commanding ofc of any Military Post within the U S. Jan 29, 1810, Jas Madison, President.

Orphans Crt of PG Co, Md. Jan 24, 1810. Prsnl est of Stephen Belt, late of said Co, dec'd. -Benj Belt, adm.

Orphans Crt of Wash Co, D C. Jan 22, 1810. Prsnl est of Capt Garrett Barry, late of said City, dec'd. -Jas D Barry, adm.

Handsome carriages for sale. -Thos Jacob, Alexandria.

WED FEB 7, 1810
Case of John B Colvin an insolvent debtor; ordered that Geo Andrews, trustee, sell goods & effects. -Wm Brent, clk. Said sale follows, furn, bks, etc at hse lately occupied by said insolvent. -Saml Speake, auct, G Andrews, trust.

FRI FEB 9, 1810
Hse o/Reps-Act to allow Jos Joshua Dyster to obtain a patent for his constructing iron bridges & other architectural purposes; 2 yrs residence shall not be required. -J B Varnum, spkr of Hse o/Reps. Jas Madison, approved.

MON FEB 12, 1810
The stallion, Oscar, late Gen Ridgeley's, will stand at Mr Vanmeters at *Ft Pleasant*, So Branch of Potomac; prop of Mr Lufborough.

For sale: a likely negro fellow. -Thos L Washington, Barry's Wharf.

An act for relief of Harry Caldwell, Amasa Jackson, Jeremiah Reynolds, Levin Jones. Violation of act to prohibit the importation of slaves. brig-*Jos Ricketson* owned by Henry Caldwell & Amasa Jackson; schn'r *Victory*, owned by J Reynolds; schn'r, *Wolfe*, of Balt, owned & commanded by Levin Jones. All penalties & forfeitures are hereby remitted. J B Varnum, spkr of Hse o/Reps. Apprv'd-James Madison.

WED FEB 14, 1810
Reward-$10 for Harry, negro boy. -Thos Harrison jr, Chappawansie, Pr Wm Co, Va. [nr Dumfries]

Died: on Jan 16, of a nervous fever, Wm Holland, 2d s/o Jas Holland, a Rep in Cong from N C; in Maury Co, Tenn; finished his educ at Greenville college, Tenn; age 20 yrs.

Died: Rev Eugene Fitzgerald Magrath, Feb 8; Bach of Arts of Univ of Dublin, skilful teacher; bequeathed property to the poor of Alexandria.

Reward-$10 for Harry, negro boy. -Thos Harrison jr, Chappawansie, Pr Wm Co, Va. [nr DumFries]

FRI FEB 16, 1810
Wm P Tuckfield has remv'd his shoe manufactory to Capitol Hill in hse occupied by Mr H Ingle as a cabinet shop.

MON FEB 19, 1810
Soc for Purpose of Encouraging Home Manufacures & Rearing Domestic Animals. Meeting at Union Tavern, Gtwn, Feb 1. John Teackle, esq-chrmn; Nathan Lufborough-sec; Osborn Sprigg of Northampton, PG Co, Md appt'd Pres of the Soc; Thompson Mason of Fairfax Co, Va-VP; David Wiley of Gtwn, D C-sec; Cmtee, viz: in Va-Dan'l Carroll Brent, John Brook of Stafford; Alex'r Henderson, Wm Tyler of Pr Wm; Wm Hayward Foote, Chas Love of Fairfax; Wilson C Selden, Wm W Bronaugh of Loudoun. In Md: Chas Carroll of C, Henry Maynadier of Anne Arundel Co; Geo Calvert, Jos Kent of PG Co; Isaac Briggs, John Bowie of Montg Co; Philip Stewart, Clement Dorsey of Chas. Dist of Col: Nicholas Fitzhugh, Wm A Dangerfield, Alexandria. Tench Ringgold, John Mason of Wash, D C.

Mrd: Hon John Pope, esq, Sen of U S, to Miss Eliza J D Johnson, d/o late Joshua Johnson, esq, of Wash, Feb 11.

For sale: land whereon I now live in Chas Co, Durham Parish, 732 acs; also a life est in 708 1/2 acs in same Co ab't 3 miles above Md Point; also ab't 30 negroes. -John Mitchell, *Holly Spring*.

Committed to goal at Fred'k Co, Md, Jim, mulatto boy; says he belongs to Mr John Crotzer, copper-smith, Harrisonburgh, Va. -Ezra Mantz, shrf, Fred'k Co, Md.

Act of relief for John N Stout, kpr of the jail of Fleming Co, Ky, for maintaining Geo Barnaby, while in his custody, as a prisoner. Pay sum due. -Apprv'd, Jas Madison.

WED FEB 21, 1810
Auction at hse of Benj Adamson, Pa Ave: furn & other articles of the cabinet mkg business. -Saml Speake, auct.

Supply of timber, 12 miles below Alexandria. -Colin Hayes agent for Bushrod Washington, esq, Mt Vernon.

Crct Crt-Wash Co, D C. Case of excs of Notly Young, cmplnts, & Jas Greenleaf & others, dfndnts. Sale of prop in Wash to raise the sum of 13,286, 7-100 dollars with int from Nov 15, 1796. -Wash Boyd, trustee.

Stolen: a coat, gold chain & locket. -John Coyle, Wash.

FRI FEB 23, 1810
In Chancery: report of Trueman Tyler, trustee, ratify sale of rl est of John Brown, dec'd, 440 acs of land in PG Co, Md, sum of $8,000. -Jeremiah Townley Chase, Chf Judge of 3d Judicial Dist. -Nichs Brewer, Reg Cur Can.

Died: Dr Rich'd Brown, s/o late Dr Wm Brown of Alexandria; age 27 yrs, Jan 20 at Chillicothe; his mthr survives him.

Sec of State notice: impressed into the British Navy: Wm Varney, Geo Beverly, Lawrence Ward, John Wilds & Jas Van-Derhorst; need proof of their Americ ctznshp. Dept of State.

Absconded: Randol, mulatto boy, prop of Mrs Mary Moreland, from Broad Creek, PG Co, Md. -Benoni Wheat, Wash.

MON FEB 26, 1810
An Act-discharging Wm Hawkins from imprisonment sent to mrsh'l for Dist of Maine; provided Hawkins pay all costs arisen on part of U S in said prosecution. -J B Varnum, spkr of Hse o/Reps. Apprv'd, Jas Madison.

Treaty bet U S & Indian tribes, Delawares, Putawatimies, Miames & Eel Rvr Miamies; at Ft Wayne on Sep 30, 1809. Sgnd by: Wm Henry Harrison, in presence of: Peter Jones-sec; John Johnston-Indian Agt; A Heald-Capt U S A; A Edwards-Surgs Mate; Ph Ostrander-Lt U S A; John Shaw; Stephen Johnston; J Hamelton-shrf of Dearborn Co; Hendrick Aupaumut; interpreters-Wm Wells, John Conner, Jos Barron, Abraham Ash. Seal-Jas Madison, Jan 16, 1810. [Indian marks & names were included in the article.]

For sale-*Blenheim*, S W Mt, Albemarle Co, Va; 2,890 acs; apply to Capt John Harris-Albemarle Co; Col Robt Gamble-Richmond; Jas Patton-Alexandria; Mr MacDonald & Ridgely, Balt; or Jas Ross, Fredericksburg, Va.

WED FEB 28, 1810
Wanted-person to superintend the carding, spinning, [by billies & jennies] & weaving. Ltr to Moses Young, Pres of Manufacturing Co, City of Wash.

For sale: one negro man, formerly the prop of Barbara Freeman, late of Calvert Co, dec'd. -Geo Gray, adm, Upper Marlboro.

Ranaway-Jim, black man; from John R Sasser, nr Lower Brick Chr, PG Co, Md.

FRI MAR 2, 1810
French papers contain details of the divorce of the Emperor of France from Josephine; consent of both parties.

Western Iron Works on Licking Crk, nr Zanesville, Muskingum Co, Ohio; erected by Moses Dillon.

MON MAR 5, 1810
Jos Walker has commenced the blacksmith business on 13th St W.

James Banbridge, or the *Irish Adventurer* has been executed by a blind gentleman of Wash, is now ready for press.

Mrd: on Feb 22, Hon Wm B Giles, Sen in Cong of U S, to Miss Frances Ann Gwynn, eldest d/o late Thos Peyton Gwynn of Va, in Gtwn, by Rev Dr Gantt.

A bay horse broke from the stable; reward-$5; deliver to Th B Dashiell at Mrs Willson's, Capitol Hill, Wash.

WED MAR 7, 1810
Dirs of the ofc of Disc & Deposit-Wash:

John P Van Ness	Wm Stuart	Thos Tingey
Wm Brent	Jos Nourse	Jas D Barry
Lewis Deblois	Thos Monroe	David Peter
Walter Hellen	John Tayloe	Elias B Caldwell
Jas Sanderson	-Mar 1, 1810	

Black horse: strayed or stolen from dwlg place of Henry Irwan, living on Bridge St, Gtwn, next door above Isaac Johnson's *Sign of the Red Lion*; deliver to above place or to Mr Stettinius' Tavern on Pa Ave; to Mr Thos Duval's store in Bladensburg, or to Thos Jones Sr, living in PG Co nr Mr P Snowden's Mills, Patuxent.

Reward-$300 for villain cld Baldwin; took Lewis from my plantation-purch'd him of Mr Wingate of Va. -Thos Waring jr, Waccamaw, or Mr Francis Withers in Gtwn, S C.

For sale-land on Aquia Crk, Stafford Co, Va, with dwlg hse; apply to John G Hedgman residing at Mr Lund Washington's of Wash or to Travers Daniel Sr, in Stafford Co, Va.

For sale-land where I resid, 626 acs, part of *Causin Manor* & *Wathen's Adventure*, Chas Co, Md. -Henry Digges.

FRI MAR 9, 1810
Act of Cong-John Dobbyn is authorised to erect hay scales nr Eastern Branch Mkt to weigh hay, straw & fodder. Wash.

Ordered that Rich'd Duvall , collector of County taxes for PG Co, Md, list lands with taxes due [Jan 18, 1810].
Upper Marl, Charlotte & Mt Calvert Hundreds:
Dan'l Carroll's heirs-part of *Darnell's Chance*;

Frank Lick's heirs-pt of *Darnell's Chance* & lots in Upper Marl;
Benj Brookes heirs-lots in Upper Marl;
Eliz Brookes-Rght of dower in B Brookes' lots;
Stephen West's heirs-lot in Upper Marl;
Dennis M Burgess-lots in Upper Marl;
Dan'l Dulany's heirs-lot in Upper Marl;
Thos Hamilton-*Groomes Last Shift, Addition to Groomes Last Shift, Mt Calvert Manor*
Thos Sim Lee-lot in Upper Marl;
Grace Lyon-lot in Upper Marl;
Arnold Livers-lot in Upper Marl;
Frank Leck jr heirs-lot in Upper Marl;
Hugh Maguire-pt of *Darnall 's Chance & Addition;*
John Roger's heirs-lot in Upper Marl;
Rich'd Sprigg's heirs-lot in Upper Marl;
Thos Tillard's heirs-pt of *Mt Calvert Manor;*
Saml I Coolidge-lot in Upper Marl;
Jane Urquhart-pt of lot in Upper Marl.
<u>Mattapany, Wash, Pr Fred Hundreds:</u>
Jas Bates' heirs -pt of *Cool Spring Addition* & pt of *Forrest;*
Rich'd Brightwell-*Ridgeway* or *No Name* & pt of *Padgett's Rest*;
John Campbell-pt of *Hogpen & Sasser's Green*;
Jane Eaton-pt of *Brookfield*;
Wm O Padgett-pt of *Woodbridge*;
Thos Sasser-pt of *Vineyard;*
Rd B Sansbury-pt of *White's Park & Tan Yd;*
Susanna Wailes-pt of *Brooke Crt;*
Thos Buchanan's heirs-lot in *Nottingham*;
Wm Cooke-pt of *White's Park*;
Henry Compton-pt of *Dunbar, Taghorton*, pt of do;
Jane Davis-pt of *Cool Spring Addition* & pt of *Forrest*;
Wm Grindell-pt of *Taylor's Course*;
John Hughs' heirs-pt of *Good Luck;*
Thos B Hodgkins-lot in *Ntnghm;*
Rebecca Letchworth-pt of *Brooke Crt;*
John Linthicum-pt of *Beanes' Landing* adj *Ntnghm;*
Alex Magruder's heirs-pt of *Coxhays;*
Wm Mayhews heirs-pt of *Colebrook;*
Jas Mewbern-pt of lot in *Ntnghm;*
Nichs B Sansbern's heirs-*Tanyd & Wight's Pk;*
Dan'l Smallwood-pt of *Naylor's Range;*
Geo Smith-lot in *Ntnghm;*
Jas Swann's heirs-*Ludford's Gift* & pt of *Hatchett;*
John Smith, [Chas Co]-*Wiltshire*;
Eliz Trueman-pt of *Buttington;*
Levin Watson-pt of *Poplar Hills.]*
<u>King Geo & Grub Hndrds:</u>
Rich'd Clagett-pt of *Hickory Hills*, pt of *Mkt Overton*, & *Tyler Disc*;

Henry Clarkson-*Plains Shrewsbury;*
Saml Joy-*West Qtr Enlgd*, pt of *Simpster;*
Wm Jenkins-lot in *Piscataway;*
Thos Lanes heirs-pt of *Vineyd;*
John Webster Sr-pt of the *Ridge;*
Ann Wade-pt of *Timberland & Finches Disc*;
Jas Adams-pt of *Mkt Overton*;
Josias Adams-pt of *Mkt Overton*;
John Adams [Col] lot in Psctwy;
Humphrey Belt Sr-*Plains of Shrewsbury;*
Nichl Blacklock's heirs-*Blacklock's Venture*, pt of *Widows Trouble*, pt of *Gantt's Enlargement Enlrgd*, pt of *Strife & Boson*, pt of *Strife*;
Rich'd Brandt-pt of *Mkt Overton*;
Saml Berry-pt of *Aix*, pt of *Wynns Chance;*
John Bowling's heirs-pt of *Psctwy Manor & Dowie's Neglect*;
Thos & Horatio Clarge & Mary Bond Tyler-pt of *Psctwy manor*, pt of *Stone's Delight*, pt of the *Ridge*, pt of *Aix*, pt of *Disc;*
Thos Clagett's heirs-pt of *Hazzard, Marlow's Resrvy*, pt of *Two Johns*, pt of *Lanham's Folly, Something & Merry Tho't Enlrgd, Hawkin's* lot, pt of *Grfrs Gift*, pt of *Ditto, Middleton's Lot Enlrgd*, pt of *Appledore;*
Thos Clagett & others-pt of *Psctwy Manor;*
Saml Chapman-lot in Psctwy;
Thos Clagett-lot in Psctwy;
Geo W Dent-pt of *Nick Him* in Deer range & meadows, pt of *Leith & Pittsburgh*, lot in Psctwy;
Geo Dyer-no name, pt of *Leith*, pt of *Edelen's Hogpen Enlgd*; lot in Psctwy;
Thos Dyer's heirs-pt of *Edelen's Hogpen Enlgd;*
Henry Davidson-pt of *Leith & Pittsburgh*, lots in Piscataway;
John Dyer's heirs-name unkwn, pt of *Leith;*
Theodore Glasgow-pt o/*Wynn's Middle Lot*;
Elvira Hardey-pt of *Leath;*
Eliz A Hilton-pt of *Jessamin*;
Benj Mitchell of Notley, pt of *Thos & Sarah;*
Rev Geo Ralph-pt of Simpster, *West Qrtr Enlgd;*
Rich'd B A Wester-pt of *Refuse.*
<u>Piscataway & Hynson Hndrd:</u>
Geo Hardey-pt of *Refuse;*
Chas Jones [Millwright]-*Leonard Lot;*
Edw Jenkins-pt of *Oxman Town;*
Philip Lee-pt of *Magruder's Plains*;
Jas Rudd-pt of *Magruder's Choice*, pt of *Goodwell;*
Sarah Smith-*London's Pleasure*;
Levin Summers-pt of *Calvert;*
Levin Talburt-pt of *Gleaning;*
Mary Wade-pt of *Hunter's Folly;*
Thos M Alnet-pt of *Maiden's Dower;*
Geo Beall of Geo-*Tenley's Chance*, Bayne's 1st & 2d lot;
Judson M Clagett's heirs-pt of *Dublin*, pt of *Strong Harbor*;

Rev Jos Eden-name unkn;
Jesse Greenville's heirs-pt of *Silver Hills;*
Dan'l Henley-pt of *Weaver's Delight*;
John Hepburn-pt of *Outlet*;
Thos Jenkins of Dan'l-pt o/*Oxman Town & Maiden Bradley*, pt of *Magruder's Choice*, pt of *Refuse*, pt of *What You Please;*
Wm Jenkins-pt of *Oxman town*, *Maiden Bradley*, pt of *Strife*, pt of *Leith*, *Addition to Maiden Bradley*;
Mary Jones-*Leonard Lot;*
Chas King-small parcel of svr'l tracts;
Michl Lowe & Leonard Soper-*Fishing Landing;*
Eliz M'Donaugh [Chas Co]-pt of *Major's Choice;*
Wm Mansfield-pt of *Lusby's Disc;*
Jas Moore's heirs-pt of *Silver Hills;*
Dan'l Moxly-pt of *Oxen Hill Manor;*
Chas Nevitt-pt of *Grey Eagle Enlgd*;
John T Shaaff-pt of *Prevention Enlgd*;
David Stone-pt of *Chance;*
Michl Lowe-pt of *Forest*, pt of *Soper's Rest Enlgd*, pt of *Manchester*.
<u>New Scotland, Oxen & Bladensburg Hndrds:</u>
Geo Bryan-*Burches Venture;*
Zephaniah Masters-pt of *Discovery;*
John Masters-pt of *Discovery;*
Patrick Dougherty-pt of 2 lots in Bldnsbg;
Wm Danford's heirs-1/2 ac in Bldnsbg;
Jos Gorden-pt of *Second Thought;*
John Murray-*Land Above*;
Randolph Morris-pt of *Pleasant Spring Enlgd;*
Wm Syde-Bothom's heirs-pt of *Hogpen*, lots 13 & 16 in Bldnsbg;
Wm Stewart-7 lots in Bldnsbg;
Jesse Taylor-half ac adj Bldnsbg;
Rev Notley Young-pt of *Bro's Joint Interest Enlgd.*
<u>Rock Creek & Eastern Branch Hundreds:</u>
Benj Armitage-*Att'n of the Faithful Steward*;
Wm Bailey-pt of *Barbadoes;*
Francis Deakins heirs-pt of *Rsvy on Millers Beginning;*
Roger Edmondston-pt of *Greene & Edmondston's Range*;
Geo Frank-*Francks Adventure;*
Eliz Jones-pt of *Elizabeth' Portion*;
Andrew Leitch heirs-pt of *Deakins Hall, Little Meadows Force Put & Paint Branch/*
Wm Sydebothams heirs-hse & lot in Bell-town;
Geo Wilson-pt of *Flag Botom;*
Benj Lowndes trustee for J Beall-pt of *Bros Fifth lot*, *Beall's Disc & Neglect.*

For sale: horse at Isaac Pierce's on *Rock Creek*, 3 miles from Gtwn. -David Pierce

Orphans Crt of Chas Co, Md. Mar 7, 1810. Prsnl est of Francis Dixon, late of Chas Co, dec'd. -Luke F Matthews.

For sale-lots 4 & 5, sq 77 in Wash; deed dt'd Jan 11, 1808 by late Chas Wadsworth, in trust. -Cuthbert Powel, Geo Taylor.

MON MAR 12, 1810

Orphans Crt of Calvert Co, Md; sale of one negro, prop of Barbara Freeman, late of Calv Co, dec'd. -Geo Grey, adm.

Sir Samson, sure foal-getter, will stand at farm of Thos C Bowie, nr Queen Anne, this season. -Ben Coolidge, groom.

Thos Thorpe has declined the coach mkg business & has commenced the vendue business, Wash City.

WED MAR 14, 1810

Francis Pic & myself, by deed of separation duly executed, have agreed to live separate & apart, in same manner as though we were never mrd; all contracts to be made by me, are to be made as though I were a feme sole & to impose no kind of obligation on him. -M A Pic.

Ranaway-negroes, Billy Hutton, age ab't 34 yrs, formerly the prop of Dr Rich'd Duckett, PG Co, Md; Ned Young, born & raised in Forest of PG Co, prop of Notley Young & was lately prch'd by Geo Hilleary together with his family of Mrs Cassinave of Wash; he is ab't 35 yrs of age. -Geo Hilleary, PG Co, Md.

Runaways-confined in Wash Co, D C, jail: Jas Parker, says he belongs to Jas Weems of Balt, Md; Susanna, says she belongs to Ignatius Adams of Chas Co, nr Port tobacco, Md. -C Tippet, kpr of the jail, for W Boyd, mrsh'l.

FRI MAR 16, 1810

Orphans Crt of PG Co, Md. Prsnl est of Hannibal Clagett of said Co, dec'd. -Horatio Clagett, exc.

Mrd: Dr Wm Grayson to Miss Mary Threlkeld, d/o John Threlkeld, esq, all of Gtwn, Mar 1, by Rev W D Addison, at Gtwn.

Hse o/Reps: Petition of Fregift Patchin, prisoner in Rev war in British Prov of Canada for nr 3 yrs, praying compensation; referred to committee.

Runaway-Wm Pane, negro, committed to goal at Wash Co, Md; says he be-longs to Mrs Priscilla Courts of Chas Co, Md. -Mathias Shaffner, shrf-Wash Co, Md.

Furs for sale at stores of superintendent of Indian trade in Gtwn; collected at U S factories. -John Mason, sup Indian trade.

MON MAR 19, 1810
Lumber Rvr Navigation lottery, authorised by Leg of No Car. Apply by ltr to post ofc at this place or to Larel Hill. Mgrs: D MacFarlan, Wm Ashley, Wyn Nance, Jesse Lee, Wm MacNeill, Ebenezer Ellis. -Lumberton.

Looking for 2 black men to drive carts. -Henry Tims, Wash.

WED MAR 21, 1810
C Boyle, having just arriv'd in Wash, offers his prof svcs-portrait painting, Pa Ave

Lands for sale in Ohio & Ky; virtue of will of Robt Means, dec'd; info from Mr Walter Dun residing in or nr Chillicothe, Ohio. -Dan'l Call , exc, Richmond.

Pblc auction at Jas Dall & Co, Balt, Md; closing the dry goods business.

Oath of insolvent debtor to be administered to John West, who is confined in Wash Co, D C, prison. -Wm Brent, clk.

FRI MAR 23, 1810
In Chancery-Feb 27, 1810. Petition of Wm M'Creery, acting adm of Stephen Wilson, for a preference of his claim out of the proceeds of a part of the rl est of Wm Hammond & Wm King, sold by a decree of this crt, on a mortgage to Jos Clarke. -Nichs Brewer, Reg Cur Can. [creditors of Jos Clarke; claims by Jul 1. -S Chase jr, trustee].

MON MAR 26, 1810
Died: on Mar 15, Maj John Saunders, of Corps of Artl & Eng of U S A, Commandant at Fort Nelson for past 10 yrs. -Norfolk, Mar 17.

WED MAR 28, 1810
Supreme Crt-Robt Fletcher vs John Peck. Suit instituted on svr'l covenants contained in a deed made by J Peck, dfndt in error, conveying to R Fletcher, plntf in error, land which were part of large purchases made by Jas Gunn & others, in 1795 from State of Ga.

Orphans Crt of Montg Co, Md. Mar 24, 1810. Prsnl est of Jas Wilson Perry, late of said Co, dec'd. -Josiah Jones Sr, Robt Jones,adms.

Dr N T Weems, late a surg in U S N; offers his prof svcs; residing in hse formerly occupied by Mr Edw L Smith, on Jefferson. St.

FRI MAR 30, 1810
Ranaway-Harry Shorter, negro, ab't 25 yrs of age; from G B Bitouzey, PG Co, nr *Bell Air*, Md.

Saml Stettinius, Pa Ave, dry goods & groc; will in the future be in association with Geo Kneller, who attended his store nrly 2 yrs. -Stettinius & Kneller.

Mrd: on Mar 22, Mr Wm Brent, of Stafford Co, Va, to Miss Minifred Lee, of Loudon Co, Va, by Rev Mr Dunn, at Caton, the seat of the late Col Thos L Lee.

Ranaway-Wm Addrey, ab't 20 yrs of age, apprentice. -Benj King, Navy Yd, Wash.

MON APR 2, 1810

Proposals for fresh beef for the Navy. -Tho Tingey, Super, Navy Yd, Wash.

Minister wanted. Rev Mr Barclay, presently of Wm & Mary Parish, St Mary's Co, Md, accepted a lucrative appointment in Alex. -John Mackall jr, Reg.

To lease or rent-5 lots in E St, 1 lot in 12th, 2 lots in Carrolsburgh. -G C Grammer, Wash. Henry Mayor, Gtwn.

Notice for supply of rations needed. Franklin Wharton, Lt Col Commandant M C. Hdqrtrs of M C, Wash.

Sale by order of Orphans Crt of Wash Co, D C. Sundry articles, prop of John M'Elwee, dec'd, at Chas Jones' nr the Centre Mkt, Wash. -Saml Speake, auct.

For sale, by ltr of atty executed by Thos Skelly, merchant of Phil City-all hsehld furn of late John Banks. Mrs Banks will also sell a valuable female svt. -Andrew Coyle

Fresh garden seeds from N Hingston, Alex, Va. -Al Joncherez.

WED APR 4, 1810

Orphans Crt of Wash Co, D C. Prsnl est of John M'Elwee, late of said Co dec'd. John Ott & Jas Kearney, attys of said Co. -Rebecca M'Elwee, of Phil City, admx.

Geo Beall has established a cut nail manufactory nr the Navy Yd at considerable expence.

For sale-the claims of the heirs of Dr Nicholas Way, dec'd, land in Dist of Col, cld *Arell's Falls, Amsterdam & Whitehaven*-340 acs; within 3 miles of Gtwn; Abner Cloud residing on the premises. -John Way, Wilmington, Dela.

Mr Duport will open his school at Long Rm, in hse formerly occupied by I H Barney on Apr 3.

Mrs Du Cherray will take possession of Mrs Beck's hse on Jefferson St & open a school.

Bank notes mailed from Jefferson, Culpepper Co, Va, on Feb 27th last, to Mr John Withers, Alexandria, have not been rec'd. -Pendleton & Fishback, Jefferson.

FRI APR 6, 1810
Ranaway-Jack, negro; from Benj Beaver, living in Chas Co, nr Bryan town, Md. Reward-$25.

MON APR 9, 1810

Ladies with ltrs in Wash Post ofc-Apr 1, 1810:		Mary Burch
Ann Blagden	Jane Baker	Susannah M Cartney
Agnes Cook	Eliz Drynan	Clarinda Evans
Lidia Fisher	Maria Glover	Matilda Hawkins
Harriot Jenkins	Mrs Mary Lane	Miss Eliza Lawrence
Mrs Philippi Marshal	Eliza Moreo	Eliza Morfield
Mary Ann McNantz	Eliz Minchin	Eliz M'Caidell
Nancy Pert	Eve Percy	Sarah Ross
Mary Rhoades	Margery Read	Maria Redman
Mary Shryosk	Harriot Slone	Freesy Ann Stickney
Mary Taylor	Mary Whaley	Mrs Hannah Walker
Miss Frances Webb	Mrs Fanny Wilson	Mrs Lucy West

WED APR 11, 1810
Runaway wench-Lotty; formerly the prop of Dr Edw Gantt, has lived some time past with Mrs H Hayward; well known in Wash & Gtwn. Reward-$25. [Enquire of printer of this paper]

Elegant horse-Mask, will stand at Mr Jas Rawlings, at the *Burnt Mill* & my stable, Joshua W Selby. [$5]

Poems by Thos Kennedy, Wash Co, Md-published by subscrip.

FRI APR 13, 1810
Ltr from Thos Sammons to Nt'l Intell: When young my fr remv'd from Ulster Co, where I was born, to Mohawk Rvr & purch'd a farm nrly adj Sir Wm Johnson; I first enrolled in the Militia in 1778 til end of the war; my fr was tied to a negro slave & forced to match; my mthr & srs were with-out shelter & exposed to the indians & soldiers; they escaped; nr the hse of Mr Fonda. We saw savages with his scalp; like manner I saw the scalps of Col Fisher & his 2 bros, Mr Hanson, Putman & others; my fr was released & my 2 bros carried to Canada where they escaped; hand-bills were sent to me in 1808 abusing Judge Herkemer, nphw of Genr'l Herkemer-who rec'd his death wound in the Battle of Oriskana-& commanded the Montg Militia. -Thos Sammons [excerpts of ltr which was followed by a speech, Jan 3, 1810, on resolution from the Senate]

Persons who own land in Va are compelled to enter same in the bks of the Commissioners of Revenue. -J Pleasants jr.

Bill of sale executed by Rosanna Finagan to Geo Thomson; at hse adj Saml H Smith, Pa Ave; all hsehld furn of said Rosanna Finagan. -Saml Speake, auct.

Hse o/Reps on Apr 11 were apprized of the death of Genr'l Wm Washington; late-Lt Col in Rev Army.

For sale or exchange for young negroes, my farm, whereon my bro, Mr Wm Armistead resides, in Pr Wm Co, Va, 266 1/3 acs. -Geo Armistead, at Fort McHenry, Balt, Md.

Fencing acad-to open at Mr Crawford's Htl-Gtwn. -Mr Willers.

MON APR 15, 1810
All with claims against est of Maj Wm McConchie, dec'd, to to hand them to Saml Chapman, adm, will annexed. Chas Co.

Partnership bet Thos Wheat & Jas Williams is dissolved by mutual consent; Thos Wheat to continue the bus; journey-man wheelright wanted immediately.

Rich'd Wallack-practice of law, opened an ofc with E M Lowe nr Navy Yd.

Orphans Crt of Calvert Co, Md. Apr 11, 1810. Prsnl est of Hezekiah F Duley, late of Calv Co, dec'd. -Benj H Mackall .

Orphans Crt of PG Co, Md. Prsnl est of Alex'r Magruder, late of PG Co, dec'd. -Benj H Mackall , Calvert Co, Md.

Per justices of Chas Co Crt-public sale of all land heretofore sold to Jesse Jamison, belonging to Justinian Burch, late of Chas Co, dec'd, at hse of Augustine Oliver Burch, adj Gideon Dent's & Miss Queen's lands, nr Bryantown. Nichs Miles, Jos Boarman of Leonard, Henry Cooksey, com'rs.

WED APR 18, 1810
Reward-$100 for Reuben, slave, who absconded from my farm on Rappahannock Rvr, 12 miles below Fredericksburg. -Francis Fitzhugh, King Geo Co, Va.

Having lived to a good old age, wishing to give his excs little to do, Henry Guest, New Brunswick, has prop for sale.

Act of relief for Tristram Hussey, coll of N Y-$395.40.

Miller & Staley, tanners & curriers; shop in High St, next dr to Lutzes Saddler Shop & oppo Holtzman's Tavern.

Wash Co, D C, Crct Crt, Dec term 1809. John Hoye adm d b n of Wm Deakins, & with Leonard M Deakins, exc of Francis Deakins, who was exc of Wm Deakins jr, vs Deborah Stewart, adm & others, heirs & devisees of Walter Stewart, dec'd. Ratify report of John G McDonald, trustee, appt'd Jun 28, 1808; rl est sold for $1,695. -Wm Brent, clk.

Died: Mr Rich'd Beck, age 31 yrs, Apr 2, of pulmonary complaint, mbr of Meth Episc Chr, Gtwn.

For sale-half or whole of 5 stud colts. -Ezekiel Dance

FRI APR 20, 1810

John Douglass has taken the store lately occupied by E Somerville; as a groc & shoe store, Pa Ave, Wash.

Country seat for rent-handsome hill east of Mr Barlow's within a mile from Pres' Hse, lately occupied by Mr Thos Hewitt, dec'd; 5 acs with dwlg hse. -Thos W Pairo, Wash.

For sale-Stelle's Hotel, fronts on A st & Md av, the lots are 16, 17, 18, sq 728, with pre-emption right to lot 19. -Pontius D Stelle.

Crct Crt of Wash Co, D C. Henry Pratt & others, cmplnts, vs Thos Law & Wm Campbell, dfndnts. In Chancery, Apr 14, 1810. Bill to redeem lots in Wash, mortgaged by Robt Morris & others to Thos Law in 1795, to quiet cmplnts's title against the claim of dfndnt, Wm Campbell, to part of mortgaged premises. W Campbell, not a resident of Wash. -Wm Brent, clk.

Mrs Greentree has a brdg schl for young ladies, in High St, Gtwn.

Orphans Crt of Wash Co, D C. Application of Chas H Varden, on prsnl est of Thos Jones, late of Wash City, dec'd. -Jno Hewitt, Reg.

Lost-$80 in bank notes. -Robt Orme, nr Vansville, PG Co, Md.

MON APR 23, 1810

Wm G Ridgely & Elisha Riggs have formed a Co-partnership in business; fancy & other goods; Gtwn.

Orphans Crt of Wash Co, Md. Pblc sale of all prsnl est of Thos Sprigg, late of said Co, dec'd; furn, carpenter, blacksmith & nailor tools, stock, breeds of cattle & hogs imported from Eng by Rich'd Parkinson in 1799, etc. -Wm O Sprigg, adm.

Orphans Crt of Wash Co, D C. Apr 21, 1810. Prsnl est of Thos Hewitt, late of said Co, dec'd. -Nancy D Hewitt, adm.

Reward-$50 for horse stolen from my stable. -Michl Snyder, lvng in Madison Co, Va.

WED APR 25, 1810

For sale-brick hse on sq 930 in Wash now occupied by Mr John W Brashears. apply to Maj Calhoun of Balt & Mr Clement Sewall at Gtwn Ferry. -Wm Brent.

Fred'k Cana, oppo the Navy Yd, offers 30,000 pds of Smithfield bacon for sale.

Runaways for sale: Jack, negro boy; says he belongs to John Roberts of Bond St, Balt, Md. Also Ben Taylor, negro man 22 yrs of age; says he belongs to Benj Dawson of Loudon Co, Va, by whom he was let on hire to Wm Wright of Westmoreland Co, Va. -C Tippett, kpr of the jail of D C.

Wash Co, D C. Crct Crt-In Chancery. Dan'l Dennison Rogers, Wm Smith, Wm Cranch, & John Miller jr, cmplnts, vs Claude Crommelin, Gulian Dan'l Crommlin, excs of Gulian Crommelin, the survivor of Robt Dan'l Crommelin & Gulian Crommelin, dfndnts. Bill to compel the dfndnts to account with the cmplnts for large am't of funded stock of the U S; placed in the hands of the late hse of Dan'l Crommelin & sons of Amsterdam by Watson & Greenleaf as collateral in yrs 1789 thru 1792; dfndnts do not reside in D C. -Wm Brent-clk.

Stolen or strayed-white mare, from Osborn Warner in city of Wash on Pa Ave nr the Center Mkt Hse.

I certify that Francis Boone brght before me a stray horse. -Alexius Sansbury, J P, PG Co, Md.

FRI APR 27, 1810

Sundry seamen impressed into British svc; declaring themselves natural-born ctzns of the U S:

Jas Sparrow, Norfolk, Va
John Perkington, Eliz City Co, Va
Jos Symonds, Jas Symonds, Jas Curry, Alex Luther, all-Salem, Mass
Amos Paul & John Minton, both Wash Co
Wm Frazier, Havre De Grace, Harford Co, Md
Jas Stanton, Balt
Geo Johnson, Sag Harbor, N Y
Jas M'Carty, N Y C
Saml Greaves, New Mkt, N H
John Harden, Duck Crk Cross Rds, Dela
Geo Prince, Newbury Port, Mass
Wm Smith, Thos Parker, Jas Coleman, Chas Thompson, all of N Y
Benj Shaw, Alexandria; Henry Young, Balt
John Smith, Brookhaven, L I
Thos Bailey, Portland, Mass
Michl Holbrook, Portsmouth
Thos Little, Louis Town, Pa
Cushing Mitchell, Cummington, Mass
Jas Howard, New Port, R I
Francis Edmunds, Lancaster, Va
Wm Welch, Dorchester, nr Boston, Mass
Thos Jones, Northampton Co, Va
John Runchey, Midshipman of U S N
-Jas Maury, Americ Cnslt, Liverpool, Feb 10, 1810. Dept of State, Apr 26, 1810

An Act authorising the dischg of John Kerr from his imprisonment to mrsh'l for Dist of N Car; upon an execution issued against him in behalf of the U S. -J B Varnum, spkr Hse o/Reps. John Gaillard, Pres of the Senate. Apprv'd-J Madison.

For sale-negro woman; deed of trust from the late Nath'l Gregory to Saml Burch, in Wash City May 2.

R C Weightman's bk store, Pa Ave, just rec'd-*The Law of Nations*: by Wm John Duane, Rep of Phil in Leg of Pa.

Pblc sale in Alexandria of tract of land-*Brent's Patent,* formerly occupied by Pressly Cox, & lately by Josiah Watson, on *Holmes' Run*, nr Alex, 490 acs. Apply to Col Gilpin of Alexandria or to Alex'r Kerr of Wash City.

MON APR 30, 1810
Act of relief for Moses Young, to settle his acc't, as sec of Legation to Henry Laurens, esq, on his mission to Holland in 1780. -J B Varnum, spkr of Hse o/Reps. Apprv'd-J Madison.

Ranaway-Ned, negro man, whose mthr lives at Mr Frost's hse. -Jas Wallace, Montg Co. Reward-$10.

For sale: merchant mill at Little Falls of Potomac with 15 acs of land.Apply to Mr John Hersey at the mill or to Jos Dean in Alexandria. -J Dean, Alex.

For sale-useful brdg hse furn. -Lund Washington-Capitol Hill.

WED MAY 2, 1810
Runaway, Poll, mulatto, committed to Fred'k Co, Md jail; says she belongs to Miss Bague of Balt. -Ezra Mantz-shrf.

Pblc sale-*Snowden's Manor Enlarged,* 33 1/8 acs, late the prop of John Thomas the 3d, taken at suits of Geo & Christopher Lindenberger. -Wm Candler, shrf, Montg Co, Md.

Pblc sale-right, title & int of Van Swearingen, in land cld *Bradford's Rest*-1002 acs & *Milleys Dislike*-553 acs; late the prop of Swearengen, taken at suits of Lewis Beall, Elemelech Swearingen use of Geo Riley; Lewis Beall use of Bernard Gilpin; Jas Anderson, Thos Linsted, Jas Jordane of Joshua Steward; Geo Willett & Eliz Swearengen. -Wm Candler, shrf, Montg Co, Md. [Writs of Vendo Exps]

Orphans Crt of Wash Co, D C. May 1, 1810. Prsnl est of Alex'r Ried, late of said city, dec'd. -David Watterston, David Somerville, excs.

Chancery, Apr 12, 1810-Christian T Hempstone's petition for decree to record deed; petitioner purch'd from Saml Hepburn a tract in Montg Co, cld *The Resurvey or Hanover* for 265 pounds, paid on Dec 9, 1801; wants same to be recorded.
-Nichs Brewer, R C C.

Orphans Crt of Wash Co, D C. Rl & prsnl est of Rich'd Beck, late of said Co, dec'd. -Rebecca Beck-excx, Jos Beck, Wms Nicholls-excs; all of Gtwn.

FRI MAY 4, 1810

Act by Sen & Hse o/Reps-persons to be on pension list of invalid pensioners of U S: [name-rate per month -effect date]

Gideon Griggs-	$2.50-	Dec 9, 1809
Elijah Brainard-	$5-	Nov 6, 1809
Benj Cotton-	$2.50-	Jan 30, 1809
Wm Smart-	$5-	Feb 2, 1809
John Union-	$2.50-	Dec 6, 1808
Edw Grant-	$3.75-	Jan 23, 1809
Peleg Smith-	$3.33 1/3	Jan 10, 1809
Nath'l Ladd-	$2.50-	Jan 28, 1809
John Reed-	$5-	Oct 31, 1809
Jos Slack-	$3.33 1/3	Oct 17, 1809
Saml Sterns-	$2.50-	Mar 20, 1809
Enos Petett-	$2-	Jun 5, 1809
Jonathan Perkins-	$5-	May 3, 1809
Toney Turney-	$3.75-	Jun 23, 1809
Jas Wayland-	$3.33 1/3	Jan 16, 1809
David Hurd-	$3.75-	Jun 23, 1808
Squire Boon-	$3-	Sep 9, 1809
Henry Shaw-	$2.50-	Oct 17, 1809
Quintim Moore-	$1.66 2/3	Aug 26, 1809
Robt Baird-	$10-	May 6, 1809
Geo Tennell-	$2.50-	Dec 5, 1808
Edw Lloyd-	$13.33 1/3	Jun 21, 1809
John M'Chesney-	$3.33 1/3	Feb 20, 1810
Benj Strother-	$3.33 1/3-	Oct 5, 1809
Geo Cress-	$2.50-	Aug 7, 1809
Jas Howard-	$2.50-	Jul 3, 1809
Newman Laudman-	$3.33 1/3	Jun 24, 1809
John Powell-	$3.33 1/3	Nov 20, 1809
David Hamilton-	$5-	Jan 26, 1809
Geo Benedict-	$3.33 1/3	Nov 22, 1809
Philip Philips-	$2.50-	Nov 29, 1809
Peter Conyne-	$8-	Nov 28, 1809
Jas Buxton-	$4-	Dec 22, 1809
John Crookshanks-	$2.50-	Dec 20, 1809
John Gilbert-	$2.50-	Sep 2, 1808
Simeon Gibbs-	$2.50-	Mar 28, 1808
Jas Berry-	$1.66 2/3	Sep 9, 1809
Jas Warson-	$3.33 1/3	Sep 22, 1809
Jos Shayler -	$20-	Feb 12, 1809
Jas Munn-	$10-	Mar 18, 1809
Jos Reed-	$3.33 1/3	Mar 16, 1809

Chas Kilgore-	$2.50-	Apr 28, 1809
Ambrose Lewis-	$2.50-	Jul 19, 1809
John Newman-	$10-	Oct 27, 1809
Jos Noyes-	$2.50-	Jan 28, 1809
Aaron Brinck-	$5-	Jan 26, 1809
Hackalia Doolitle-	$2.50-	Jan 25, 1809
Peter Harford-	$2.50-	Mar 8, 1810
John Wood-	$2.50-	Mar 3, 1810
Thos Goodrum-	$2.50-	Mar 14, 1810
John Smith-	$4-	Jan 28, 1809
Jared Duncan-	$5-	Dec 8, 1809
John Martin-	$2.50-	Mar 21, 1810
Gerardus Dingman-	$5-	Jan 15, 1810
Donald M'Donald-	$2.50-	Jan 20, 1810

Those already on pension list-increase in pension:

Wm Little-	$5-	Nov 22, 1809
Walker Baylor-	$20-	Dec 29, 1808
Isaac Bennett-	$3.33 1/3	Jun 26, 1809
Thos Cahart-	$5-	Feb 21, 1809
David Weaver-	$5-	Sep 4, 1809
Josias Smith-	$10-	May 11, 1809
Abiel Knapp-	$3.33 1/3	Oct 27, 1808
Peter D Damarest-	$5-	Jan 7, 1809
Kerly Ward-	$3.33 1/3	Jan 10, 1809
John Utter-	$5-	Jan 3, 1810
Lee Lay-	$6.66 2/3	Dec 4, 1809
Henry Cone-	$5-	Dec 4, 1809
Elihu Sabin-	$3.33 1/3-	Oct 3, 1809
Simon Crosby-	$3.33 1/3-	Sep 20, 1809
Wm Tarbell-	$3-	Jun 3, 1809
Jeremiah Markham-	$5-	Jun 3, 1809
John Wakelee-	$5-	Sep 1, 1808
David Orcutt-	$5-	Mar 15, 1809
Jedediah Brown-	$2.50-	Oct 14, 1808
Stephen Hempstead-	$3.75-	Feb 3, 1809
Isaac Finch-	$5-	Jul 21, 1808
Rich'd Lamb-	$3.33 1/3	May 1, 1808
Solomon Stark-	$3.75-	Feb 13, 1809
Nathan Hawley-	$3.33 1/3	May 26, 1808
Saml French-	$5-	May 26, 1808
Nero Hawley-	$3.33 1/3	May 26, 1808
Zeba Woodworth-	$5-	Sep 5, 1809
Annanias Tubbs-	$2.50-	May 15, 1809
Jonas Adams-	$5-	Feb 6, 1809
Moses Smith-	$5-	Feb 9, 1810
Abraham Sawyer-	$2.50-	Nov 16, 1809
Elias Barron-	$5-	Jun 6, 1809
Rich'd Crouch-	$5-	Apr 12, 1809

Jos Johnson-	$5-	Mar 18, 1809
Jeremiah Robbins-	$3.33 1/3	Jan 30, 1809
Abner Kent-	$5-	Jan 30, 1809
Jas Cobey-	$5-	May 16, 1809
Geo Vaughan-	$13.33 1/3	Jan 12, 1810
Statts Hammond-	$5-	Dec 18, 1809
Bartlett Hawkins-	$5-	May 8, 1810
Wm Foster-	$5-	Dec 16, 1809
Saml Johnson-	$5-	Jan 1, 1809

Sec of war is directed to place Andrew Pinkerton on pension list of invalid pensioners-$3.33 1/3-Aug 25, 1809. -J B Varnum-spkr of Hse o/Reps. John Gaillard, Pres of Sen -Pro Tempore. Apprv'd-Jas Madison.

Passed at 2d session of Eleventh Cong of U S: [those with surnames only were extracted] Act of relief for: Wm & Elias Rector;
Wm Hawkins; Joab Garret;
Tristram Hussey; John Kerr;
Wm Baynham; Moses Young;
Jos Joshua Dyster; John N Stout;
Wm W Weymouth & Jos P Weeks; P C L'enfant;
Henry Caldwell & Amasa Jackson, Jeremiah Reynolds & Levin Jones;
Arthur St Clair, Mgt Lapsley, Robt Robinson.
Bills re-read a 3d time. For relief of Grove Pomeroy, Arthur St Clair, David Blackwell, Lucy Dixon & John Murray. Bill of relief for Amy Dardin-rejected.

MON MAY 7, 1810
For sale-land on mouth of Wicomico-200 acs; with dwlg hse. -Jno D Locke, St Mary's Co, Md.

WED MAY 9, 1810
Sixth anniv of Arlington sheep shearing was celebrated Apr 30; cups were adjudged to Dan'l M Chichester & John C Scott, esqs for best tup & pr of ewe lambs; Mr Custis presided; also named-Rich'd M Scott, Jonathan Swift & Mr Chacon.

FRI MAY 11, 1810
Spanish merino sheep for sale at *Broonlawn*, nr Alexandria. -Jas H Hooe.

Ranaway-Jim, black; Frank, not so very black; & Isaac, black. -Gerrard T Greenfield, PG Co, nr Nottingham, Md.

Appointments by Pres of U S-J Madison:
Buckner Thruston of Ky, Assist Judge of Crct Crt of D C;
Wm H Harrison, Gov of Indiana Terr;
Cornelius P Van Ness of Vt, atty for Vt;
John Willard of Vt, mrshl;
Jos Crockett of Ky, mrshl of Ky;
Return J Meigs, com'r to hold convention bet Ky & Chickasaw indian Nation;

John Eppenger of Ga, mrshl-Ga;
Alex'r Montg, David M'Caleb, Thos Barnes, Jos Robert & Jos Carson, all Miss Terr, to be mbrs of Leg Cncl of same;
Henry M Queen, Nathan Luffborough & Walter S Chandler, J P for Wash Co, D C;
John M'Cambell of Tenn, atty for E Tenn;
Obadiah Jones of Ga, Judge of Miss Terr;
Stanley Griswold, Judge of Ill Terr;
John B C Lucas of Pa, Judge of La Terr; Otho Shrader of Pa, Judge of same;
Francis Xavia Martin of N C, Judge of Orleans Terr;
John E Beck of Tenn, atty for W Tenn;
Geo Wash Park Custis, Justice of Peace for Alexandria Co, D C;
Benj Howard of Ky, Gov of La Terr;
Tully Robinson of Orleans Terr, atty of Orleans;
Oliver Fitts o/N C, Judge o/Miss Terr; Ebenezer Knight Dexter o/R I, mrshl of R I;
Parke Walten of Miss Terr, recvr of pblc monies-land west of Pearl Rvr, Miss Terr;
Lewis Sewall of Ga, Reg of land ofc east of Pearl Rvr;
Levin Wailes of Orleans Terr, Reg of land ofc for western part o/same:
Jesse Somers of N J, coll of Great Egg Harbor;
Amos Spafford of Ohio, coll of Miami Dist;
Thos H Williams of Miss Terr, coll for Miss Dist;
Archibald S Bulluck of Ga, coll for Savannah;
Parker Barnes of Va, coll of Folly Landing Dist;
Jas Spark of Va, coll of East Rvr Dist;
Peter Isaackson of Norway, Consul at Christiansand;
Thos English of Pa, Consul at Dublin;
John B Davy of Pa, Consul for Port of Rangoon in Birnian Empire;
Chas Harris of Ga, com'r of Loans for State of Ga.

MON MAY 14, 1810

John Geo Baxter, Blockly Twnshp, Phil Co, offers for sale his patent mach for carding, roving & spinning cotton. Certificates: Geo N Skipwith, Hickory Hall , Cumberland Co, Va. Apr 14, 1810; John Kelso-same; T Robertson, M D, Farmville, Apr 13, 1810. Orders taken by: Geo N Skipwith, esq, Hickory Hall, Cumberland Co; Pugh W Price, esq, Pr Edw Co; Messrs M'Kenzie, Christian & Co, merchants, Petersburg.

Appointments in Naval establishment of U S: Jacob Jones-Mstr Cmndant in Navy; Geo Logan of S C & Amos A Evans, now Surg's mates to Surgs in Navy: Henry H Ford, Jas H Boyle & Jos Forster, 2d lts to 1st Lt Marines.

Acting Lts to Lts in Navy:

Alex'r Wadsworth
John Pettigrew
Geo W Rodgers
Henry E Ballard
Jesse D Elliot
Geo C Read
Thos Gamble

To 2d Lts-Marines:

Nichs Martin of Md
Saml G Hopkins of Ky

Nath'l Allen of Ga
Jos Woodson of Tenn
Robt B Riddell of Md
Jas M Broom of Dela
Alex'r G Sevier of Tenn
Francis D Cummings of Ga
Francis Thornton of Va
Jos Moseley of Ky,
Chas S Hanna of Ky
John Randal to be Navy agent at Annapolis;
Constant Tabor to be Navy agent at Newport, R I.

For sale-3000 acs of Loudon land, Va. -Henry Ashton, my resid in St Mary's Co, Md. [Chaptico]

Mrd: on May 8, Howell Cobb, esq, Rep in Cong from Ga, to Miss Martha J Rootes, d/o Thos R Rootes, esq of Fredericksburg, Va.

Roger Nelson, esq, Rep in Cong from Md, appt'd Assoc Judge of 5th Judicial Dist, vice, Wm Clagett, dec'd.

Strayed or stolen-sorrel mare from nr Great Hotel, Wash City; return to Thos Kelly, at the Wash Factory. Reward-$10.

Wm Ward, F St, *Sign of the Fan*-dry goods for sale. Wash.

WED MAY 16, 1810
Partnership bet Saml Hanson of Saml & Thos C Wright, is dissolved, May 7, 1810. Payments to Thos C Wright, Wash City.

Died: Genr'l Benj Lincoln, May 9, at his seat in Hingham, Mass, late coll of the port of Boston & Charleston.

Died: Admr Collingwood, at Cadiz, ab't Mar 24.

For sale-prop at Orange Crt Hse, Va, being occupied as a tavern for upwards of 50 yrs, with 200 acs. -Paul Verdier.

FRI MAY 18, 1810
Seamen impressed into British svc, who state they are ctzns of U S, Dept of State: May 15, 1810:
Henry Marsh, Exeter, N H;
Thos Fithian, Queen's Co, N Y;
Jos Symonds & Jas Symonds, Salem, Mass;
Saml Graves, New Mkt, N H;
John Thompson, Phil-his bro lives at Manhattan, N Y;
Philip Spinks, Chas Thomson, Edw Golson, Wm Smith, Solomon Sinclair, all N Y; Jas Coleman, Thos Juferson, Chas Simmes, all Phil;
Elezear Clark, New Bedford;
Henry Hones, Dennis, Mass;
John Barker, Dresden, Mass;
John Pinkinson, So Hampton, Eliz City Co, Va;

Thos Baily, Portland;
Mich'l Holbrock, Rockingham, N H;
Jos Ransam & Dan'l M'Guire, both Balt;
Wm Fravier, Hartford Co, Md;
Jas M Hoyt, Stamford, Conn;
Wm Smith, Petersburg, Va;
John White -Southfield, Orange Co, N Y;
Grelle Eastman, Concord, N H;
Alex'r Luthers, Swanses, Mass.
Jan. 1810: Wm Morris jr, Berwick Mass; John C Sutton, N Y
Feb 6, 1810: Geo Coffin, Nantucket; John Sleight, New Brunswick, N J.
Feb 10: Wm Patterson, Marlborough, Arundel Co, Md; Jos Thomas, New Bedford.
Feb 13: John Cochran, Marblehead.
Feb 14: Thos Hopkins, Talbot Co, Md; Peter Working, Balt, Md; Wm Conner, Chester, Md.
Feb 13: John Allen, Wiscasset.
Feb 21: John Harrison, Phil.
Feb 22: John Miller & Vincent Shore, both Fell's Point, Balt, Md; John Horsman, Dorchester Co, Md; Peter Campbell, Twnshp of Fairfield, N J.
Feb 23: John Morse or Moss, Saml Grimes, both N Y C; Jas Taylor, Newark, Essex Co, N J; Alex'r Welden, Phil.
Mar 1: Timothy Stanwood, Newburyport, Mass; Wm Lewis, Old Bark St, Norfolk; Sylvester Brown, Hartford Co, Conn; Asa Pendleton, Ayleysbury, Hancock Co, Mass; Chas Adams, Kensington, Pa; David Higgins, Phil; Jas Gordon, Lichfield, Linc Co, Mass.
Mar 2: Russel Brainerd, Haddam, Conn; John Albert, Benington Co, N J; Geo Bissel, Saratoga, N Y; Jas Smith, N Y C; John Taylor, Balt. Md..
Mar 3: Jacob Ferris, Belville, N J; Rich'd Penny, N Y; Edw Olingsworth, Portsmouth, N H.
Mar 5: Rich'd Hill, Phil; Robt Thompson, N Y C; David Smith, Hemstead, Queen's Co, N Y.
Mar 6: John Thomas, New Haven, Conn; Jas Prinfield, Centerville, Queen Ann's Co, Md; John Gold, Phil.
Mar 10: John Maines, Shrewsbury, Monmonti Co, Middlesex, N J; Henry Myars, Phil, Pa.
Mar 14: Benj Hartis & Isaac Belsey, both Balt; Thos Holland, Fell's Point, Balt; Robt Farmer, Charleston, S C; Rich'd Conner, Little Water St, Phil; John Lewis, Alex, Va, s/o Fielding Lewis. -Americ Cnsl, Liverpool, Mar 18, 1810. Jas Maury.

Mrd: on May 17, Mr Thos B Dashiell to Miss Keziah A Couzins, both of Wash, by Rev Mr Addison.

Wm Gamble, insolvent debtor, confined to Wash Co, D C, prison, for debt.
-Wm Brent, clk.

SAT MAY 19, 1810 Extra
Ltr from Wm Pinkney, esq, to R Smith, esq, Sec of State, dt'd London, Mar 21, 1810.

MON MAY 21, 1810
Geo Boyd has remv'd his store to one of the new hses lately built by Ross & Getty, above Union Tavern, Gtwn.

WED MAY 23, 1810
Longevity-Mrs Eliz Clayton, wid of Mr Jacob Clayton, is now living in this county, 129 yrs of age; ntv of this country. -Fredericksburg Herald.

Genr'l Moreau now resides in New York City.

Runaways, committed to Wash Co, D C jail: Negress Hessey; says she belongs to Levi Gantt of PG Co, Md; also negress Beck; says she belongs to Benj Mackle of PG Co, Md. -C Tippet

Jas M'Cormick jr, has rec'd a collection of goods for sale.

Chas Vinson has opened a new store in Bridge St, adj the stand of the late Rich'd Beck; seasonable goods. Gtwn

Partnership bet Aquila Beall & Wm Steuart, Gtwn, dissolved by mutual consent for some time. Settlement to Wm Steuart alone.

Proposals for receiving beef & pork for the Navy; apply to Paul Hamilton, Navy Office.

Promotions in Army of U S:
Regt of Artl-1st
Lt Francis Newman to Capt, vice Wm A Murray, rsgnd
2d Lt Thos Bennet to 1st Lt, vice Jos Kimball, rsgnd
2d Lt Ethan A Allen to 1st Lt, vice Francis Newman, prmt'd
1st Regt of infty:
Ensign Jas W Bryson to 2d Lt, vice John Read, rsgnd
Ensign Robt C Page to 2d Lt, vice Wm Lithgow, dec'd
Ensign John Campbell to 2d Lt, vice Louis Loramier, rsgnd
Ensign Dixon Stansbury to 2d Lt, vice Nath'l Pryor, rsgnd
2d Regt of infty:
1st Lt Wm Lawrence to Capt, vice John Brahan, rsgnd
2d Lt Wm F Ware to 1st Lt, vice Benj S Smoot, rsgnd
2d Lt John Davis to 1st Lt, vice Wm Lawrence, prmt'd
Ensign Robt Cherry to 2d Lt, vice Wm F Ward, prmt'd
Ensign John T Wirt to 2d Lt, vice John C Carter, dec'd
Ensign Evert Bogardus to 2d Lt, vice John Davis, prmt'd
Ensign Hezekiah Bradley to 2d Lt, vice Francis W Small, rsgnd

Regt of Light Dragoons:
Lt Col Leonard Covington to Col, vice Wade Hampton appt'd Brig Genr'l
Maj Electius Backus to Lt Col vice Leonard Covington, prmt'd

Capt Jacint Lavall to Maj, vice Electus Backus, prmt'd
1st Lt Bille Williams to Capt vice Jacint Lavall, prmt'd
1st Lt Thos A Helmes to Capt, vice Clement Biddle, rsgnd
1st Lt Arthur P Hayne to Capt, vice Alex'r F Rose, rsgnd
1st Lt Asa Morgan to Capt, vice Isaac A Coles, rsgnd
2d Lt Silas Halsey to 1st Lt, vice Bille Williams, prmt'd
2d Lt Saml M Lee to 1st Lt, vice John F Bowie, dec'd
2d Lt Alex'r Cummings to 1st Lt, vice Thos A Helms, prmt'd
2d Lt Wm Littlejohn to 1st Lt, vice John M Barclay, rsgnd
2d Lt Geo Haig to 1st Lt, vice Arthur P Hayne, prmt'd
Cornet Levi Hukill to 1st Lt, vice Asa Morgan, prmt'd
Cornet Elijah Boardman to 2d Lt, vice Silas Halsey, prmt'd
Cornet John Hollingshead to 2d Lt, vice Saml M Lee, prmt'd
Cornet Jos Kean to 2d Lt, vice Geo Nicholls, rsgnd
Cornet Henry Whiting to 2d Lt, vice Jonas Munroe, rsgnd
Cornet Robt P M'Kelvey to 2d Lt, vice Alex'r Cummings-prmt'd
Cornet Geo Birch to 2d Lt, vice Wm Littlejohn, prmt'd

Regt of Light Artl:

1st Lt Thos Pitts to Capt, vice Dan'l Guno, rsgn'd
1st Lt Alex'r S Brooks to Capt, vice Geo Peter, rsgn'd
1st Lt John H Testes to Capt, vice Jos Chandler, rsgn'd
2d Lt Andrew M'Dowall to 1st Lt, vice Thos Pitts, prmt'd
2d Lt Saml Newman to 1st Lt, vice Alex'r S Brooks, prmt'd
2d Lt Luther Leonard to 1st Lt, vice John H Testes, prmt'd
2d Lt Henry Lenud to 1st Lt, vice Saml Watson, rsgn'd

Third Regt of infty:

1st Lt Wm Butler to Capt, vice John Darrington, prmt'd
1st Lt Cadwallader Jones to Capt, vice Abner Pasteur, rsgn'd
2d Lt Saml W Butler to 1st Lt, vice Robt M'dougall, dismissed
2d Lt Henry Chotard to 1st Lt, vice Wm Butler prmt'd
2d Lt Wm Johnson to 1st Lt, vice Cadwallader Jones, prmt'd
Ensign Saml C Mabson to 2d Lt, vice Edw Mason, dec'd
Ensign John Burnett to 2d Lt, vice Saml W Butler, prmt'd
Ensign Joel Lyon to 2d Lt, vice Chas C M'Kensie, rsgn'd
Ensign Sterling Anderson to 2d Lt, vice Henry Chotard, prmt'd
Ensign Wm Lavall to 2d Lt, vice Wm Johnson, prmt'd

Fourth Reg of infty:

Maj Zebn M Pike of 6th inf, to Lt Col, vice John Whiting, prmt'd to Col of 5th Regt of inf
1st Lt Josiah Snelling to Capt, vice Isaiah Doane, dismissed
1st Lt Robt C Barton to Capt, vice David Byers, dismissed
2d Lt Chas Larrabee to 1st Lt, vice Josiah Snelling, prmt'd
2d Lt Ebenezer Way to 1st Lt, vice Saml Haines, rsgn'd
2d Lt Minor Huntingdon to 1st Lt, vice Alden Cushman, dismissed
2d Lt Jackson Durant to 1st Lt, vice R C Barton, prmt'd
2d Lt Saml Borden to 1st Lt, vice Nicoll Fosdic, rsgn'd
Ensign Fred'k Conklin to 2d Lt, vice Chas Larrabee, prmt'd
Ensign Abraham Hawkins to 2d Lt, vice Eben Way, prmt'd

Ensign Geo P Peters to 2d Lt, vice Minor Huntingdon, prmt'd
Ensign Jonathan Simonds to 2d Lt, vice Lewis Harrington, rsgn'd
Ensign John Smith to 2d Lt, vice Jackson Durant, prmt'd
Ensign Lewis Peckham to 2d Lt, vice Saml Borden, prmt'd
Fifth Reg of infty:
Lt Col John Whiting of 4th Regt, to Col of 5th Regt, vice Alex'r Parker, rsgn'd
Capt Gilbert C Russell of 7th Regt to Maj of 5th Regt, vice Tully Robinson, rsgn'd
2d Lt Wm Henshaw to 1st Lt, vice Jas Fonerdon, rsgn'd
2d Lt Le Roy Opie to 1st Lt, vice Mordecai Griffith, rsgn'd
2d Lt Rich'd H Beall to 1st Lt, vice Roger A Jones, rsgn'd
Ensign Robt Carson to 2d Lt, vice Wm Henshaw, prmt'd
Ensign John Jamison to 2d Lt, vice Le Roy Opie, prmt'd
Ensign Jas Saunders to 2d Lt, vice Rich'd H Beall, prmt'd
Sixth Regt of infty:
Capt John Darrington of 3d Regt, to Maj in 6th Regt, vice Z M Pike, prmt'd
1st Lt Ebenezer Bebee to Capt vice Chas F Lott, rsgn'd
1st Lt John Christie to Capt, vice Benj Walton, rsgn'd
1st Lt John Machesney to Capt, vice Ebenezer Cross, rsgn'd
1st Lt Geo Nelson to Capt, vice Wm Pennell, rsgn'd
1st Lt John T Arrowsmith to Capt, vice John T Bentley, dec'd
1st Lt Gad Humphreys to Capt, vice Wm Cock, rsgn'd
1st Lt John Walworth to Capt, vice Thos Davis, rsgn'd
2d Lt Clement Sadlier to 1st Lt vice Eben Bebee, prmt'd
2d Lt Wm Nicholas to 1st Lt, vice John Christie, prmt'd
2d Lt Robt Sterry, to 1st Lt, vice J Machesney, prmt'd
2d Lt Jas Eamstrs to 1st Lt, vice Geo Nelson, prmt'd
2d Lt Chauncey Pettibone to 1st Lt, vice Jas Chambers, dec'd
2d Lt Henry Philips to 1st Lt, vice J T Arrowsmith, prmt'd
2d Lt John I Plume to 1st Lt, vice Gad Humphreys, prmt'd
2d Lt Jas I Vooris to 1st Lt, vice John Walworth, prmt'd
Ensign Neil Shaw to 2d Lt, vice Clement Sadlier, prmt'd
Ensign Edw Webb to 2d Lt, vice W Nicholas, prmt'd.
Ensign Chas K Gardner to 2d Lt, vice Robt Sterry, prmt'd
Ensign Henry Shell to 2d Lt, vice Jas Eamstrs, prmt'd
Ensign Jacob Sinn to 2d Lt, vice Chauncey Pettibone, prmt'd
Ensign Jacob Heet to 2d Lt, vice Henry Philips, prmt'd
Ensign John Reigart to 2d Lt, vice Abel Morse, rsgn'd
Seventh Regt of infty:
1st Lt Uriah Blue to Capt, vice Gilbert C Russell, prmt'd
1st Lt Rich Oldham to Capt, vice Jas Desha, rsgn'd
1st Lt Jas Doherty to Capt, vice Edw Hord, rsgn'd
2d Lt Alex'r White to 1st Lt, vice U Blue, prmt'd
2d Lt Thos S Jessup to 1st Lt, vice Rich'd Oldham, prmt'd
2d Lt Elisha Edwards to 1st Lt, vice Martin Durald, rsgn'd
2d Lt Narcissus Brontin to 1st Lt, vice Jas Doherty, prmt'd
Ensign Jas S Wade to 2d Lt, vice Alex'r White, prmt'd
Ensign Saml Vail to 2d Lt, vice Duff Green, rsgn'd
Ensign S M'Cormick to 2d Lt, vice Alex'r Smith, rsgn'd

Ensign Geo C Allen to 2d Lt, vice Thos S Jessup, prmt'd
Ensign E Montgomery to 2d Lt, vice Elisha Edwards, prmt'd
Ensign David M'Clelland to 2d Lt, vice Narcissus Brontin, prmt'd
Regt of Riflemen:
1st Lt Abraham A Massias to Capt, vice David Findley, dec'd
1st Lt Thos Spencer to Capt, vice Alex'r S Walker, dismissed
2d Lt Ludowick Morgan to 1st Lt, vice Geo Morrison, dec'd
2d Lt Dan'l Appling to 1st Lt, vice A A Massias, prmt'd
2d Lt Joshua Hamilton to 1st Lt, vice Thos Spencer, prmt'd
2d Lt Thos A Patterson to 1st Lt, vice Chas Potterfield, dec'd
Ensign Elias Stallings to 2d Lt, vice Lodowick Morgan, prmt'd
Ensign Arthur W Thornton to 2d Lt, vice Dan'l Appling, prmt'd
Ensign Francis Stribling to 2d Lt, vice Horace S White, rsgn'd; Ensign Jas Johnson to 2d Lt, vice Lewis Weir, dec'd

To rent: store rms & cellar, latley occupied by Capt Edgar Patterson, Wash City. -Francis Clarke, living in adj hse.

For sale-lands in Ohio & Ky, last will of Robt Means, dec'd. apply to Mr Walter Dun, residing in or nr Chillicothe, Ohio. -Dan'l Call , exc of Robt Means, dec'd.

Partnership bet Saml Hanson of Saml & Thos C Wright is dissolved this day; settlement to Thos C Wright, Gtwn.

Wm Gamble, insolvent debtor, confined in Wash Co, D C, prison for debt. -Wm Brent, clk.

Benj Edes & Co, of Balt, propose publishing a new work entitled, *A Universal Dictionary of Commercial Geography*.

Simond Adams, negro man, committted to Fred'k Co, Md, jail-as a runaway. -Ezra Mantz, shrf

Runaway-Reuben, slave; from Francis Fitzhugh, King Geo Co-Va.

FRI MAY 25, 1810
Patent obtained by Jos Hawkins, of Balt, for preparing pitch, turpentine, by a chemical process.

For sale-one half interest or the whole in 5 well bred stud colts. -Ezekiel Dance

Columbia Agricultural Soc met at Gtwn on May 16 & held their first exhibition. Judges for the sheep: Henry Maynadier & Brice J Worthington of A A Co, Md; Wm Hall of PG Co, Md; Geo Graham of Fairfax Co, Va; & John Cooke of StafFord Co, Va. Best 2 toothes ram-Solomon Cassidy of Alex Co, D C-1st Premium $100. 2d Pre-$80: John C Scott of *Strawberry Vale*, Fairfax Co, Va. 3d Pre-$60: Wm Marbury of *Blue Plains*, Wash Co, D C. Judges for domestic manufactures: Wm Marbury & John Cox of Wash Co, D C; Wm A Dangerfield of

Alex Co, D C; Gerard Brooke of Montg Co, Md; Jos Cross of PG Co, Md. 4th Pre-$30: best cotton cloth-men's coats, Mrs Martha P Graham of Dumfries, Pr Wm Co, Va. 5th Pre-$30: best fancy patterns-vests, Mrs Sarah Mc C Mason of *Hollin Hall*, Fairfax Co, Va. 6th Pre-$30: best cotton cloth for pantaloons & small clothes, Mrs Anna M Mason of *Analoston Island*, Wash Co, D C. 7th Pre-$20: cotton counterpane, Mrs Eliz Maynadier of *Bellevoir*, A A Co, Md. 8th Pre-$10: cotton stockings, Miss Kitty Shackelford of Culpeper Crt Hse, Va. 9th Pre-$30: hempen or flaxen sheeting, Mrs Sarah Chichester of Newington, Fairfax Co, Va. 10th Pre-$30: hempen or flaxen shirting, Mrs Eliz Gunnell of Fairfax Co, Va. 11th Pre-$30: flaxen table linen, Mrs Anna M Mason of Analoston Island, D C. 12th Pre-$10: flaxen thread stocking, Mrs Dennison of Fairfax Co, Va. 13th Pre-$20: twilled bagging, Mrs Sarah Mc C Mason of Hollin Hall , Frfx Co, Va. 14th Pre-$20: bed ticking, Mrs Sarah Mc C Mason of do. 15th Pre-$15: shearing a sheep in neatest, safest, expeditious manner, Mr Edw Eno of Wash Co, D C. Exhibited lambs: Mr Cassidy, Mr Scott, Mr Marbury, W H Foot, Chas Love, Rinaldo Johnson, Bern'd Gilpin, John C Scott, Isaac Duckett, Mr Chichester & Jos Kent. -David Wiley, sec.

Richmond Enquirer: Edw Livingston, ctzn of N Y, now of New Orleans, has brought a suit against Thos Jefferson on ground of having ejected him from the batture of N Orleans, while Mr J was Pres o/U S; damages at $100,000; John Wickham took writ out in name of E L. -W Mann, Dpty Mrshl, set out for Monticelo, to serve it.

Order of Orphans Crt-sale of valuable female svt, appy to Mgt Banks at Dr Chas Beatty's, Gtwn.

Crct Crt of Wash Co, D C. Henry Pratt & others, cmplnts, vs Thos Law & Wm Campbell, dfndnts. In Chancery, Apr 14, 1810. Bill to redeem lots in Wash City, mortgaged by Robt Morris & others to Thos Law in 1795, to quiet cmplnts title against the claim of Wm Campbell, who does not reside in D C. -Brent

Wm Jenkins is a missionary among the Oneida Indians. -Windsor

Archduke Francis, bro of the Empress of Austria, is to marry Maria Augusta-Antoinette, Princess Royal of Saxony; & will be created King of Poland.

Orphans Crt of Wash Co, D C. May 23, 1810. Prsnl est of Stephen Osborn, late of said Co. dec'd. -Cath Osborn, admx; Nathan Gray, adm.

MON MAY 28, 1810

For sale-land, part on which I reside, late the seat of Wm Briscoe, esq; 288 acs, on rd that leads from Chaptico to Newport. -Sally S Briscoe, Chas Co, Md.

Mrd: Mr Jeremiah W Bronaugh to Miss Eliz H Mitchell, d/o late Capt John Mitchell, all of Gtwn, May 22, by Rev Mr Addison.

Died: on May 17, Gustavus A Clagett, age 26 yrs, of PG Co, Md.

WED MAY 30, 1810
Camp meeting-Meth Episc Chr, nr Isaac Landsdel's mill in Montg Co, adj the lands of Col Henry Gather.

For sale: land on which Mr David Lacey now lives, Loudoun Co, Va; decree of Superior Crt of Chancery, Richmond, Va, May 26, 1801 & Feb 20, 1810. -E I Lee, John Keene, Rich'd Henderson, Acting com'rs.

Orphans Crt of PG Co, Md. May 28, 1810. Prsnl est of Henry Smallwood, formerly of Chas Co, Md, dec'd. -John Spalding-adm.

Crct Crt of Wash Co, D C. In Chancery, Apr 14, 1810. Godfrey Haga vs Chas Cist's heirs. Ratify sales made by Phineas Bradley, trustee, lots in Wash City; Mary Cist, wid o/Chas Cist, dec'd, to receive 1/7th of proceeds. -Wm Brent-clk.

FRI JUN 1, 1810
Geo Johnson has erected the *Columbia Mills* on Rock Creek, 2 miles from Gtwn; grinding of indian corn & plaister of Paris.

Order of U S Crt for 5th Crct & Va Dist, Jun 21, 1809, amended May 24, 1810; in suit wherin John Lloyd, exc of surviving partner of Capel & Osgood Hanbury was plntf, & Robt Patton & others, dfndnts. Sale-est cld *Mansfield*, subject to dower rights of the elder Mrs Page; nr Fredericksburg; Mrs Page's dower is in 1014 1/2 acs; part held by tenants of Robt C Page, 672 1/2 acs; also ab't 1200 acs on Massaponax, devised by the late Col Page to his son John T Page; sale at Wm Henderson's Tavern, Fredericksburg, Va. -Benj Botts [Map at Mr Alsop's at Mansfield]

For sale-land in Ohio Co, Ky, on Green Run; when surveyed they laid in Jefferson Co, since the division, now in Ohio Co, Ky. -Everard Gary

Ctzn's of 4th ward to meet at hse of Sylvanus Shumway, Fri.

MON JUN 4, 1810
PG Co, Md. Gen Robt Bowie brought before me astray bay mare. -Jas G Wood

Strayed or stolen, sorrel horse & small mare. -Jos Stone, St Clement's Bay, St Mary's Co, Md. Reward-$10.

Robt Witherspoon, now Rep in Cong from S C, has declined re-election to that station.

WED JUN 6, 1810
Geo Page, of PG Co, Md, insolvent debtor, confined for debt. -Jno M Gantt, Chief Judge of 1st Dist.

Stolen-gray horse, from Jacob Kieser, living nr Hardy Crt Hse, Va.

Elected to City Cncl of Wash: Phineas Bradley, Chas Jones, John Hewitt, Jas Hoban, John Davidson, John Graham, Walter Hellen, Jas H Blake, Sam N Smallwood. Also ran-Mathew Wright, Gustavus Hidgen, John Dobbyn. [1st Chamber] Elected for 2d Chamber: Nicholas King, Henry Herford, Peter Lenox, Geo Andrews, Toppan Webster, John M'Gowan, Jas M'Gowan, Jas Birth, Peter Hagner. Also ran: Wm James, C H Varden, John Chalmers, Geo Blagden.

FRI JUN 8, 1810

Robt Polk, will practice law in the Crct Crt of this Dist; has opened an ofc on Pa Ave, nr the Treasury Dept.

For sale-150 barrels of whiskey. Jos Forrest, Commercial Co of Wash; at Barry's Wharf.

For sale-farm, 130 acs, in Montg Co, Md; adj the est of Thos Cramphin, esq; good dwlg hse. Apply to Thos Brown on the premises; Robt Brown in Wash City.

Wm Dorsett, of PG Co, Md, confined as debtor. -John Read Magruder jr, clk. Also, John Henry Hall , of PG Co, Md,-debtor.

Dan'l Mandell, insolvent debtor, confined to Wash Co, D C, prison, for debt. -Wm Brent, clk.

Jas Hillhouse has resigned his seat in the Senate of U S, & accepted the ofc of com'r of the school fund, conferred by the Leg of Conn.

Stray horse came to Mr R Forrest's farm nr the Great Falls of Potomac; apply to Z Holsey.

MON JUN 11, 1810

Farm cld *St Osyth*, offered for sale sometime ago, is still unsold; 700 acs. Apply to Dr W Baker, Gtwn, or Jon. B Carr, Charlottesville, Albemarle Co, Va; title is unexceptionable.

New packet boat from Barry's Wharf for Alex & returning the same day; packages to go at Mr Jas Van Zandt's in Wash City & at Cooper's in Alex. -Dan'l Adlington.

Bath or Warm Springs, Berkley Co, Va. Boarding hse for visitors this season. -Wm Throckmorton.

Six cents reward for Joel Wenfield, youth indented to the saddling business; from John Poynor, living in Mecklenburg Co, Va.

Jas Crawford of Basil, of PG Co, Md; confined as insolvent debtor for debt. -Jno M Gantt.

Robt Brent, esq, re-appt'd Mayor of Wash City.

WED JUN 13, 1810
Runaway-Miel, negro man; says he was sold by Henry T Compton, of PG Co,Md, to Mr Broomsfield, living in N Orleans. -John Ireland, shrf of Calvert Co, Md.

FRI JUN 15, 1810
Orphans Crt of PG Co, Md. Est of Jas Nowell, late of said Co, dec'd. -Eliz Nowell, excx.

MON JUN 18, 1810
Sir Francis Burdet has been committed to the tower of London, for an alledged breach of the privileges of the Hse of Commons; he is mrd to Miss Courts, by whom he has chldrn.

Persons wishing to apply for a patent or marble, see Rev Robt Elliot, Capitol Hill; or Jos Lefever, Strasburg, Lanc Co, Pa.

Orphans Crt of PG Co, Md. Jun 8, 1810. Prsnl est of Thos Magruder, late of said Co. dec'd. -Polly B Magruder, John H Beans, adms.

Society meeting of the Sons of Erin. -Henry Whetcroft, sec.

Intended marriage: Emperor Napoleon with Arch Dutchess Maria Louisa of Austria. St Petersburg, Mar 21.

Died: on May 25, Gen John B Caradeux, age 70 yrs, at his seat in St Thos' Parish; ntv of St Domingo; arrv'd here in 1797. -Charleston, Jun 6.

Ltr directed to Jos Janney containing $200, & put into the Winchester Post ofc at Winchester in Jul 1809, advertised as lost by Dan'l Lee last summer, has been found; ltr was directed to Balt instead of Alexandria by the writer.

White or Bowyers Sulphur Springs, Greenbrier Co, Va; season begins Jul 1, 1810 under c/o Mr Jas Frazer. -Wm Herndon & Co.

WED JUN 20, 1810
Orphans Crt of Chas Co, Md. Jun 14, 1810. Prsnl est of Henry Bishop Morris, late of said Co. dec'd. -Caleb Hawkins, exc.

Jas Monroe of Va, Morgan Lewis of N Y, & John T Gilman of N H, elected mbrs of their respective State Legislatures-all srv'd in capacity of Governor & at the same time.

Jacob Gibson, esq, of Talbot Co, Md, lately advertised Marengo sheep for sale in the Evening Post.

Treasurer's sale-hse & prop of Henry Tims, for tax due by said H Tims to Corp of Wash. -Henry Whetcroft, Treas, Wash.

Reward-$10 for runaway, Ben, negro man. -Nichs L Queen, Wash.

FRI JUN 22, 1810
Reward-$20 for Anthony Smith, negro; I lately purch'd from est of late Thos Hewitt, esq, formerly of Bladensburg, Md. -Wm Simmons.

Wanted-able teacher, in Richmond, Va. -L H Girardin, Richmond, Va.

Orphans Crt of St Mary's Co, Md. Jun term, 1810. Mildred Walker, admx of Bennet Walker, late of St M Co, dec'd, is to give notice required for creditors. -Jas Forrest, Reg of wills for St Mary's Co. Notice followed signed by Mildred Walker-admx of Bennet Walker.

MON JUN 25, 1810
Saml Stettinius, Pa Ave, nr the Centre Mkt, will carry on the business in assoc with Geo Kneller; grocery & dry goods.

For sale-land in Randolph Co, Va, 4777 acs. -Wm Waters, Wash.

WED JUN 27, 1810
Pblc sale-5 lots of ground, 1 mile from the Pres' Hse; 20 to 60 acs; on Bladensburg Rd. Apply to Mr Wm Smith or to Thos Peter, Gtwn.

Orphans Crt of Wash Co, D C. Jun 25, 1810. Prsnl est of Jas Tootle, late of said city, dec'd. -Wm Whann, adm.

Count Pahlen, Russian Minister, has arrived in Wash City.

FRI JUN 29, 1810
Ranaway-Randel, mulatto boy; from Mary Moreland, living at Broad Creek, PG Co, Md. Reward-$8.

Long's Hotel to rent; now occupied by Robt Long; also tavern formerly occupied by Mr Stelle. -Dan'l Carroll of Dud.

Theodore Count Pahlen, Russian Minister, presented to the Pres of U S; with Mr Poletica-Counsellor of Leg & Mr Ivanoff,-sec.

Court Martial was held at Marine Barracks, by order of Lt Col F Wharton, for trial of Lt Thos H Pinkney of the Marines, for charges against him by Lt Archibald Henderson of same Corps; not guilty.

Reward-$10 for red purse with $260, lost about Brooke's Tavern, in Alexandria, or on rd to Wash Bridge. -Wm Dudley Digges.

Meeting of Columbia Dragoons, Long's Htl. -Saml Burch-1st Sgt.

MON JUL 2, 1810
New dry good store. Wm M'Kenney & Joel Brown, have entered into Co-partnership, nr Union Tavern.

Absconded, negro Tom, from Henry Basford, mgr at farm of Mr Isaac Ducket, on So Rvr, nr Annapolis. Tom was purchased of Capt John S Brooks ab't 5 yrs since.

Clermont sheep shearing celebrated at the mansion of Hon Robt R Livingston, on Jun 15, in Clermont; Mr L introduced the Merino sheep to this country. Toasts by: Saml L Mitchill, VP of the Soc; Elkanah Watson of Mass; Stephen Van Rensselaer; Dittmar Basse Mulier, late of Germany, now of Pa.

Madame Stael Von Holstein, authoress of Corrinna, intends to bid adieu to Europe & reside in N Y. Mr Wm Schlegel will accompany her thither. -Bos Gaz.

Gallant exploit-Oct 6 last, Capt Saml Green of the ship *Polly*, bound from this port to Falmouth, was captured by a French privateer nr Scilly islands; ship plundered & prize-mstr & 4 men were put on board; ship's crew except for Capt G & his apprentice were taken from the *Polly*; Oct 9th Capt G seized a moment & recaptured the ship; Oct 19 he arrv'd in Bristol, Eng. -New York.

Sale of livestock, at Cold Stream; may be seen at my Springfield plantation on Liberty town Rd & my mills on Phil Rd. -Wm Patterson, Balt.

Va coal wanted. D Easton, Treas Dept, at his dwlg, G St, nr Mr Duvall 's.

WED JUL 4, 1810
Died: Ann Sylvester, at Falmouth, Jamaica, Jun 15, at age 133 yrs; a free black woman.

Norfolk, Jun 25-Ltr from H M S Princess, Port of Liverpool. *Impressed seamen*:
Jas Sparrow, born in Pr Ann Co, Va
Rich'd Peter Tongue, B. Sep 23, 1782, age 27, Norfolk Co, Va
John Perkinton, B. Aug 22, 1778, age 31
Jos Symonds, B. Sep 25, 1787, age 22, Salem, Mass
Jas Symonds, B. Oct 27, 1782, age 27, Salem, Mass
Jas Curry, B. Jan 16, 1773, age 37, Ditto
Alex Luther, B. Oct 26, 1787, age 22, Ditto
Amos Paul, B. Apr 31, 1779, age 30, Wash Co
John Minton, B. Dec 28, 1787, age 23, Ditto
Wm Freazier, B. Jul 16, 1785, age 23, Havre De Grass, Hartford Co, Md
Jas Stanton, B. Dec 5, 1790, age 19, Balt Co
Geo Johnson, B. Dec 16, 1788, age 21, Sag Harbour, N Y
Benj Hutchings, B. Aug 26, 1782, age 27, N Y C
Jas M Carty, B. Dec 25, 1776, age 33, N Y C
Saml Greaves, B. Oct 13, 1787, age 22, New Mkt, N H

John Harden, B. Jun 5, 1779, age 30, Duck Creek, Cross Rds, Dela; Geo Prince, B. May 29, 1789, age 29, Newbury Port, Mass
Wm Smith, B. May 29, 1773, age 36, N Y C
Thos Bailey, B. Jun 1, 1790, age 19, Portland, Mass
Thos Parker, B. Jun 1, 1782, age 27, N Y C
John Roberts, B. Mar 14, 1791, age 18, Reding, Pa
Jas Colemen, B. Mar 14, 1774, age 35, N Y C
Benj Shaw, B. Jan 14, 1787, age 21, Alex
Henry Young, B. Aug 5, 1788, age 21, Balt Co, Md
Chas Thompson, B. Jan 25, 1786, age 23, N Y, N Y
Jos Pitty, of Balt, Mate of the ship *Hercules*-released by a Habeas Corpus. [The above need proof of ctznship of U S]

FRI JUL 6, 1810
London paper of May 19: Princess Amelia, y/d of the King, born in 1783, was in very critical state last night, attended by Princess Mary & his Majesty.

Runaway, Geo Jones, negro, ab't 45 yrs of age, committed to my jail. -John Darnall , shrf, PG Co, Md. Also Wm Harriss, negro, ab't 23 yrs of age.

For sale-hse on 19th St West, bet F & G. -Wm Cocking, Wash.

MON JUL 9, 1810
Sale of entire stock of dry goods by middle of Sept; bks to be settled.
-Romulus Riggs.

Wilmington, Jul 4. John Rowland, Old Cape Henlopen pilot, on Jun 25 boarded the British sloop of war *Avon,* Henry T Frazer, Comder; unlawful intercourse suspected. Take care ctzns, you are influenced by British gold than by the laws of your country-there is a day of retribution. -Watchman.

Wm Perkins, of PG Co, Md, brought before me astray bay gelding. -Thos Magruder, one of the Justices of the Peace-PG.

Turtle dinner to be srv'd at Sebastian Spring. -John Austin.

Ranaway-Wm Harriss, negro, ab't 23 yrs of age; says he srv'd appr of four yrs with Jos Priggs of Harford Co, Md, to shoe making bus. -John Darnall , shrf, PG Co, Md. Also, Geo Jones, negro, ab't 45 yrs of age; says he lived in Mathews Co, Va.
-John Darnall, ditto.

For sale-2 story brick hse nr Marine Barracks. -Buller Cocke.

Lost-Morocco case. -Peter Dent Moore, Treas ofc.

WED JUL 11, 1810
Auction-stock in trade of Mr Edw G Handy, cabinet mkr, Pa Ave -Andrews & Jones, Auc'rs.

Ladies with ltrs in Wash Post ofc-Jul 1, 1810:

Mrs J S Blount,	Miss Biscoe
Mrs Ch Cozens	Mrs Charity Eastin
Nancy-living with Col Freeman	Matilda Gross
Miss Johnson-Stelle's Hotel	Eliz Lewis
Cath M'Mullen	Mrs M'Lawmany
Mrs Ann Norris	Miss Mary Percy
Mrs Mgt Shats	Miss Jane Taylor
Mary Whaley	

FRI JUL 13, 1810

Died: on Jul 7, Mr Wm Bushby, age 64 yrs, at his hse nr the Navy Yd, long a respectable ctzn of Alex; last 6 yrs a resid of Wash; hsbnd & father.

For sale-lot & hse whereon Eleazer Standage now lives, on Eastern Branch of Potomack. Also 4 lots being part of the est of the late Matthew Wigfield, dec'd; ab't 20 acs. -Zeph Farrell, Wash City.

Reward-ten cents-for Michl Murphy, ab't 12 yrs of age, appr to shoemkg business. -John Minchin, N J Ave, Wash.

MON JUL 16, 1810

Jas Rvr Canal: a contract has been made by the Jas Rvr Co with Capt Abiel Cooley, of Springfield, Mass, with a view of commmunicating the basin with tide water-completion May 1812.

Univ of Pa: Dr Caspar Wistar is elected the Prof of anatomy; Dr Thos C James, Prof of midwifery, & Robt Hare jr, Prof o/natural philosophy. -Phil, Jul 5.

Mr Jos Sigfried has lately discovered a bed of stone, in Allen township, of quality superior to the French burstone.

Rio Janeiro, May 15, 1801-Extract of a ltr: Spanish Prince Don Pedro will be mrd to the Princess Royal of Portugal, niece to his Catholic Majesty Ferdinand the VIIth.

Copperplate printing at next door to Mr Dan'l Reintzel, in Bridge St, Gtwn. -Edw Davis.

Reward-$20 for some person who defaced the tomb recently erected over the grave of the late John Leathall, in sq 109. -Geo Blagden, Nichs King.

Caution-Dec 16 last I purch'd lots 9 & 10 in sq 168 in Wash City, sold as the prop of A. Lindo. I believe they are again offered for sale by the said Lindo. -H Aborn.

WED JUL 18, 1810
N Battiste, in 7th St, nr the Navy Yd, has ice creams prepared at his hse on 2 days in the week, Sun & Tues; he also makes cakes and goes out to cook dinners.

Union Bank of Gtwn: resolved that the conduct of Robt Beverly, Pres of the Bank, in relation to a dispute with Edgar Patterson, respecting the bank paper, is a gross misrepresentation. From minutes of the board. -David English, cashier.

Proposals to be rec'd for erecting a banking hse. -Fred'k May, chrmn; Wash City.

For sale-negroes, at the hse of John C Moore, at the Eastern Branch bridge; prop of Capt John L Naylor. -John B Kerby.

FRI JUL 20, 1810
Orphans Crt of St Mary's Co, Md. Jul 20, 1810. Prsnl est of Jos Turner, late of said Co, dec'd. -Henry Turner, Josias Turner, excs.

Drawing School. David Boudon, limner from Geneva, Switz, has opened a school at the hse of Mr John Gardiner, Pa av

Robt Marion, esq, Rep in Cong from S C, has declined re-election; area comprehends Charleston.

For sale-hse & lot now occupied by Dr Sim, prop of Mr S T Anderson of N Y. -Matthew Greentree, Gtwn.

Died: on Jul 19, Mrs Eliz M'Kee, Consort of Mr Wm M'Kee, of Wash, of a severe illness; funeral & burial at Christ Chr.

MON JUL 23, 1810
For rent-hse in occupation of Mr Jas D Barry, nr Barry's wharf. -Dan'l Brent, Wm Brent.

Orphans Crt of Montg Co, Md. Jul 11, 1810. Prsnl est of Aquilia Coventy, late of said Co. dec'd. -Jesse Leach-adm.

Fletcher vs Peck; Supreme Crt at Wash, Feb term, 1810. John Peck, principal owner of land in Miss Terr under grants of the State of Ga; title adjudged valid in said case.

Sale of Merino sheep. -Jos Dougherty, Wash.

Merino sheep-for sale; shipped by Wm Jarvis, esq, U S Consul at Lisbon; apply to 53, Long Wharf, Boston. -Cornelius Coolidge & Co.

Chas J Catlett, Alexandria, wishes to engage 50,000 bushels of wheat, delivered in Oct & Nov

Orphans Crt of Wash Co, D C. Jul 23, 1810. Prsnl est of Thos Jones, late of said city, dec'd. -Philip O'Mara, adm.

For sale-a lease of 13 yrs, of the sugar hse adj dwlg hse at mouth of the Canal. -Corns Coningham.

WED JUL 25, 1810

Longevity in N H:

1-In Dover, Howard Henderson, died in 1772, age upwards of 100 yrs, was a seaman & srv'd on board the fleet of Sir Cloudesly Shovel in 1704.

2-In Durham, John Buss, unordained preacher for 33 yrs, died in 1736, age 108.

3-Family of Col Jas Davis: fr died. in 1749, age 88; his chldrn: Jas-age 93; Thos-age 88; Saml [in 1788]-age 99; Dan'l-age 65; Sarah-age 91; Hannah-age 77; Eliz-age 79; Ephraim [in 1791]-age 87; Phebe-age 85 & the wid of Saml, age 102, were living in 1779.

4-In Londonderry, Wm Scoby, died. at age 104.

5-In Chester, Jas Wilson died. in 1793-age 100 yrs.

6-Jas Shirley, in 1654, age 105.

7-Wm Craige & his wife, died in 1775, ea age-100 yrs.

8-In Newmarket, Wm Perkins, died in 1742-age 116, born in west of Eng; his son died. in 1757-age 87.

9-In Atkinson, Eben-Ezer Belknap, died age 75 & his wife at age 107.

10-In Wakefield -Robt Macklin, ntv of Scot, died in 1787, age 115; lived svr'l yrs in Portsmonth, a baker, he walked from Portsmouth to Boston, then 56 miles, in one day & returned the next.

11-In 1775, Mrs Lear died at Portsmouth, age 103 yrs; & Mrs Mayo, age 106.

Runaway-Reward $5, for Watt, negro man, prop of Dr Casine, of Port TobacCo, Md. -Gilbert Docker.

Runaway-Hetty Baylor, yellow woman, age 22 yrs; says she is free; I believe her name is Mary & she belongs to Mr Beverly Roy, of King & Queen Co, Va. -C Tippett, kpr of jail, Wash.

Reward-$50 for mulatto wench, Lotty; she absconded with a man srvnt belonging to Dr Edw Gantt, of Loudon Co, Va. Deliver to John Travers, auct, in Gtwn, D C.

FRI JUL 27, 1810

New Orleans, Jun 16, 1810-ltr to Capt Porter. Testimony of respect & esteem...Signed: Lts-M B Carroll, Jos Bainbridge, Benj F Read, John D Henley; Wm Carter jr, Act Lt; Sam W Heap, Robt S Kearney, S Hambleton.

Montreal, Jul 9. Jul 5, Donald Mac Kenzie embarked at La Chine, with Mr W P Hunt, & a crew of 16, in one canoe, for the N W coast with a view of opening a new trade.

Died: Rev Saml Webber, D D Pres of Harvard Univ, in Cambridge. [No date-appears recent.]

Died: Chevalier Chas Genevieve Louis Auguste Andre Timothe D'eon, in Eng, age 84.

Seth Pease, esq, appt'd one of the assist. Post-Mstr Genr'l.

For sale: mercant & saw mill, in Loudon Co on Goose Crk, Va; ab't 300 acs total. -Wm Brent jr, nr Aquia Post ofc, Va.

MON JUL 30, 1810

Chevalier D'eon, born in Honnere, Burgundy, on Oct 27, 1827 of an ancient family; assumed the female dress from 1777 until his death & was regarded as a woman; recent death revealed he was a man. Mr D'eon has left 2 or 3 nphws by name of O Gonman, related to the noble family of Thomond, in Ire. Burial in St Pancras Churchyard.

Orphans Crt of St Mary's Co, Md. Jul 10, 1810. Thos Billingsley & Jas B Latimer, excs of Allen Billingsley, late of said Co. dec'd, ordered to give notice to creditors. -Jas Forrest, Reg of wills. Said notice followed. -Latimer & Billingsley, excs.

German emigrants from N Y paper: the Harmonic Soc ab't 5 yrs ago, came to this country & planted themselves in Butler Co, Pa; Mr Geo Rapp with others, arrv'd at Zelinople in Dec 1804; they bought ab't 4,700 acs of land; in 1805, consisting of 50 famlies they laid out the town of Harmony; Soc now consists of 780 persons; 140 families.

Crct Crt of Wash Co, D C-Jun term, 1810. Eliz Robertson, cmplnt, vs John Jackson & Letitia his wife, Maria Mitchell & Matilda Mitchell, Co-heiresses of Electius Mitchell, Dan'l Renner & Dan'l Bussard, dfndnts. Bill to obtain a sale of rl est of Electius Mitchell, dec'd, for his debts, & claim due from Electius, for judgment obtained in Montg Co, Md; Electius died with rl est in Gtwn, leaving Maria & Matilda his heirs at law, under age of 21 yrs; both reside out of D C. -Wm Brent, clk.

Orphans Crt of Wash Co, D C. Jul 10, 1810. Prsnl est of Wm Bushby, late of said city, dec'd. -Mary Bushby, excx.

Partnership of Boarman & Wm Magee is dissolved; persons not to pay Boarman until arrangements have been made. -Wm Magee.

WED AUG 1, 1810

Stockholders of the Va Copper Mine Co, are to pay up $15 per share, to Jeremiah W Bronaugh, Gtwn. -Dan'l C Brent, Pres.

Memorial from the merchants of Boston: Jas Lloyd jr, John Coffin Jones, David Greene, Geo Cabot, Arnold Welles, Thos H Perkins, David Sears; Attest-Isaac Winslow jr, sec.

Wash Monument lottery of Balt, Md-mgrs:

Jas A Buchanan	Robt Gilmor jr
Robt Miller	Isaac M'Kim
Geo Hoffman	Edw J Coale
Lemuel Taylor	Wash Hall
John Frick	Jas Partridge
Wm Gwynne	Wm H Winder
Nath'l F Williams	John Comegys
David Winchester	Jas Barroll
Levi Hollingsworth	Fielding Lucas jr
R H Mulhkin	Jas Calhoun jr
Nichs G Ridgely	Dr Jas Cocke
Jas Williams	

Lottery ofcrs: Eli Simkins, sec, Balt;
Messrs Ridgely, Riggs, McKinney & Osborn, Gtwn;
Dan'l Rapine, Wash City;
Jas Wisffing, New Mkt
Geo Beux & Caspar Mantz, Fredericktown;
John & Geo Harry, & Rich'd Ragan, Hagerstown,
Johnson & Bowles, Hancocktown;
Wm McMalon, Cumberland;
Wm Holliday, Winchester.

FRI AUG 3, 1810
Hses & lots for sale on north F St, nr St Patrick's Chr. -Thady Hogan.

Reward-$5 for bay horse that strayed from Commons in Wash; Geo Watson at John Moore's, N J Ave, Wash City.

Wm Ward, at the *Sign of the Fan* on F St, just rec'd fancy goods.

MON AUG 6, 1810
Reward-$5 for black mare that strayed from the Commons in Wash. -Ambrose Moriarty, nr Centre Mkt, Wash City.

WED AUG 8, 1810
For sale-hse where I now live; oppo the Marine Barracks, in Wash City. -Wm P Tuckfield.

In Chancery-Walter B Smallwood & John H Beans against Chas Smallwood. Bill to obtain conveyance by dfndnt to cmplnt, John H Beans, part of a tract of land in Chas Co cld *Friendship;* 1803 dfndnt con-tracted to sell same to cmplnt, Walter B Smallwood; said land has since been sold to Beans. Chas Smallwood is a non-resid of Md. -Nichs Brewer, Reg C C.

Orphans Crt of Wash Co, D C. Philip Mara, adm of Thos Jones, dec'd, ordered to sell prop of dec'd. -John Hewitt, Reg.

Lost-gold locket. -Harriot Davis, Gtwn.

Reward-one half cent for runaway, Rich'd Kenney, age 20 yrs, apprentice. -John Hebron, Navy Yd, Wash.

Wash Co, D C. Certify that Geo L Dixon, of said Co, brought before me a stray bay horse. -Rich'd S Briscoe, Justice o/Peace.

FRI AUG 10, 1810
Died: Capt John Vincent, an Indian, age 95 yrs, at Parkertown, Vt.

Benj Betterton, insolvent debtor, confined in Wash Co, D C prison, for debt. -Wm Brent, clk.

Ranaway, Andrew, Jacob & Bob, 3 negroes; from Mills Holladay, residing in *Days Neck*, Isle of Wight Co, Va.

Orphans Crt of PG Co, Md. Sale at dwlg hse of Seth Hyatt, prsnl prop of Aderson Conaway, dec'd. -Elenor Conaway, admx.

Pblc sale-all stock of greenhse plants; also unexpired lease of 4 yrs & 4 mos; 2 1/2 acs. -Peter Billy.

MON AUG 13, 1810
Salem Gaz-Apr 10th. Sailed from Naples in ship *Mgt,* of Salem; passed thru gut of Gibraltar Apr 22; May 21-squall, capsized; got the long boat & Mr Saml Crafts, of Derby, Conn, repaired hole in her bottom; left the wreck in the long boat. -Wm Fairfield, Robt Peele, Edw Richardson & John Hayman, of ship *Mgt,* Alex Thompson, Nahum Warren, Wm Graves, John M Peck, Louis Barney, Z Kemp, Joshua Safford, John Tyler, Rufus Wilkins, Jacob Shultz & Alex'r M'Kenzy. May 28th-gale, lost all provisions but salt meat & wine; Capt Janvrin & myself took care of provisions; Jun 3d-Green Perry, of Salem died. Jun 4th-Geo E A Carpenter, clk of ship *Hercules*-Salem, John Brown, seaman of ship *Trent*-Boston; Isaac Choate, cook of schr-*Syren*; Maybury Orion of schr *Kite*-Balt; John Jones of same; Henry Gill 2d mate; John Brackley, appr of schr *Uranio*-N Y; Saml Crafts, mate of schr *Ousitanick*, Derby, Conn; Geo Cogswell of schr-*Peace*, Newburyport; Dan'l Cahill of the *Mgt;* Louis Josias, appr of Capt Fairfield; Hanson Wilson, cook of the *Mgt*; Geo Jones, shipped at Naples-all died. Jun 4th-Stephen Valpy, seaman of the *Mgt,* died. Jun 7th-those who left the wreck: John C Very, E A Irvine & Jepthah Layth, of Salem, John Treadwell, of Ipswich & myself-in a yawl. Left on board the ship: Henry Tucker, of ship *Francis*-Salem; Capt Janvrin, mstr of schr *Syren*-Newburyport; Benj Peele, seaman of brig *Victory*-Salem; John Merrill, seaman of schr *Peace*-Newburyport; Edmund Wingate, same; Nath'l Sheffield, of schr *Ousitonack*-Derbey, Conn; Jacob Fowler, of brig *Two Betsies*-Beverly; Jas Sinclair, of schr *Kite*-Balt; Alex'r Marshall, brig *Nancy-Ann*-Newburyport; Wm Burrill, of schr *Syren*-same Jun 28th -Layth died. Jun 30th-came along side the schr, *Genr'l Johnson* of Gloucester, from Lisbon, commanded by Capt Stephen L

Davis, who rec'd us on board; Jul 21-arrv'd safe at Gloucester. -Henry Larcom. Beverly, Aug 2, 1810.

Copper mine found on farm of Mr Benj Bowen, 5 miles from this City, on Falls Turnpike Rd. -Balt, Md. Aug 9.

Died: John Broome, Lt Gov of N Y, Aug 9, age 72 yrs. -New York.

For sale-*Sudley;* estate whereon I now reside, 1,000 acs, Fairfax Co, Va; anxious to remove to the Western country. -Lewis Beckwith, *Sudley Farm.*

WED AUG 15, 1810

Mr Boudet has opened a painting rm on Capitol Hill; he is not Mr Boudon & Mr Boudon is not Mr Boudet.

Died: Mrs Mary Gibbon, formerly of Phil, Aug 8, in Wash, age 80 yrs.

Reward-$50 for runaway, Chas Parker, negro, ab't 26 yrs of age; has a forged pass as a free man under the name of Wm Thornton; srv'd as a waiter with Mr S Meyer & Mrs Wadsworth in this city. [no name] -Wash. [Elener Beall -Aug 17 paper]

For sale-land in Montg Co, Md, 300 acs. -Robt Wallace, for the heirs of W Wallace, dec'd.

FRI AUG 17, 1810

Died: Lt Tripp, of U S N, at sea on his passage from Havana to this port; had command of the brig *Vixen.* -New Orleans

Reward-$50 for Merino ram lamb taken away from me by force by 4 men on my return from Alexandria, Aug 12. -John Threlkeld, Gtwn.

For sale-2 story brick hse on sq 930 in Wash, now occupied by Mr John W Brashears. -Wm Brent. Apply also to Maj Calhoun of Balt & Mr Clement Sewall at the Gtwn Ferry.

MON AUG 20, 1810

Marriage of Prince Christian Fred'k of Denmark, with the Princess Charlotte Frederica of Mecklenburg, is dissolved, at the desire of both parties. The Princess continues to reside at Horsens in Jutland.

If Mr John Rodolph Faesch, s/o late Mr F Rodolph Faesch, a ctzn of Basle & an ofcr in svc of Eng, who settled in S C in 1768, & was in N Y in May 1782, is yet living, he will hear something to his advantage by applying to the Dept of State. If he is dead & has left chldrn, they should apply.

Pblc sale by order of Crt of Chancery of Md, at Lewyllyns warehse on the premises, all the rl est of Rich'd Jordan, late of St Mary's Co, dec'd-*Brambly,* 450 acs; also 150 acs; subject to the dower of Mrs Jordan, which she will sell, rent or lease. -Jas Cooke, trustee.

Orphans Crt of PG Co, Md. Payments to the est of Eleazer Lanham, shd be paid to Thos Owen. -Thos Fenley, exc.

Rev John T Kirkland is chosen Pres of Harvard Univ

WED AUG 22, 1810

Died: Tingey Anna Margaretta Wingate, only child of Jos F Wingate, grdght of T Tingey, all of this city, on Aug 20.

Ranaway-Harrison, mulatto boy. Reward-$10. Apply to Mr Hugh Drummond, Wash City, or Gwyn Page, residing in Pr Wm Co, Va, nr Hay-Mkt. -Saml Pryor

FRI AUG 24, 1810

Orphans Crt of PG Co, Md. Ltrs of adm d b n, on prsnl est of John Brashears, of said Co, dec'd. -Benedict Brashear, exc.

Persons indebted to est of Wm T Beall, late of this city, dec'd, are to make payment. -John Coyle, adm.

Education. Rev A T McCormick, will teach chldrn or wards; apply to him at his seminary, Capitol Hill, Wash.

For sale: dwlg hse on F St; enquire of Mr B Bowling on the premises, or of Mr Alex Cochrane, Wash.

For sale: lands. Per will of John Gibson, dec'd, at plantation in Fairfax Co where Lewis Jenkins is now overseer; & land adj est of John Gibson, dec'd, ab't 1437 acs, on Castle Branch & Jonnymore Run; and at the hse of Capt Geo Williams, in Dumfries, plantation in Pr Wm Co-724 acs; also 900 acs. Mr Elisha Jenkins, lying thereon will show *Slaty Run.* -John Spence, Jas Reid, excs of John Gibson, Dumfries.

Madam De Cherray will open her acad on Mon. Gtwn

MON AUG 27, 1810

PG Co, Md. Dr Wm Baker, Francis Tolson & Col Wm Lyles, comrs, sold the lands of Jas Moore, dec'd, & have the money to divide among said heirs. I have purch'd of Wm Moore, one of the said heirs, all his rights.& forewarn all persons from purchasing from said Wm Moore any right he may attempt to set up to said land or lands. -Philip Spalding

Col Anthony New, esq, is elected to Cong from Ky, vice, Matthew Lyon, esq.

Orphans Crt of PG Co, Md. Sale at hse of Eliz Nowell, excx, in Nottingham; prsnl prop of Jas Nowell, dec'd. -E Nowell-excx.

For sale-2 healthy country born slaves. -Edw Dawes, Gtwn.

WED AUG 29, 1810
Pblc sale-small farm nr the Middle Battalion ground in PG Co, Md-100 acs, with small dwlg hse; apply to Francis Magruder, esq, living nr the same. Dwlg hse & lot in Wash City wld be rec'd in the barter. -Sarah Shanly, Wash.

Pblc auction-prop of Saml Russ, insolvent debtor. Creditors exhibit their claims to Benj Bryan. -Saml Speake, auct.

Reward-$20 for Fred'k Cromwell, negro, age 30 yrs. -Aquila D Hyatt, Pa Ave, Wash.

Wm H P Tuckfield has remv'd his shop from the Navy Yd to Capitol Hill-boots & shoes. At the same place, Mr Hemler has an assortment of fashionable hats.

For sale-land on which the late Judge Jones resided, 2,000 acs, on Little River, Loudon Co, Va. -Jas Monroe, Albemarle.

Appt'd assessors for Wash, D C:
1st ward-Alex'r Kerr, Jos Brumley
2d-Thos H Gillis, Eariel McDaniel
3d-Jno T Frost, Henry Ingle
4th-Henry M Queen, Wm Walker
-Robt Brent-Mayor

One cent reward for Betsey Innes, indented mulatto svt girl, ab't 12 yrs of age. -Alex'r Cochrane, north F St, Wash.

FRI AUG 31, 1810
Saml H Smith has transferred the establishment of the Nat'l Intelligencer to Jos Gales jr.

Died: Mrs Sarah Shanly, Aug 28, after a short & painful illness. She leaves a sister & 2 dghts.

Sale of prop advertised for sale by Mrs Sarah Shanly, recently dec'd, has been postponed.

Thos Crawford of PG Co, Md, brought before me a stray horse. -Andrew Hamilton, a Justice of the Peace for PG Co, Md.

Orphans Crt of Chas Co, Md. Prsnl est of Ignatius Ryan, late of Chas Co, dec'd. -Roger Dunnington, adm will annexed.

Orphans Crt of Chas Co, Md. Aug 23, 1810. Prsnl est of John Robertson, late of said Co. dec'd. -Alex'r Greer, exc.

Death of the late John Robertson, of Chas Co, Md, renders the closing of various mercantile concerns; his partner, Alex'r Greer, has the task of enforcing payment; settlements to Mr Wm Greer at Pomonkey & Mr John Edw Ford of Port TobacCo.

For sale-*Eagle's Nest,* ab't 1,056 acs, in Nanjemoy, Chas Co, Md, the resid of late John Robertson, dec'd. -Alex'r Greer.

For sale-Merino sheep, rec'd from Spain per the brig *Louisa*, Capt MacNamara. -John Muncaster, Alexandria.

John Brown, esq, Rep to Cong from Md, declined re-election.

MON SEP 3, 1810

Runaway, Jerry Bryan, negro man, committed to Fred'k Co, Md, jail; says he is free & drove a dray for Mr Robt Cark in High St, Gtwn, D C. -Ezra Mantz, shrf of Fred'k Co, Md.

History of Printing by Sen Mr Thomas, of Worcester, Mass, is now completed at the press.

Dentist from Paris, J Huau, offers his svcs at the hse or he may be seen at Lewis Morin's, Pa Ave, Wash City.

For sale-2 farms, on rd from Gtwn to Fredericktown; 140 acs & 93 acs. -Wm Cocking, F St, Wash City.

Lewis Deblois has Marsella wines for sale at his store nr the Navy Yard.

Peter Baudy, nr Wilmington, Dela, owns 600 Merino sheep.

WED SEP 5, 1810

Mrd: lately, Jas Turner, esq, Sen of U S from N C, to Mrs Johnson, of Warren Co, N C.

Mrd: on Aug 11, Lemuel Sawyer, esq, Rep in Cong from N C, to Miss Mary Snowden, of Camden Co, N C.

Died: on Sep 4, in Wash, Col John Whiting, of the Fifth Regt of U S infantry, age ab't 54 yrs, leaves a numerous family of chldrn to lament his loss; Rev soldier. [ntv of Mass]

Jas I Wigfield, insolvent debtor, confined in Wash Co, D C, prison, for debt. -Wm Brent, clk.

Died: Col Dennis Ramsay, age 56 yrs, at Alexandria, Aug 31.

Runaway-Moses Amenger, negro, committed to Wash Co, D C, jail. -C Tippett, kpr of the jail for W Boyd, mrsh'l.

For sale-brick hse on Va Ave, ab't half an acre. Apply to Saml Smallwood, next dr, or to E Dempsie at Wm Emack's Hse, on Capitol Hill.

FRI SEP 7, 1810

Died: John Muir, at Annapolis, on Aug 23, Pres of the Farmer's Bank of Md.

Died: Col Levin Powell, of Loudon Co, age 73 yrs, on Aug 23, at Bedford, Pa, on his way from the Springs; leaves a fmly.

Died: Pierre Rousseau, age 66, Aug 8, at his farm, half a league above New Orleans; Capt in the Navy-Rev war.

Died: Simon Southward, age 82, in Horsham Goal, formerly of Boxgrove, nr Chichester; miller by trade; in 1766 fancied himself Earl of Derby; 1767 arrested on a small debt & released 43 yrs 4 mos 8 days later, by the hand of death, on Wed last.

Died: Maj Genr'l Jos Walker, of Stratford, Conn, age 55 yrs, on Aug 12, at Ballston Springs where he had gone to recover his declining health; Grad of Yale Univ in 1774; Rev Sldr until the peace of 1783; retired a Capt.

Died: Hezekiah Rogers, of the War Dept, age 57 yrs, on Sep 4, in Wash City; ofcr in Rev Army; interred with Military Honors.

Henry Dangerfield, esq, of Va, appt'd by Pres of U S, sec of the Miss Terr, vice Thos H Williams, appt'd coll of the Port of New Orleans.

Obit of late Col John Whiting; ntv of Mass; took arms in his 18th yr; in action on Oct 7, 1777 at capture of Burgoyne; retired into his family after the war & conducted a bk store at Lancaster, Mass. Whiting once more offered his svcs when America was again provoked by belligerents; he arv'd in Wash in 1809. Burial in the pblc ground nr the Navy Yd after having lain in Military State.

For rent-hse I now occupy on N J Ave, $275. -S Hanson of Saml.

In Chancery-Md, Sep 3, 1810. Nicholas Lingan, surv partner of Henry Marbury & Co, vs Colin Hunter & Henrietta his wife, & others, heirs of Thos Dent of Chas Co, Md, dec'd. Bill to obtain a decree for sale of rl est of said Thos Dent, dec'd; said Dent died indebted to said Lingan; T Dent's prsnl est not sufficient to pay his debts; Colin & Henrietta Hunter are residents of Wash, D C. -Nichs Brewer, Reg Cur Can.

Died: Rt Hon Wm Windham, of *Felbrigge Hall*, Norfolk Co, Jun 4, age 60 yrs, at his hse in Pall Mall. -London Paper, Jun 5. He left no issue.

For sale-brick hse on sq 929, L St So. -Jas B Potts

For sale-brick hse & lot on 8th St West, sq 432. -Thos Young.

MON SEP 10, 1810

Dr Jos Kent, of PG Co, Md, is selected as Rpblcn candidate for Congress, for the Dist now represented by Archibald Van Horn, esq, who declines a re-election.

Mr Barnabas Bidwell, atty Genr'l of Mass, is charged with peculation, in the ofc of the Treasurer of Berkshire Co; in the amount of $1000; he has secreted himself & sent ltr of resignation. Perez Morton-nominated to take his place.

Died: on Aug 31, Mrs Mary Shaaf, consort of Dr John T Shaaf, at Annapolis, age 34 yrs.

Died: Mr Thos Jacob, age 50 yrs, at Alex, on Sep 6.

Died: Col Saml Postlethwaite, age 72, on Aug 24, at Carlisle.

Wanted-young man to assist in editing the *Watchman*. -Jas Wilson, editor, Wilmington, Dela.

Strays-mare & gelding, at my place on *Greenleaf's Point*. -John Chalmers, Wash.

Orphans Crt of Wash Co, D C. Prsnl est of Wm Wilson Thomas, late of Wash City, dec'd. -John Hewitt, Reg.

Gentleman teacher wanted-school nr completion. -Walter D Addison, Gtwn.

Died: Caleb Whitefoord, esq, lately, in England, author.

WED SEP 12, 1810

Bankrupts-London, Jul 14: Nath'l Cranch of Exeter; John Fanshaw of Liverpool; Thos Godwin of Queen St, Cheapside; Jas Willis, Geo Morss Jakes, Jas Grey Jackson & John Langley, of Salisbury sq, Fleet St.

Died: Jos De Montgolfier, age 70, Jun 26; inventor of fire balloons. -Picadilly, Jul 19, 1810.

Died: Dan'l Haragan, in New Orleans, on Jul 23; formerly assistant Qrtr-Mstr Grn'l of Legionary Army of U S, under Maj Gen Wayne.

Died: Capt Jas Williamson, Aug 4, at Natchez, cmndng U S Gun Vessel No. 19.

Died: Hon John Hubbard, age 50, on Aug 14, in Hanover, Prof of math & natr'l phil-Dartmouth college; formerly of Walpole.

Died: Col Philip Skene, at an advanced age, at Addersey-Lodge,nr Stoke Goldington, Bucks, Eng, on Jun 9; formerly of Skenesborough; ofcr in British Army from 1739 'til 1787; his grfr, John Skene of Halyards, in Fifeshire, Scot, was mrd to Eliz, d/o Sir Thos Wallace, of Craigie, in Ayre-Shire, nearest collateral descendent of celebrated but unfortunate Wm Wallace. Col S has left a son & 2 dghts. [From a London paper]

Cash sale-all right & title of Jos Bentley, in frame hse on sq 907, Wash City; at suits of Rich'd Barry, John Hayre & Stephen Perry. -David Bates, Constable, Wash City.

Orphans Crt of Wash Co, D C. Sep 12, 1810. Prsnl est of Saml Jones, dec'd. -Ann Jones.

Flea bitten grey horse was taken from the pastures in Wash. Reward-$5. -Godfrey Smith, nr the Great Htl, Wash.

FRI SEP 14, 1810
Mr H H Harwood, esq, elected Pres of Farmer's Bank of Md, vice Mr Muir, dec'd.

Edw St Loe Livermore, esq, Fdrl Rep in Cong from Mass, New-Buryport Dist, has declined re-election.

Mrs Durang will open an academy for young ladies on N J Ave, in hse lately occupied by Mrs Lee.

For sale-20 boxes of lemons. John Ott, druggist & chemist. -Gtwn.

Died: Mr Jas Williamson, sailing-mstr in U S N, at Natchez. [No date-appears recent.]

MON SEP 17, 1810
Died: Lt Geo Marcellin, of consumption, on board the frig, *President*, off Sandy Hook, Sep 10.

Died: Lt John Nicholson, of U S N, Sep 1, in Talbot Co.

Died: Peter Hoffman Sr, at Balt, on Sep 12.

Fire buckets-ctzns of Wash are notified to have their fire buckets in complete order. -John C Shindle, inspector.

Wash Co, D C. Oswald Clements brought before me a stray sorrel gelding.
-Saml N Smallwood, a Justice of Peace. [Oswald Clements lives nr the Eastern Branch bridge.]

Lt Thos Ramsey, of U S Army, arv'd at Nashville on Aug 20.

WED SEP 19, 1810
Reward-$5 for runaway-Andrew, black fellow. -Rich'd Delphey, *Greenleaf's Point*, Wash.

Conveyance & notary public-ofc at his dwlg oppo Rhodes Hotel. -Thos Herty.

FRI SEP 21, 1810
Rpblcn Ticket for the assembly in PG Co, Md: Col Jos Cross, Wm Bowie of Walter, Robt Wm Bowie, Humphrey Belt jr.

Benj Pickman jr, Federal Rep from Salem, Mass, has declined re-election.

Died: Wm Cushing, age 77 yrs, on Sep 7, at Scituate, Mass; Assoc Judge of U S.

Died: Jas Cox, esq, Sep 12, Rep from N J.

For sale: *Cornwallis' Neck*, bet 500 & 600 acs, on Mattawoman Swamp, with large dwlg hse. Also 3 lots in Wash City-lots 1, 2, 3; Mr Wm Worthington resides on these lots & will show same. -W Jameson, *Hardship*.

Wash Co, D C. John O'Connell, insolvent debtor, confined in prison for debt. -Wm Brent, clk.

Reward-$40 for runaway, Isaac Bluefoot, negro, age ab't 23 yrs. -Chas Binns, Leesburg, Loudon Co, Va.

Dissolution of partnership bet Benj Burns & Ninian Beall, is dissolved by limitation. Benj Burns will continue the business on N J Ave, Wash City.

For sale-hedge plants. -Thos Main, Main's Nursery, Gtwn.

MON SEP 24, 1810
John Francis Mercer, esq, is announced in the Md Gaz, as a candidate for Cong to rep PG & A A cos, Md.

Died: Chas Fleurriau, at his plantation nr New Orleans, ntv of that country, age 80 yrs; had been an ofcr in French svc & deputy from prov of La to the Synod at Havanna. [No date-appears recent.]

Messrs Bogle & Sommerville, & Bogle, Jemieson & Co John Nicholas & Robt Rose, adms of Gavin Lawson, dec'd. Take notice that at the hse of Enoch George, Lancaster Co, Va, depositions to be read in evidence in suit now pending in Sup Chancery Crt for Williamsburg Dist; we are plntfs & you are dfndnts. -Helen Gilmour, John M Gilmour, Robt Gilmour, Lancaster Co, Va.

Died: Jas Cheetham, Sep 19, nr N Y, editor of Americ Ctzn.

Orphans Crt of PG Co, Md. Sale of negro boy ab't 5 yrs old, prop of Jesse Hellen, dec'd; to settle his debts. -Thos Wall , living nr Philips's Mill.

Died: on Aug 26, Col Mose M'Lean, sldr o/Rev, at Chilicothe, Ohio.

Mrd: on Sep 16, Mr Tobias Matthews, of Wash, to Miss Sarah Ann Boose, of PG Co, Md.

WED SEP 26, 1810
Notice-my wife Jane Ward, formerly Jane Collard, has left me without sufficient provocation; I shall pay no debts she may contract. -Wm H Ward, Wash City.

Stolen or strayed-bay mare, from the Commons in Wash City. -Wm McKee, Navy Yd, Wash.

FRI SEP 28, 1810
Ltr written from Norfolk, Sep 1810. Passing thru Wash City a few wks ago I found a chapel built by a Mr Jas Barry, late of that place, on one of his own lots, for his Catholic brethren who were remote from the Parish Chr; my informer added that Mr Barry & his dghts were all dead, & buried in the vault beneath the chapel; there was no memorial. G B [Referring to: Mr Jas Barry, his dghts Anne & Mary, & Mrs B, wid of Mr J B]

Died: Mrs Martha Wise, consort of Mr Geo Wise, of *Abingdon*, nr Alexandria; at Mr Jos Newton's nr Leesburg, Sep 19.

Strays, a cow & calf came to my plantation. -John M Wight.

R Ballad, adj the store of J Wheaton, F St, wishes to employ svr'l good workman-journeymen taylors.

Dinner was given on Aug 29 at Wash, Miss Terr, by Rpblcns, to Geo Poindexter, their delegate in Congress.

West Fla-Convention appt'd: Robt Percy of New Feliciana; Fulwar Skipwith of Baton Rouge; & Shepherd Brown of St Helena; to be Assoc Judges of Superior Crt. Jos E Johnson of New Feliciana, shrf; & Andrew Steele of Baton Rouge, Reg of land claims for this Jurisdiction.

Matthias Rich'ds has declined a re-election to Cong from Pa.

American Consulate, Liverpool, Jul 26, 1810. Stephen Rose, Americ seaman in Plutarch, Capt Rossiter, from Phil, was dischgd at this place a few days ago, & lawful deposit of wages made in this ofc by said mstr. S Rose died before receiving his quota from me. S R was ntv of Eastern Shore of Md, mrd in Phil, in George's St, bet So & Shippen Sts Notice to the heir or heirs of Stephen Rose. [Dept of State.] -Jas Maury.

MON OCT 1, 1810
Moses Tabb, esq, has declined an election to Congress from Fred'k Dist, Md, in favor of Genr'l Saml Ringgold.

Mrd: Hon Wm Eustis, sec at war, to Miss Caroline Langdon, d/o late Hon Woodbury Langdon, of Portsmouth, N H, on Sep 24, by Rev Dr Buckminster, in Portsmouth, N H.

Mrd: Lt Satterlee Clarke to Miss Frances Whetcroft, on Sep 23, at Annapolis.

Died: Nicholavs Anciaux, esq, age 67 yrs, Oct 1, at the Social Circle, Bulloch Co, N Y; ofcr in svc of France, joined the Legions of our country when Americ Rev broke out; after the war he mrd & settled in N Y State.

Appointments apprv'd by the Govn'r-Baton Rouge, Aug 25, 1810.
Gilbert Leonard of Baton Rouge, Bryan M'Dermott of New Feliciana, & Dan'l Rainer of St Helena, to be Civil Commandants.
Ofcrs of Militia: Philemon Thomas-Col Cmmndnt; Isaac Johnson-Maj of Cavalry.
1st Regt of infty: Saml Fulton-Col; Geo Mather-1st Maj; Reuben Curtis-2d Maj.
2d Regt: Wm Spiller-Col; Jos Thomas-1st Maj; Abraham Speers-2d Maj.
3d Regt: Aquilla Whittaker-Col; Robt M'Causland-1st Maj; Robt Young-2d Maj.

Reward-$100 for runaway, Frank, negro. -G T Greenfield, residing in PG Co, nr Nottingham, Md.

PG Co, Md. Eversfield Bowie, confined in prison as insolvent debtor. -John Read Magruder jr, clk

John Spalding has commenced bus in the shop formerly occupied by Jos Bently, Navy Yd: clock & watch mkg & silversmith business.

Auction sale of Merino sheep at Canton, country seat of the late Col O'Donnell. -Robt Barry, Balt.

Last notice to those persons indebted to the late firm of Morin & Moore. -Lewis Morin, Geo Moore.

WED OCT 3, 1810

Balt City, Md, elections:

Mbrs of Cong:

Nicholas R Moore	Alex'r M'Kim	Peter Little
Joshua Barney	all Rpblcns	

City assembly

Theodorick Bland	Jas Martin	Robt Steuart

W H Stroud has silk, cotton & woollen dyer from London, for sale at Col Van Ness' warehse, mouth of Tyber Creek.

I am authorisd to sell the right of using John Herrick's patent *water elevator* in D C & PG Co, Md. -Thos Patterson.

The body of a drowned man was found by Thos Lindsay, on shore of Warburton, nr the fort on Sep 29. -Alexandria

T Craven has sold his stock of dry goods to Silas Butler.

FRI OCT 5, 1810

Diving machine has been constructed by Mr Saml Farmer, of Portsmouth; will descend at any wharf in Boston & proceed to Ft Independence. -Bost Cent.

Ladies with ltrs in Wash Post ofc-Oct 1, 1810:

Mrs I L Blount	Mrs Mary E Bacot
Miss Mariah Betagh	Mrs Eugenia Bacot
Miss Harrit Butler	Anne Boothe
Mrs Ch B Cochran	Mrs Alsa Collins
Mary Davis	Marget Gibbs
Mrs Allatha Holmead	Mrs Bailee Holy
Miss Gilyard	Mrs Jenkins
Miss Harriott Jenkins	Miss Eliz Murdoch
Mrs G Musgrave	Mrs G McDonald
Mrs Nancy Parsons	Deborah RayJohn or Mary Rice
Mrs Eliz Sandford	Mrs Jno L Wilson
Mrs Susannah Wheatly	Mrs Martha Young
Sally Young	

Meeting to examine the principles & utility of Mr Fulton's torpedoes, at City Hotel on Sep 21: Robt R Livingston, Oliver Wolcott, Col Williams, Dr Kemp, Morgan Lewis, C D Bolden, Mr Garnet, Cmdor Rodgers, & Capt Chauncey. -The Columbian

Mr John M'Gowan was chosen Pres of Commercial Co of Wash, vice Jos Forrest, resigned.

Died: Jos Otis, esq, age 83 yrs, Sep 23, at Barnstable; s/o late Jas Otis, of same, & bro of a distinguished statesman & lawyer; was a Brig Genr'l in Militia & coll for said Dist.

Died: Mr Jos Spear, age 47 yrs, Sep 28, at Balt, merchant in that city.

Orchard Cook, has declined re-election to Cong from Mass.

MON OCT 8, 1810

John G Jackson, esq, Rep in Cong from Va, rsgn'd bec of the state of his health.

Died: Baruch Duckett, age 66 yrs, suddenly on Oct 2, at his seat in PG Co, Md; hsbnd, parent, fr-in-law, mstr & friend.

Died: Col Wm A Washington, age 53 yrs, at Gtwn, Oct 2; remains were deposited in the vault at Mt Vernon.

Federalists in Chas Co, Md. elected to Hse o/Delegates: Clement Dorsey,
John Parnham Thos Rogerson Wm H MacPherson.
For Congress-Col Stewart-no opposition.
Fred'k Co: Joshua Cockey John Schley Rich'd B Cooke
Jos Swearengen. All Rpblcns.
For Congress- Saml Ringold Benj Galloway.
Harford Co: John Montgomery for Cong.
Delegates: Stevenson Archer, John Forwood
John Street Elijah Davis, all Rpblcns.

Died: Maj Wm Brown, of the Rev war, on Sep 21, at Savannah.

In Chancery of Md. Anthony Reintzel, adms & heirs of Peter Cassanove, & against Amy Thruston, Thos Robinson, Wm Robinson, Wm Pollard, Saml Crawford, John Barclay, Jacob Spier, Clement Biddle, Clement B Penrose & Wm Hutchinson. For sale at Mr Henry Ruth's Tavern, High St, Gtwn; the right & est of the heirs of P Cassanove in lot 7, 2d addition to Gtwn with improvements. -Dan'l Renner, trustee.

WED OCT 10, 1810

Md election cont'd: [See Oct 8, 1810]
Caroline Co-Alumby Jump, Henry Driver, Peter Willis, P G Bayard, Rpblcns.
Worcester Co for Cong: Fed-C Goldsborough; Rpblcn-Dr Williams. Delegates: E K Wilson, R H Handy, T N Williams, Lit Quinton, Wm Quinton, Josh Prideaux, Zadock Sturges, T R Handy.
Wash Co: John Bowles, Wm Downey, Thos B Hall & Wm B Williams, Rpblcns-Delegates.
Gen Saml Ringgold elected to Cong from Fred'k, Alleghany & Wash cos.
St Mary's Co: Dr Henry Ashton & Dr Thomas, both Rpblcns.

Mr Myer Moses, nominated at Charleston, to the Legislature of S C; he is a Hebrew & first of his nation elected to ofc in this country. -Columbian.

Jos Harwood, esq, appt'd Judge of Orphans Crt of A A Co, Md, vice Jonathan Sellman, dec'd.

Notice-committed to Montg Co goal, Isaac, negro; says he was the prop of John Greenpage, in Va; sold by him to a man named Roberts, living in Ky. -Wm Candler, shrf.

Notice-Ned, black man, committed to Wash Co, D C, jail; says he formerly belonged to Barbary Freeman, dec'd & was left by her in c/o Geo Gray of Lower Marlboro, Calvert Co, Md. -C Tippett, kpr of the jail.

Post Ofc dept appointments:
Denton, Md-Montg Denny, vice Thos Culbreth, rsgn'd;
Darnes, Md-Aron Offut, vice John Chandler, rsgn'd;

Hamptonville, N C-Thos Hampton, vice Hampton Bynum, rsgn'd;
Millville, N J-Nathan Lake, vice Jas M'Clong, mv'd away;
Saccarappa, Maine-Hezakiah Winslow, vice Enoch Truman;
Wallingford, Vt-Lent Ives, vice Rufus Buckland jr, rsgn'd;
Laytons, Va-David W Pitts, vice Wm Roy, rsgn'd;
Round Bottom, Ohio-John Smith, vice Thos Regan, rsgn'd;
Burlington, Conn-Waite Lowrie, vice Sylvester Norton, rsgn'd;
Augusta, Maine-Nathan Weston jr, vice Saml Fitcomb, rsgn'd;
Berkshire, Vt-Josiah Wheeler, vice Jesse Badcock, rsgn'd;
Nescopeck, Pa-Wm Baird, vice Geo K Harrison, rsgn'd;
Loyds, Va-B H Munday, vice Jas Sale, rsgn'd;
Balise, Orleans Terr-Wm Allen, vice G W Stackpoole, dec'd;
Russia N Y-Hobart Graves jr, priv rte;
Pittstown, N J-Edw Wested, vice Robt E Foreman, rsgn'd;
Vergennes, Vt-Abel Tomlinson, vice John Green;
New Salem, Mass-Obediah Townsend vice Saml Frazer jr, rsgn'd;
St Michaels, Md-Rich'd Harrington, vice Jas Dodson, rsgn'd;
Bridgeport, Conn-Jesse Sterling, vice Ch Bostwick, rsgn'd;
Carnesville, Ga-Maxfield H Payne, vice John R Brown, rsgn'd;
Templeton, Mass-Lipha French, vice Caleb Leland, dec'd;
Pendleton, S C-John T Lewis, vice Jas Cooper, rsgn'd;
Martin's Creek, Pa-Andrew Whitesell, vice Jos Bowman jr, rsgn'd;
Canonsburg, Pa-John Roberts, vice Henry Westbay, rsgn'd;
Concord, N C-Jos Young, vice John Phifer, rsgn'd;
Occoquan, Va-N Elliot, vice B P Gilpin, rsgn'd;
Rocky Springs, N C-Jas H Deering, vice Jos Ladd, rsgn'd;
Bellfont, Pa-Robt G Steward, vice J Dunlap, rsgn'd;
Epson, N H-Saml Morrell, vice Jas McClary, dec'd;
Lower Sandusky, Ohio-Wm Matthews-appt'd;
Lower Blue Lick, Ky-Jos Ellerbeck, vice Wm Williams, rsgn'd;
Mackaysville, N C-Jno Mackay-appt'd;
Lisbon, N Y-Jas Thompson, vice Geo C Conant;
Enfield, N C-Jno Branch, vice Wm Bradford, rsgn'd;
Pelham, Mass-Constant Ruggles, vice Isaac A Conkey, rsgn'd;
Epping, N H-Wm Plummer jr, vice Wm Plummer, rsgn'd;
Lincolton, Ga-Thos Lamar, vice Peyton Harris, rsgn'd;
New London Rds, Pa-John W Conyngham, vice David Corry, rsgn'd;
Schoharie Bridge, N Y-Jos C Blanchard, vice J Cleveland, remv'd from the place;
Franconia, N H-John Punchard, vice Chester Farman, rsgn'd;
Columbia C H, Ga-Jas Cary, vice John Cole, rsgn'd;
New Madrid, La Terr-P A Laforge, vice Jos Mitchell, dec'd;
Hungary Town, Va-Jno H Knight, vice Fielding Ellis, rsgn'd;
Blackstock, S C-Wm Daniel, vice Simion Bevens, rsgn'd;
Ravenna, Ohio-Wm Tappan, vice F Wadsworth, rsgn'd.
New ofcs established: Stafford, C H, Va, Stafford Co-Jas Ford;
Dauphin Co, Pa-Henry Bowman;
Columbus, Coenango Co, N Y-Jos H Dwight;
Amissburg, Culpepper Co, Va-Thos Amiss.

Post ofcs discontinued: Sommerville, Va; Neilsville, Va; Ashes Store, S C; Browns x Rds, Ga; Deerfield, Warren Co, Ohio.

FRI OCT 12, 1810

Sep 8, The *Fredonia* was boarded by the British frig, *Malampus*, Capt Hawker; the following were impressed: Saml Little, farmer, 29; John Fearburn, a child, coming to reside with his uncle; Jas Sutloff, farrier, 22; Chas Ruley, clk, 24; Dan'l Lodger, 20; Thos Fitzpatrick, 24; Wm Ballard, 26; Peter Flinn, 20; Thos Kinsela, 26; Matthew Kinsela, 20; John Raney, a boy. The ship departed with their prey. -N Y paper.

For sale-*Woodberry Harbor*, residence of the late Burditt Hamilton of Chas Co, Md -ab't 175 acs, in Nanjemoy. -Pliny Hamilton.

Orphans Crt of St Mary's Co, Md. Creditors to exhibit their claims; Thos Cole, adm of Geo Cole, late of St M Co, dec'd. -Jas Forrest, Reg wills. Thos Cole, adm of Geo Cole.

John C Sceverman, insolvent debtor, confined in Wash Co, D C prison for debt. -Hon Wm Cranch, Chf Judge.

MON OCT 15, 1810

Phil, Sep 18, 1810. Ltr from Thos Boyd, impressed seaman; from N Y. -I sailed on the brig *Sussex,* bound for St John's, in Island of Antigua & there was impressed; had my protection with me-they wld not look at it; impressed for 3 yrs; eventually came to Phil in Americ ship; my mthr lived in New-Bern, N C when I left home; have not heard of my bros or mthr since I left home; inform them where I am. -Thos Boyd.

Sale of furn, etc, at home of Henry Timms on Capitol Hill, Wash City. -Andrews & Jones, aucts.

Died: Rich'd Stoddert, age ab't 18 yrs, at Bladensburg, Oct 10, s/o Benj Stoddert, esq.

Died: Wm Macklin, esq, on Sep 24, at his farm in Blount Co, Tenn; late Sec of State of Tenn.

Notice-Joe, negro, committed to Fred'k Co, Md, jail; says he belongs to Mr Henry Peak, who owns a mill on Crooked Branch in Stafford Co, Va. -Ezra Mantz, shrf.

Orphans Crt of Montg Co, Md. Sale of prsnl est of Basil M Perry, late of said Co, dec'd. -Robt Edmondston, acting adm.

Died: Alex'r Martin, in N Y, ntv of Boston, age 33 yrs.

WED OCT 17, 1810

For rent-that place where Mr John Stephen lives, nr the Glass Hse; large wharf attached. -Mls Ths Kirk, Gtwn.

Mrd: on Oct 13, Mr Eliry Chauncey, of Phil, to Miss Henrietta Teackle, of Gtwn, at resid of John Teackle, esq, in Wash, by Rev Dr Addison.

High Crt of Chancery. Will of Thos Pleasants; sale on the premises of valuable mill seat, 40 acs on Hawlings Rvr, nr Unity, in Montg Co, on rd to Balt. -W H Pleasants, trustee.

FRI OCT 19, 1810

Mgrs of ball to be held at Union Tavern: Wash Bowle, John Cox, John W Bronaugh, Geo Johnston, Robt Johnston.

Wash Co, D C. Mary Lane brought before me a stray bay horse. -Henry M Queen, a Justice of the Peace.

Robt Wharton chosen Mayor of City of Phil.

Shoes for sale at new store on F St, Wash. -Jos Wheaton.

MON OCT 22, 1810

For rent-two hses in the occupation of John Graham, esq, Wash City. May be entered into immediately. -Thos Peter.

Wm F Reed, insolvent debtor, confined in Wash Co, D C, prison, for debt; trustee appt'd. -Wm Brent, clk.

Runaway Ellick Howard, mulatto man ab't 24 yrs of age. -Matthias Shaffner, shrf of Wash Co, Md. [Hagerstown]

Orphans Crt of Wash Co, D C. Oct 12, 1810. Prsnl est of Jos Wheat, late of said city, dec'd. -Rachael Wheat, admx; Elects Middleton, adm.

WED OCT 24, 1810

Mr Wm S Green is appt'd clk of A A Co Crt, vice Nicholas Harwood, esq, dec'd. [Maryland]

Mrd: Capt Wm Davis, of Phil, to Miss Mgt Matilda Heig, Oct 13, at Charlotte Hall, St Mary's Co, Md, by Rev Dr Bowman.

Mrd: on Oct 9, Dr Edw Gantt to Miss Maria Blake, d/o Col Jos Blake, all of Calvert Co, Md, by Rev Mr Sutton, in Calv Co.

Died: on Oct 17, Mrs Dorcas Dearborn, at Roxbury, Mass, consort of Hon Henry Dearborn, late Sec of War.

For rent-wharf on Eastern Branch & all hses in my occupation; intending to move to my farm in St Mary's Co. -Jeremiah Boothe, Wash.

Died: on Oct 11, Gen Saml Benton, at Hillsborough, N C.

Wash Co, D C. Garner Sherman brought before me a stray bay horse. -Rich'd S Briscoe, a Justice of the Peace.

Pktbk lost-Benj M Belt, Pa Ave, nr the theatre, Wash.

FRI OCT 26, 1810
Pblc sale-farm whereon I reside, adj Leonard Town, Md, ab't 300 acs-plantation & hses; also ab't 100 acs whereon Jas Johnson now lives; also all my prsnl est. -Mary Lansdale.

Died: on Oct 25, John Little, age 65 yrs. Funeral from his late dwlg hse on G St this afternoon.

Jas McLachlan Sr has disposed of his stock to his son, Jas McLachlan, who will continue the boot & shoe mkg business.

Baton Rouge, Sep 26, 1810-Declaration that the Terr of W Fla be a free & independent state. Signed: John H Johnson, John Mills, John W Leonard, Wm Barrow, Philip Hicky, John Morgan, Edmund Howes, Thos Lilley, Wm Spiller, John Rhea-Pres, Andrew Steele-Sec.

MON OCT 29, 1810
Pblc auction-all furn of Jos Whait, lately dec'd, nr Barry's Wharf. -Nicholas L Queen & Co.

Wash Co, D C -Stephen Potter, of said Dist, hath deposited a bk which he claims as author: *A New Grammatical Sytem of the English Tongue, in Three Parts....* .
-G Deneale, Clk of D C.

Strayed or stolen from race ground nr this city, a bay horse. -John Tarrence, pump-mkr, nr Centre Mkt, Wash.

WED OCT 31, 1810
Died: on Oct 13, John Heath, in Richmond, Va, mbr of Privy Cncl.

Died: on Oct 10, Rich'd Matthews of Herford Co, age 103 yrs, 2 mos, 11 days; born in Va, has resided in N C for 60 yrs.

Died: on Sep 29, Col Jas Richardson age 76 yrs, at his plantation in Bladen Co; born in Stonington, Conn; fought in the Americ Rev

Reward-six cents for appr boy, Rich B Brashears, who absconded Oct 25.
-Fred A Wagler, Wash City.

Balt Americ: R C C Diocese of Balt, which comprehended the whole of the U S, is now erected into an Archbishopric & 4 new dioceses are est; suffragans to the See of Balt. Bishops now to be consecrated: Rt Rev Dr Egan-Bishop of Phil, Oct 28; Rt Rev Dr Cheverus, of Boston, Nov 1; celebrated in St Peter's Chr; Rt Rev Dr Flaget, of Bairds' Town, Ky, on Nov 4, in St Patrick's Chr, Fell's Point. The late Rt Rev Dr Concannon, Bishop of N Y, died before he cld take possession to the other new diocese. -Balt, Oct 26, 1810.

West Fla-New Orleans, Oct 8: last Sun, the inhabitants of Bayou Sarah, headed by Genr'l Philemon Thomas, attacked & took the fort & town of Baton Rouge & hoisted the American Flag.

Orphans Crt of Montg Co, Md. Oct 31, 1810. Prsnl est of Peter Becraft, late of said Co, dec'd. -Mary Becraft, admx.

FRI NOV 2, 1810

For sale-cordage of every kind. -John Chalmers, at his Rope Factory, lower end of *Greenleaf's Point*, Wash.

Wanted: a gardener, at the place of Capt Josias M Speake, nr the seat of Joel Barlow, esq. -Saml Speake.

Orphans Crt of Montg Co, Md. Pblc sale of prsnl est of late Rebecca Offutt & Jas Offutt: 30 negroes, stock, furn, waggons, etc; at late plantation of aforesaid Rebecca Offutt. -Jas Offutt of Wm, adm of Rebecca Offutt & adm D B N of Jas Offutt.

Strayed or stolen-bay horse; reward $10. -Barton Duvall, mgr of Mrs Sarah B Craufurd, Greenwood, PG Co, Md.

For sale-Chas Co, Md-Hardship; part of tract cld *Cornwallis' Neck,* bet 500 & 600 acs, 68 cld *McAtter's Luck;* 53 negroes, stock, all my hsehld furn, dwlg hse, coachee bought by me from Mrs Peter of Gtwn; 3 lots in Wash City. Mrs Wm Worthington resides on premise. On Mattawoman Swamp I will sell the farm I bght of Capt Wm Marbury of Gtwn for $6000 & farm on Zachiah Swamp which I bght of Nicholas Biles for $6000; bonds, notes & judgments ab't $10,000; those not pd by Jan 1-to be put in hands of Clement Dorsey, Atty. -W Jameson-Gtwn

MON NOV 5, 1806

Died: on Oct 28, Col Edw Carrington, at Richmond; a Revolutionary worthy & a man of sterling integrity.

Died: on Oct 11, Alfred Moore, in N C; late as Assoc Judge of Sup Crt of U S.

Died: on Oct 28, Cmdor Saml Barron, at Norfolk; seized with a fit of apoplexy.

Henry Childs opened a dry goods store below Union Tavern-Gtwn.

Wm M'Kenney has returned from Phil with supply of seasonable goods; his new establishment, Bridge St, Gtwn.

Auction sale-at hse of Mr Chester Bailey, Pa Ave, adj hse of late Maj Swans; furn & milch cow. -Andrews & Jones, aucts.

WED NOV 7, 1810
Died: on Oct 31, John Brown, esq, at Richmond, clk of Crt of Appeals.

Stevensburg Acad has a vacancy for a gentleman of science. -Chas Stuart Waugh, Pr, Culpeper Co, Va.

Jacob Swoope, esq, Fed Rep of Va, declined re-elec to Cong.

Edw Johnson, esq, re-elected Mayor of Balt City, Md.

Pblc auction of all prsnl est of Jas Ord, dec'd, consisting of ship-carpenters tools, eliptic moulds, builder bks; at the Old Billiard rm on Maddox's lot. -N L Queen & Co, aucts.

Just rec'd at J Milligan's bk-store, Gtwn: *The Rival Princess,* by Mary Anne Clarke; narrative of facts relating to Mrs M A Clarke's political acquaintance with Col Wardle, Maj Dodd, etc, concerned in the charges against the Duke of York.

Orphans Crt of Wash Co, D C. Ltrs of admin obtained by Isabella Thompson & myself on the prsnl prop of Geo Thompson. -W Morton

Trustee's sale by deed in trust made by Geo Thompson, viz. 2 brick dwlgs on Falls St; dwlg & store where Mrs I Thompson now resides in Gtwn. -Wm Morton, trustee

Runaway, Robin, negro, committed to PG Co, Md, jail; says he belongs to Mr Zachariah Creddenton, of Middlesex Co, Va & was bght by him of Thos Rose, of same Co. -John Darnall, shrf.

Sale by deed of trust, from Dan'l M'Carty & Margaretta Matilda Snowden, his wife; land in Loudon Co, Va, cld *M'Carty's Island, & Sugar Land Tract;* prop shown by Mr John W Bronaugh in Gtwn, or Mr Danl M'Carty, on the premises. -Elisha Janney, Jas Keith jr.

FRI NOV 9, 1810
Mrd: on Nov 4, Mr Wm B Scott, late a Lt in U S N, to Miss Ann Holton, of St Mary's Co, Md, by Rev Mr Derosey.

Mrd: on Nov 3, Gurdon S Mumford, esq, Rep of N Y in Congress, to Miss Letitia Van Soren, at N Y.

Navy Dept-ofcrs of Navy & Marine Corps shd wear crape in memory of late Cmdor Saml Barron. -Paul Hamilton, Sec of Navy.

Order of Orphans Crt of Calvert Co, Md. Sale of one negro man, formerly prop of Barbara Freeman, late of said Co, dec'd. -Geo Gray-adm.

Death of Mr Abraham Goldsmidt, one of the great contractors for the loan; shot himself at his hse at Merton; cld have been depressed over recent death of Sir Francis Baring; depressed over the futures; 2d suicide in Mr G's fmly; stock exchange was crowded to excess. [Appears under N Y heading]

Wm Williamson has been chosen principal of Wellington Acad; parents unable to pay tuition are to apply to Saml H Smith, Thos B Gillis or Jas Laurie.

Wanted-journeymen shoemkrs; apply to Alex'r Harper, on Capitol Hill next to Dr Ewell's Shop.

TUE NOV 13, 1810

Maryland-Tobias E Stansbury was chosen spkr of the hse of Delegates, & John Brewer, clk.

Chain Bridge over the falls above Gtwn has been carried away; in the act of getting drift wood, Mr Wm H Stroud, a silk & cotton dyer, was unfortunately drowned. -Tue Nov 13.

Died: on Oct 27, Mr John Ridgeway, age 64 yrs, at his seat in Calvert Co, Md; his chldrn have lost the best of fathers.

Literary notice-I intend on publishing a small volume on midwifery. -Thos Ewell, Wash.

For sale-40 2/3 acs of land nr the Eastern Branch Bridge, in Wash, D C. -John Masters.

Notice-John Gassaway, negro boy, ab't 17 yrs of age, was committed to the Fred'k Co, Md goal, as a runaway; says he belonged to Mr John Myers, of Kent island, Md, who sold him to a man going to Natchez. -Ezra Mantz, shrf, Fred Co, Md.

For sale-decree of Crct Crt o/Wash Co, D C as Crt of Chancery; part of lot 18 sq 127, with 2 brick hses fronting on I St, prop of the late Chas Cook, dec'd. -Chas Glover, trustee.

Died: on Oct 28, Wm Todd, esq, age 68 yrs, at Greensburg, Pa.

THU NOV 15, 1810

Mrd: on Nov 13, in Wash, Thos H Blount, esq, of N C, s/o John Gray Blount, esq, to Miss Eleanor Mgt Brown, of Chas Co, Md.

Joel Brown, Bridge St, has just rec'd an assortment of hats & shoes from N Y, Phil & Balt, for his store.

Orphans Crt of Wash Co, D C. Nov 13, 1810. Prsnl est of John Little, late of said city, dec'd. -Saml Brock, adm.

SAT NOV 17, 1810
Died: Francis Hamersly, esq, age 60, of apoplexy, in Fairfax Co, Va. [No date-recent.]

Horse & gig stolen from before the Post Ofc door in Gtwn; reward-$20. -Abraham Bradley jr, Wash City.

Pblc sale-order of Orphans Crt of St Mary's Co, Md-all prsnl est of Jas Thompson, late of said Co, dec'd, except negroes; sale at the tavern, the late resid of the dec'd, at Leonard town. -Genet Thompson, admx, Leonard town.

TUE NOV 20, 1810
Notice-sale of 2 story brick hse with all his hsehld furn, nr the Navy Yd Gate-Saml Young. -N L Queen & Co, aucts.

Mrs Chisholm has taken the hse lately occupied by Mr Michl Nourse on I St, where she can accomodate a few boarders.

For sale-ab't 150 acs with dwlg hse where I live; 2 1/2 miles from the Capitol in Wash City; also 100 acs on opposite side of the road. -Jas Clerklee

Orphans Crt-ordered that John Minchin, adm of Edmund Scannell, dec'd, sell the prop returned in the inventory at public auction. -John Hewitt, Reg. Notice followed: sale on the premises nr the Navy Yd Mkt Hse-ideal for the groc or liquor business having been carried on there heretofore. -John Minchin, adm of E Scannell, dec'd. -Andrews & Jones, aucts.

Died: on Nov 18, Mrs Cornelia De Krafft, Nov 18. Funeral at 3 o'clock.

THU NOV 22, 1810
Died: on Nov 9, Walter Bowie, esq,, age 62 yrs, at his seat in PG Co, Md, after a long & painful illness; patriot of Rev

Died: lately, Rich'd C Hooe, s/o M Bernard Hooe, late o/Pr Wm Co, Va, age 19 yrs.

For sale-brick hse, formerly occupied by Jas Madison, esq, now in possession of Paul Hamilton, sec of the Navy; also adj store & hse; the 2 story brick hse in which I live, adj Mr B H Latrobe; also 3 hses on 7th St; also 2 hses nr Mr McLeod's Seminary, with 5 vacant lots adj; intending to retire to my farm in Va. -Capt S N Smallwood or N Voss.

Meeting of the young men o/Wash City, at Davis' Htl, to form an assoc for relief of the poor. -Rich'd Wallack, chrm -Christopher Andrews, sec. Geo Sweeny, Jos Gades, & Richmond Johnson, committee.

SAT NOV 24, 1810

Mrd: on Nov 20, Mr Robt Boyd, bkbinder, of Wash, to Miss Betsey Bailey, of Alexandria, by Rev Mr Roberts.

Died: Mr Jacob Motte, s/o Maj Chas Motte who was killed in 1779 leading his regt, the 2d Reg Regt of S C, to the attack of Savannah. J Motte died Nov 3.

Died: on Nov 16, Capt John Heth, very suddenly, in Richmond, entered into Rev Army very young, continued till the close of war; belonged to the Soc of Cinc; buried with honors of war.

Census of Wash City: inhabitants in 1803 were 4352; in 1807 were 5652; in 1810 were 8620. -Alexandria Daily Gaz.

Geo St Clair, of Wash Co, brought before me a stray bay horse. -Dan'l Rapine.

Charlotte Hall School-boarding hse ready for ensuing yr, Mr John Kilgour, Steward. -D Donlevy, Principal.

Nov 6 in the U S Crt for the Dist of N Y, Dr Wm Jas Mac Neven, formerly an eminent patriot in Ire, was admitted a ctzn of the U S, before his Honor Judge Talmadge.

For sale, at Tyber Spring Gardens: poplar, pear, & English walnut trees.
-Alice Hepburn.

TUE NOV 27, 1810

Mrd: on Nov 6, Dr Wm Adams, to Miss Sarah Eppes Goodwyn, all of Columbia, S C, by Rev Isaac Tucker, at Columbia, S C.

Mrd: on Nov 22, Dr John Spence, physician at Dumfries, Va, to Mrs Mary F Muschett, of same place, by Rev Chas O'Neal, at Dumfries, Va.

Died: on Nov 24, Mrs R Polk, consort o/ Mr Chas P Polk, in Wash, age 44 yrs; wife & mthr.

Died: on Nov 26, Mrs Rachel Ridgely M'Cormick, cnsrt of Jas M'Cormick jr. Funeral from her late dwlg, E & 9th Sts, today.

Orphans Crt of PG Co, Md. Nov 21, 1810. Prsnl est of Ann Clarke, late of said Co, dec'd. -Benj Hodges, adm, will annexed.

Reward-$30 for runaway, Wm Wootten, negro man, ab't 43 yrs of age. -Benj Belt of Stephen, living nr Up Marl, PG Co, Md.

Orphans Crt of PG Co, Md. Pblc sale of all prsnl est of Stephen Belt, late of said Co, dec'd. -Benj Belt, adm.

THU NOV 29, 1810

For sale: two hses in Wash City, one lately occupied by Gen Tureau, French Mnstr; other now occupied by Mr Alex'r Kerr; also lots in Gtwn. -Walter Smith.

St Patrick's Chr, Wash City: next Sun, Rev Dr Callagher, from Charleston, S C, will preach in this chr; collection that day is to defray the expense of the grand organ of the church.

Genr'l assembly of N C: Gen Riddick chosen spkr of Senate; Wm Hawkins-spkr of Hse of Commons.

Jos Forrest, esq, appt'd Justice of the Peace for Wash Co, D C. Jesse Crampton, late of Guilford, Conn, has taken a hse nr Stelle's Htl, recently occupied by Dr Ewell as a druggist shop, where he has opened a boot & shoe manufactry.

Orphans Crt of PG Co, Md. Nov 27, 1810. Prsnl est of Mary Mackall Hellen, dec'd. -Geo Beall.

Land for sale-by authority of heirs of late Wm Thrusher, of Montg Co, dec'd; land whereon he lived-84 acs, nr Mr John Rabbit's Tavern, in Montg Co, Md. -Leonard P Osbourn.

Orphans Crt of PG Co, Md. Nov 27, 1810. Prsnl est of Rich'd Mulliken, dec'd. -Ann Mulliken, admx; Horatio Beall, adm.

Michl Grimes, insolvent debtor, confined in Wash Co, D C, prison, for debt. -Wm Brent, clk.

SAT DEC 1, 1810

Happy to announce the arrival of Wm Jarvis, esq, [son of late Dr Chas Jarvis] our Consul at Lisbon with his fmly. -Patriot

Sale-of all hsehld furn of Robt Armstead, at his hse on Navy Yd Hill, oppo Mr Lindsey's store. -N L Queen & Co, aucts.

Mrd: on Nov 27, at Balt, Capt Geo Armistead, of U S Army, to Miss Louisa Hughes d/o Christopher Hughes, esq, of Balt.

Died: Mr John Hays, gunner at Navy Yd, Gosport, nr Norfolk, some days ago.

Died: on Nov 15, Wm Dunbar, esq, at his seat nr Natchez.

Orphans Crt of PG Co, Md. Adms of Thos Woodward will sell at his late dwlg-svr'l negroes & other articles. -Abraham B Woodward, Wm R Woodward, adms. PG Co, Md.

Reward-$20 for runaway, Jack Brown, negro ab't 21 yrs of age. -Elias Gray, PG Co, 3 miles from Eastern Branch Bridge.

Runaway-John Jack, black man ab't 50 yrs of age, committed to Montg Co, Md-goal; says he is free & born in France. -Wm Candler, shrf.

Money lost-$200 in bank notes directed to Augustine Newton of Alexandria. -G & J Smither, Wash, Culpeper Co.

TUE DEC 4, 1810

Runaway-Frank, black man, committed to Wash Co, D C jail; says he belongs to Wm Patterson, of Balt, Md. -Cartwright Tippet, kpr of the jail.

Died: on Nov 19, Matthew Whiting, esq, of Pr Wm Co, Va, at his seat, *Snowhill,* after a short illness; he wanted but 2 days of 80 yrs of age. -Alex Gaz.

L J M Littlejohn has opened a Hair Dressers Shop on Pa Ave

Mr John Horne Tooke, born Jun 1736, has prepared a vault for his remains nr Wimbledon Common; he is now in alarming state of health. -London Paper.

Columbian Agric Soc met at Union Tavern in Gtwn on Nov 21, Premiums were adjudged to Geo Calvert, of PG Co, Md;
Osborne Sprigg, of same;
Wm Stinbergen, of Shenandoah Co, Va;
Mrs Ann M Mason, of *Analostan island*, Wash Co, D C;
Mr Geo M Conradt, of Fred'k town, Md;
Mrs Martha P Graham, of Dumfries, Pr Wm Co, Va;
Mrs Sarah M'Carty Mason, of *Hollin Hall*, Fairfax Co, Va;
Miss Patsey Shackleford, of Culpepper Crthse, Va;
Mrs Eliz Gunnel, of *Minorca*, Fairfax Co, Va;
Mrs Eliz Maynadier, of Belvoir, A A Co, Md.
Ofcrs appt'd: Osborne Sprigg, of Northampton, PG Co, Md-Pres;
Thomson Mason, of *Hollin Hall*, Fairfax Co, Va-VP;
David Wiley, of Gtwn, D C-sec.

Land sale-per last will of Dr Henry Rose, dec'd, late of Fairfax Co, Va; at hse of Nehemiah Morris; 3 tracts each in said Co; adj lands of Judge Fitzhugh Wm Moss, the reps of John Moss, dec'd, Giles Fitzhugh & others; 7 miles from Wash; 670 acs total. Apply to Robt I Taylor of Alexandria; shown by Mr Wm Moss nr the premise. -Alex'r F Rose, exc.

Teacher wanted at the Rockville Acad. -Jos Elgar jr, sec, Montg. Crt Hse, Md.

For sale-negroes, order of Orphans Crt of PG Co, Md; at Ranter's Tavern nr Nottingham, late the prop of Rachel H Brooke, dec'd. -Stan Hoxton, exc.

THU DEC 6, 1810

History of the American Revolution by David Ramsay, M D, is revised & corrected, ready for the press; covers from 1607 down to the present time.

Francis Heuson, of Montg Co, Md, brght before me a stray mare. -Thos Gittuegs, a Justice of the Peace for Montg Co.

Jas Melvin, merchant taylor, Gtwn, Bridge St, has rec'd cloths from Phil & Balt. also-to rent, brick hse adj Mr Peter Hagner's, nr Pa Ave, lately occupied by Mrs Handy.

SAT DEC 8, 1810

Mrd: on Dec 6, Mr David Somervill to Miss Jane Underwood, both of Wash.

Post ofc appointments:
Denton, Md-Montg Denny, vice Thos Culbreth, rsgn'd
Darnes, Md-Aaron Offutt, vice John Candler, rsgn'd
Brownsburg, Ga-Wm Booker, vice S Marshall, rsgn'd
Hamptonville, N C-Thos Hampton, vice Hampton Baynham, rsgn'd
N Y, Va-Nath'l Landraft, vice Wm Stewartson, rsgn'd
Culpepper C H, Va-John C Williams jr, vice B Shackleford, dismissed
Boardman, O-Saml Clark, vice E J Baldwin, rsgn'd
Fork o/Muskingum, O-Wm Lockard, vice Thos L Rue, rsgn'd
Lancaster, Ky-Jos P Letcher, vice Jos C Keane, rsgn'd
Spencer, Ms-Isaac Jenks jr, vice Isaac Jenks, rsgn'd
Greensboro, Va-Ephraim Strong, vice Peter Brown, rsgn'd
Northampton, N Y, John Fay, vice Jacob Shaw, situation inconvenient
Penn's Store-Va, Hardin Hairston, vice Jas Penn, mv'd away
Port Gibson, Miss Tery-Jas Wood, vice Rye, dec'd
Williamsville, N C-Currey Barnett, vice Jas Barnett, rsgn'd
Stroudsburg, Pa-Peter Barker, vice Peter Hollingshead, rsgn'd
Taunton, Ms-Jas L Hodges, vice Mr Hodges, dec'd
Lunenburg C H, Va-John Taylor, vice Henry Astrop, rsgn'd
Waterbury, Con-Wm K Lamson, vice Mr Lavensworth, dismissed
White Plains, Ten-Wm Quarles, vice Danl Alexander, rsgn'd
Port Eliz, N J-Stephen Willis, vice Jas Lee, rsgn'd
Hillsboro, Md-Francis Sellers, vice John Tillotson, rsgn'd
Dingman's Ferry, Pa-Henry Jackson, vice D W Dingman, rsgn'd
China Grove, S C-Matthew Allen, vice L Gasque, rsgn'd
West Liberty, Va-Alex'r Berryhill, vice Wm M'Kinley, rsgn'd
Saugatuck, Con-Morehouse, vice Stephen Barlow, rsgn'd
Richmond C H, Va-Benj Boughton, vice John Tayloe, rsgn'd
New London, Va-Jas Penn, vice Saml White, rsgn'd
Lincolnton, Ga-Pierson Pettit, vice ___ Lamar, left the place
Rocky Mt, Va-Peter Saunders jr, vice Edmond Dennis, rsgn'd

Franconia, N H-Caleb Baker, vice Wm Punchard
Wilmington, Vt-Saml Thompson, vice Mr Tobey, dec'd
Christianville, K-Signal Abernathy, vice Wm C Wall, rsgn'd
W Stockbridge, Ms-Amusa Spencer, vice Ethel Burch, rsgn'd
Oxford, P-Saml Ross, vice D Dickey, rsgn'd
Varennes, S C-Mark H Collins, vice Malder Reves, rsgn'd
New Mkt, N C-Wm Britton, vice Drew S Whitmell, rsgn'd
Amherst C H, Va-Arthur B Davies, vice Jas Allen, rsgn'd
Selins Grove, Pa-Fred'k Dearing, vice Jacob Lechner, rsgn'd
Hardenburg, K-John McClarty, vice John H McClarty, dec'd
Eastham, Ms, Hardin Knowles, vice Saml Freeman, rsgn'd
Red Hse, N C-Wash Jeffries, vice Chas Wilson, rsgn'd
Norfolk, Con-Jos Jones, vice Mich'l F Mills, rsgn'd

Ofcs discont'd, Nov 1810:
Elk Run Chr, Va; Greenbrook, N J; Orange Hall, S C.
New ofcs est'd Nov 1810 & Post Mstr appt'd:
Acton, Middlesex Co, Mass-David Perhum
Litchfield, Herkimer Co, N Y-Jno Pendergraft
Mill Hall, Centre Co, Pa-Benj Harvey
Poole's Store, Montg Co, Md-Dennis Lackland
Berkshire, Del Co, O-Thos Brown
Mystic Rvr, New London Co, Ct-Zabdial Rogers
Boat Run, Claremont Co, Ohio-Ebenezer Newton
Euclid, Cayahoga Co, O-Wm Coleman
P O to commence operation in Jan 1, 1811:
Anson, Cumberland Co, Maine-Jas Collins
Bowdoinham, Linc Co, Maine-Simms Gardner
Hennicker, Hillsboro Co, N H-Joshua Darling
Hopkinton, Hillsboro Co, N H-John Harris
Northwood, Stafford Co, N H-Jno Harvey
Whiting, Addison Co, Vt-Amos E Walker
Hubbartston, Rutland Co, Vt-Danl Meeker
Assonet, Bristol Co, Mass-Stephen B Pickens
Troy, Plymouth Co, Mass-Abraham Bowen
Sturbridge, Worcester Co, Mass-Simeon Burt
Charlemont, Hampshire Co, Ms-Saml Rathbone
Tiverton, Newport Co, R I-Wm Norton
Kent, Litchfield Co, Con-Lewis St John
Cornwall, Litchfield Co, Cont-Wm Lewis
Warehse Pt, Hartford Co-Chas Reynolds
Enfield, Hartford Co, Con-Wm Dickson
Woodstock, Windham Co, Con-Wm Bowen
Willton, Fairfield Co, Con-Wm Comstock
New Windsor, Rockland Co, N Y-Jos Merrill
Canterbury, Rockland Co, N Y-Nath'l Barton
Cohecton, Sullivan Co, N Y-Ebenezer Taylor
Monticello, Sullivan Co, N Y-Saml F Jones

Bloomingsburg, Sullivan Co, N Y-Maj Bailey
Providence, Luzerne Co-Pa, Benj Slocum
Waterford, Mifflin Co, Pen-Enoch Anderson
Concord, Mifflin Co, Pen-Edw Doyle
Landisburg, Cumberland Co, Pen-Wm Wilson
Douglass Mills, Cumberland Co, Pen-David Moreland
Mt Pleasant, Wayne Co, Pen-Oliver Granger
Burgettstown, Wash Co, Pen-Thos Miller
Head of Chester, Kent Co, M-Jas Bradshaw
Crugerstown, Fred'k Co, Md-Fred A Hase
Jonasville, Cumberland Co, Md-John Jonas
Fredericktown, Knox Co, O-Abner Ayres
Piquatown, Miami Co, O-Armstrong Brandon
Burton, Geauga Co, O-Peter Hitchcock
Aurora, Portage Co, O-Ebenezer Sheldon
Delaware, Dela Co, O-Leonard H Coles
Derby, Franklin Co, O-Jas Ewing
Hartford, Trumbull Co, O-Titus Brockway
Smithfield, Trumbull Co, O-Jeremiah Wilcox
Kinsman, Trumbull Co, O-John Kinsman
Emersonville, Ind Ter-Jesse Emerson
Little Sandy Salt Works, K-Amos Kibby
Greenup C H, Greenup Co, K-Joshua Bartlett
Lewis C H, K-Rowland Perkins
Rose Creek, Ten-Reuben Thornton
Istapachy Riser, Miss Ter-Laughlin McCoy
Rhea C H, Ten-Dan'l Rawlins
Highwassee Garrison, Ten-Geo Smith
Bledsoe C H, Ten-Saml Terry
Warren C H, T-Jos Colville
White C H, T-John McCarrick
Hickman's C H, T-Wm Early
Humphries C H, Ten-Robt German
Pulaski, Giles Co, Ten-Gabriel Bumpass
Fayetteville, Linc Co, Ten-John McConnel
Huntsville, Madison Co, Miss Ter-Peter Perkins
Thrasher's Store, Loudon Co, Va-Elias Thrasher
Hamilton's Mill, Loudon Co, Va-John Hamilton
Smith's store, Fauquier Co, Va-Hewes
Arnold Old place, Fauquier Co, Va-Thos Barber
Gibson's store, Fauquier Co, Va-Wm Gibson
Cattlettsburg, Greenup Co, K-Horatio Catlet
Framingham, Worcester Co, Ms-Jonathan Maynard
Sutton, Worcester Co-Ms.Estes Howe
Herculaneum, La T-Moses Austin
Shawnee town, Ill T-Geo Robinson
U S Saline, Ind T-Leonard White
Long Creek, Caldwell Co, K-Vincent Anderson

Mrd: on Dec 6, Mr John C Vowell, merchant, to Mrs Mary Jaqueline Taylor, at Alexandria, both of that city.

Died: on Nov 26, Jos Russell, esq, at Boston, pres of the No American Ins Co.

Died: Maj Jos Scott, at Richmond, on Dec 1, mrsh'l of the District of Va.

Pblc sale, deed in trust from Osborn Warner, dt'd Apr 23, 1810, to secure the payment of money to Andrew Scholfield; all right, title of Osborn Warner, in lot 7 sq 576, Wash City, on Md av. -John Hewitt, trust. Andrews & Jones-aucts.

TUE DEC 11, 1810
Notice-ltrs of adm on rl & prsnl prop of Mary Roby, late of Chas Co, Md, dec'd. Dec 8, 1810. -Wm S Roby

Henry Polkinhorn, insolvent debtor, confined in Wash Co, D C prison, for debt. -Wm Brent, clk.

Pblc sale-order of Orphans Crt of PG Co, Md; at dwlg hse of Leonard Deakins on Balt Rd, all the est of the dec'd Dan'l Barron. -Mary Barron, admx, of Dan'l Barron.

THU DEC 13, 1810
Orphans Crt of PG Co, Md. Nov 24, 1810. Prsnl est of Alex'r Gibbons, dec'd. -Levin T Gibbons, adm.

Hse o/Reps: Petition of John & Edw Tauner, of La Terr; aid in opening a canal & rd for internal communication in La.

Sale for cash-all right, title & claim of Thos Nevitt, in & to Harry, a black man, virtue of 4 writs of fieri facias, to satisfy Wm Wood, Notley Maddox, Jeremiah Booth & Dan'l C Brent, levied Dec 6, 1810. Cash sale on sq 690, next dr to Rev M'Cormick, all right, title, & claim of Thos & Theodore Hagen, in a plank work shop, by 2 writs to satisfy Enos D Fugason & Geo Walker, levied Dec 10, 1810. -David Bates-cnstb.

Benj Smith was chosen Governor of N Carolina for the ensuing yr.

SAT DEC 15, 1810
Saml Francis, a crew mmbr of the frig the *Constitution* drowned while on duty; the crew collected $1250 for his widowed mthr in Phil.

Hse o/Reps: Petition of Simeon Knight, whilst acting paymstr in U S A, under authority of late sec at war-Genr'l Henry Dearborn, pd to Brig Genr'l Jas Wilkinson, $1,450, extra rations allowed him as Cmder of a separate post whilst at N Orleans; settlement by the war ofc was withheld; praying relief.

Gen Andrew Moore is appt'd mrsh'l of State of Va.

Wm H Crawford, esq, chosen a Senator of U S from Ga.

For sale-4 farms & 120 shares of Union Bank stock. -John Goulding, Gtwn, Potomac.

Mrd: on Dec 13, Mr John Tarrence, of Wash, to Miss Nancy Godman, of PG Co, Md.

Died: Edw Carter Stanard, a few days ago, at Leesburg, editor of the Spirit of '76.

Died: on Nov 23, at N Y, Col Saml Griffin, of Williamsburg; an old & meritorious Rev ofc.

Orphans Crt of Wash Co, D C. Dec 15, 1810. Ltrs test on will & prsnl est of Patrick Deery, late of said city, dec'd. -Bridget Deery, excx. Jas Hoban, Wm Brent, excs.

Edw Loe Mills & Robt Coudon Stone, insolvent debtors, confined in Chas Co, Md, prison-for debt. -Edmund Key, one of the Judges of the first Judicial Dist of Md.

Saml Davis, black man, committed to Fred'k Co, Md, jail; says he is free & srv'd his time with Col Butler & Col O'Hara, in or nr Chambersburg, Pa; has a cert of freedom signed by Robt Allison, & another of his marriage with Molly Lucas, signed by D Denny. -Ezra Mantz, shrf, of Fred'k Co, Md.

John Tyler, esq, is elected Governor of State of Va.

TUE DEC 18, 1810

Robt Marion, esq, Rep from S C, has resigned his seat in Cong, having been taken severely ill on his way to Wash.

Died: Mr Benj Perkins, on Dec 7, at Phil, formerly a resid of Wash.

Leg of Ohio-convened on Dec 3 at Zanesville; Thos Kirker was chosen spkr pro tem to the Senate & Edw Tiffin, esq, to the Hse of Reps.

Gen John Armstrong, our late rep in France, given a dinner on Dec 13 in Phil.

Died: a few days ago, Israel Smith, esq, late Gov of Vt, formerly a Sen in Cong from Vt, a worthy patriot.

Jos Joshua Dyster, late of Eng, now a resid of Phil City; has obtained a patent right for constructing iron tubular bridges by special act of Congress passed Feb 5, 1810.

Francis Pic continues his groc store business; residing next door to Mr Claxton's on Capitol Hill.

Wm Woodward, who srv'd his time as appr to Thos Carstairs, hse carpenter in Phil City, remv'd with his family to Phil & from thence in summer of 1806 to Ohio; in Sep 1809 he sent his family back to Wash City; Nov 1809 went down the Ohio to Cinc; set out for the Falls of Ohio; purposed to go to New Orleans in the spring & thence to Wash City. Need info ab't Wm Woodward, apply to Mr Robt Underwood.

THU DEC 20, 1810
Creditors of John H Barney are to meet at Semme's Tavern in Gtwn, on Mon.

Dennis Mahoney, Priv in U S Marines, was chg'd before a Crt Martial with mutiny, having run a bayonet thru Lt Wainwright with intent to kill him, was convicted & sentenced to death; mercy was granted by the Pres of the U S in consequence of some symptoms of insanity which occasionally appeared in his conduct & manners; pardon granted Dec 13.

Placard posted at N Orleans: Edw Livingston was deprived of his prop on the batture of the suburb St Mary; claims of the city lately claimed no title thereto; he has resumed the actual possession of his said property. -Nov 16.

H C Lewis to issue in a publication in Wash, in a few days, of a wkly mscl paper, *The Hive* or *Repository of Literature* .

Chas Boarman, late Prof of Languages in Gtwn College, intends to open school in Wash City on Jan 2, 1811 in white hse lately occupied by Maj Bowling on F St nr St Patrick's Chr.

For sale or rent: hse which I occupy on Pa Ave; apply to Elias B Caldwell, esq, Wash City or Wm Morgan, Gtwn. Also to dispose of: a negro girl ab't 18 who has 2 yrs to srv & a negro boy ab't 11 who has 14 yrs to srv. -Josiah Fox.

SAT DEC 22, 1810
Philip Pyfer jr has commenced the hatting business, Pa Ave, in hse lately occupied by Vincent Dougherty.

The Batture that Edw Livingston, esq, gave notice of has been taken possession of by order from the Dist Atty; and expelled Mr Livingston from the same.
-N Orleans Gaz of Nov 22.

For sale-Wash or Americ thorn seed; apply to M Morgan at W Morgan's store in Gtwn, or to Evan Evans, Wash City.

Congress-Petition of Larkin Smith, coll of the Dist of Norfolk, Portsmouth, Va, for relief of the collectors of ports of Norfolk, Balt & Phil-passed to a 2d reading.

Jos Sim of PG Co, Md, writes for benefit as insolvent debtor; he is now in confinement for debt. -John Read Magruder jr, clk PG Co Ct.

Henry Middleton is elected Governor of the State of So Carolina.

TUE DEC 25, 1810
R Bainbridge, vet surg from Eng, to practise horse & beast farriery in Wash City & vicinity; leave order with Mr Cocking's, 19th St West.

Harry, mulatto man, committed to Fred'k Co, Md, jail; says he belongs to Mr Wm Valandigam of FairfaxCo, Va. -Ezra Mantz, shrf.

I have remv'd my medical shop to Timms's brick bldgs, adj my dwlg hse, Capital Hill-Jas Ewell.

For sale-warranted hse clocks made by Aaron Willard jr of Boston, Mass.
-Saml Speake, at my hse on Pa Ave,

Wm H Hamer has commenced the hatting business on Pa Ave

THU DEC 27, 1810
John Hemler, at his old stand on F St, continues the manufacture of hats of every description.

Mrd: on Dec 26, Mr Richd H Litle of Alex, to Miss Eliz Talbott of Wash, at Friends Meeting Hse.

Died: on Nov 9, Richd Wall, very suddenly; coll of the Port of Savannah, Ga.

Died: on Dec 16, in Chas Co, Md, Mrs Sarah Russell Contee, w/o Rev Dr Benj Contee, d/o the late Philip Thos Lee, esq.

Geo W Erving, esq, appt'd by Pres of U S, Spec Minister to the Court of Denmark; is now in Wash.

Rev John Andrews, D D, elected Provost, & Robt Patterson, esq, vice Provost of the Univ of Pa.

John Marsters brought before me a stray bay horse. -Henry M Queen, J P-Wash Co, D C.

For sale-freight or charter, the capital ship *Amazon*, Geo Turner, mstr. Apply to Wm Hartshorne, Alexandria.

Wm O'Brien, merchant tailor, 7th St, nr the Navy Yd, Wash.

SAT DEC 29, 1810
Died: on Dec 21, at Richmond, Va, Col W Terry, Del to Leg from Halifax Co.

Mrd: on Dec 27, Mr David Dobbins & Miss Rachael Coleman, of Alexandria.

—A—

—B—

—C—

—D—

—H—

—L—

—M—

—Q—

—R—

—S—

—T—

—U—

—V—

—W—

—Y—

—Z—

Other Heritage Books by the author:

National Intelligencer *Newspaper Abstracts, Special Edition: The Civil War Years, 1861-1863*

National Intelligencer *Newspaper Abstracts 1846*

National Intelligencer *Newspaper Abstracts 1845*

National Intelligencer *Newspaper Abstracts 1844*

National Intelligencer *Newspaper Abstracts 1843*

National Intelligencer *Newspaper Abstracts 1842*

National Intelligencer *Newspaper Abstracts 1841*

National Intelligencer *Newspaper Abstracts 1840*

National Intelligencer *Newspaper Abstracts, 1838-1839*

National Intelligencer *Newspaper Abstracts, 1836-1837*

National Intelligencer *Newspaper Abstracts, 1834-1835*

National Intelligencer *Newspaper Abstracts, 1832-1833*

National Intelligencer *Newspaper Abstracts, 1830-1831*

National Intelligencer *Newspaper Abstracts, 1827-1829*

National Intelligencer *Newspaper Abstracts, 1824-1826*

National Intelligencer *Newspaper Abstracts, 1821-1823*

National Intelligencer *Newspaper Abstracts, 1818-1820*

National Intelligencer *Newspaper Abstracts, 1814-1817*

National Intelligencer *Newspaper Abstracts, 1811-1813*

National Intelligencer *Newspaper Abstracts, 1806-1810*

National Intelligencer *Newspaper Abstracts, 1800-1805*

www.ingramcontent.com/pod-product-compliance
Lightning Source LLC
LaVergne TN
LVHW020540100826
845148LV00010B/1553